A POET AT WAR

EDGELL RICKWORD
A POET AT WAR

Charles Hobday

CARCANET

Acknowledgements

Thanks are due to the following authors or their representatives and publishers for permission to quote: Francisco Campbell Custódio and Ad. Donker (Pty) Ltd. (Roy Campbell, *Broken Record* and letters); Roy Fuller and Collins Harvill (*Memoirs of Childhood and Youth*); Lawrence and Wishart Ltd. (Georgi Dimitrov, *Selected Articles and Speeches*); Jack Lindsay and The Bodley Head (*Fanfrolico and After*); John Lucas and Harvester Wheatsheaf (*The 1930s: A Challenge to Orthodoxy*); the Oxford University Press (Wilfred Owen, *Collected Letters*); J.M. Dent and Sons Ltd. (Herbert Palmer, *Post-Victorian Poetry*).

C.H.

First published in 1989 by
Carcanet Press Limited
208-212 Corn Exchange Buildings
Manchester M4 3BQ   U.K.

British Library Cataloguing in Publication Data

Hobday, Charles
  Edgell Rickword: a poet at war.
  1. Literature. Criticism. Rickword, Edgell, 1898-1982
  I. Title
  801'.95'0924

  ISBN 0-85635-883-5

The Publisher acknowledges financial assistance from the
Arts Council of Great Britain.

Typeset in 10pt Sabon by Bryan Williamson, Manchester
Printed in England by SRP Ltd., Exeter

Contents

Preface

EDGELL Rickword is a key figure in the history of twentieth-century literature, and a paradoxical one. The youngest of the trench poets of the First World War, he produced war poems which although influenced by Sassoon's realism were in a manner distinctively his own. Temporarily associated after the war with the traditionalists of the "Squirearchy", and regarded as a possible candidate for inclusion in Edward Marsh's Georgian anthologies, he moved on to write erotic and satirical lyrics, at once witty and passionate, which demonstrated how completely he had absorbed what Donne and the Metaphysicals on the one hand and Baudelaire and the Symbolists on the other could teach him, and was described by an early critic as "the only complete and satisfactory English Symbolist". Among the poets of the 1920s he emerged alongside T.S. Eliot, Edith Sitwell, D.H. Lawrence and Hugh MacDiarmid, yet he abandoned lyric poetry before he was thirty. Neglected by critics and anthologists for forty years, and almost unknown to the poetry-reading public, he remained a poets' poet, admired by contemporaries including Basil Bunting, William Empson, Stephen Spender, John Betjeman and Roy Fuller, and by poets of each subsequent generation.

As editor of *The Calendar of Modern Letters* from 1925 to 1927 he was at the heart of the Modernist movement. This remarkable journal, of which a reviewer said when it was reprinted in 1966 that it had failed because it had been "too good for any possible audience", included Lawrence, Wyndham Lewis, Aldous Huxley, E.M. Forster, Robert Graves and Edwin Muir among its contributors, and would have published part of *Finnegans Wake* if the printers had not objected to what they considered its obscenity. It introduced such American poets as Hart Crane, John Crowe Ransom and Allen Tate to British readers, and published stories by European writers such as Luigi Pirandello, Isaac Babel and Leonid Leonov, as well as the first English translation of Chekhov's *The Wood Demon*. Its critical essays and reviews, especially Rickword's own, provided the inspiration and model for the criticism of F.R. Leavis, who acknowledged his debt when he edited a selection from *The Calendar* under the title *Towards Standards of Criticism* and borrowed the name of his own journal, *Scrutiny*, from the series of "Scrutinies" of contemporary writers which Rickword had published, first in *The Calendar* and then in book form.

Rickword's political development was typical of many of his generation. Converted to Socialism in boyhood, partly by his reading of Morris, Shaw and Wells, he was confirmed in his beliefs by his wartime experiences, and became a contributor to George Lansbury's *Daily Herald*. Under the impact of the General Strike and the Slump of 1929 he abandoned lyrical verse for Swiftian satire, and during the Spanish Civil War wrote "To the Wife of Any Non-Intervention Statesman", one of the great political satires of the language. After joining the Communist Party in 1934 he edited *Left Review*, which sought to rally writers of all shades of Socialist and Liberal opinion to the struggle against Fascism. Gradually becoming disillusioned with Stalinism, he found a new source of inspiration, long before he left the Communist Party in 1956, in the English tradition of libertarian radicalism, and by his writings on this theme contributed to the emergence of the Eurocommunist New Left and the brilliant Marxist school of English historians.

Both Rickword's poetry and his criticism merit much fuller examination than they receive in this book, which is a biography rather than a critical study. The most important events in any author's life are his writings, however, and I therefore attempt to relate his life to his writings and his writings to his life. As politics played a large part in both, I trace in some detail the development of his political outlook from his schooldays to his last years, and the influence upon it of public events including two World Wars, the General Strike, the Home Secretaryship of Sir William Joynson-Hicks, the Slump, the rise of Fascism, the Spanish Civil War, Stalin's purges and the Soviet invasion of Hungary.

My primary source for Rickword's life down to 1965 has been his unpublished memoirs, written in his old age. For reasons discussed in Chapter XVII these are defective in many respects, and have had to be supplemented or corrected from other sources, published and unpublished, written and oral. I owe a particular debt of gratitude to five people, without whose help the writing of this book would have been almost impossible. Beatrix, Rickword's companion for the last seventeen years of his life, allowed me free access to his papers, willingly answered countless questions, read the manuscript of this book and enabled me to correct some misleading statements. Dr Jane Grubb, his daughter, placed at my disposal George Rickword's unpublished history of his family, her father's letters to her and family photographs, and answered many of my questions either personally or in correspondence. Three of his friends – Arnold Rattenbury, David Holbrook and Jack Beeching – supplied me with copies of their correspondence with Rickword, as well as other documents and information which proved invaluable, especially for Rickword's later years. With these I wish to associate the name of Jack Lindsay, Rickword's friend since 1928, with whom I had two long and enjoyable talks at his Cambridge home.

I deeply regret that A.L. Morton, another of Rickword's friends of many years, did not live to see the completion of this book, in which he had taken a keen interest.

I have been fortunate in the co-operation which I have received from many others who knew Rickword or could supply me with information about him. E.H. Markham, the Honorary Secretary of the Old Colcestrian Society, and Herbert Beckett, a contemporary of Rickword's at Colchester Royal Grammar School, allowed me access to their files of *The Colcestrian*, and Geoffrey Martin, the historian of the school, replied to my inquiry about *The Idler*. J.R. Maddicott, archivist of Exeter College, Oxford, sent me information on J.G. Worth; Mrs Naomi van Loo, deputy librarian of Pembroke College, established that Rickword was at the college for three terms, not four; and Miss M. Macdonald (Oxford University Archives), Miss Maria Croghan (St Hilda's College), Dr Susan Wollenberg (Lady Margaret Hall), Mrs M.E. Rattue (St Anne's College) and Ms Susan Purver (Somerville College) all assisted in my vain search for Margaret McGrath among the students of the Oxford women's colleges. Mrs Paddy Garman sent me a full account of the career of her husband, Douglas Garman, and John Rickword replied at length to my questions about his father, Cecil Rickword. Charles Seaton, librarian of *The Spectator*, introduced me to the paper's records, thereby enabling me to identify many of Rickword's unsigned contributions.

For information on his activities in the 1930s I am indebted to Sir Stephen Spender, who helped me to reconstruct the movements of the delegates to the 1937 Writers' Congress; to Stephen Hayward and the staff of Lawrence & Wishart Ltd., who talked to me about the history of the firm and showed me the minutes of the pre-war directors' meetings; to Mrs Olive Parsons, who wrote to me on the same subject; to Margot Heinemann, who answered my questions about John Cornford; and to Julius Lipton. Mrs Judith Williams sent me copies of Rickword's letters to her father, Randall Swingler, and of some of his unpublished poems, including what appears to be the only surviving copy of "Presumption". George Matthews and Sam Aaronovitch replied to my inquiries about aspects of Communist Party history, and Elizabeth Shaw talked of her experiences as an artist contributing to *Our Time*. Stanley Mitchell supplied me with a précis of Rickword's *British Ally* article on Milton from the Russian text.

Many people contributed to my account of Rickword's later years. Paul Allen told me a great deal about his life in the 1950s, Jonny, Hayter Preston and his other friends of that period, and Peter Chalk and Mrs Irene Chalk reminisced about the days when he shared their flat. Alan Young sent me the script of a broadcast which included recordings of an interview with Rickword, and Daniel Kirkpatrick, of

10 Preface

the St James Press, let me have copies of his replies to requests for information for his entry in the first three editions of *Contemporary Poets*. Among those who sent me copies of letters or other information were Roy Fuller, David Craig, Jeremy Hawthorn, H. Gustav Klaus, Donald Mitchell, Frederick Grubb, Eric Homberger, Michael Marland and Bernard J. Balkin. I would like to thank all those named, and to apologize to anyone whom I may have inadvertently omitted. I owe a special debt to Fred Beake, who, although he was himself planning a book on Rickword's poetry, not only stood aside in my favour but gave me the benefit of his wide knowledge of English and French poetry.

I am grateful to the Authors' Foundation of the Society of Authors for a grant towards the cost of the research for this book. In my researches I have benefitted from the assistance of the staffs of the British Library, the Colindale Newspaper Library, the Imperial War Museum, the Record Office at Kew, the Army Records Centre, the Colchester Public Library, the London Library and the Kensington Central Library.

My greatest debt of all is to Helen, my wife, who good-humouredly accepted Edgell as a member of our household for over two years, read each chapter as it was completed, gave me advice which I was usually glad to accept, and which perhaps I should have accepted more often, and throughout my work on the book was a constant source of encouragement and inspiration.

I. Colchester

WHEN in April 1896 Colchester town council appointed its first borough librarian, the post went to George Rickword, who had already been a non-councillor member of the public library committee for five years. The appointment proved to be a great success. Rickword combined a passionate love of books with administrative ability, and discharged his duties to general satisfaction until his retirement in 1926, at the age of seventy. During that period he established a reputation as a local historian, contributing many articles to the *Transactions of the Essex Archaeological Society*, which he edited for some years, the *Essex Review* and other journals. It was not his published writings which gave him most pleasure, however, but his *Annals of a Family of No Importance: Materials for a History of the Rickword Family and its Connections*, which he began compiling in 1887 and on which he continued to work until his death 47 years later.

Although he was able to trace the family name back to 1140, the earliest Rickword whom he could identify with certainty as an ancestor was John Rickword, husbandman, of Chailey in Sussex, who died in 1598. Five generations of Rickwords continued to farm for the next two centuries, at first in Sussex and later in Wiltshire, until the pattern was broken by William Shotter Rickword, a veterinary surgeon by profession, who settled in Colchester about 1812. His grandson, George Rickword, built up a flourishing business as a cabinet maker, upholsterer, auctioneer and undertaker. By his first marriage he had three children, Emily, George (the future librarian) and Henry. After his wife's death he appeared inconsolable, yet six years later he shocked his friends and relations by suddenly marrying a woman nearly thirty years his junior, who bore him seven more children. His children by his first wife deeply resented his remarriage, believing that as a result their education had been neglected and their financial prospects endangered. To make matters worse, he drew heavily on his capital to rebuild his business premises, shortly before the agricultural depression of the 1870s struck a heavy blow at trade in country towns such as Colchester.

The younger George's brooding resentment at the situation is clearly apparent in his family history, written many years later.

> All three of us received a fair education, though my brother Henry's was cut unduly short at fourteen, but we should all have had better chances in life if we had had a longer training. Unfortunately my Father was obsessed with the idea that the business was sufficiently flourishing to provide for all of us – that is to say – a family of ten!! He gave us no

special business training, and the few years' experience we had away from home was not of a character to give us much insight into the management of so complex a concern. His vigorous personality induced him to keep everything as far as possible in his own hands and to give neither information, control nor responsibility to anyone else.

When his father died in 1886 the younger George took over the management of the business, but he was glad to relinquish it on receiving the offer of the borough librarianship ten years later.

The difference between father and son is amusingly illustrated by their religion and politics; the father's were those of a shopkeeper, the son's those of a minor poet. The younger George wrote of his father:

Without being exceptionally spiritually minded, he was a deeply religious man... He belonged to the old reticent High and Dry school so far as he took any definite line, and acquiesced tacitly in the ceremonial revival... He was a keen politician on the High Tory side – hating Radicals and Dissenters theoretically, and long suspicious of Disraeli. Bright and Gladstone were his aversions.

The son, on the other hand, was an Anglo-Catholic Tory of a romantic and sentimental type, a lover of lost causes, to whom the ritual of the Anglican Church whispered the last enchantments of the Middle Ages. After visiting Piddinghoe, in Sussex, in search of ancestors he noted in his diary: "Made my devotions on Holy Cross day Sept. 14, 1923; Church of St. John properly appointed, with Catholic adjuncts", and later the same day he "said a paternoster and ave" in the nearby church of Southease. In his family history popish recusants become "adherents of the Old Faith", Charles I "the Royal Martyr", the Stuarts even after 1689 "the legitimate line", an eighteenth-century Oxford don "a link in the chain between the Catholic churchmen 'of good King Charles's golden days' and John Keble", and David Morgan, a Welsh Jacobite executed in 1746, "one of the last persons to suffer for the Cause". Five pages are devoted to Morgan, on the flimsy grounds that he was a cousin of Mrs Rickword's great-great-great-grandfather. Toryism of this type clearly bore little relation to twentieth-century politics, and although in early life, perhaps under his father's influence, George Rickword had often addressed Conservative election meetings, he made his appointment as borough librarian the pretext for giving up political activity. He continued to vote Conservative, but his commitment became so tepid that even his son Edgell, who was at the other end of the political spectrum, could describe his position as "conventional moderate Tory".[1]

In 1883 he married Mabel Thomas Prosser, the daughter of a local chemist of Welsh descent, and in the next eight years four children were born: Evan George in 1885, Gerald Owen in 1886, Margery

Prosser in 1888 and Barbara May Bevan in 1891. Then, after a seven years' gap, John Edgell was born at the family home at 28 Head Street* on 22 October 1898, and was christened in St Martin's church. It is typical of George Rickword's historical romanticism that all his children were given the names of ancestors of their mother; John Edgell was named after a great-great-grandfather of Mrs Rickword's, who in the eighteenth century had pursued the unromantic trade of butcher and grazier at Trowbridge, in Wiltshire. To his family he was always "Jack"; it was only after he began to write for publication that he took to using the name by which he is generally known.

Colchester was in many respects a birthplace to stimulate the imagination of a future poet, especially one with a sense of the past. With 38,373 inhabitants in 1901 and 43,452 in 1911, it was large enough to have an economic and cultural life of its own, and small enough for every street to be within a few minutes' walk of green fields. Its half-urban, half-rural character was reflected in its industries, engineering and the manufacture of clothing, boots and shoes side by side with corn-milling, brewing, brick-making and rose-growing. London was near enough to be within easy reach, and too far away to threaten Colchester's independence.

Town and country met on market days, when the farmers with their wives flocked in from miles around. As Colchester was a garrison town, young Edgell could hear the noonday gun fired in Abbey Field, and when the troops paraded for inspection could enjoy the pageantry of red-coated linesmen, green-coated riflemen, kilted highlanders and dandified hussars. A mile down the Colne, where the river was tidal, Thames barges from London with huge brown sails unloaded their cargoes of timber and coal at The Hythe. At the river's mouth were the famous oyster fisheries, and every year in October, when the fishing season began, the mayor presided over the oyster feast, at which George Rickword was regularly among the guests. A few miles to the north the Stour flowed past Dedham church and Flatford Mill beneath skies which Constable had often painted.

With an antiquarian for a father, the young Edgell can hardly have failed to realize that Colchester had a longer recorded history than any other English town, a history reflected in its buildings – the earthworks of Camulodunum, where Shakespeare's Cymbeline had his capital, the walls of the Roman *colonia*, a Saxon church tower, the keep of the Conqueror's castle, a ruined Norman priory, seven medieval churches, the gatehouse of a Benedictine abbey and houses of every century since the fourteenth. He would have heard much from his father about the stubborn defence of the town by the royalists in 1648, and how after

* Now renumbered 15.

they surrendered their leaders were shot, martyrs for the Stuart Cause. He probably heard less about Colchester's other martyrs – the Lollards burned in 1428, the Protestants burned in 1557, the nineteen-year-old Quaker James Parnell, who died in the castle in 1656 after a long and cruel imprisonment. Colchester was a town with a long tradition of political and religious radicalism, a hotbed of Lollards, early Protestants, Puritans, sectaries and pioneer trade unionists, where John Ball had preached, where seditious talk had been rife in Mary's reign and priests had been called "knaves" in the streets, where in 1642 "the rude sort of people" had risen *en masse* against royalists and papists, and where striking weavers had rioted in 1724. It was with this tradition, rather than the Tory Anglican tradition his father loved, that Rickword was to identify himself.

"We were a harmonious family," he recalled in his old age.[2] The age-gap between himself and his brothers and sisters meant that he was something of a family pet, and "was treated with more affection and less rivalry than if I had been one of a close-knit batch". In early childhood he saw most of his sister Barbara, who tended to treat him as a living doll, dressing him up and pushing him round in a little cart. He saw little at this time of his other sister, who usually lived with Grandmother Prosser to relieve the strain on the small house, or of his brother Evan. But despite the twelve years' difference in their ages he was always on friendly terms with his second brother, Gerald, who took a kindly interest in him. In later years Gerald followed in their father's footsteps as a local historian, and their common love of books drew them more closely together.

While his brothers and sisters were at school or at work Rickword was forced to amuse himself, which may have helped to develop his imagination, or was thrown back upon his mother's company. A deep affection developed between them. He had few male companions of his own age except his cousin Cecil (the son of George Rickword's brother Henry), a year younger than himself. The enveloping atmosphere of feminine affection in which he lived, he later believed, made him extremely sensitive, with the result that he over-reacted to any rebuke or criticism from his father or Evan, but in general his relations with both his parents were happy. Although he early rejected their religion and politics, they continued to take pride in his literary achievements, and until his mother's death when he was forty he rarely failed to come home to Colchester for Christmas. When he was over sixty he wrote to a friend: "My Mother was central to my emotional life in the formative years, and beyond. I still feel remorse that I gave her a lot of anxiety and did not adequately express my love for her. But perhaps she felt it was there."

As a public official George Rickword was expected to maintain a middle-class standard of living on a salary little more than a skilled workman's wage. In the early 1900s the family moved to 38 Wellesley Road, one of a row of small bow-windowed houses built in drab brick, of a type which was mass-produced all over Victorian England as homes for Mr Pooter and his peers. George Rickword owned this house and three more adjoining it, which brought in a rent of ten shillings a week, but as he had to pay rates on all four the profit was not great. At this time, when Evan had already gone out to work, he gave his wife £9. 0s. 0d a month for housekeeping, out of which she had to feed and clothe four children. The fact that the Rickwords sometimes had a maid living in is less inconsistent with their status of genteel poverty than it may seem; in Edwardian England servants were plentiful and cheap, and even the lower middle class regarded at least one maid as a virtual necessity.

The Rickwords employed a girl from the country, who received £15 or £16 a year and her food, and who kept an eye on little Edgell while his mother was resting or otherwise engaged, adding to the feminine atmosphere which surrounded him. The cost of keeping a servant, of course, contributed to the financial tensions which, Rickword later believed, helped to make him a poet. "A sense of being on the edge certainly influenced my young life and gave me a sense of insecurity," he wrote in his memoirs, "to counter which I began to establish a kind of extra – it's rather difficult to describe – a sort of super-ego, which began to find expression in scribbling and writing fantastic scraps."

The Rickwords' social status demanded that Edgell should begin his education, not at a board school, but at a private school. When he was four or five he was sent to a dame-school run by a Miss Abbott and her starved-looking assistants at 10 Crouch Street, a few minutes' walk from Wellesley Road, where twenty or twenty-five children sat round tables on the first floor of a three-storeyed early-Victorian house, and in return for a small fee were instructed in the three Rs. He found the endless writing on slates and learning by heart boring and the hours very long, but at least two features of school life relieved the monotony; the Bibles used in the scripture lessons, which featured largely in the curriculum, had fascinating illustrations, and the spelling books had metal edges to enable them to withstand wear and tear, which meant that they could be used as weapons.

"Undoubtedly the proximity of my cradle to a bookstack helped to decide my destiny," he wrote as an old man. His interest in books began even before he went to school, when he studied the pictures in books handed down to him by his brothers and sisters or given to him as presents. Some of them lingered in his memory throughout his life – *Shock-headed Peter*, Grimm's *Fairy Tales*, with Cruikshank's plates, Randolph Caldecott's *John Gilpin*, Kipling's *Just So Stories*. The interest

in Cruikshank aroused by the illustrations to Grimm was still alive
when he wrote on the artist over sixty years later. When he progressed
from looking at pictures to reading he discovered poetry. "We had
poetry about the house," he recalled. "Not highbrow stuff; father sometimes read aloud Macaulay's *Lays*, and mother liked Tennyson, which
I read to her sometimes whilst she did the mending, so poetry wasn't
strange or sissy."[3]

Life contained other pleasures for a boy. There were three seaside
resorts within easy reach of Colchester, each with a character of its
own. There was Clacton, with donkey rides, "open-fronted shops dis-
pensing all kinds of luxuries, such as little saucers of whelks in vinegar
and Clacton rock," and as excursion trains emptied a "seething mass
of East-Enders having a jolly good day out". As for the other two,
"Walton-on-the-Naze provided none of the exciting vulgarities of Clacton, but its beach and cliffs were better fun for children who wanted
an open-air holiday. Frinton was a case by itself – almost policed by
guardians of gentility. Even the errand boys ceased to whistle as they
went on their rounds." As Rickword grew older there was the additional
pleasure of long country walks with Gerald and sometimes with their
father. They considered a walk of ten or twelve miles an enjoyable form
of exercise, and the pleasure was all the greater when they stopped for
lunch at a public house (one Sunday it was rabbit pudding at Peldon
on the way to Mersea Island, Rickword remembered), with half a pint
of beer for Gerald and lemonade for himself.

From Miss Abbott's school Rickword progressed in 1908 to Colchester Royal Grammar School, where two years later he won a foundation
scholarship. The school was founded by Henry VIII in 1539 and granted
a new charter by Elizabeth I in 1584, and when Rickword entered it
was being dragged into the twentieth century by a dynamic headmaster,
P. Shaw Jeffrey. When he assumed the post in 1900 there were only
29 pupils, and the buildings erected in 1853, consisting of a large school-
room and two small and badly lit classrooms (towards the cost of which
Rickword's grandfather had subscribed five guineas), were in a state
of decay. By 1914 the number of pupils had risen to 200, and a new
hall, classrooms and laboratories had been built, new subjects introduced into the curriculum, a modern side established, playing fields
provided and a cadet corps and boy scout troop formed.

The modest account of his scholastic achievements which Rickword
gave in later life ("I wasn't very good at school. I was lazy"[4]) is hardly
borne out by his school record, which shows that he received form
prizes for scripture and English in 1909, a bronze medal for English
and form prizes for science and mathematics in 1911, form prizes for
science and Latin in 1912, and the governors' prize for English literature
and form prizes for science and scripture in 1913. The subjects in which

he particularly distinguished himself – English, science and scripture – formed a useful combination; familiarity with the mythology and rich imagery of the Old Testament was an asset for a future poet, and a sound scientific training counteracted any temptation to take his religious studies too literally.

The Royal Grammar School also taught him about the English class system. The foundation scholars, who had sat for the scholarship examination while fee-paying pupils at the Grammar School or at private schools, wore gowns and square caps "like mortar boards with no stuffing in" at prayers and civic functions, unlike the county scholars (scholarship boys from the board schools) who, although often among the most gifted boys in the school, were generally looked down on. By the time he was in the fourth form he had learned that any breach of social convention in such matters as speech or dress was likely to expose one to ridicule. Contempt for poverty and contempt for the unconventional together produced one especially painful incident. At a time when the Rickwords were in financial difficulties Mrs Rickword received a parcel of clothes from a relation whose children had outgrown them, including some woollen combinations which had belonged to a girl cousin and had been adapted to allow for the development of her breasts. As these fitted Edgell he was compelled to wear them in cold weather. While he was changing for gym one day they were noticed by a classmate, who roared with laughter and shouted "Look at Ricky, he's growing bubs!" Fortunately the term was near its end, and during the holidays the incident was forgotten by everyone except Rickword himself.

After receiving instruction from a soft-hearted curate, he was confirmed by the Bishop of Colchester on 2 March 1913. A fortnight later his brother Evan, who was also his godfather, sent him a letter which combined much hearty good advice ("it may help you in your endeavours to live the Straight Life if you think of it as you would of a hard-fought game of footer or cricket") with distinctively Anglo-Catholic pious sentiments ("when you feel most miserable and wretched and think that you can do nothing right then go to the altar and meet there Jesus in the Blessed Sacrament"). Religious teaching of this type, however well-meant, produced the contrary effect. Rickword had been brought up to believe that some magical virtue resided in the rituals of confirmation and holy communion, but after receiving his first communion at Easter he was disappointed to discover that he remained the same unregenerate boy as before.

He reacted by taking to a career of crime. Together with two classmates a year or two older than himself – Walter Town, the son of another local government official, and Eric Brand, whose father owned a children's outfitter's shop in the High Street – he formed a gang which

raided the school tuck shop and broke into empty houses, where they
had feasts of sweets and soft drinks. They abandoned an attempt to
steal a chicken from a run on discovering how much noise it made
when they tried to seize it, but succeeded in stealing three pigeons from
a loft, which they sold to a fishmonger for ninepence each. Rickword,
who acted as the gang's treasurer and kept its accounts in code, used
the proceeds to buy the next evening's feast.

At about this time he discovered the opposite sex. During the summer
of 1914 he conducted a correspondence simultaneously with a girl
named Gladys White in Clacton and another named Trixie in Felixstowe. Of Gladys he could remember little in later life, except that she
wore a red overcoat and had a kind heart. While the friendship lasted
he often saw her, as Clacton was within easy cycling distance of Colchester, but it soon petered out. His affaire with Trixie, a girl two years
older than himself who worked in an office and was better educated
than Gladys, was more serious, and they continued to correspond at
least until he joined the army. Letters which Town wrote to him in
1915 and 1916 make it clear that he was also flirting at the same time
with several girls in Colchester.

With stealing and flirtation, both forms of adolescent rebellion, went
a conscious rejection of his parents' politics. In January 1914 the
employees of the Britannia Iron Works at Colchester were locked out,
and between fifty and sixty families were reduced to such distress that
the mayor organized a relief fund. Rickword was so shocked by the
suffering caused by the employers' action that from that time forward
he felt himself a Socialist.* His conversion was almost certainly not a
sudden emotional reaction to a particular situation, for Socialism had
been in the news at Colchester during 1913. In the spring of that year
the Rev. F.H. de Courcy-Benwell had become rector of St Martin's,
the church which the Rickwords attended and at which George Rickword was people's warden. Despite his aristocratic name, the new rector
not only declared himself a Socialist and a supporter of women's suf-
frage, but gave a lecture on Socialism in July to the Colchester branch
of the Independent Labour Party, and even addressed an open-air
Socialist meeting in August.

Even more shocking, a Socialist candidate won a seat on the town
council for the first time at the November elections. The *Colchester
Gazette*, a dyed-in-the-wool Conservative and Anglican journal which
normally concentrated on the wickedness of Liberals, Radicals, Home
Rulers, Papists and Dissenters, promptly turned its fire on the Socialists,

---

* In his memoirs and the account of his life contributed to *World Authors* Rickword
dated these events about 1911, but the lock-out of the Britannia Works is the only one
that fits his description. This date is confirmed by his statement in *Poetry Nation* I, p.77,
that his political commitments began when he was "about 15 or 16".

with a campaign intended to prove that Socialism was a conspiracy for the propagation of atheism. As some of the best-known Socialists in Essex were either Anglo-Catholic priests like de Courcy-Benwell and Conrad Noel of Thaxted or Primitive Methodist ministers, this was not easy, but it continued to labour the subject for several weeks. George Rickword unconsciously furthered his son's political education by bringing home the public library copy of the Fabian *New Statesman* after it had completed its week's service in the reading room; his sole interest was in the book reviews, which gave him suggestions for library acquisitions, but Edgell read the political articles as well. At the same time he read the Socialist writers that were available, notably Morris, Shaw, Wells, Jack London and Gorky, and his reading of realist novelists – Dostoevsky, Hardy and Frank Norris among them – influenced him in the same direction. In his search for a new and more just society he began making a collection of Utopian stories.

In those early months of 1914, when he was rejecting his parents' certainties, there was a sense of crisis in the air, even in peaceful Colchester. The Ulster Protestants were demonstrating their loyalty to the Crown by openly preparing for armed rebellion, while Unionist Party leaders stumped the country preaching sedition. In March Rickword and about sixty other Grammar School cadets took part in a field day at Great Bromley, where they were ordered to round up a company of "Ulster Volunteers". The great strike movement of those years made an impact on Colchester; a six-day strike at Mumford's engineering works in May won the employees a two shillings increase in their minimum weekly wage, and in the surrounding countryside the agricultural labourers went on strike. A general strike, civil war in Ireland, war with Germany: any or all of these seemed possible. Meanwhile at the Grammar School lessons and examinations went on as usual. Rickword had passed the Cambridge local examinations in a number of subjects in July 1913, with distinction in religious knowledge, and took more subjects in the following July, receiving third class honours with distinction in English. As three of the other entrants gained second class honours and eight, including Town and Brand, received passes, it was a respectable but not a brilliant result.

When the school broke up at the end of July 1914 the cadet corps left for its annual camp. Before they had been away for a week war was declared, and the boys were sent home. Rickword, however, wrote to his parents that his company commander had been moved to the regimental depot at Felixstowe and wanted Rickword to accompany him for a few days as his runner. At the same time he wrote to Trixie to tell her of his imminent arrival in Felixstowe. In her reply on 5 August she wrote: "I wonder if I shall hear the guns tonight. I expect so if there are any to hear. It's really impossible to grasp the situation, but I'm feeling a bit nervous now. Aren't you?" Nervous or not, he went on to Felixstowe, where he found that many of the inhabitants were leaving in panic and the lights on the promenade had been switched off for the duration. He amused himself as best he could while Trixie was at work and spent the evenings with her at a cinema or café. After three days his money was running out. He returned to Colchester.

The war brought changes to the Grammar School. Most of the sixth form promptly volunteered. Town had joined the Essex Regiment before Christmas, and Brand enlisted in the Rifle Brigade in May 1915. Rickword went to London with Gerald in the same month in an attempt to join the Artists' Rifles, although he was only 16 at the time. The doctor who examined him made no pretence of believing his claim to be almost 18, and told him to come back in a year's time.* The departure of so many of the senior boys probably meant that he was promoted to responsible posts in the school earlier than he would otherwise have been; by the time he left in July 1916 he was a prefect, a member of the second cricket eleven, captain of his house football, cricket and shooting teams, a sergeant in the cadet corps and a member of the debating society committee.

The fact that he was appointed only a Queen's Prefect, which placed him below the King's Prefects in the school hierarchy, suggests that the authorities did not entirely approve of his activities, political or amorous. In March 1916 he was conducting an *affaire* with a pupil at Miss Dobson's boarding school for young ladies, and one night was discovered climbing up to her dormitory window. "My mother received a stinging letter from the headmistress demanding my abject humiliation and punishment," he recalled in his memoirs.

> In answer I concocted a Shelleyan tirade of indignation against the wicked tyranny exercised by schoolmistresses and proprietors of boarding schools, smothering the natural exuberance of youth under hypocritical restrictions and denying them the freedom that nature had created for them. My mother remarked sharply that this was not an apology, and ordered me to go back and write something entirely different. I realized that I must admit defeat, and produced an insipid expression of regret for my behaviour, giving assurance that I would not behave in the same way again, which was accepted by the headmistress.

For a seventeen-year-old with a distinction in English who was in rebellion against his parents' politics and religion and in love with several girls at once, the obvious next step was the writing of verse. From his mother's favourite, Tennyson, Rickword had moved on to

---

* In his memoirs Rickword dates this incident in the early autumn of 1915. It is dated earlier here on the evidence of a letter from Trixie of 2 June 1915, in which she says: "How disappointing for you to be told you were not eligible! No doubt you were thought to have run away from home, that is if you went to town alone."

Swinburne, finding something intoxicating in the sentiment and the rhythm of "Thou hast conquered, O pale Galilean; the world has grown grey from thy breath". Swinburne led on to the sensuality of Rossetti and the Aesthetes, from Pater to Wilde. His taste for such verse could have embarrassing consequences, as when he wrote in a girl's autograph album:

> As balmy as the breath of her you love
> When deep between her breasts it comes to you.

Her reaction was to tear out the page and return it to him with the comment "You're barmy all right".

His knowledge of contemporary poetry was extended by J.G. Worth, a young Australian who joined the Grammar School staff as English master in 1914. Worth violently disapproved of the Aesthetes in general and Wilde in particular, and held up as healthier models the work of Rupert Brooke, Flecker and other Georgians. Rickword was able to read verse by some of the Georgians, and particularly those who later became known as the Squirearchy, in the *New Statesman*, which under the literary editorship of J.C. Squire published in 1916 poems by W.J. Turner, John Freeman, W.H. Davies, Francis Brett Young, Joseph Campbell and Squire himself. According to his later recollections, however, Swinburne remained the dominant influence on the verse which he wrote before joining the army.

Only one specimen of his early work seems to have survived, an untitled and unfinished draft written on the back of a letter from Worth dated 15 November 1915:

> Though I should see thee ne'er again
> Thine image in my heart will dwell
> For thou must know I love thee well
> Though I should see thee ne'er again.
>
> One word from lips for love full meet
> One glance from modest hazell eyes
> Of Hazell*
> Raised up to mine in modest wise
> And thou hadst fettered me Oh Sweet.
>
> Unknown, unknowing thy dear form
> Flower of the forest glade & pure
> Free from the taint of gross pursuer…

These lines may have been intended for Trixie or another of his girl friends, but the emphasis on modesty and purity suggests that they were the "scrap of a poem" which he wrote for the daughter of a Mrs

---

* These two words should have been deleted.

Mustard, a child of five or six. The fact that they can be interpreted as addressed either to a young woman or to a little child indicates the imprecision of their conventional pre-Georgian archaisms. Although his other early work has disappeared, he certainly wrote a great deal of both prose and verse, which he later referred to as "doggerel, scribble", in the first two years of the war.

He made his début as an editor in 1914 with a magazine called *The Idler*; no copies seem to have survived, but it was apparently a Grammar School publication of a less formal character than the official *Colcestrian*. References in letters from Town and Brand suggest that it included contributions from old boys in the army describing their experiences. More ambitiously, late in 1915 he sent a work entitled *The Ruler* to Cassell's with a view to publication; on their card acknowledging its receipt he wrote many years later "I don't remember what this was, unless a verse drama in Swinburnian style". A few months later he wrote a poem protesting against the execution of the leaders of the Dublin Easter Rising of 1916. His model may have been Swinburne's "An Appeal", which pleaded in vain for mercy for the Fenians condemned to death in Manchester in 1867. He probably chose this subject as the theme of his first known political poem at a time when Pearse, Connolly and their comrades were generally regarded in England as traitors in German pay who had met their just deserts, influenced by the protests against the executions published in the *New Statesman*, particularly that by Shaw. The sympathy with Irish republicanism displayed here he was to retain throughout his life. In 1945 he wrote: "We can never think of Easter now without bringing to mind the Easter Rising."[5]

Worth joined the Royal Army Service Corps in the summer of 1915, but he continued to correspond with Rickword. Although twelve years older than Rickword, in the seven long letters which have survived he treats him as his intellectual equal and shows respect for his critical judgment. Reporting that he has tried to read Henry James's *The Outcry*, he adds "I would like to know if you think 'The Outcry' is good *English*". Rickword's Socialist enthusiasms are evident from Worth's replies, which contain such sentences as "Was very interested in your remarks on Morris" and "So you are still at grips with social problems!" His comments on society, although vague and muddle-headed, here and there express ideas on such topics as the unity of art and life and the possibility of a genuinely popular culture which seem to have lingered in Rickword's mind and contributed to his later thinking. On Morris he writes: "What one admires most about him is that he succeeded in transmuting his ideas into action even beyond the writing of poetry which in itself would be sufficient justification". When Rickword asks who is to do the unpleasant work in a Socialist society, Worth comments:

"The Athenian citizen could be joyous and develop his 'self' because slaves did the menial work for him! We *must* make labour dignified and sweet – as it should be. Browning wanted grocers to read poetry – and perhaps live poetry – why shouldn't they?"

The letters suggest that Worth's feelings for Rickword contained a sexual element of which he himself may not have been fully conscious. In one of them he devotes two pages to a hysterical attack on Wilde, and then continues: "I would sooner read Walt Whitman...Have you read the Calamus poems?" That a bachelor of 29, immediately after violently denouncing Wilde, should recommend to a seventeen-year-old youth poems in which homoerotic love is thinly disguised as "the dear love of comrades" suggests that he was attempting to sublimate feelings about which he harboured a sense of guilt.

The homosexual element in another of Rickword's friendships of this period was not sublimated at all. Early in the war his father introduced George Coombe to his family, a young man of some education serving in the Royal Army Medical Corps and stationed a few miles outside Colchester. Coombe struck up a close friendship with Rickword, conducted a correspondence with him on literary matters and lent him a number of books by Wilde, whom, unlike Worth, he greatly admired. One of his letters to Rickword ends: "I am longing to see you again my dear boy, it seems ages since we met...With love and best wishes Yours affectionately Georges." The conclusion of another is even warmer in tone: "Adieu, sweetheart, until tomorrow. Yours very affectionately G." One evening after a meal with the Rickwords Coombe deliberately or accidentally stayed late enough to miss the last train, whereupon George Rickword, who had an innocent mind, suggested that he should share his son's bed. During the night Coombe made a determined assault on his bedmate's virtue, which was vigorously repelled. The friendship ended abruptly, leaving Rickword with the distaste for homosexuality which is discernible in some of his poems.

Worth's high opinion of Rickword's abilities was shared by the headmaster, Shaw Jeffrey, who suggested that he should work for a university exhibition. He accordingly sat for scholarships to both Oxford and London universities on a number of occasions in 1915 and 1916, but felt no great disappointment when he failed. Most of his friends were already in khaki, and he was impatient to join them. Conscription, in any case, was introduced in February 1916, and even if he had won an exhibition he would have been called up before he could reap the benefit of it.

From the vantage point of the late twentieth century his eagerness to plunge into the slaughter seems incomprehensible, and incompatible with his Socialism. That was not how he saw it. In 1940, recalling "the naïveté of our state of mind at home in 1915", he wrote:

It is doubtful if the younger generation of today, familiarized for years by the news-reels and illustrated papers with the destructiveness of modern warfare as practised on the bodies of the Jonah-countries, can realise the virgin ignorance of their counterparts in 1914-15. We were inured to colonial wars, pacifications of backward peoples (our toy soldiers had significantly light armaments), which only differed from the more risky and expensive forms of sport in the degree of danger and hardship involved.[6]

At sixteen or seventeen he was still child enough to regard the war as a great adventure in which the other members of his gang had the good luck to be taking part and from which he was unfairly excluded. "War seemed to open up exhilarating experiences," he said as an old man. "War fever is a real disease."[7] The fact that Gerald, then approaching thirty, assisted his attempt to enlist when under age and that their parents must have been aware of their action suggests that the older Rickwords saw the war in similar terms. What, after all, did they really know about it? Colchester's only first-hand experience of war had been a stray bomb dropped in a back garden one Sunday evening in February 1915, which had broken a good many windows and damaged some sheds but caused no casualties.

Little enlightenment was to be gathered from the press. The events of 1 July 1916, the first day of the offensive on the Somme and the bloodiest day in the history of the British Army, were reported by the weekly *Colchester Gazette* on 5 July under the following headlines:

ANGLO-FRENCH ADVANCE
MANY FORTIFIED POSITIONS TAKEN
THIRTEEN VILLAGES CAPTURED BY
FRENCH AND BRITISH TROOPS

The next issue, on 12 July, reported the continuing slaughter under equally cheering headlines:

IMPORTANT BRITISH AND FRENCH SUCCESSES
GERMAN FIRST LINE CAPTURED

A glimpse of reality creeps into a paragraph lower down on the page:

> a large contingent of wounded soldiers, numbering over 300, the result of the great offensive in the west, arrived at Colchester during the last week-end. Their high spirits were very noticeable, many of the cases being only minor ones caused, apparently, by charging barbed wire entanglements. The incessant and awful din of conflict had shattered the nerves and in some cases temporarily weakened the minds of the poor fellows.

The reporter's desire to tell the truth had clearly come into conflict with his duty to write what was expected of him, with the result that the wounded combined high spirits with shattered nerves and weakened minds, but probably few readers, eager for reassurance, noticed the contradiction. So far from deterring Rickword, as he recalled when writing his memoirs, "the bloody battles of the early summer of 1916 roused one's impatience to get into the army".

His Socialism did not necessarily conflict with his desire to fight. The majority of Socialists in Britain and France, and even some in Russia, supported the war as one of self-defence against Prussian militarism. The majority of German Socialists supported it as a war of self-defence against Russian tsarism, and could quote those ardent Russophobes Marx and Engels in support of their attitude. It was the active Fabian propagandist Rupert Brooke who welcomed the war with the cry "Now, God be thanked Who has matched us with His hour". The minority of British Socialists who opposed it mostly did so as Christian pacifists; revolutionary Marxist opponents of the war formed a minority within a minority.

There was certainly some anti-war feeling in Colchester. "The outbreak of the war, allegedly to free the world from the tyranny of Prussian militarism, was rapidly followed by the virtual suspension of the democratic rights which had been won with so much effort," Rickword wrote over twenty years later.

> As the effects of the Defence of the Realm Act became felt, with the intrusion of the police and the bureaucracy and amateur tribunals of local big-wigs and die-hard dug-outs into every aspect of the people's private lives, deep resentment was aroused. It was realized, particularly by the working class, that these anti-democratic measures were not being used to ensure the most efficient conduct of the war, but to safeguard the profits of the same monopolists who held up progress in peace-time.[8]

When he wrote this he may have had in mind a resolution adopted in May 1916 by the Colchester trades council and Labour Representation Committee, which condemned conscription of manpower without conscription of wealth and declared "undying opposition to Prussian methods, militarism and acts of repression, recently adopted in this country".[9] There is no evidence, however, that he had any personal contact with any Socialist organization in Colchester; his statement that he "felt" himself a Socialist after the 1914 lock-out suggests that his Socialism at this stage of his life was an emotional attitude rather than a reasoned position.

An afternoon in mid-September 1916 lingered in his memory sixty years later. "I remember going down to Dedham one afternoon in early autumn within one or two weeks of my call-up," he wrote,

> and addressing the calm river as it flowed towards Manningtree and then to sea. The leaves were fluttering off the pollard willows that studded

the banks of the Stour in the stretch from Dedham to Flatford. Was it then or later that I came upon the line of Edward Thomas, "The hundred last leaves stream upon the willow"? I don't remember whether it had yet been published, but that was what I thought of as I meandered along the towing path.

In fact Thomas had not yet written "The Long Small Room", which concludes with this line, but several months earlier he had written another line which, if Rickword had known it, he would have found even more apt:

Now all roads lead to France...

II. War

In 1860, when a panic fear of French invasion was sweeping the country, a group of painters, architects, writers and actors formed a volunteer organization, the Artists' Rifles. Its most prominent members were two future presidents of the Royal Academy, Frederick Leighton and John Everett Millais, but Rossetti, Holman Hunt, Morris, Burne-Jones, Swinburne and G.F. Watts also joined, and Ruskin was an honorary member. The artistic element in its membership declined in time, but it remained a predominantly middle-class body.

On the outbreak of war it was assigned the dual role of fighting unit and officers' training corps, to be drawn on to supply officers to other units. A second battalion was raised at the end of August 1914, and a third on 1 January 1915, which received official recognition as an officers' training corps in November. The battalion had a special attraction for ambitious young men who hoped to obtain a commission quickly. For those of artistic and literary tastes the attraction was strengthened by its historical associations. Edward Thomas enlisted in July 1915 and Wilfred Owen in October, after writing excitedly to his mother: "Lord Leighton, Millais, Forbes Robertson were in Artists' Rifles!!"[1] Both factors had no doubt contributed to Rickword's attempt to join it in 1915, which he now repeated, with success.

On 25 September 1916 he reported to a depot in Bunhill Fields, where he passed his medical examination, was sworn in, received a number (762491) and was issued with his uniform and kit. After spending the night with friends of the Town family in Maida Vale he joined his squad of recruits at Liverpool Street station. They were taken on to Hare Hall Camp, Gidea Park, Romford, the headquarters of the 3rd Battalion. The camp was overcrowded, for the battalion was often over 3,000 strong, and Rickword had to live, eat and sleep in a hut shared with about thirty other men. Having learnt the rudiments of military drill in his school cadet corps, he found some of the training course easy, though boring, but as he was not deft with his hands the winding of his puttees and the folding of his blankets to meet the army's standards of neatness were something of a nightmare. He evaded pre-breakfast physical jerks by getting himself appointed batman to one of the officers; unfortunately the officer in question was responsible for training the recruits in trench-digging, and Rickword had to remove thick deposits of Essex mud daily from his top boots.

To compensate for this drudgery, the peculiar nature of the Artists' Rifles gave him a better chance of finding congenial company at Hare

Hall Camp than he would have had in another unit. A few months earlier Privates Thomas and Owen had been stationed there at the same time without being aware of each other's existence, but Thomas had struck up a friendship with the young painter Paul Nash. Early in December, while in the camp hospital with an infected arm caused by a smallpox inoculation, Rickword chanced to hear the name "Turner, W.J." at a roll call. The name struck a chord, for W.J. Turner had regularly contributed music criticism to the *New Statesman*, and between June and October four of his poems had appeared there, including the much-anthologized "Romance" and a poem inspired by recently discovered cave-paintings, "In the Caves of Auvergne", which had impressed Rickword. When an opportunity occurred he asked "Are you the Turner who writes in the *New Statesman*?". When Turner said he was, Rickword told him how much he admired his poems. This meeting, his first encounter with a published poet, was to have important consequences, for Turner, an Australian nine years his senior, had a range of contacts which were to prove valuable to Rickword when he was beginning his literary career. For the time being each found the other's company stimulating. As the winter of 1916-17 was exceptionally severe and they had nowhere to spend their spare time except a crowded hut or canteen, they rented a room, complete with a fire, in a house in Gidea Park for seven shillings a week. Their quiet evenings there provided an escape from army routine, but when Turner was transferred to an artillery course early in 1917 shortage of money obliged Rickword to give up the room.

In June he was sent to an officer cadet battalion at Farnborough, Hampshire. He found the course more interesting than his basic training. It included subjects such as map-reading and elementary tactics which required some brainwork, in addition to shooting, grenade-throwing, trench-digging, night exercises and a great deal of square-bashing. Although the life was hard, there were more amenities than at Gidea Park; meals were served in a mess room, the huts were less crowded and a well-lit room was provided for study in the evenings. Farnborough was a pleasant town with a good bookshop, where Rickword found Constance Garnett's new translations of Chekhov's short stories. It also lingered in his memory as the place where he lost his virginity, seduced in a field by a country girl whom he had never seen before and never saw again – an event which he remembered as "more than confirmation and first communion rolled into one".

After passing his final examination he went back to Colchester on leave pending gazette. He had applied to be posted to the Essex Regiment, in which Town and several of his other friends were serving, but on 25 September he was gazetted to the Royal Berkshire Regiment. After some delay his papers came through, and towards the end of

October he reported to the headquarters of its reserve battalion at Portsmouth, which he found a gloomy place. Here he formed a friendship with James Rowe, another young subaltern from the Artists' Rifles, which was to end tragically.

In the wake of the Easter Rising, Irish garrisons in Ireland were being replaced by English regiments, and in November the Berkshires were transferred to Dublin. Portobello Barracks, where they were stationed, had a sinister reputation because of the murder there, after the Rising, of the pacifist Sheehy Skeffington by an officer who was later found to be deranged. Life had some uncomfortable features, such as a four-day gas course. Dublin offered compensations, however. The subalterns were astounded at the quantity and quality of the ham, beef and butter available at the buffet lunches, and tucked in so greedily that the adjutant frequently reprimanded them. On a higher level, Dublin had a lively cultural life; Rickword saw a play by Maeterlinck, he remembered, "in a salon in O'Connell Street just by or underneath a piano shop". He was delighted by the friendliness of the Irish, who showed no resentment at the damage inflicted by the army during the suppression of the Rising. Although he sympathized with Irish national aspirations, he was surprised to find that no one appeared particularly interested in the subject; it does not seem to have occurred to him that in 1917 no Irish republican was likely to disclose his beliefs to an English officer.

In December Rickword and Rowe were gazetted to the 5th Battalion of the Royal Berkshire Regiment, a new battalion formed in August 1914 which had been serving in France since May 1915. Together with the 7th Norfolks, the 7th Suffolks and the 9th Essex, it formed part of the 35th Infantry Brigade, one of the three brigades which made up the Twelfth (Eastern) Division, then attached to General Sir Henry Horne's First Army. Rickword and Rowe crossed the Irish Sea at night, and travelled by train to London and thence to Southampton. After crossing to Le Havre on 12 December they had a slow and dreary journey to Robecq, where five days later they reported for duty at battalion headquarters.

Rickword was assigned to B Company, and having reported to company headquarters just had time for a quick wash and shave before joining his fellow-officers at mess. Dinner was not a very lively meal, and he was glad to get back to his billet in a small cottage for a good night's rest. "As I walked down the road I realized for the first time that I was on my own and actually at war," he recalled in his old age. "Way in the south the sky was alight and there was a rumbling of the distant bombardment, too far off to hear the individual explosions. I suddenly felt extremely lonely and vulnerable in this flat countryside with no hedges, no trees for a long way round and a strange bed to go to."

During the last ten days of November the 5th Berkshires had suffered heavily in the Cambrai offensive, losing thirteen officers and 462 other ranks killed, wounded or missing, and on 2 December they had been withdrawn from the line and moved north to the Béthune area. When Rickword joined them they were licking their wounds and enjoying a well-earned rest. On 21 December they marched to the small town of Merville, where they were able to celebrate Christmas in some comfort; there were even performances in the local theatre by the divisional concert party, the Spades, who took their name from the divisional emblem, the Ace of Spades. Christmas dinner in the officers' mess, according to the menu which Rickword preserved among his souvenirs, consisted of *huîtres, consommé à la reine, soles frites, dindes rôties, petits pois,* Christmas pudding (a dish for which no French name exists), *fromage, fruits, desserts* and *café.*

His first experience of front-line service did not come until 21 January 1918, when the Berkshires relieved the 7th Sussex in the Fleurbaix area, south of Armentières, in the sector of the line between two trench systems known as New Bond Street and Brompton Road. Their stay in the trenches, which lasted a week, was unexciting enough to be summed up in the battalion's official war diary in the words: "Very quiet sector and good accommodation for all ranks. Casualties – 2 O.R. wounded." War, Rickword decided, wasn't so bad, though very uncomfortable. The biting cold, hard frosts and deep snow with which 1917 ended and 1918 began on the Western Front seemed the worst enemy to the young recruit, though more experienced soldiers preferred them to the mud in which so much of their lives was spent.

The Twelfth Division was reorganized on 6 February, when the 5th Berkshires were transferred to the 36th Brigade, which also included the 9th Royal Fusiliers and the 7th Royal Sussex. Meanwhile the front remained almost uncannily quiet, except for an incident on 17 February when A Company of the 5th Berkshires was shelled out of its billets and four men were wounded. From 5 March onwards, however, the Germans greatly increased their shelling and made sporadic trench raids. Everyone knew that an offensive was coming, and when not in the line the Berkshires were kept busy constructing new defences, harassed by enemy shelling.

On 19 March Rickword and Rowe, who had been put in charge of a working party, were talking together when a shell exploded nearby. Both were hit by flying splinters. They were taken to the base hospital at St Pol, where Rowe died on 17 April, although the wound in the shoulder which Rickword had received was found to be comparatively slight. St Pol was some miles behind the lines, but it still came under fire. Rickword later recalled that "the Germans were bombing the railway station by day, testing, with fair success, a long-range gun on the church in the square, and brightening our evenings with air-raids on the dumps surrounding the hospital". He also remembered a visit to the hospital by a concert party, and commented: "For the courage which faced these dangers and the skill which organized it no praise could be extravagant".[2]

While Rickword was being kept under observation, Ludendorff on 21 March launched his long-awaited offensive on the Somme front, which at first swept all before it. During the night of 24-25 March, just after Rickword had rejoined his battalion, the Twelfth Division was hurried southward in buses to Warloy, west of Albert, to reinforce the 5th Army. The 36th Brigade spent 25 March marching in various directions in intense cold and periodically receiving changes of orders, but by dawn on the 26th it had taken up its position along a railway embankment north of Albert, with the Berkshires in reserve at the village of Martinsart. The brigade's situation seemed desperate. Its position was commanded by higher ground to the east, and although the River Ancre ran between none of the bridges over it had been destroyed. The old trenches were useless, and the brigade had few entrenching tools, no barbed wire, no grenades and no Very lights. Soon after noon the Germans were seen advancing into the river valley, and by the evening they had occupied Albert.

On the morning of the 27th they launched an attack from the north, which was halted by rapid fire from a platoon of the Berkshires, and a counter-attack by a brigade of the Naval Division drove them back. In the late afternoon another German attack from the south, assisted by aircraft, forced two platoons to withdraw, but the Berkshires succeeded in forming a strong line on a ridge to the south of Martinsart. After a third strong attack on the following morning had been repulsed a lull followed until the brigade was relieved during the night of 29-30 March and withdrawn to Warloy. In the previous five days' fighting the Berkshires had lost eleven men killed and 67 wounded.

After three days out of the line, which were spent working on new defences, the battalion returned on 2 April to the front, which now ran due west of Albert. B Company was on the right of the line, within sight of the Hanging Virgin, the gilded statue crowning the tower of the modern basilica at Albert, which as a result of shelling was bent over at a right angle to the tower. A belief had grown up among the troops on both sides that when the statue fell the war would end; in fact British artillery fire would soon bring down the tower to prevent the Germans from using it as an observation post, with seven weary months of war still to go. On the evening of 4 April Rickword shocked the major in command at mess by circulating the port in the wrong direction; however grave the military situation, regimental tradition had to be upheld. As he left the mess he heard a rumbling in the east, to which he drew the major's attention before rejoining his platoon.

The platoon spent a miserable night, crouching in the bottom of a trench as the barrage of which he had heard the first rumble grew heavier and the drizzle in the air turned to rain. One man suffered an hysterical seizure, grovelling on the ground until he was taken out of earshot of the guns by two medical orderlies.

At 9.30 on 5 April the Germans launched an attack on the sector of the line to the left of that held by B Company; this was repulsed, but in a second attack at noon they gained control of about 600 yards of the trenches held by A and C Companies. Three platoons of reserve troops which were sent to restore the situation lost half their men killed or wounded by enemy machine-gun fire; a counter-attack by the Royal Sussex was only partly successful, and it took a second counter-attack by the Fusiliers to drive the Germans out. When the division was relieved on the 7th the Berkshires had lost 255 men killed, wounded or missing in five days, and A and C Companies had suffered so heavily that the battalion had to be reorganized as two companies instead of three. But the German offensive had been held.

After a fortnight of training and work on defences the Berkshires returned to the front line in the Beaumont Hamel sector, to the north of where they had previously been operating, in the last week of April. During this period the two sides confined themselves mainly to an exchange of artillery and trench mortar fire, but after the Berkshires had again returned to the line an enemy patrol made a raid on their trenches on 12 May in which Rickword was wounded. Although his wound was not dangerous, it was serious enough for him to be sent back to England on 26 May.

He spent some pleasant weeks in the military hospital at Reading, catching up on his arrears of reading, writing a great deal of verse, which he found much easier than prose, and punting on the Thames when he was sufficiently recovered to leave the hospital grounds. On 19 June he heard from his parents that Gerald, who had been put in a low medical category and was serving as a sergeant in a labour battalion of the Berkshires, was in Colchester on embarkation leave. As this was possibly his last chance of seeing his brother alive he applied for 48 hours' leave, which was refused on the ground that "the reason given is not sufficient to justify special leave".

Deciding that family loyalty took precedence over military pedantry, he returned to Colchester without leave. Next morning the military police arrived at his home while he was out having a drink with Gerald, and left a message with his bewildered mother that he must return to the hospital without delay. In fact he spent another night at home, and on his return to Reading was put under house arrest. As his offence was not serious he was let off with a reprimand, but when in the following week he was passed fit for service he was given only ten days' leave instead of the usual three weeks.

Before returning to France he was sent for another spell at Portobello Barracks. Little had changed except that the rations were not quite so lavish as in the previous year. His duties were light, being confined to drilling men, leading an occasional route march and commanding the guard posted at the Bank of Ireland. His sexual education had progressed since his initiation at Farnborough, and he acquired a girl friend. His literary education was also progressing. One day he asked in a Grafton Street bookshop for James Joyce's *Portrait of the Artist as a Young Man*, of which he had read a favourable review in the *New Statesman*. After hesitating for a moment (in Dublin Joyce was not considered respectable) the assistant asked him to call back later, and when he returned produced a copy already wrapped from under the counter.* But the war could not be put entirely out of mind, as he was sharply reminded when he learned that his friend Eric Brand had been killed in action on 23 August, at the age of twenty-two.

Whatever his views on the war – and they had certainly changed radically in the last year – when he was recalled to France in September he went willingly, drawn by the same loyalty to his comrades which had sent Siegfried Sassoon and Wilfred Owen back to the line.

While passing through London for the second time on his way from Dublin to France he stopped at Fred Henderson's bookshop in Charing Cross Road, the Bomb Shop, which was prepared to display any piece of literature hostile to the establishment, whether Radical, Fabian, Marxist, Anarchist, syndicalist, pacifist, vegetarian or anti-vivisectionist. In the summer of 1917 it had distributed printed copies of Siegfried Sassoon's letter to his commanding officer protesting against "the political errors and insincerities for which the fighting men are being sacrificed", until all the remaining copies were seized by the police. There Rickword picked up another work of Sassoon's, a slim red-covered collection of poems called *Counter-Attack*. It was not the first collection of war poems which he had read. He had bought Robert Graves's *Over the Brazier* in the Colchester branch of W.H. Smith's, and later his *Fairies and Fusiliers*, both of which had delighted him. He had also read Robert Nichols's *Ardours and Endurances*, which he found theatrical and wordy, though he kept the book until his death. *Counter-Attack*, however, came as a revelation of how war could be dealt with "in the vocabulary of war", and gave him "a start towards writing more colloquially, and not in a second-hand literary fashion". He also took another book to France with him, the two-volume Muses' Library edition of Donne's poems, and like the soldier in "Trench Poets" read Donne on the Western Front.

* The memoirs date this incident in 1918, but in the interview in *Poetry Nation* I (p.76) Rickword suggests that it occurred during his first stay in Dublin.

When he rejoined his battalion in the second half of September Haig's offensive had been in progress since 8 August, and the Twelfth Division, now attached to Sir Henry Rawlinson's Fourth Army, had been in the thick of the fighting. Its losses had been heavy, and Rickword found few of the men in his company who had been there only four months earlier. The exact date of his return is not recorded; the 5th Berkshires were fully occupied from 18 September to the end of the month, and the officer responsible for keeping the battalion's war diary merely noted in his summary of events that 2Lt J.E. Rickword "joined during the period". It was certainly not later than 23 September, when he wrote "Epéhy. September 23rd 1918" on the flyleaf of the first volume of his Donne, and was probably several days earlier.

On 18 September the Twelfth Division launched an attack on Epéhy, a strongly fortified village forming an outpost of the Hindenburg Line. It was defended by the Alpine Corps, a crack German unit consisting of twelve *Jäger* battalions, who had been ordered to hold it to the last. The 35th Brigade succeeded in clearing the enemy out of the southern part of the village, but some still clung to a line of posts on its northern edge and others hid in cellars. As the brigade had suffered heavy casualties the 5th Berkshires were sent in as reinforcements, and by the evening had helped to clear the ruins of the village. Rickword seems to have taken part in this battle, for many years later he wrote underneath the word "Epéhy" in his Donne: "An outworks of the Hindenberg [sic] Line. Bloody Hell."* Beyond Epéhy lay numerous German posts, defended by trenches and barbed wire and strongly held by riflemen and machine-guns. At midnight on 21-22 September, a bright moonlit night, the 5th Berkshires made a bayonet charge against one such post, Little Priel Farm, and captured it after an hour's fierce fighting; in the ruins they found fifty dead Germans and forty machine-guns. On 24 and 26 September they twice attacked Dadas Loop, another strong German position on the crest of a spur overlooking the River Escaut. Each attack was repulsed, and it was not until 30 September that the 6th Royal West Kents finally took the post.

By the end of September the Hindenburg Line had been broken, but the Twelfth Division had suffered so heavily in the process that it was unfit for active operations until reinforced. The 5th Berkshires alone had lost some 250 men killed, wounded or missing since 18 September. The division was therefore relieved on 30 September, and on the following day was transferred to General Horne's First Army. Till the end of his life Rickword kept among his war souvenirs a copy of General Rawlinson's farewell message to the division, which praised its "high standard of discipline and efficiency" and its "endurance and tenacity",

* In his old age Rickword gave this book to his friend David Holbrook.

and concluded: "A long list of successes, including Morlancourt, Car-
noy, Maricourt, Hardecourt, Maurepas and Nurlu, culminating in the
capture of the strongly fortified village of Epéhy, constitutes a record
which has seldom been equalled". Rickword had not taken part in any
of the engagements named, with the probable exception of the taking
of Epéhy, and seems to have kept this document primarily out of respect
for his wartime comrades.

The 5th Berkshires were taken by bus on 1 October to the camp at
Proyart, where they had three days' rest, by train on 4 October to a
camp near Arras and by bus on the following day to the Vimy Ridge
area. On 9 October they were back in the line, pushing forward east
of Lens. After a temporary delay at the Drocourt-Quéant Line, which
was evacuated by the enemy on 11 October, they resumed their advance,
and in spite of stubborn opposition cleared the village of Dourges on
13 October. They now found themselves confronted by the Haute Deule
Canal; all the bridges had been blown up, and the retreating Germans
occupied a strong position on the eastern bank. During the night of 14
October the British positions on the west bank were heavily shelled,
and although the shell fire diminished on the following day any further
advance was still impossible.

It was now that Rickword distinguished himself, perhaps because in
the presence of his fellow-soldiers he felt a sense of shame at having
passed the summer in comfort while they were fighting and suffering.
He volunteered to cross the canal and make a reconnaissance, and
swam across at a point called Pont à Sault. Although his presence was
discovered by the enemy, who kept him covered with their machine-
guns, he worked his way along the east bank, making careful note of
the enemy's positions, then swam back with his information. Acting
on this, B Company forced a crossing at Pont à Sault on 16 October
and established a bridgehead, under cover of which a pontoon bridge
was constructed during the night. The Germans were still holding a
wood on the east bank in strength, but at 5.30 a.m. on the 17th patrols
reported that they had withdrawn. The 36th Brigade crossed by the
pontoon bridge, and the advance was resumed.

By now it was more like a triumphal march than a battle. Three
villages – Malmaison, Leforest and Cordela – were cleared in the course
of the day. Previously the retreating German forces had compelled the
local population to evacuate their homes, which were then systemati-
cally demolished; their withdrawal was now becoming too hasty to
allow time for this, and the Twelfth Division were welcomed by the
inhabitants into undamaged villages decorated with the tricolour. In
one village Rickword found a notice printed in French and German
and signed by Generalleutnant von Trotta, which announced that
evacuated villagers who returned to their former homes without an

official pass would be liable to a year's imprisonment, a fine of 4,000 marks or both, "without prejudice to the more severe penalties laid down by other laws". The notice was dated 4 October, but the events of the last fortnight had already rendered it out of date. Rickword added this specimen of German military bureaucracy at work to his growing collection of souvenirs.

The 36th Brigade was relieved by the 37th on 18 October, and remained out of the line until 27 October, when it took over the whole of the divisional front. An attempt to establish a bridgehead over the Canal de l'Escaut on the following day came up against strong enemy opposition, and the 5th Berkshires had five men wounded. These were the battalion's last casualties, and when it was relieved at 10 p.m. that evening its active service ended. On 29 October it moved into billets at Flines, where two days later it was inspected by General Horne and the Prince of Wales. On 11 November Rickword received an order of the day which he read to his platoon: "Hostilities will cease at 1100 Hours Nov. 11th. Troops will stand fast on line reached at that hour which will be reported to Corps Headquarters. Defensive precautions will be maintained. There will be no intercourse of any description with the enemy." At 11 a.m. the entire 36th Brigade attended a church parade, and after the service the massed brigade bands played the national anthems of the allies.

Looking back on those closing weeks of the war, Rickword wrote in 1935: "Our rulers were not war-weary, but the ordinary people who were suffering on the home and battle fronts were thinking: Not another winter of this! I know that was the feeling among the troops in Flanders in October 1918."[3] This might be regarded as wisdom after the event, an attempt to attribute his political views of the 1930s to his wartime comrades, if it were not supported by independent evidence. The German Chancellor, Prince Max of Baden, had telegraphed President Wilson on 4 October seeking an immediate armistice and the opening of peace negotiations. This aroused so much speculation on the possible imminence of peace that General Rawlinson issued a special order of the day on 10 October declaring that "Peace talk in any form is to cease in the Fourth Army. All ranks are warned against the disturbing influence of dangerous peace talk".

The German government accepted Wilson's terms – adoption of his Fourteen Points and withdrawal from France, Belgium, Luxembourg and Italy – on 12 October. On the same day Horatio Bottomley, hitherto the army's favourite journalist, asserted in *John Bull*: "I have no intention, as far as I have any power, of allowing the Gentlemen of Whitehall to come to an arrangement with the Kaiser. I don't want any more talk of not being out to destroy the German nation – that is just what I am out for". In a letter to his mother Wilfred Owen reported on 15 October that this article "had had the effect of turning the whole army against its John Bull at last"; that "every officer and man left" was hoping for peace before he went into the line again; and that "Christmas is the Limit of our Extreme Patience".[4] Bottomley had his poetic counter-parts; Kipling warned in *The Times* of 24 October against any "parley with the foe", and in the *Daily Mail* of 1 November Gilbert Frankau put forward the slogan "No truce with the Beasts in Gray".[5] In the end it was the German rather than the allied forces' war-weariness which ended the war, but one wonders what would have been the British Army's reaction if peace had been delayed much longer.

After the armistice the Twelfth Division settled in a mining district east of Douai. The 5th Berkshires on 25 November moved into winter quarters at the village of Erre, near Valenciennes; the battalion mess was established in a small mansion, where lunches and dinners were accompanied with traditional ceremony, and Rickword enjoyed a com-fortable billet in a house near by. The most important duty which came his way was supervision of loading and unloading of goods at the marshalling yard, in an attempt to prevent the wholesale pilfering which normally accompanies military operations. Diversions were organized for the bored troops; the Spades resumed their performances, football, rugby, boxing and cross-country competitions were held on a divisional basis (the 5th Berkshires were beaten 3-1 at football by the 9th Essex), and a pioneers' battalion constructed a race course where two race meetings took place. The officers of the 5th Berkshires clubbed together to buy a cinematograph; a hall was built by battalion labour and was first used for Christmas dinner, which was followed by a film show. Amid these activities Rickword still found time for writing, and acquired something of a reputation in his company. The company com-mander told him one day: "You ought to pay a visit to E Company. There's another scribbler there." The scribbler of E Company, he later discovered, was Lieutenant Edmund Blunden of the Royal Sussex Regi-ment, who was stationed in the next village and was to become his close friend.

Rickword developed a high respect for the commanding officer of his battalion, Lieutenant-Colonel E.H.J. Nicolls, who took an elder-brotherly interest in him and recommended him for a decoration for his reconnaissance at Pont à Sault. The recommendation was approved at headquarters, and on 10 December divisional orders announced that Rickword had been awarded the Military Cross "for conspicuous gal-lantry and initiative". The same honour had previously been awarded to Siegfried Sassoon, who was also recommended for the Victoria Cross; Herbert Read, who also received the Distinguished Service Order; Edmund Blunden; and Wilfred Owen. The trench poets did not lack courage.

Towards the end of December Rickword suffered an accident. It did not seem serious at the time, but on 4 January 1919, his batman found it impossible to wake him. The doctor was sent for, and ordered his immediate removal to the field hospital at Bois de Montigny. For several days he remained in a heavy fever, but one morning, when he was fairly lucid, two doctors came to his bedside. They gently broke the news that they had diagnosed his illness as a general vascular invasion which had resulted in general septicaemia, and that his left eye was so badly infected that they thought it necessary to remove it to prevent the infection from spreading to the other eye. Although he only half understood what he was being told, he gave the necessary consent; the infected eye was removed and replaced by a glass one (for which he was charged three guineas), and the other remained in working order for nearly sixty years, although with impaired vision.

While he was recovering from the operation he received a visit from Gerald, who had hitch-hiked many miles to see him.* Shortly afterwards he was moved to a hospital for officers at Douai, where Gerald again visited him. As he was only a sergeant he had some difficulty in obtaining admission, but he finally succeeded, and the two brothers had dinner together before the younger left for England on 30 January. After a long cold journey he came to his senses in the hotel at Paddington station, which had been taken over as a military hospital. The great influenza epidemic was raging, and every two or three days the body of one or other of the three officers with whom he shared a room would be removed. When he had entered the convalescent stage he was transferred to another military hospital on Millbank, near the Tate Gallery, and after a week or two was allowed to go out into the streets, which enabled him to stock up with books. He had determined to wipe out any recollections of army life, and when a man from his company visited him he had no idea what to talk to him about.

On his discharge from hospital in March he was granted three months' convalescent leave, much of which he spent in Colchester. As technically he was still an officer he drew full pay and could impress the girls by swaggering round in uniform; he even had some three months' accumulated back pay which he had not drawn while he was in hospital. When he looked round for old friends with whom to spend some of it, however, he found that besides Eric Brand many others had been killed, while Town's family had moved away. Only the dullest of his schoolfellows, whom he had no desire to see, seemed to have survived the war and returned to Colchester. Fortunately the girls were still there and most of them still unmarried, and he was able to fill in his time with a little flirtation. But he had outgrown Colchester, and was eager to move on.

* Gerald was probably stationed at the base port of Rouen, to which the labour battalions of the Berkshires had been sent.

On 17 June he resigned his commission, and was granted the honorary rank of lieutenant. He applied to the War Office for the wound gratuity to which he was entitled, and three months later was granted £250, plus a refund of the three guineas which he had paid for his glass eye. His military career was over.

Memories of the war haunted him until his death, in the form of recurrent nightmares that he was back in the trenches, influenced his writing in verse and prose and helped to shape his political thought. If in the poem "Grave Joys" he seems much possessed by death, it is because before he was twenty he had seen more dead men than Webster and Donne saw in their entire lives. Not only seen them, but smelt them. The dead in his poems do not lie peacefully as if asleep; they stink, their faces are mud, they gape, mackerel-eyed, their bodies are scattered like offal, they are eaten by rats and worms. There are real experiences behind these horrors. The dead white-shirted Boche of "Moonrise over Battlefield" – who are they but the fifty Germans lying dead in the moonlight at Little Priel Farm, some of them, no doubt, still in their shirt sleeves as they had risen from sleep to repel the Berkshires' attack?

In his memoirs Rickword does not attempt a consecutive narrative of his experiences at the front. He could not muster the necessary concentration for so painful a subject; instead he records isolated incidents as they occur to him – his friend Rowe mortally wounded at his side; a grey-faced young soldier lying on the parapet of a trench, his left hand sliced off by a shell fragment; an elderly German found dead in a shell hole. For those who escape death war can bring humiliations equally dehumanizing; a shell-shocked soldier grovels on the ground like an animal, a military hospital is a haunted place "where, with child's voices, strong men howl or bleat". When war came again his mind went back to his dead schoolfellows, "that lost generation, bewildered and storm-tossed...who are now earth of Flanders". In one of his last-published poems the washerwoman's son drowns in mud on the Somme. The fact that this, the only one of his poems set in Colchester, was not published until sixty years after he left it suggests that he could never separate his childhood from the horrors that ended it.

He does not pretend that war is all horrors. In "War and Peace" he recalls how

> In sodden trenches I have heard men speak,
> though numb and wretched, wise and witty things;
> and loved them for the stubbornness that clings
> longest to laughter when Death's pulleys creak.

Even in a satire he pays tribute to the public school boys who are

> strong to die
> quite admirably for a lie –
> as might have been observed in Flanders,
> at least in subaltern commanders.

But the tribute is double-edged; it is the subalterns who risk their lives, not the base-wallahs who send them to their deaths, and it is for a lie that they die so heroically. "It was not the suffering and slaughter in themselves that were unbearable," he wrote in 1940, "it was the absence of any conviction that they were necessary, that they were leading to a better organization of society."[6] The search for a means of preventing a repetition of the suffering and slaughter and for that "better organization of society" was to occupy his mind for the rest of his life.

III. Oxford and Marriage

RICKWORD now faced the problem of choosing a career. He knew that he wanted to write, otherwise his ideas were vague. He was prepared to acquiesce in his parents' wish that he should go to a university, but when his mother hinted that he might study for holy orders he was obliged to assure her that he had no vocation. His religious beliefs had begun to wither away after his confirmation, and his war experiences had completed the process. His parents' ignorance of this suggest that he was unwilling to hurt their feelings by revealing his real opinions. The question of his future was solved for the time being when the Government introduced a system of scholarships for ex-officers whom the war had prevented from taking or completing a university course. They were now to be allowed to receive a degree after taking a two-year course in a single subject. Rickword applied for a grant, and on 9 September 1919 was informed that for two years from 1 October he would receive an annual maintenance allowance of £130 and tuition fees of £40, to allow him to take a course in modern languages at Pembroke College, Oxford.

The six months between his leaving hospital and entering the university he divided between Colchester and London, where he renewed his friendship with W.J. Turner. Turner, who had a wide acquaintance in the literary world, introduced him to his hero Siegfried Sassoon, then literary editor of the *Daily Herald*, who in turn introduced him to his fellow-scribbler of the 36th Brigade, Edmund Blunden. It was probably on Turner's advice that he sent his poem "Winter Warfare" to the weekly *Land and Water*, which published it in its issue of 10 July. "Winter Warfare" the first published, has remained the best-known of Rickword's poems, thanks to its popularity with anthologists of First World War verse. A reminiscence of the Western front during the winter of 1917-18, it was written at the very end of the war or shortly after,* and is closer to the experience which inspired it than any of his other war poems. It differs from Sassoon's poems in that it is not merely a photograph of the sufferings of the troops; the personification of the cold gives it an archetypal quality which recalls the manner of Hardy.

Rickword's writing at this time was not confined to verse. As early as his period at Hare Hall in 1916-17, perhaps under Turner's influence, he had been "struggling, between drill and duties, with imitative prose

---

* Rickword states in the Poetry Book Society Bulletin, no. 88, that it was written "at the end" of the war, but in *Poetry Nation* I he says that all his war poems were written "after the end of hostilities" (p.73).

fantasies, heavy with Paterian ecstasies".[1] The element of fantasy predominates in his few surviving short stories; of the seven published in 1929 under the title *Love One Another*, only two are conventionally realistic. His first published story, "The Cow", is set in a fairy-tale world described in richly sensuous imagery similar to that of his early poems. In this fantasy many elements – a consciousness of the strength of man's sadistic instincts born of the writer's wartime experiences, reflections on the relationship between art and sex and cruelty – are blended into a harmonious whole. It appeared in October in the second issue of *The Owl*, a handsomely produced periodical edited by Robert Graves. As Turner was closely associated with this venture, it is probable that once again it was he who suggested that Rickword should send his story to it.

During this summer he made the acquaintance of Roy Campbell, a South African three years his junior who had arrived in England in February with the intention of entering Oxford, and a friendship developed which was to last for some fifteen years. In almost every respect they formed a striking contrast, physically and morally. Rickword was of average height, slight, soft-voiced and modest; he was not a great talker (as he himself admitted, he had no small talk), but for that very reason when he did express an opinon, usually in few words, it was listened to with respect. Campbell was tall and strongly built, unconventional in dress, loud-voiced, highly imaginative about his own achievements, flamboyant, pugnacious, fond of playing the part of the wild colonial boy. What united them was a common dedication; each recognized that the other took poetry seriously.

The university term was due to begin on Friday, 10 October, and the two friends arranged to meet for a meal and then travel to Oxford together. A few days before, however, Rickword rang one of his girl friends (he had several in London, none of whom meant much to him), who suggested that they should spend the weekend at the seaside. He agreed, and invited Campbell to join them at his expense in a trip to Brighton. They stayed at the Metropole Hotel, where Campbell caused a disturbance by challenging Rickword after midnight to a wrestling match in the corridor outside their bedrooms. When he made his belated appearance at Pembroke College Rickword increased his offence by explaining that he had not realized that universities had the same standards of discipline as the forces. This the bursar regarded as impertinence, especially as Rickword still looked more like a sixth-former than a veteran officer.

His attitude towards his studies did not appeal to the college authorities. His choice of French literature as a subject for study was in itself surprising, as French was not one of the subjects in which he had distinguished himself at school. While in France he had managed to get hold of some books, and had increased his knowledge of the language by reading French novels. Of French poetry he had read little or nothing, although his interest in Baudelaire had been aroused by Swinburne's elegy "Ave atque Vale", and he had been introduced to Verlaine by Ernest Dowson's and Arthur Symons's verse translations. When he looked at the course syllabus he found that it ended with Victor Hugo, and decided that he was not interested. He paid occasional visits to his tutor, who would give him a glass of sherry and then talk about Montaigne or Descartes, and on rare occasions he attended a lecture, but most of his knowledge of French literature he acquired from voracious private reading. Baudelaire and Verlaine he read first of all, in defiance of his tutor, who assured him that they were not in the syllabus, and some Rimbaud, although he did not start reading him thoroughly until two or three years later. Baudelaire proved as exciting a discovery as Donne had been; to discover these two, who were to become the strongest influences on his own verse, he felt, was to be "irremediably changed in mind".[2] He went on to acquire a broad knowledge of modern French poetry and prose, and to read back into the main traditions of French literature from the Renaissance, finding particularly congenial Rabelais, Montaigne, Voltaire and Anatole France, who had "built up and propagated the great impulse of scepticism".[3] At the same time he was extending his knowledge of English poetry, especially the Elizabethan dramatists and the Metaphysicals.

Oxford was a stimulating place during the academic year 1919-1920. It was also a crowded one. For the first time for six years there was the normal intake from the public and grammar schools, and in addition hundreds of ex-officers had taken advantage of the Government's scheme. The number of undergraduates had risen to 3,588, of whom 1,440 were freshmen, against the normal pre-war figure of about 1,000 freshmen. The housing problem was so acute that it was impossible to find unfurnished houses to rent; army huts were erected in the grounds of Keble College, and the regulation requiring students to live within a mile and a half of Carfax had to be relaxed, the distance being extended to three and a half miles. Whereas the freshmen normally were almost entirely boys straight from school, they now included lieutenants, captains, majors and even colonels, some of them mature men, others, like Rickword, young men made wise beyond their years by their experiences. A passage in his later story "Orders to View", obviously autobiographical, sums up the attitude of many of them:

> And this had been followed by the boy's feverish lust for knowledge, naively believed the concomitant of power and love, a monstrous target to offer to a war-frenzied world! For the boy had taken that vast idealism to the trenches with him, which was like wearing a huge blown-up diver's suit there. Though the body inside might, as it happened, not be

hit for all the hurtling metal, such an envelope was bound to be pierced
by the fear and the surrounding agony, and it now sagged ludicrously
about him like an elder brother's clothes.*[4]

The effects of this influx were felt in many ways. The University Dramatic Society selected for its annual production Hardy's *The Dynasts*, and
the soldiers and sailors of the Napoleonic Wars were acted by men
who had themselves served in a greater war.

There was a new radicalism in the air. A University Labour Club
was founded in November 1919 (there is no evidence that Rickword
was a member), and began publishing a paper, *The New Oxford*. The
undergraduates at St John's revolted against the college's catering
department, formed a "soviet" and succeeded in winning reforms. The
Oxford Union adopted a resolution opposing intervention in Russia,
although it later demonstrated its fundamental political soundness by
resolving "That the return to power of the Labour Party would be a
national disaster" and rejecting a resolution (moved by the youthful
Beverley Nichols) in favour of a capital levy. The ultra-Tory *Morning
Post* was sufficiently alarmed by the situation, however, to issue a solemn
warning against a plot by the Labour Party to infiltrate the universities.

Rickword's circle of friends included several who were to achieve
distinction as writers or scholars, among them Edmund Blunden and
Robert Graves, the novelists L.P. Hartley and Louis Golding, the poet
Alan Porter, the literary historians Vivian de Sola Pinto and Jacob
Isaacs, and the art historians T.W. Earp and Anthony Bertram, almost
all of whom had served in the war. His closest friend in the university
was an Australian three years younger than himself, Bertram Higgins,
of whom Roy Campbell wrote that he was "the most interesting of all
the poets at Oxford, but concerned chiefly with disillusionment".[5] Outside the university Rickword's literary friends included Campbell, who
was attempting without success to learn the minimum of Greek then
required for entrance to the university, and the short-story writer A.E.
Coppard, who had recently given up his job as a clerk to devote himself
to writing. Almost all his friends wrote verse, even those who are now
remembered exclusively for their prose writings, and most had published or were shortly to publish at least one slim volume. "We were
a singing colony at Oxford in those distant days after World War I,"
Pinto wrote to Rickword in 1962, echoing Dr Johnson's description of
Pembroke College as "a nest of singing birds", and added: "I always
thought you had more of the authentic fire in you than any of us".

Our main evidence of Rickword's poetic development while at
Oxford comes from Campbell, not always a reliable witness. In an

---

* The final image is clearly derived from Rickword's memories of his shabby-genteel
childhood.

undated letter to his father, after surveying the English poetic scene
with disapproval, he continued:

> The last school is that of very young people like Rickword and myself.
> We have had the shell broken for us by futurism. We accept *Wheels* as
> a very necessary but badly-written hypothesis on which to work our
> theorems. We apply our work closely to the life that goes on around
> us. We read the French symbolists, modern futurists, the Elizabethans,
> modern scientists, the Roman poets and as much as we can of the Greeks.
> No one can say we are not as widely read as any of the Georgians or
> Futurists, most of whom turn their backs on science.[6]

This is probably not too far from the truth, though no doubt Campbell
exaggerates the breadth of their reading. In his later autobiography,
Broken Record, he tells a very different story. In this version Campbell
and his friends T.W. Earp and the composer William Walton are the
only champions in Oxford of the "new poetry" of Eliot and the Sitwells.
Campbell writes "imitation Eliot", which is criticized by Rickword,
who has "more time for Flecker or Turner" than for Eliot. Campbell
and Earp visit Paris in the vacation (apparently the Christmas vacation
of 1919-20) and there collect all Valéry's poems which have appeared
in magazines. Campbell makes six typed copies, probably "the first
collection of Valéry's poems that ever came to England", and gives one
to Rickword.[7] His portrayal of himself, at the age of eighteen, as a
lonely pioneer in English appreciation of Eliot and Valéry is not convincing. We know what he was writing at the beginning of 1920, and it
was not imitation Eliot. Two of his poems, "Gigue Macabre" and
"Absinthe", were published in the *Oxford Chronicle* in January and
February; they are intended as imitations of Baudelaire and Verlaine,
but in their conscientious decadence they irresistibly suggest Max Beer-
bohm's Enoch Soames.

One literary activity in which Rickword and Campbell were involved
was a club for reading old plays, which held its first meeting, a reading
of *Love for Love*, on 12 February 1920. The president, according to
the *Oxford Chronicle*, was a South African who "happens to speak
Zulu most fluently" – obviously Campbell, although his claim to fluency
in Zulu, and perhaps even his claim to be the club's president, can be
taken with a pinch of salt. In addition to Rickword and Campbell, the
members included Coppard, Porter, Golding, Isaacs, Pinto and two
other poets, Wilfred Rowland Childe and Richard Hughes, whilst even
W.B. Yeats, then living in Broad Street, occasionally took part. Childe,
a convert to Catholicism who reminded Campbell of "a rapt mediaeval
monk",[8] wrote sentimental poems glorifying a Catholic Merrie
Englande that never existed. In later years Campbell thought his verse
underrated, and even Rickword, who must have been amused by

eccentricities so similar to his father's (on one occasion Childe took Campbell to a Jacobite celebration), treated his verse sympathetically in a review, praising his "simple devotion to the beauty of the past".[9]

At the club, which met every Thursday evening in the saloon bar of a public house, Elizabethan and Jacobean plays were most commonly read, but the members also experimented with Otway and, at Porter's suggestion, with Beddoes, a former Pembroke College man whose verse interested Rickword and may have influenced his own. "These readings were often uproarious," Campbell later recalled. "Coppard laughs easily, like myself, and I remember laughing until it became almost agony and paralysis over some of the scenes in Thomas Heywood's farce of Lucrece, notably the scene of Valerius and the clown. Sometimes it would end in a rough-house...It was by far the most spontaneous literary gathering I ever knew."[10] In the end the authorities became aware that a group of undergraduates was defying the university regulation which forbade them to frequent licensed premises after 9 p.m. unless accompanied by an M.A. One evening the reading was interrupted by the entrance of a Proctor, who took the names of those present. Hughes hurried off to inform Yeats, who wrote to the Proctors assuring them of the respectability of the club's proceedings, and its members were let off with a nominal fine of half a crown, on the understanding that they would find a more suitable meeting-place. The meetings were accordingly transferred to the attic of a club called The Hypocrites, but finally ceased when the room was found to be infested with fleas.*

Like undergraduates in all ages, Rickword and his friends derived as much intellectual benefit from their social life and their interminable arguments as from their formal studies. "When I read Evelyn Waugh's diaries of his early days in Oxford I thought how much more sober things were in my day," he later recalled. "We did have a good time though, even rather sybaritic. I remember strawberries and champagne in the afternoon...I don't think anybody did much work; we were still too dazed at being alive at all."[11] One social occasion which lingered

---

* The accounts of the club in the *Oxford Chronicle* for 20 February 1920, Roy Campbell's *Broken Record* (1934), A.E. Coppard's *It's Me, O Lord!* (1957), Vivian de Sola Pinto's *The City that Shone* (1969) and Rickword's memoirs disagree on its name, its meeting-place and other details. The *Chronicle* calls it the Oricrusians, which suggests that it held at least its first meeting at the Golden Cross in Carfax. Campbell and Pinto state that it met at the Jolly Farmers, and are supported by Isaacs, who wrote in a poem addressed to Porter "Their Mermaid Tavern you with Jolly Farmers crowned" (Alan Porter, *The Signature of Pain*, 1930, p.11). According to Campbell, the club was known in consequence as the Jolly Farmers, but Coppard and Rickword say that it was called the New Elizabethans. Coppard gives the name of its meeting-place as the Paviour's Arms, whilst Rickword, whose account seems to be a combination of Campbell's and Coppard's, mentions both pubs. The description of the end of the club given above is Coppard's; Pinto states that Yeats was present when it was raided by the Proctor, and that the members were fined two guineas each.

in his memory was a party in a senior undergraduate's rooms in Pembroke College, at which Campbell, in the course of an argument with a subaltern in the Scots Guards, was heard to say loudly "Fuck the King!" The guardsman, who was wearing the King's uniform at the time, felt bound to avenge this treasonable sentiment, and bloodshed was averted only when the others present forcibly separated the two antagonists.

From the discussions between Rickword and his friends the idea emerged of a literary review, to consist of contributions from young writers at Oxford and Cambridge. The result was *The Oxford and Cambridge Miscellany*, the first and only number of which was published in June, at the end of the academic year. The Oxford section included poems by Blunden, Graves, L.A.G. Strong, Golding, Porter, Higgins and three non-members of the university, Campbell (represented by "Absinthe", of which he was evidently proud), Robert Nichols, who "haunted Oxford for a time as a poetic personality",[12] and Edith Sitwell, and short stories by C.H.B. Kitchin and Blunden. Rickword contributed a poem, the macabre "Dead of Night", and a story, "Grey Pastures". The latter seems intended as a companion-piece to "The Cow", an impression confirmed by the fact that he altered the title to "The Bull" when it was published in *Love One Another*. "The Cow" is concerned with male sadism and the relationship between a man and two women, "Grey Pastures" with female sadism and the relationship between a woman and two men. The setting, one of marshes and grey mudflats stretching down to the sea, evidently suggested by Rickword's memories of the Essex coast, contrasts with the lush green of the forest and the orchards in the earlier story.

Work by Rickword and his contemporaries was also brought together in *Oxford Poetry 1920*, which appeared in November. Twenty-three poets are represented, among them Blunden, Campbell, Golding, Graves, Hartley, Higgins, Hughes, Pinto, Porter and Strong. The result is disappointing, for most of the contributions are unadventurous lyrics, and even when a writer attempts something more ambitious, matter and form remain rigidly traditional. There are few references to the war and little satire, so that Vera Brittain's embittered "Lament of the Demobilized" comes as a welcome relief from so much sweetness, despite its slender poetic merits. It is the three trench poets who dominate the book, Blunden with "Sheet Lightning" and "Forefathers", Graves with "Morning Phoenix" and Rickword with "Intimacy", "Grave Joys", "Advice to a Girl from the Wars", "Yegor" and "Strange Elements". For the rest, only Campbell, whose two contributions ("The Porpoise" and "Bongwi's Theology") have a characteristic panache, and Strong with the forceful "Christopher Marlye", make any particular impression.

Reviewing the book, Louis Golding, himself a contributor, recognized the quality of Rickword's poems, and suggested that his wartime experiences had deepened his sense of reality. After asking "Why is the latest volume so conspicuous a success?" he continued:

> Is it that such poets as Mr Blunden and Mr Rickword have had time to perfect their art in places where their senses were not dulled by the "tapers, acolytes, and Magdalen," which give the impression that so many of their predecessors are babbling from a drugged sleep?...Mr Rickword has a mind vivid and swift as a swooping bird. His pungent fleshliness might have been an amalgam of Donne and Rossetti if Mr Rickword were not firmly establishing himself as one of the least derivative of our poets.[13]

Shortly before the academic year ended, Rickword was brought into direct contact with the class struggle. At a time of soaring prices, busmen in Oxford were shamefully underpaid; whereas in London a driver received £4 10s. and a conductor £3 10s. for a 48-hour working week, at Oxford a driver received £2 14s., a conductor £2 and a woman worker £1 15s. for a 54-hour week. After negotiations for an increase had dragged on for seven months without result, on 19 May the bus company's employees went on strike. The local press and public opinion were strongly on their side, especially after the Ministry of Labour's offer of arbitration was accepted by the busmen's union but rejected by the bus company. Support for the busmen was strengthened by the fact that, as the press pointed out, "three-parts of the strikers have served in the war, and many have Military Medals for bravery and good conduct while in the army. Some are wearing the 1914 star".[14] Sympathy for ex-servicemen who were being denied a square deal helped to rally many ex-officers such as Rickword behind them.

On the evening of Saturday, 29 May, undergraduates who supported the strikers held a meeting in St Giles's Street, which was addressed by a don and students from Ruskin College. By eight o'clock the street was packed with a dense crowd, which included Rickword, and blackleg drivers were being hooted. At Carfax the crowd surrounded a bus, forced the driver to get down and then put the bus out of action; the Oxford Chronicle commented that "the crowd was very good-humoured, and there was a great deal of laughter as it turned down the High".[15] In the High Street the crew of another bus hastily deserted it on finding themselves surrounded, but in Longwall Street a driver rashly tried to drive his bus into the crowd. Their mood immediately changed, and the driver was thrown out of his cab none too gently. After the crowd, now some 2,000 strong, had held a demonstration outside the house of the bus company manager in Iffley Road, the word passed around that a Ruskin student had been arrested for obstruction, on a charge of trying to pull a blackleg driver off his bus. A shout went up "Let's get him out!", and the crowd marched on the police station in St Aldates Street and threatened to storm it.* The police finally released the prisoner on bail, but demonstrations continued until the early hours of Sunday morning. The story ended happily; the bus company agreed on 3 June to grant wage increases, the strike was called off, and five days later the magistrates dismissed the case against the Ruskin student.

Rickword did not return to Oxford after the long vacation.† By November 1919 at latest he had become the lover of an Irish girl nine months younger than himself, Margaret McGrath. He celebrated the event by writing "Intimacy", one of the great English love poems of the twentieth century:

> Since I have seen you do those intimate things
> that other men but dream of [...]
> I have not troubled overmuch with food,
> and wine has seemed like water from a well.

Peggy, as he always called her, is an elusive figure. Their relationship ended tragically; her children grew up knowing nothing of her, and to the very end of his life he found it painful even to speak of her. We know that she was the daughter of a Catholic farmer, John McGrath, and came from Kilkee, in County Clare. There are slight indications that she and Rickword met, and possibly became lovers, in Dublin in the summer of 1918. In addition to "Intimacy" he addressed at least two poems to her, "Grave Joys" and "The Gift (To Peggy)", but they tell us little about her except that she was beautiful and had dark curly hair. There are hints that she had a capriciousness which he sometimes found trying, as when he speaks of her "proud and mocking curls" and calls her "most lovely, vile, adorable of girls". The fact that he thanked her for her help with his life of Rimbaud clearly suggests that she was educated and intelligent and had a good knowledge of French, and other references confirm that she appreciated poetry. Apart from this, she is only a name to us.

By the end of the academic year she was well advanced in pregnancy. Rickword was willing to marry her, but he knew that his scholarship and his disability pension would be far from enough to support himself, Peggy and their child. This did not greatly disturb him, as he had £100,

---

* Rickword stated over fifty years later that the would-be rescuers found the road barred by members of the ultra-Conservative Bullingdon Club, "hefty Blues in their dinner-jackets" (*Poetry Nation* I, p.77). This detail is not confirmed by the contemporary *Oxford Chronicle* report.

† In several autobiographical statements (e.g. *Poetry Nation* I, p.75) he said that he was at Oxford for four terms, but Pembroke College records show that he was in residence only for Michaelmas Term 1919 and Hilary and Trinity Terms 1920; Michaelmas Term 1920 is marked "not kept".

few debts and high, and as it proved unrealistic, hopes of the possibility of supporting a family by freelance journalism. He left Oxford with no great regret; he had had a good time there, but he was eager to move on. He expressed his feelings in the witty "Complaint of a Tadpole Confined in a Jam-jar", of which many years later he wrote: "The jam-jar, it would seem, stood for an Oxford college, and the lines were a paradigm of my ambivalent response to encapsulation therein".

> No strife to propagate the Kind,
> but leisure to improve the Mind!
>
> Yet curious sensations range
> about the tail, and hint at change [...]
>
> Whilst in the valleys pipers play
> *Over the hills and far away.*

On leaving Oxford he settled with Peggy in a furnished flat in Queen's Club Gardens, a middle-class neighbourhood in West Kensington. He was no doubt anxious that she should bear their child in comfortable surroundings, but the rent was to prove far higher than he could afford. Here on 19 August their daughter was born, and was given the names Joan Madeleine. Although he and Peggy were not yet married, when registering the baby's birth on 29 September he gave the mother's and the child's surname as Rickword, showing that he already regarded Peggy as his wife. The marriage took place on 25 October at the nearest Catholic church, St Thomas's, Fulham, a depressing example of Victorian Gothic with a spire and a cemetery attached. As the two witnesses were both strangers, it would seem that none of Rickword's family attended the wedding. This was not because of religious bigotry, from which George and Mabel Rickword were completely free. The probable explanation is that Rickword was too embarrassed about his child's birth and his subsequent marriage to break the news of either to his parents until well after the event; this is supported by the fact that when drawing up a family tree George Rickword gave the date of Joan's birth as 29 November 1920, over three months after the real date.

IV. *Behind the Eyes*

WHEN registering his daughter's birth, and again when signing the marriage register, Rickword gave his occupation as "journalist". He was entitled to do so, for since July he had been contributing regularly to the *Daily Herald*, which under George Lansbury's editorship had become the organ of the left wing of the Labour Party. Himself largely self-educated, Lansbury wished to use the paper for purposes not only of agitation but of popular education, and its weekly book page was one of its strongest features. Sassoon had been appointed the literary editor in March 1919, and when he resigned at the beginning of 1920 was succeeded by W.J. Turner, who collected a remarkable team of contributors. During the two years when Rickword wrote for the paper the reviewers of political books (among them G.D.H. Cole, Leonard Woolf, R.W. Postgate, H.W. Nevinson, H.N. Brailsford, R. Palme Dutt, Bertrand Russell and Maurice Dobb) represented a very broad cross-section of the Left. The literary side was equally strong and even more catholic in its representation of different schools of thought. Reviews and essays were contributed by, among others, Edmund Blunden, David Garnett, Katherine Mansfield, Havelock Ellis, Osbert and Edith Sitwell, Virginia Woolf, Robert Graves, Lascelles Abercrombie, Wyndham Lewis and Aldous Huxley. It may have been through Rickword's influence that a number of his Oxford friends – Louis Golding, A.E. Coppard, Alan Porter and Roy Campbell – were also recruited as contributors.

His first contribution appeared on 14 July 1920, and up to the end of March 1921 he published a total of eighteen items. Thereafter the frequency of his contributions declined as he found new markets for his work, but he continued to write for the *Herald* occasionally until August 1922. Although the bulk of his reviews were of poetry and novels, he also contributed three notable reviews of critical works (T.S. Eliot's *The Sacred Wood*, J. Middleton Murry's *Aspects of Literature* and Robert Graves's *On English Poetry*) and three on miscellaneous topics. One suspects that it was a practical joke of Turner's that he was asked to review Marie Stopes's *Radiant Motherhood*, and that his review ("There is much that is good sense, but on the whole, the book leaves the impression of sentimentality and want of balance") appeared on 27 October 1920, two days after his wedding. His opinion of Oxford is pungently expressed in his review of *University Reform: Recommendations of the W.E.A. submitted to the Royal Commission on the Universities of Oxford and Cambridge*:

Oxford and Cambridge are not national but class institutions, because
the tests to be satisfied before admission are intellectually low and financially high...The most intelligent members of the community, irrespec-
tive of their class and income, should have the first claim on places of
higher education. Unfortunately, the W.E.A. regards examinations as
an adequate intellectual test. The more real, the farther removed from
mere fact-cramming education becomes, the more useless are examinations.[1]

The most interesting of his reviews, however, are those dealing with
poetry. It was the *Herald* which taught him the art of reviewing; as the
space at his disposal was limited, he learned to go to the heart of the
matter and to seize on the essence of a writer's achievement, as he did
in his review of Edward Thomas's *Collected Poems*. No two poets
would seem on the surface to have less in common, but there was much
in Thomas which profoundly appealed to Rickword – the directness,
the freedom from "hyperbole and periphrase", the keen "sense of the
harmony of words", the vividness and freshness of the descriptions,
and an Englishness which had nothing of jingoism in it.[2] We learn much
of Rickword's views on the practice of poetry in these short pieces,
which are often written with a pungent wit. In reply to F.S. Flint's
advocacy of *vers libre* he comments: "We think that theories about the
way to write poetry are utterly useless, and when borrowed from the
French (whose material requires handling so differently) positively a
nuisance. It is so obvious that poetry may be written in a hundred ways,
in the rhythms of normal speech, of prose, of a merry-go-round, or
even in cadence".[3] Edmund Blunden is praised for making "all his detail
significant and contributory to the meaning of the poem".[4] Reviewing
a collection of translations of Asian verse, Rickword admires the "detached irony" of Chinese poetry and "a contact with reality that ensures
a freedom from emotional hysteria" in Indian and Arabic poems.[5] On
John Freeman's poems he observes that "austerity of thought and passion
is not equalled by an unflinching regard for the mere donkey-work of
the art", and refers to "that objection which some have, and which we
can only consider sentimental, to working on a poem when the first
glow of creation has cooled".[6] In a similar comment on the poems of
G.H. Luce he remarks: "It appears that he has thought more than he
has felt, which is a good fault in a poet and has been rare since the
metaphysicals. Unhappily, his intellect has been brought to bear on his
matter at the expense of his style".[7]

One of the major features of the book page was the regular series of
essays on "Great Names" in literature, science and philosophy, which
began on 25 August 1920. The contributors usually dealt with figures
whom they found congenial; Sassoon wrote on his friend Thomas
Hardy, Blunden on Charles Lamb and Leigh Hunt. Between September

1920 and June 1922 Rickword supplied seven essays in this series, on Morris, Swinburne, Keats, Poe, Baudelaire, Donne and Verlaine. In these brief studies, each of some 400 words, he sought to communicate what he had gained from these men to whom he owed so much. The most fascinating and the most imperfect is that on Swinburne, in which he is torn between his desire to make the best possible case for his former idol and his recognition that Swinburne's poetry is not as good as he had once thought it. "To obtain the real savour, the intoxication, of Swinburne," he sums up,

> he should be read in early youth, when the effect will be devastating, but worth while. Even in colder years he can flood the reader with the magnificence of his language, and if he loses control sometimes of the meaning of his words, he is always master of their sound, and out of the clash and echo of vowels and consonants creates something greater than their mere literal meaning will allow.[8]

He had rejected Swinburne as a model in favour of Donne, "the most modern of all poets", of whom he wrote: "He said the truest and bitterest and wittiest things about the mechanics of love, the tenderest and most ecstatic about the spirit of it…Sentiment is the husk of passion, and it is this outside his wit strips off, to expose, white and dazzling, the true matter".[9]

His last contribution to the *Daily Herald* was published on 23 August 1922. Faced with an advertisers' boycott, the paper had struggled hard to survive. Meanwhile, the Labour leaders had become increasingly worried by the left-wing policies advocated by the *Herald*, the only daily paper supporting the party; Lansbury welcomed the formation of the Communist Party in 1920, for example, and urged its affiliation to the Labour Party. A settlement was reached in September 1922, whereby the Labour Party and the T.U.C. assumed financial and political responsibility for the *Herald*. Lansbury resigned, and was succeeded by a Fleet Street professional, Hamilton Fyfe, under whose editorship both the paper's Socialist militancy and its literary standards drastically declined. The space devoted to books was greatly reduced, and in 1923 Turner resigned.

The *Herald* could not afford to pay its contributors well, and Rickword eked out his income during the second half of 1920 by placing an occasional poem. In addition to those published in *Oxford Poetry 1920*, "Outline of History" appeared in Middleton Murry's *Athenaeum* in November and "A Dead Mistress" in *Coterie* in December. *Coterie*, six issues of which appeared between May 1919 and December 1920, was published from Henderson's shop in Charing Cross Road, where Rickword had bought Sassoon's poems and was himself to be employed many years later, and was largely produced by his Oxford contemporaries.

T.W. Earp was on its editorial committee, and poems by Wilfred Rowland Childe, L.A.G. Strong, A.E. Coppard, Edmund Blunden and Roy Campbell appeared in its pages. It was very much an organ of the avant-garde; T.S. Eliot, Aldous Huxley, Wyndham Lewis, Richard Aldington and the artist Nina Hamnett (a future friend of Rickword's) sat on the editorial committee at various times, and it published poems by Eliot ("A Cooking Egg"), Huxley, Aldington, Herbert Read, all three Sitwells and the Americans Conrad Aiken, John Gould Fletcher, H.D. and Amy Lowell, as well as drawings by Henri Gaudier Brzeska, Walter Sickert, William Rothenstein and Amadeo Modigliani.

Even when augmented by a guinea for a poem now and then, Rickword's earnings from the *Herald* were not enough to live on, and he abandoned the expensive West Kensington flat for a cottage in the country. Early in December the landlord tracked him down, and he was faced with a bill for arrears of rent totalling £20 or £25 – an enormous sum for a young father who was having to warm his cottage with firewood from the hedgerows. Summoned before the county court, he was granted a year in which to pay off the debt; in fact, as he later recalled, not more than about a quarter of the monthly instalments were ever paid. Life in the country, although cheaper than in London, made it more difficult to get reviewing work, and early in 1921 he took a flat in King's Road, Chelsea, consisting of a ground floor and basement with a front and a back garden, which although shabby was roomy and comfortable.

Once again it was W.J. Turner who came to his rescue financially. Turner, who was still the *New Statesman*'s music critic, recommended him to Desmond MacCarthy, who had succeeded J.C. Squire as its literary editor. Rickword, who remembered MacCarthy with affection, wrote of him in his memoirs:

> He made a great success of his side of the paper for a dozen years or more. It had been anticipated that he would not get the paper out on time, as he could never finish a thing to order. As it happened he did conquer this little maladjustment and became an efficient editor, and one who was deeply matured and mellowed in the literature of the European languages. His choice of "Affable Hawk" as pseudonym was a very wise one, and very representative of its producer. He was generous and friendly to the younger intellectuals who came under his notice, and when he knew I was a drifting freelance he offered me a desk in his room on the second floor of the *New Statesman* offices in Great Queen Street. For several months I used to turn up there and do a lot of reading, and received the benefit of his conversation and general insight into the workings of the literary magazine. MacCarthy's profound literary sensibility did not extend, or at least so he said himself, to modern poetry, and he would often throw something across to me and ask me did it mean anything? This was a question which was frequently difficult to

answer, and I would do my best to tell him in prose terms more or less what it was trying to say. I had to deal in this way with one of Bertram Higgins' poems which he had sent in. Although it was rather an obscure poem I did make enough sense out of it to make MacCarthy feel that he should give it the benefit of the doubt, and he did include it in his columns. For some months he let me deal virtually alone with the new poetry as it came in.

Rickword's first contribution to the *New Statesman*, an unsigned review of Harold Nicolson's life of Verlaine, appeared on 19 March 1921; it is noteworthy that his main criticism of the book concerns what he considers to be the writer's unsympathetic attitude towards Rimbaud. Between April and August he contributed four unsigned reviews of collections of verse, in addition to his first signed article, an essay on the poetry of Tristan Corbière, which appeared on 16 July. His critical method is well illustrated in a review of four collections in which each writer's style is subjected to a careful and witty analysis. Elizabeth Bridges (better known as Elizabeth Daryush), we are told, "handles her lines like a metrist (which is rare nowadays), and not like a rhapsodist". The minor Georgian Martin Armstrong "uses rhyme for cymbals. He rhymes persistently, unfalteringly and polysyllabically". Rickword's criticisms of his friend Louis Golding are administered with a humour that removes their sting:

> If there were a House of Correction for erring poets, Mr Golding should be chained to the floor with a hundredweight or two on his chest, and constrained to scratch his poems on the ceiling with his big toenail. Some such mediaeval discipline would be entirely for his own good. "What a flow of inspiration, what a measure of divine afflatus!" as they used to say. He would beat us into submission with his clashing rhymes and war-like imagery, and then to shame us for our unyielding, offers us such an irrefusable gift as "Lyric in Gloom" – which is all a lyric should be, an almost inconsequent thing.

Finally, on Marianne Moore he writes: "We confess we do not understand her always, but we do not conclude, therefore, that she is tremendously profound, nor that she is talking nonsense. Her book is quite the most interesting of these four, because she is trying to do something which has never yet been done, though it may be impossible to achieve".[10]

This review appeared in the same issue of the *New Statesman* as Rickword's short story "Love One Another", which gave its name to his later collection of tales. Guy, a young officer on leave in Ireland, receives a letter from Hylda asking him to visit her before he returns to the front. Although his interest in her has waned, he goes to the village where she is staying because he does not wish to hurt her feelings. She welcomes him warmly and introduces him to her friends, including the young squire, Seumas. After Guy has left, "thinking of her pain on

the morrow", she says to her friend Eileen: "I simply have to be nice
to that poor, dear dull Guy. I could not hurt him just before he goes
out to the trenches again…but it is hard, indeed. When will Seumas's
brother be coming back, I wonder?"[11] One is left wondering whether
the setting is merely a reminiscence of Rickword's visits to Ireland in
1917-18, or whether some tension in his relations with Peggy underlies
the story. With its neat final twist it is the most conventional of his
tales, yet the keen observation and the humour in the depiction of Irish
life arouse regret that he did not develop this vein.

He kept up his output of verse while contributing to the *Herald* and
the *New Statesman*; six of his poems were published in as many different
magazines between May and November 1921, and six more were
included in *Oxford Poetry 1921*, edited by Alan Porter, Richard Hughes
and Robert Graves, which appeared in November. His representation
in this anthology was in itself a compliment, for not having been in
residence since June 1920 he was not strictly eligible, and Graves, who
was no doubt the dominant figure among the three editors, was an
exacting critic. The number of contributors was reduced to ten, most
of whom were represented by five or six poems, but it was again Blunden, Graves and Rickword who dominated the collection. Rickword's
six poems represented a cross-section of his work to date; "Trench
Poets" was a specimen of his war poetry, "Desire" and "Winter
Prophecies" of his early Romantic manner, and "Complaint of a Tadpole", "Regret for the Depopulation of Rural Districts" and "Complaint after Psychoanalysis" of the more mature style which he was
now developing.

In the same month, November 1921, his first collection of poems,
Behind the Eyes, was published by Sidgwick and Jackson. It contained
36 poems, 22 of which had been published before; always a stern critic
of his own work, he omitted three others which had previously appeared,
"Advice to a Girl from the Wars", "Strange Elements" and "A Dead
Mistress", although ten years later he relented and included the first in
Twittingpan and Some Others. He was wise to exclude the other two,
both of which are of psychological interest for their disconcerting streak
of sadism and necrophilia but of little artistic value. In "Strange Elements"
he compares his girl to a shark and a water-snake and she compares
him to a tiger, whilst in "A Dead Mistress" he gloats over the spectacle
of a woman's body being devoured by insects. This theme seems to have
obsessed him in 1920, for he dealt with it again in "Grave Joys", with
a wit, imagination and tenderness which the other poem entirely lacks;
it is noteworthy that both poems were published within two months
of their author's wedding, and that "Grave Joys" was originally dedicated
to Peggy. He had abundant precedents for his treatment of this subject
– in Donne and the Metaphysicals (Marvell's "then worms shall try /

That long-preserved virginity" surely suggested his "the weird embraces of the worm"), in the Jacobean dramatists, in Beddoes, in Swinburne, and above all in Baudelaire, whose *Une Charogne* provided the model for "A Dead Mistress". Whatever the psychological factors involved, a combination of these literary influences with an obsession with death originating in his war experiences explain in part his choice of this theme.

The book included four of his war poems, which stand apart from those of the other major trench poets. Those of Sorley, Graves, Sassoon, Owen and Rosenberg were written in France or on periods of leave or hospital treatment before returning to the front, and bear the impact of immediate experience; the long narrative poems, Herbert Read's "The End of a War" and David Jones's "In Parenthesis", although based on personal experience were written many years later. Rickword's war poems, with the possible exception of "Moonrise over Battlefield", were all written within three years of the armistice, and could rather be described as post-war poems. "Winter Warfare", the earliest and most conventional, concentrates on a single aspect of war. "The Soldier Addresses his Body" summons up a mood, that of the nineteen-year-old subaltern contemplating the possibility of extinction before he has experienced what the earth has to offer. The horror is extracted from the thought by describing the experiences for which he longs in terms of the Romantic properties of Rickword's own early verse, which is subtly burlesqued by setting the description within a framework of army slang. "War and Peace", dealing with the transition from one to the other, may have been modelled on Sassoon's "Dreamers", which tells how soldiers dream of commonplace things like "going to the office in the train". Rickword, remembering his comrades' courage in the trenches, sees with regret how they

> lay stubborn courage by,
> riding dull-eyed and silent in the train
> to old-man stools –

perhaps an expression of his disappointment that they had not shown themselves more politically militant after the war.

By far the most powerful of the four, however, is the nightmarish "Trench Poets". Contemplating death in war as he had seen and smelt it, his mind turns to Donne who had written so eloquently on death, whose poems he had taken to the Western Front and whom he had read, perhaps aloud, with Campbell at Oxford. This memory suggests two others: that Donne is the poet not only of death, but of the mechanics of love; and that Rickword had also read Tennyson aloud to his mother at Colchester. His anger and disgust at war are re-created, and in the white heat of this process a whole complex of ideas – death, decay, sex, Donne, Tennyson – is fused into a poetic unity, in which war and love and poetry are seen as equally futile in the face of death. It is not surprising that a poet who in his early twenties was so conscious of the ignominies to which death subjects the human body should have developed into an admirer of Swift.

The war poems are all reprinted in the collected editions published in 1947, 1970 and 1976, but only five of the remaining thirty-two poems in *Behind the Eyes* appeared in all three, and eleven more were never reprinted. Rickword's attitude towards the rest vacillated; seven poems excluded in 1947 were readmitted to the canon in 1970 and eight more in 1976, but "Regret for the Depopulation of Rural Districts", included in the previous collections, was omitted in 1976, perhaps by mistake. There are several reasons for this indecision; the weakest of these poems can be dismissed as juvenilia, and one or two others he probably did not reprint because they had painful personal associations for him. The rest belong to a tradition of Romantic verse (inherited from the Elizabethans, through Keats, Tennyson, the Pre-Raphaelites, the poets of the 1890s, Yeats and the Georgians) against which he reacted violently soon after *Behind the Eyes* was published, yet which he could not reject entirely without repudiating a valuable part of his own poetic achievement. Hence the wholesale purge of 1947, followed by the partial rehabilitations of 1970 and 1976.

The chronology of these poems presents a problem. It would be natural to assume that he began by writing in a highly derivative style which he gradually outgrew as he found his own voice, but the publication dates of the poems, which are our only evidence, do not suggest any such neat and tidy process. "Winter Warfare", published in July 1919, and "Intimacy" and "The Soldier Addresses his Body", published in March 1920, are mature in style and appeared in the collected editions with little alteration; on the other hand, "Beauty Invades the Sorrowful Heart" did not appear until December 1920 and "Foreboding" and "Singing at Night" until May 1921, although they are among the poems in which the Romantic element is strongest and were never reprinted by Rickword. It would appear that throughout 1919-20, and to a lesser extent well into 1921, he worked naturally in a Romantic idiom from which he escaped only when dealing with experiences – military in "Winter Warfare" and "Trench Poets", sexual in "Intimacy" and "Passion" – for which he found it inadequate.

The origins of his Romanticism are complex. The Elizabethan and Keatsian elements are strongest in that strange fantasy "These are Strange Woods that Call"; it was unmistakably a young man steeped in Keats's odes who wrote this stanza:

> Naked I stand in terror; what are these
> Immense green waters hissing at my feet

That drag me into darkness? Is there peace
In their deep caverns? There will Beauty greet
Her brother with glad whispers? Is her wraith
  More than her body sweet?
Do these white petals on the waves her waving tresses wreathe?

There is a strong Yeatsian element in this and many of the other poems, even in such a title as "Beauty Invades the Sorrowful Heart", which Rickword later regretted. "Somehow one got hold of that volume of Yeats, the *Poems*, which had all his Celtic-twilight stuff – melodious, evocative and all that, but not a very good influence, really," was his judgment in later years.[12]

The influence of the Georgians is more difficult to assess, if only because the forty contributors to *Georgian Poetry* differed so fundamentally from one another, but those whose influence is most apparent seem to be Walter de la Mare, whose music is discernible in the lyrical poems, J.E. Flecker and W.J. Turner. When in 1973 Rickword said that after being introduced to the Georgians by J.G. Worth in 1914, "I very soon lost interest in them",[13] his memory was deceiving him. In a passage already quoted, Roy Campbell states that in 1919-20 Rickword "had more time for Flecker or Turner" than for Eliot, and "funnily enough was at that time one of the hopes of the Squirearchy".[14] There is certainly some basis for both these statements. J.C. Squire thought sufficiently highly of his poems in 1920-21 to publish "Intimacy", "The Soldier Addresses his Body", "Revery" (later renamed "Sea Sash") and "Regret for the Passing of the Entire Scheme of Things" in *The London Mercury*. We know that Rickword already admired Turner's poetry before he met him in 1916, and for at least six years his admiration remained strong enough to evoke comment not only from Campbell but also from Robert Graves. In a letter of June 1922 to Edward Marsh, the editor of *Georgian Poetry*, Graves suggested "E. Rickword, when he is not playing at being Turner" as a possible contributor for the next volume, together with Blunden, Frank Prewett, Herbert Palmer and Peter Quennell.[15] Marsh in fact invited Blunden, Prewett and Quennell to contribute to *Georgian Poetry 1920-1922* but not Rickword or Palmer, which suggests that by that time the older generation of Georgians at least were beginning to regard Rickword as a modernist.

The three collections of poems which Turner published in 1916, 1918 and 1921 are dominated by a dreamy Romanticism. His favourite words are "dream" and "moon", which occur in twenty-six and twenty-three respectively of the fifty-nine poems in the three books. Other recurrent properties are sun, stars, clouds, sea, foam, streams, fountains, pools, woods, trees, flowers (especially roses), exotic animals (tigers, lions, reindeer, gazelles, antelopes and giraffes) and birds (swans, parrots and parroquets), ships, spirits and music. Exotic and sonorous place-names (Chimborazi, Cotopaxi, Popocatepetl, Yucatan, Chagóla, Khangavar, Coromandel) are heard. Colour adjectives are splashed on; "white-limbed", "yellow", "purple", "mauve", "silver" and "greenish gold" occur in the first eleven lines of a single poem. Bring all these mannerisms together, and the result can sound like this:

> The stone-grey roses by the desert's rim
> Are soft-edged shadows on the moonlit sand.
> Grey are the broken walls of Khangavar
> That haunt of nightingales, whose voices are
> Fountains that bubble in the dream-soft Moon. ("The Princess")[16]

Verse of this sort can be infectious as the measles, and it was not only young poets like Rickword who were in danger of catching it. In fairness to Turner, it should be said that he outgrew these mannerisms, and his later verse is radically different.

Although Rickword shared many of Turner's Romantic properties, he used them in a fundamentally different way. The moon, forests and the sea are frequently referred to, often in conjunction, but as symbols rather than ornaments. The moon may be cold, sinister, even "clownish" ("Winter Prophecies"), it may be a symbol of passion, swaying men's minds like waves; it is never merely a piece of stage lighting. A mind at ease may be "a rich forest...of blooms deep-scented and gay-plumaged birds" ("Beauty Invades the Sorrowful Heart"), but more often Rickword's forests are terrifying places, "beast-haunted...Where the savage flowers scream" ("Tryst"). A woman's hair is a "sinister dark forest" ("Intimacy"). If in "These are Strange Woods that Call" the trees house laughing dryads, in "Lovers" they are withered men waiting to snatch away souls.

There is surprisingly little evidence in *Behind the Eyes* of the influence of Donne and Baudelaire, his avowed masters. For a young man it was easier to imitate their surface mannerisms than to absorb their essential qualities, and it seems to have taken two or three years before their influence finally ousted that of his earlier models. In the poem where the Metaphysical note is most evident, "The Gift (To Peggy)", Marvell's influence is more apparent than Donne's. His first attempt at imitating Baudelaire, "A Dead Mistress", was so unsatisfactory that he excluded it from *Behind the Eyes*. It was easier to come to terms with Verlaine; his lyricism has always lent him a special appeal for the English reader; in an early essay he praises Verlaine as "the French poet most pleasing to our ears, for he has a melodiousness too often absent in the regular classic verse",[17] and in such poems as "Winter Nightfall" and "Foreboding" Verlaine's influence blends easily with that of de la Mare.

In a number of poems Rickword moves away from his Romantic

bases towards a more personal style. In addition to the poems reprinted in 1947 – "Regret for the Depopulation of Rural Districts", "Intimacy", "Passion" (later renamed "Obsession"), "Regret for the Passing of the Entire Scheme of Things", "Cosmogony", "Complaint after Psycho-analysis" and the war poems – "The Gift (To Peggy)", "Blindness", "Complaint of a Tadpole Confined in a Jam-jar", "Grave Joys", "Outline of History" and "Meditation on Beds" fall into this category. In "Blindness" Romantic symbols acquire a new strength, handled with the intense feeling arising from Rickword's fear of losing the sight of his remaining eye. In "Regret for the Passing of the Entire Scheme of Things" the Romantic imagery of

> Winter's white-armoured horsemen on the hills
> take from the virgin Frost their stirrup-cup

can exist side by side with the realistic detail of "drone of mowers on suburban lawns". Such peaceful coexistence would be inconceivable in the earlier poems. In "The Soldier Addresses his Body" and "Complaint after Psycho-analysis" fauna even more exotic than Turner's – hippogriffs and wyverns, unicorns and jewelled birds – are invoked in a spirit of burlesque.* In "The Gift (To Peggy)", a poem equally indebted to Marlowe and Marvell, the spirit of Swift suddenly intrudes in the line "The frightened nations gibber like mad apes". Finally, in this poem, as in "Complaint of a Tadpole", "Grave Joys", "Outline of History" and "Complaint after Psycho-analysis" an ironic Metaphysical wit is counterpointed with the Romantic elements in such a way as completely to transform their nature.

One of the most striking features of the book is its technical variety and ingenuity. Rickword experiments with sixteen different stanza forms of four to nine lines, many of them of his own invention, and most of them handled with skill. Each of the three sonnets in the book ("Sick Thoughts", "War and Peace" and "Moon-talk") uses a different rhyme-scheme. In addition to blank verse poems, there are unrhymed triplets ("Regret for the Passing of the Entire Scheme of Things") and unrhymed quatrains ("Cosmogony"). That this is not mere ingenuity for its own sake can be illustrated from poems in which the metre or stanza-form is changed within the poem. As the tone of "The Gift (To Peggy)" develops from playfulness into passion octosyllabics are replaced by heroic couplets (the quick-moving open Elizabethan or Caroline couplet, not the closed Augustan type), like a stream broadening

---

* There is similar burlesque in the last line of Section III of "Outline of History" as it was revised for publication in the 1976 collection, where "throned princesses gay as singing-birds" becomes "Bakst Princess gay as parakeets". The revised text is more self-consciously of the age of the Diaghilev ballet and *Wheels* than the original text of 1920.

Behind the Eyes

into a river. The rhyme-scheme of the first of the two eight-line stanzas of "Passion", dealing with the silence that follows love-making, is completely regular (abbabaab), its regularity being underlined by strong assonance (*enclosed, snows, slow*); that of the second, in which the lover's mood becomes one of deepening agitation, is chaotic (abccdbad). "Outline of History" begins with a picture of primitive man in two regular five-line stanzas. The second section, a vision of a pastoral golden age, is written throughout in eleven-syllable lines to which the unstressed endings give a swift, light-hearted movement; an unrhymed opening line is followed by four rhyming quatrains and a final couplet:

> like moonlight shadows
> the laughing dancers swept across the meadows.

The third section, depicting an over-ripe civilization, consists of two quatrains rhyming emphatically on long syllables;* this is the shortest section, as if to emphasize that periods of civilization make up a very small part of human history. The final section, which may owe something to Byron's "Darkness", shows mankind facing extinction under a dying sun. In contrast to the full rhymes of the previous section, the first eighteen lines rhyme imperfectly, with assonances or consonances; one couplet ironically repeats the concluding rhymes of the second section, substituting hopelessness for joy:

> the stagnant rivers rot in sombre meadows;
> the flowers are harsh and grey, the trees are shadows.†

The last eleven lines, in which mankind dully wait for darkness, are in blank verse, as if even the attempt to rhyme, however crudely, had been abandoned as too great an effort. These subtle variations in rhyme and metre are clearly the work of an artist fully conscious of what he is doing.

The reviews of *Behind the Eyes* give the impression that the reviewers did not quite know what to make of it. Alan Porter in the *Daily Herald* of 4 January 1922 compared it favourably with *Seeds of Time* by John Drinkwater, one of the founding fathers of *Georgian Poetry*, and the anonymous reviewer in the *New Statesman* of 25 March preferred it to *Music* by John Freeman, another card-carrying Georgian and a pillar of the Squirearchy. Perhaps inevitably, it was the familiar elements in the book that were welcomed. As a favourable example of Rickword's style Porter quoted from "Singing at Night"; the *New Statesman*

* The effect is partly concealed in the 1976 text by Rickword's alteration of "singing-birds" in the last line to "parakeets".

† There is another ironic repetition in the revised 1976 text, in which the "dark-haired girls" in the final section become "tousled girls" – the same adjective that is applied to the caveman's mate in the opening section.

reviewer commended "Moon-talk"; and Amabel Williams-Ellis in *The Spectator* of 17 December 1921 singled out for praise "Beauty Invades the Sorrowful Heart", from which she quoted at length, "Sick Thoughts" (surely the feeblest poem in the book) and "These are Strange Woods that Call" – all poems which Rickword himself was later to reject. All three had criticisms to make. Porter, who as an old friend gave him the best review, lumped together the Keatsian "These are Strange Woods that Call", rather oddly, with the highly original "Meditation on Beds" and "Outline of History" as "too much like exercises or self-imitations". Amabel Williams-Ellis found "a certain sameness about the general tone of the verse" (another surprising judgment) and complained, more justly: "There are too many 'jewelled birds' and 'white petals'. Above all, there are too many assorted girls. Sometimes they are 'sea-cold', sometimes 'flat-breasted', sometimes 'low-laughing' sometimes 'dark-haired'. However adjectived, they swarm in the less successful poems". The *New Statesman* critic was harsher, and condemned the book's "decadent affectations: a striving after bizarre Donne-like effects, a determination to shock". All three, however, finally brought down the balance in Rickword's favour. "Mr Rickword starts with a clean and steady imagination, a deep and personal thought, and struggles against the obscuring ineptitude of words. If you prefer never to think, avoid Mr Rickword's poems as you would the plague; but the man of alert mind will obtain from them a vast and satisfying delight" (*Daily Herald*). "Mr Rickword's book of poems is one that will make his reviewers write his name down in that little list that I suppose we all keep – the list of writers whose next productions are to be watched for ... His verse is sometimes clumsy, but time will cure that. It is never thin and never forced" (*Spectator*). "If in the sonnets 'War and Peace', 'Moon-talk', 'Passion' it is, as we believe, his own voice that we hear, if the lovely lines in 'Intimacy': 'Since I have seen your stocking swallow up, / A swift black wind, the flame of your pale foot,' are something more than a happy accident, Mr Rickword's second volume may be a considerable contribution to the poetry of our day" (*New Statesman*).

The longest and oddest review appeared in *The Times Literary Supplement* of 5 January 1922. It began by commending the poet for not being too modern:

> Mr Rickword's poetry is perhaps best described as the poetry of surprise. There lies beyond it, in a region of extravagant surprises, a poetry which we might call the poetry of consternation – the poetry we associate with the names of Mr Sacheverell Sitwell and some others. Mr Rickword is not with those, at least he is not with them at present, and we conjecture that he never will be. In the forms of his verse he might fairly be called a traditionalist; we see him experimenting in various familiar styles, in the style of Blake, in the style of the "metaphysical" poets, in the style

of Keats, and might even suggest that he is insufficiently on his guard against conventional repetitions on this side of his work. Will he believe that, in this slim volume of his, he three times gives us the rhyme of "girls" and "curls"?

Having this pointed out to him seems to have come as a shock to Rickword; he later suppressed two of the poems in which this rhyme occurs – "The Gift (To Peggy)" and "These are Strange Woods that Call" – permanently, and the third, "Grave Joys", until 1976.

In an acute analysis of his methods, the review continued:

> His aim in general would seem to be to use the familiar forms as an apparatus for the administration of eye-opening shocks... Mr Rickword is serious and his fabric is all of a piece; yet it embodies something of the parodist's contrast between the actual and the ideal, in that it uses the associations of poetry for the presentment of what would commonly be regarded as unpoetical material. The spectral horror of a midnight orgy, the tangled meditations of a victim of psycho-analysis, the imaginary sensualities of corpses after burial are themes which he treats in sombre rhymed verse of a prevailingly Elizabethan flavour.

Having patted Rickword on the back for "his sense of style, his love of the music of the phrases", the writer apparently feared that his head would be turned, and devoted the rest of the review (over half of it) to a lecture on morality. "How curious it is to reflect," he complacently mused, "that in the whole of the love poetry of France the poet praises his mistress, whereas in the whole of ours he praises the woman who is or will be or might have been his wife!" (Much virtue in "might have been"; presumably the Dark Lady might have been Shakespeare's wife if they had not both been married already.) As he had married Peggy a year earlier, Rickword thought the implied rebuke rather unfair. The review no doubt strengthened the distaste which he had already expressed for "the admitted flabbiness of present-day reviewing" and "the fuddled ranks of contemporary critics",[18] and his conviction of the urgent need for the application of more rigorous critical standards.

His belief that the book promised better things to come is clear from his modest inscription in the copy which he gave his parents: "To my Mother and Father, to whose loving care I attribute any achievement which may be mine in the future, these seedlings". He made no more money out of it than most poets do from a first collection. "Though the book had as many favourable reviews as it deserved, its influence on my financial position was negligible," he recalled in later life.[19] That was not the important point. He entered 1922 no longer merely a journalist, but a published author and a recognized poet.

V. Reviewing and Rimbaud

IN an essay on Thomas Lovell Beddoes Rickword wrote in 1923: "Beddoes was now in a dangerous condition – a promising young man on the outskirts of the literary community. Journalism was then more directly if less insidiously dangerous to an original talent than it is now, and might involve the compulsion of 'writing anything for £15 a sheet'."[1] Much the same might have been said of Rickword's position after the publication of *Behind the Eyes*. He was still writing for the *Daily Herald*, though less frequently than in the past, and for the *New Statesman*, and had recently begun reviewing for *The Times Literary Supplement* and the *Spectator* as well. This made his financial position easier, but brought with it the danger that he would become too dependent on ephemeral journalism to have the time or energy for original work.

The editor of *The Times Literary Supplement*, Bruce Richmond, to whom he had been introduced by Desmond MacCarthy, at first showed some caution in employing him. His first contribution, a review of Louis Cazamian's *L'Evolution Psychologique et la Littérature en Angleterre, 1660-1914*, which appeared in October 1921, looks rather like an examination paper intended to test both his command of French and his knowledge of English literature. This was followed in December by a review of a book on jewellery which constitutes his only venture into art criticism, apart from his much later essay on George Cruikshank; he has little to say on the artistic aspects of his subject, but makes some interesting comments on its psychological and social significance. After a graceful review of a minor French poet had appeared in April 1922 and a full-blooded appreciation of Thomas Dekker's prose in July, Richmond seems to have decided that he had served his apprenticeship, and from October 1922 to January 1925 he was a fairly regular contributor. This connection was an extremely useful one, as *The Times Literary Supplement* paid three guineas for a thousand words, a guinea more than most other papers, and gave its contributors a fair amount of space. "In good months," he later recalled, "I earned about £20 from the *TLS*"[2] – in the 1920s a reasonable income.

In December 1921 he also began contributing to the *Spectator*. Its editor and proprietor, John St Loe Strachey, had given it too Conservative a tone for his taste, but Strachey's daughter Amabel, who acted as literary editor, was a more congenial personality. Amabel, who was married to the architect Clough Williams-Ellis, worshipped her brother John, and under his influence was to move away from her father's

politics, first toward Socialism and then Marxism. She presided over
the weekly distribution of books to reviewers at the paper's Gower
Street offices, which Rickword described in his memoirs:

> We were a motley collection, rather starveling crows I would think, and
> it was rather like a board school's prize-giving. However, Amabel could
> be very warm and encouraging, and though one never felt quite at home
> and never took very much away, it was all a job. The only one to receive
> a great deal of the week's book output was J.B. Priestley, who put his
> hand up for pretty well everything that was of any interest. Of course,
> he didn't get everything he asked for, but he got quite a lot of subjects,
> and one envied his encyclopaedic knowledge.

To make the atmosphere even more reminiscent of eighteenth-century
Grub Street, the editor gave regular luncheons for his contributors.
Rickword was invited only once, and when Bertram Higgins went
he disgraced himself by using the wrong knives and forks.

Rickword's statement that he "never took very much away" is
misleading; between December 1921 and February 1924 he wrote
about seventy reviews for the *Spectator*, far more than he contributed to the *New Statesman* or *The Times Literary Supplement*.
All but two of these were published anonymously, and it is impossible to identify with certainty all the contributions to "Some Books
of the Week" or "Other Novels" for which the paper's account
books record payments. As the rate of pay (about three shillings a
column inch) was not generous and his monthly earnings averaged
only £2 6s. 8d., he found it necessary to review books on subjects
in which he had little interest. His highest earnings for any one
month, £5 13s. in December 1922, consisted of payments for reviews
of *French Essays and Profiles* by Stuart Henry ("There is no reason
why this book should not have appeared twenty years ago. None
of its ideas and few of its facts have any connection with the twentieth century"[3]), a book on fireworks and three novels; he was no
doubt anxious to earn a little extra money for Christmas, for in the
same month he reviewed five books for the *New Statesman* and one
for *The Times Literary Supplement*. The *Spectator* paid a higher
rate for verse than for prose; for the twenty-four lines of "Toilet,
or The Art of Poetry" (later renamed "Dream and Poetry") he
received £2, and for the sixty lines of an incomplete translation of
Rimbaud's *Bateau Ivre* £2 10s.

During the first eleven months of 1922 he published nothing in
the *New Statesman*,* and reviewing for the *Spectator* and *The Times
Literary Supplement* formed his main source of income. He also did

---

* The reviews signed E.R. which appeared in the *New Statesman* in 1922-3 were by Ellis
Roberts. To distinguish his work from Roberts's Rickword signed his reviews J.E.R.

some work for the *Daily News* (his review of a book on the Dodecanese Islands appeared in the issue for 27 April), but as most of the reviews in the paper were unsigned it is impossible to identify his contributions. Although in general his writings for the *Spectator* are of less interest than those for *The Times Literary Supplement* and *New Statesman*, an exception is his review of a reprint of Holbrook Jackson's *The Eighteen-Nineties*, in which he stated:

> We have not been able to match, in the work of the first fifteen years of this century, the intellectual virility, the active concern for the finest and rarest in art and life, the audacity (though sometimes but effrontery of convention) of theme, technique and criticism, concentrated in the last decade of the nineteenth century. The survivors went their ways; some wilted and a few that grew to full height are now our giants, but the Edwardians themselves and the early Georgians played for safety rather than distinction.[4]

Evidently Worth's attempt to convince Rickword of the superiority of the Georgians to the Aesthetes, whatever temporary success it may have achieved, had failed in the long run.

From the summer of 1921 onwards he renewed his contacts with his Oxford friends as they came down from the university. Several became contributors to the *Spectator*, including Higgins, who was appointed its film critic. Roy Campbell, who since leaving Oxford had travelled in France, Italy and North Africa, reappeared in London in September 1921, and shortly afterwards met Mary Garman, one of the seven daughters of a well-to-do Midlands doctor. They became engaged, and were married in February 1922. As a result of their meeting Rickword received a visit in the autumn of 1921 from a tall, handsome man about four years younger than himself, who introduced himself as Douglas Garman, the brother of Campbell's fiancée. Rickword invited him in and offered him tea, but as neither knew what to say to the other the meal was eaten in an embarrassed silence. It was only when they stood on the doorstep again saying goodbye that a conversation really began, from which it emerged that Garman fully shared Rickword's literary interests. This seemingly unpropitious meeting was the beginning of a lifelong friendship.

From Chelsea Rickword moved to Denbigh Street, Pimlico, where in March 1922 his second daughter, Pamela Jane, was born. A week or two later the family moved again, to a cottage at Chipstead in Surrey, which Turner had provided for them. This had its disadvantages (neither electricity nor gas was laid on, and sanitation was primitive), but Rickword found the large living room a pleasant place to work in. As money was short and Turner was charging them a high rent, Peggy put her Irish peasant skills to good use by planting a patch of ground with potatoes, cabbages and beans, and a partridge which nested at the bottom of the garden provided free eggs. Other attempts to augment their income were less fortunate; three goats which they tried keeping ate rings of bark off Turner's fruit trees, and a notice announcing that teas were served in the garden attracted only one customer, who queried his bill.

Early in September Campbell sent handwritten copies of his first long poem, "The Flaming Terrapin", to Rickword and two of his other friends, the painter Augustus John and the composer Philip Heseltine (Peter Warlock), in the hope that they would use their contacts to find it a publisher. On 9 September Rickword sent his opinion of it to Campbell:

> I have waited three days and three nights in order to be able to tell you quite coolly that the poem is magnificent. One doesn't often find anything to overwhelm one's expectations, but this does completely. I don't know that it's any good elaborating on this subject, and I want to avoid the appearance of ceremonial congratulations but really you knock the wind out of all the other "singers" as they are called by some reviews. I know of *no one living* who could write in such a sustained and intense poetical manner and by poetical I don't mean flowery but something profounder. Lots of things might have weighed against my liking it (particularly your philosophy of sweat) but the sheer fecundity of images ravished my ladylike prejudices. I soberly do not think there is anything of the kind in Corbière which can come up to your description of the voyage (poor inadequate word) round the Horn. If only one were a Bob Nichols and able to say "Hail, brother poet"! As it is I stifle as well as I can my jealousy and pray you to write, if only for the benefit of one humble admirer. Peggy and I spent a breathless evening over the manuscript and she has most carefully taken it to a typewriter in Redhill, who will do it as quickly as possible... I shall probably make some technical observations when I see the poem in type, but you can light your pipe over them. Good luck and ten thousand thanks for such a poem.

Reporting Rickword's reaction to the poem in a letter to his mother, Campbell wrote: "He is the one man among the younger poets whose opinion I revere at all and I only expected rather a cold-blooded criticism from him. I simply fell down on my bed and howled like a baby when I got it".[5] Rickword did not confine his attempts to help Campbell to getting the manuscript typed, but showed the poem to MacCarthy, who shared his enthusiasm and offered to write an article on it in order to interest publishers. This proved to be unnecessary, for Augustus John showed it to T.E. Lawrence, who persuaded the publishing firm of Jonathan Cape to accept it.

Rickword's enthusiasm is not surprising. "The Flaming Terrapin" is an intensely exciting poem, especially at first reading, written with the gusto of a young man not yet twenty-one, and is unlike anything else which was being written at the time, whether by Georgians or Modernists. He instinctively singled out for praise its amazing "fecundity of images", drawn from the entire natural world, from biblical and classical mythology and from everyday life. When he reviewed it for *The Times Literary Supplement* in 1924 he recognized its weaknesses of construction and diction, thereby causing Mary Campbell some offence, but he still paid it a tribute no less enthusiastic, though more balanced, than that in his letter.

There is something idyllic about the six months or so which the Rickwords spent at Chipstead. Despite their poverty, they were enjoying a rural life in happier circumstances than in their previous stay in the country in 1920-21. Peggy, a country girl by upbringing, probably felt more at home at Chipstead than in Chelsea, and took pride in being able to contribute to the family income by her gardening. The tone of Rickword's reference to her enjoyment of "The Flaming Terrapin" suggests that she had a genuine appreciation of poetry and could share in his intellectual pleasures. He evidently found the atmosphere stimulating, for while at Chipstead he wrote at least three of the most successful of his earlier poems, "Terminology", "Annihilation" and "Beyond Good and Evil". There were disadvantages to Chipstead, however; not only did he need to visit editorial offices and bookshops regularly, but they might have a long, dark and bleak winter to face if they stayed there. In the autumn, therefore, they moved back to Chelsea, where they rented two ground floor and two basement rooms in Sydney Street. It was the last home which all four members of the family were to share.

The happiness which Rickword derived from his marriage and the depth of his feeling for Peggy are apparent in the poems which he wrote in 1921-22. An early draft of "Terminology" contains the lines:

> We know not ecstasy in our quiet homes
> Except a strangeness from the nameless comes
> And that bright creature, sharer of our life,
> Glistens beneath the habit of the wife.

Perhaps the tenderest of all his poems is "Phenomenon in Absence", written in the autumn of 1921 while she was visiting her mother in Ireland:

> The mountains are bleak and bare,
> Unlovely stone,
> Once in the darkening air
> She is gone.

Effort can bring no bloom
    To hang there, nor water
To lighten the gloom
    In solitude, of matter.

Thought stirs not the rock
    Of mind, that mountain;
But her pale crumpled frock,
    A moonlit fountain

Whence the faint fragrance falls
    Of her love in past hours,
Plashing the stony walls
    Sets moss there with flowers.

Another poem apparently addressed to her, "The Pause" (later renamed "Strange Party"), which appeared in the *Spectator* in July 1922, is indebted to Verlaine, for the epigraph, the properties from Watteau – the masked and disguised dancers, the lute, the fountains, the moonlight – and the basic image are derived from his "Clair de lune":

"Votre âme est un paysage choisi."

On this lawn's most secret shade
    The masked Joys droop in their dance
As though the spirit of the maid
    Wearied beneath the lute's light nonchalance.

Their arms gay gestures still intend,
    Gently their voices lapse, and cold
The cascades of the moon descend
    On silvery dancers with false cheeks of gold.

Discreetly mocking in the dusk
    The masqueraders bow and twirl
In quaint disguises harsh of musk
    Among the fountains of your heart, sad girl.

This disturbing poem reads like a premonition of her approaching tragedy.

Through "Terminology" Rickword became involved in a controversy over the alleged obscurity of modern verse. The *Spectator* published on 30 December 1922, a letter from a reader complaining that Edith Sitwell's "Promenade Sentimentale", which had recently appeared in its pages, was completely incomprehensible. Amabel Williams-Ellis defended the poem, and took the opportunity to comment on "Terminology", which was printed in the same issue. At

first, she admitted, it had conveyed little or nothing to her, but on
re-reading it she had realized that "the poem was about the inability
of words to express meanings 'in the round', that names and words
are, so to say, a two-dimensional medium and leave out a great deal
about the thing spoken of".[6] Rickword's poem came out of the controversy rather well; one correspondent singled out for praise the lines

> Speech is most precious when the words we use
> Leap to an end the speaker did not choose,

and Philip Heseltine wrote:

> I regret to find the fashionable vendors of gingerbread verse, jugglers of
> little coloured balls of verbiage, associated in the columns of the *Spec-
> tator*, even by implication, with the author of "Terminology", a poet
> of real vision and creative imagination allied to an acute and penetrating
> intellect, whose little book *Behind the Eyes* is, in the opinion of more
> than one reader, the most significant contribution of the last ten years
> to English poetry.[7]

It was MacCarthy who realized that there was a danger that apart
from publishing an occasional poem Rickword would dissipate his
talent on journalism, and urged him to get a book commissioned.
As he had already written for the *New Statesman* on Verlaine and
Corbière, MacCarthy suggested that he should write on a French
poet, preferably Rimbaud. The suggestion was a wise one. On the
one hand, Rimbaud's work was much discussed at the time; reviewing a collection of writings by Etonians, Rickword wrote: "As Rimbaud said, of whom there is naturally mention in this volume, 'Il
faut être absolument moderne'."[8] On the other, there was no full-
length book on Rimbaud in English, and indeed very little writing
of any sort except two essays by George Moore and Arthur Symons,
both well over twenty years old. Rickword received further encouragement from T. Sturge Moore, a friend of MacCarthy, who had
published translations of Rimbaud's "Sensation" and "Les Cher-
cheuses de Poux" as long ago as 1899 and gave him permission to
include them in his book. At MacCarthy's suggestion Rickword
approached Heinemann's with a proposal for a biography of Rimbaud. This was accepted, and he proudly carried home to Peggy his
first contract, under which he was to be paid £25 on receipt of his
manuscript.

In the summer of 1923 he paid his first visit to Paris, together
with Peggy, in order to carry out some research for his book. They
took a room in the students' quarter, a few steps from the Odéon,
where they found that life had changed little since the previous
century; water carts came down to the Seine to fill up for the farms

just outside the city, and milkmen led goats with jingling bells round their necks from door to door, milking them into canisters on the doorstep. They took a day excursion to Charleville, Rimbaud's birthplace, which made a very unfavourable impression on Rickword. "Charleville is surely the least attractive town between Paris and the frontier," he wrote in his biography,

> though its Siamese neighbour Mézières, with its steep paved streets, obsolete fortifications, and deep moat is not without distinction. But only the presence of the Meuse saves Charleville itself from utter desolation, and even then it is the dustiest town in Western Europe. Today (though something must be forgiven on account of its unlucky record in the last two wars*) his name is unfamiliar in the few poor bookshops, even though there is a bustless monument to his memory in the Station Square. The bronze head presented to the town by Parisian men of letters on their own initiative was removed by the Germans during their occupation, but walking from the station through the pleasant little garden with bandstand and fishponds, the same which he described in *A La Musique*, the stone still confronts one with the sole justification "Explorations en Afrique". Only on closer examination may one detect the other leaves in his wreath of glory: "Illuminations, Bateau Ivre, Voyelles, Saison en Enfer". But it seems these shopkeepers lack even the commercial enterprise necessary to draw profit from their involuntary connection with a poet. There is a public library, open during the holidays for two hours a week, but perhaps the town does not possess a second Rimbaud to fret at this meagre ration of knowledge.[9]

In the sardonic comment on the town's library service we seem to hear the voice of George Rickword's son.

While working on his book Rickword continued to contribute to the *New Statesman* up to July 1923, and to *The Times Literary Supplement* and *Spectator* throughout that year. Much of his work for the first two was concerned with French literature; he wrote essays on Laforgue, Mallarmé and Rimbaud and reviews of translations of Huysmans and Anatole France for the *New Statesman*, and reviewed Valéry's poems, translations of Cyrano de Bergerac and various French novels, and books on French verse, Baudelaire and Rimbaud for *The Times Literary Supplement*. He also did some reviewing of English verse for both, and made his only appearance as a dramatic critic when he wrote on a production of *Arthur*, a verse tragedy by Laurence Binyon. On the character of King Arthur he made the interesting comment:

> Arthur has tempted many modern poets because he was evidently the type of man in whom the civilising instincts are stronger than in his contemporaries. In the parley outside Joyous Gard, Malory says: "King

---

* The reference is to the wars of 1870-71 and 1914-18.

Arthur would have taken his queen again, and would have been accorded with Sir Lancelot, but Sir Gawaine would not suffer him by no manner of means". Arthur is the first of our race to attempt the intellectualisation of the passions, and his amorousness was only skin deep.[10]

By far the most important of Rickword's writings on poetry of this period is his review of *The Waste Land*, which appeared in *The Times Literary Supplement* on 20 September 1923. The publication of Eliot's poem in *The Criterion* in October 1922 and in book form, first in New York in the following December and then in London in September 1923, provoked a heated controversy among critics on both sides of the Atlantic. Some were openly hostile. The *Manchester Guardian* dismissed it as "a mad medley". J.C. Squire suggested that it represented "a faithful transcript, after Mr Joyce's obscurer manner, of the poet's wandering thoughts when in a state of erudite depression", and commented that "a grunt would serve equally well".[11] This view was shared by other Georgians, including Ralph Hodgson, who described the poem as "literary leg-pulling",[12] and Sassoon. F.L. Lucas poured donnish scorn on "this unhappy composition", and declared it inferior to Tennyson's "Vision of Sin". Other reviewers, while fully recognizing the power of the poem, were critical of its structural weakness and its patchwork of quotations; the parody of Goldsmith's "When lovely woman stoops to folly" was singled out for particular censure. John Crowe Ransom commented on its "extreme disconnection", and called the Goldsmith parody "a considerable affront against aesthetic sensibilities". National feeling underlay much of the unfavourable criticism, especially in the United States, where there was felt to be something un-American in Eliot's pessimism and his obsession with the culture of a decadent Europe. Some of his admirers (and he was already the centre of a cult) asserted the poem's greatness while ignoring the very real problems which it raised. When it was first published in *The Criterion* an anonymous reviewer in *The Times Literary Supplement* wrote: "We have here range, depth, and beautiful expression. What more is necessary to a great poem?" Some declared it great despite its structural weakness, among them Edmund Wilson, who held that "the poem is – in spite of its lack of structural unity – simply one triumph after another", while others convinced themselves that its weakness was really its strength, that, in Conrad Aiken's words, "the poem succeeds – as it brilliantly does – by virtue of its incoherence, not of its plan".[13]

Rickword would have none of this special pleading. He had been familiar with Eliot's work at least since his Oxford days, and in 1920 had hailed him as the greatest living critic writing in English, but precisely because of the greatness of Eliot's achievement he had to be judged by the highest standards. Rickword remarked that "his emotions hardly ever reach us without traversing a zig-zag of allusion", and that there was a danger that "if the apparatus of reserve is too strongly constructed, it will defeat the poet's end". The central theme – "the toppling of aspirations, the swift disintegration of accepted stability, the crash of an ideal" – was clear enough, but the poet's purpose was defeated by his method of communication.

> Set at a distance by a poetic method which is reticence itself, we can only judge of the strength of the emotion by the visible violence of the reaction. Here is Mr Eliot, a dandy of the choicest phrase, permitting himself blatancies like "the young man carbuncular". Here is a poet capable of a style more refined than that of any of his generation parodying without taste or skill – and of this the example from Goldsmith is not the most astonishing. Here is a writer to whom originality is almost an inspiration, borrowing the greater number of his best lines, creating hardly any himself. It seems as if *The Waste Land* exists in its greater part in the state of notes.

Despite the excellence of particular passages, Rickword concluded, "we do not derive from this poem as a whole the satisfaction we ask from poetry".[14] Today, when Eliot is a figure sufficiently remote to be seen in perspective, it is possible to assent to this conclusion.

Rickword's contributions to the *Spectator* in 1923 included a number of reviews of the work of minor poets, who, because they were of less importance, were judged by less exacting standards than Eliot. He picks out their strong points for praise, and his good-humoured comments often have a dry wit. "Mr Forster's sonnets... will delight the amateur gardener who combines a literary culture with the other. Miss C. Fox Smith's sea-songs...are brinier than the most crusted old salt and more rollicking than the jolliest tar."[15] He also reviewed novels, short stories, plays, critical works, essays and a large number of travel books, beginning with D.H. Lawrence's *Sea and Sardinia*, on which he commented that "the exasperation, the bad temper, is no doubt the price that we must pay for the exceptional sensitiveness of his recording apparatus".[16] Despite the wide range of subjects covered, his writing can rarely be described as hackwork, and memorable passages may occur at any time. Reviewing Lady Gregory's plays of Irish peasant life, for example, he writes:

> As anyone who heard both will remember, conversation in the ranks of the war-time Army was on a much higher level, aesthetically, than that in the officers' messes; not because there were many literate men in the ranks, but for the opposite reason. Speech, with the illiterate, is their highest form of expression, and they put their best into it, till it rings

like good money flung down. Those who live more remotely, the cultured, are apt to regard it as a necessary, but sometimes wearisome,
system of exchange, for which leaden counters will suffice.[17]

In view of his later political opinions, Rickword's reviews of two
books on Russia are of particular interest. As a young officer he
had welcomed the revolution, even though there was a danger that
it would release German troops to fight on the Western Front, and
later opposed British intervention in Russia. By 1923, however, his
enthusiasm had waned. In his review of *Through the Russian
Revolution*, an eyewitness account by the American Socialist Albert
Rhys Williams, he treated the author's unqualified admiration with
some irony: "Reading this book one would say it was quite the
nicest Revolution in history, and that the number of casualties bore
such a small proportion to the population of Russia that it might
be called bloodless".[18] A few months later he reviewed *Russia and
Peace*, by Fridtjov Nansen, in which the great explorer and humanitarian advocated that the Western countries should grant credits to
Russia to enable her to buy machinery and manufactured goods in
exchange for agricultural produce. "Russia spent her savings in that
disastrous experiment Communism," Rickword caustically commented, "and now she cannot, without external help, both repair
the wastage and build up new reserves of vitality."[19] By "Communism" he apparently meant the "War Communism" which the
Bolsheviks had practised during the civil war, and which had been
abandoned in 1921 in favour of the New Economic Policy, rather
than Communism in general, but the sentence is certainly not one
which a fellow-traveller could have written.

His last contributions to the *Spectator*, apart from two poems,
appeared early in 1924, and included his first two signed reviews
for the paper – an indication of his growing authority as a critic.
Discussing the poems of Wilfrid Scawen Blunt, whom he admired
as a poet combining profound patriotism with a passionate hatred
of imperialism and racialism, he wrote: "His antagonism to Anglo-
Saxondom, in a time when a dominant Imperialism clothed itself
in fine phrases, does not prevent him from being one of the most
English of English poets".[20] In the other review he considered the
work of eight poets, singling out the very dissimilar Arthur Symons,
"Michael Field" and W.H. Davies for praise.

His prose writing during 1922-23 was not confined to the three
weeklies. Although he admitted to being "tone-deaf and completely
ignorant of musical techniques", he reviewed W.J. Turner's *Music
and Life* for *Isis*, praising it for its stylistic qualities; on the same
page Higgins reviewed Turner's latest collection of poems and
Behind the Eyes, which he considered "probably the best first volume

published in England since the war".[21] Rickword contributed an essay, "The Birth of a Classic", to *Marcel Proust: An English Tribute*, which appeared in the autumn of 1923 and also included contributions by – among others – Compton Mackenzie, Clive Bell, J. Middleton Murry, Joseph Conrad, George Saintsbury, Arthur Symons and Arnold Bennett.

A more important work was an essay on Thomas Lovell Beddoes, published in the *London Mercury* in December 1923. Rickword's comments on Beddoes's poetry are of interest not only for their own sake, but because they reflect the change in his own verse that had occurred in the past four years. "His impulsiveness must have driven him romantic, considering the nature of the influences he suffered, but under continual self-criticism he would have become aware that this romanticism was super-imposed and not in accord with his true personality", he wrote, and maintained that Beddoes had become "sick beyond patience with the comforting illusions of romance", quoting as an example his reference to "fat mother moon". The phrase is certainly remote from the Romantic moon of Turner's poems, but it comes very close to the "fat-cheeked moon" of Rickword's own "Ode to a Train-de-luxe". "His anatomical studies," he continued,

> rendered him intimate with processes more private than those of the toilet, and destroyed in him that reverence for the flesh it is a communal labour to maintain, in face of the actuality. Such a thing has happened to other writers, to Swift and to Baudelaire; these and their like depend on more gracious qualities for any popularity they may win. A grotesque such as no other poet has is Beddoes' contribution to literature.[22]

Rickword's own reverence for the flesh, as "Trench Poets" reminds us, had been destroyed on the Western Front, and although he had outgrown the crudity of "A Dead Mistress" he retained his conviction that a healthy poetry needed to be able to deal with all aspects of life, not merely the pleasant ones.

At about the time this essay was published he suffered one of the most painful experiences of his life, when Peggy lost her reason. The story is best told in the words of his memoirs:

> Soon after we came back from France, the circumstances of my existence became less amenable to an orderly programme of work and relaxation, as my wife was developing very volatile and unpredictable mannerisms, being at one time perfectly amiable and at the next very antagonistic to myself and sometimes physically attacking me, and also being very jealous whenever I went out to go up to Fleet Street to get some books to review. I began to think that I must get a cheap room somewhere out, as I could no longer concentrate on my writing. In fact, Peggy's suspicions grew, enveloping everything else, common sense and all, and she used

to resort to sewing up my flies and sewing my shirt to my trousers or vice versa. When I went out I might get my face scratched, and that would lead to very awkward situations in company.

I believe that Peggy did not know she had done these things when she came out of the mood in which she had acted in that way, yet I think I can truly say that she became aware of something menacing her. She went to her parish priest and had some sort of talks with him, and then of course there was confession. I don't know to what extent sexuality was involved, but she certainly tried to get release from the rule that no attempt must be made to inhibit conception. Yet it was too much like a rationalization to believe that this was the primary cause of her distress. It must have had a much deeper seat, perhaps stemming from her very early life.

Suddenly one evening she turned towards the children rather than myself, as it were menacing them and looking on them with a suffering look, and not knowing what to do to avoid their being punished by some exterior power. She kept making the sign of the cross over them. Finally the doctor arrived and instructed that she be sent to hospital. I communicated with my family in Colchester by telegram the next morning; neither of us were on the phone in those days, but the telegraph was almost as quick. I think it must have been the same evening after the catastrophe that my younger sister Barbara arrived and took things in hand. When I found that Peggy had been transferred to a mental hospital I immediately thought of the new science of psycho-analysis and wrote off to ask for an interview with Dr Ernest Jones as soon as possible. The interview was unproductive.

It was some days before I was allowed to visit my wife. It was a longish journey to some suburb, where I was shown into the hospital. After passing through many wards we came to a small unfurnished cell with very little light. On the bed in the corner there was an almost invisible human being lying under the canvas. Under this covering a small, white, emaciated face was all that could be seen or, rather, barely distinguished. Peggy was not going to have Christmas with us, which I'd hoped would help to drive away the anxieties which beset her, and which she was never to be free from again.

The clumsiness of the writing is evidence of the reluctance with which Rickword recalled these events. One reason why little is known about Peggy is that in old age he still found the memory so painful that he was unwilling to speak of her, even to those nearest to him, and if these were his feelings over half a century later, his sufferings at the time must have been extreme. Two years earlier he had recorded his loneliness during her visit to Ireland in "Phenomenon in Absence"; now he defined his desolation in two other poems, published together in 1925 under the common title "Absences", behind the second of which clearly lies the memory of his glimpse of her in the mental hospital:

Now that you lie in lonely pain,
O Moon in no flower-clouded bed,
What shall evoke our Joy again?
O Tears, rain Tears on Pleasure dead!

Under their sharp caressing stroke
The foliage of our love revives,
Though your face pale when anguish broke
Alone on Night's dead sea survives.

Another poem, possibly unfinished, which he never published, seems
to refer to the evening when her sanity finally broke down:

Pain beat black wings against the wall and rent
With tossing beak the tenderest of her kind;
And all that night the droning wind
Crept through the darkened garden and rack went
Scudding across few mournful stars that sent
Pale pitiful gleams down the compassionate mind.
And pity wept that night till eyes were blind
And her balm spent.

Gradually he was forced to accept the fact that their separation
might be permanent, and would inevitably imply separation from
his children as well. It was impossible for him simultaneously to
earn his living, run a home and look after two baby girls, and early
in 1924 he entrusted them to foster-parents. Joan, the elder girl,
was brought up by a brother of Rickword's mother and his wife,
who lived in Kent, and Jane by two sisters living in Berkshire who
were friends of the Rickword family. Although he contributed what
little he could towards their keep, he could not afford to visit them
often, and the two girls grew up virtually in ignorance of their
parents – a fact which Jane at least greatly resented as a child. To
complete the break with the past, the lease of the Sydney Street flat
expired in March, and after a visit to his parents in Colchester he
moved into a Bayswater boarding house with Bertram Higgins, who
was supposed to be reading law.

It was fortunate for his sanity that his life of Rimbaud fully
occupied his mind at this time. The manuscript was completed and
delivered in March, and before the end of the month the proofs
arrived. He rewrote the book so thoroughly that after he had submitted his corrected proofs he was sent another set, with a letter
suggesting that in view of the expense involved he should correct
them again, making only essential alterations. He tried to comply
with this request, but he still ran up a bill of nearly £10, which was
deducted from his £25 advance. In this form *Rimbaud: The Boy
and the Poet* appeared in June.

Rickword emphasized, consciously or unconsciously, the points of resemblance between Rimbaud's career and his own, which were certainly striking. Both came from provincial families which were "by no means wealthy but not penurious either, *petit bourgeois* most exactly". Both were given a pious upbringing, and remained deeply religious until after they had taken their first communion. The imaginations of both were stimulated by their childhood reading of the Bible. Both rejected Christianity in their middle teens and adopted Socialist views. Both were strongly affected by the outbreak of war when they were fifteen, and developed a fierce hatred of the war-makers. Both were influenced at this stage of their careers by a young schoolmaster with literary interests and progressive views. Each experienced "great shocks which unsettled the idealistic structure on which he had built his mind". Rimbaud's attitude to Paris, as described by Rickword, resembled his own attitude to London: "He loved it for its inexhaustible variety, its indifference, its brutality. For the anonymity which, like an invisible cloak, permits splendid liberties". And both, although Rickword did not know it, were to provoke much speculation by ceasing to write poetry, entirely or almost entirely, while still young.

How far Rickword's identification with Rimbaud affected his writing can be seen from his treatment of Rimbaud's politics and his sexual life. He described the young Rimbaud as "a rather doctrinaire Communist",[23] and chronicled his school essays in praise of Marat and Robespierre, his draft of a communist constitution and his eloquent revolutionary poem *Le Forgeron*. He also accepted the legend, supported by apparently excellent authority, that he had joined the forces of the Paris Commune. In the second edition of 1963 he qualified his description of Rimbaud as a "Communist" by pointing out that in his day the word "did not imply membership of a political party", and rejected the story that during the Commune, with little or no money to buy food, he had walked the 150 miles from Charleville to Paris in six days, which in 1924 he had accepted without question, as "too fantastic".[24] Clearly in 1924 his feeling that Rimbaud should have fought for the Commune, for which he expressed strong support in his letters, had prevailed over his judgment.

His experience with George Coombe had given Rickword a strong prejudice against homosexuals, and Rimbaud's relationship with Verlaine caused him some embarrassment. In his book he emphasized the heterosexual feeling of some of the early poems which gave expression to "the feverish desires of adolescence", whereas his only reference to homosexuality was the bald statement that Verlaine's wife had demanded a divorce, "alleging in particular immoral relations between the two friends".[25] As Edmund Gosse remarked with some justice, he "gives a plaintive impression of not knowing, as people say, what to think'."[26]

It is true that in the 1920s the subject was virtually taboo, but that had not prevented him from dealing with it sensibly in his essay on Beddoes, where he remarks that "there is no indication that he was ever interested in any woman, or in the sex", and notes without comment that "the only company he would tolerate" while living in Frankfurt was that of the young baker Konrad Degen, separation from whom led to his suicide.[27] The only explanation of his failure to discuss Rimbaud's sexual life in a similar spirit would appear to be that he was too emotionally involved with Rimbaud to accept the idea that he ever indulged in homosexual practices. In the 1963 edition he had to take into account the obscene sonnets known as *Les Stupra*, which were first published while his book was being written, but he virtually absolved Rimbaud of responsibility for them by arguing that "they are parodies of Verlaine's style of homosexual braggadocio and were almost certainly a combined operation, an opportunity for that infantile exhibitionism to fits of which Verlaine was subject".[28]

His comments on Rimbaud's verse technique often cast light on his own theory and practice. His explanation of why Rimbaud rejected his early poems would serve equally well for his own rejection of the Romanticism of *Behind the Eyes*:

> Unadulterated aesthetic enjoyment is not only very rare, after infancy, it is not more desirable than sugar-icing. The percentage of artist in a poet is generally very high, but it is always in the great poets subordinated to a preoccupation of the sensibility which is outside the aesthetic. So as our taste matures we cast off the delights of sound and sweetness and "feed on that which to weak tastes seems tough". The strongest poems, we shall find, are those in which the aesthetic make-up (rhythm, imagery, colour, rhyme) is not more pronounced than the emotion which gives it life. There are many poems almost wholly made of pleasing colours and images through which the emotion scampers like a mouse in the Crystal Palace. That is why a poem, pleasing in all its external characteristics, may be quite repulsive.

He is not, of course, condemning rhythm, imagery, colour or rhyme in verse; he has no use for "the theorists who say that one must not scan, or rhyme, which is a tyranny worse than that of the formal prosodists". Rather he holds up as a guide "the classic (theory) of saying as much as possible in, it is a matter of elementary politeness, the fewest possible words", and develops this theme when he says of Rimbaud: "We see him not trying to decorate his ideas, as an insincere writer would do, but to strip them of all the expressions that were merely fanciful or of secondary interest until one can say that his final version is the idea itself, which, with a word more or a word less, would not be at all the same thing".[29]

Rickword's own artistry is apparent in the revision to which

Rimbaud was subjected in the 1963 edition. Phrases which he had come to consider chauvinistic or racist were removed. Where he had compared Rimbaud to "the best type of English explorer" the word "English" was omitted; "nigger" was altered to "savage"; and in the phrase "Latin and Greek, the base of civilization" "our" was inserted before "civilization".[30] But the bulk of the changes were inspired by aesthetic motives. An image which a reviewer had criticized as illogical, although defensible, was removed; words were replaced by others which expressed the intended sense more exactly; sentences or whole paragraphs were compressed or omitted. Even this drastic revision did not satisfy him. On many pages of his own copy of this edition proposed emendations are written in the margins, some of which were incorporated in the text of the chapters included in *Essays and Opinions* in 1974.

In normal circumstances Rickword would probably have dedicated his book to Peggy; instead he dedicated it to his parents. In an introductory note, after thanking Sturge Moore and MacCarthy for their help and encouragement, he wrote: "Towards my wife I am a more intimate debtor, though I cannot at present express my gratitude for her sympathy and devotion". The words "at present" suggest that in the spring of 1924 he still hoped that she would recover her reason.

George Rickword was proud of his son's achievement, and carefully hoarded reviews and other press cuttings about the book. It had a mixed reception. The warmest welcome came from *The Times Literary Supplement*, which praised alike Rickword's "admirable" literary criticism, his "careful and industrious research" and the "imaginative skill" with which he had reconstructed Rimbaud's family life, as well as his translations of some of the prose poems.[31] J.C. Squire in the *Observer* criticized his style and proof-reading, but considered these "the only serious blots on a very good book which gives a conscientious account of the subject, and is full of hard, tight criticism of ideas and art".[32] Hugh l'Anson Fausset in the *Spectator* praised the "great insight" of Rickword's analysis of Rimbaud's psychology,[33] but Sydney Waterlow in the *New Statesman* was distinctly patronizing: "Mr Rickword's enthusiasm for his subject has enabled him to write an attractive and, indeed, a lovable book, although partly because he confines himself to Rimbaud's artist period, we hardly think that he has got to the root of the matter".[34] The book received its roughest handling from Edmund Gosse, then one of the grand old mandarins of literature, though he is now remembered solely as the author of *Father and Son*. In a bad-tempered review in the *Sunday Times* he accused Rickword of misusing words and images, bad grammar, lacking a fresh viewpoint and imitating Lytton Strachey, and concluded with a violent attack on Rimbaud, who, he declared, "thought the readers of poetry were imbeciles, and that he would frighten them with horrors like 'Le Dormeur du Val'."[35]

Rickword probably concluded that the opinions of a critic who could write such a sentence need not be taken too seriously.

A more informed judgment on his book was given thirty years later by Enid Starkie, then regarded as the leading British authority on Rimbaud, who wrote:

> After Arthur Symons we must wait a quarter of a century to find a penetrating study of Rimbaud in England, and that is in the book by the poet Edgell Rickword, published in 1924, which was the best, if not the very best, which had appeared up to date in any country, even in France, and it holds interest even for modern readers. Rickword shows a comprehension of the poet which was rare at that time. It was the first time that any attempt had been made to give a psychological interpretation of his nature. He was particularly interested in the human personality of the man, and that is why the biographical part is the longest.[36]

This tribute can be accepted still as an authoritative assessment of the book's merits.

George Rickword included among his collection two cuttings from local papers which were flattering to his family pride. The *Essex County Telegraph*, which a week before had published an article by Gerald Rickword entitled "Old-time Cricket in Colchester and East Essex", commented on 21 June 1924, that Rickword had "long given evidence of a remarkable talent, of original and sometimes wayward thought, and a desire for the untrodden paths of literature", and had now "taken his place amongst the other members of a literary family with whom the readers of this journal are well acquainted". The *Essex County Standard* of the same date recalled that besides being "a poet of distinction – and of daring – and a literary critic of considerable repute", he was "a native of Colchester, and son of Mr GEORGE RICKWORD, F.R.Hist.S."

The publication of the biography did not completely exorcize Rimbaud's ghost, which continued to haunt both his prose and his verse. His short story "Orders to View" is a free adaptation of the prose poem "Ouvriers" in *Les Illuminations*. The central episode of the dream-fantasy "Pioneers, O Pioneers!", published in 1925, in which a dreamer, travelling through a polar landscape, comes upon a thousand-storey hotel, is an expansion of one sentence in Rimbaud's "Après le déluge": "Et le Splendide-Hôtel fut bâti dans le chaos de glaces et de nuit du pôle".[37] Above all, his study of Rimbaud drew his attention to the story of Faustus.

The comparison between Rimbaud, with his craving to make himself a seer, "le grand malade, le grand criminel, le grand maudit, – et le suprême Savant",[38] in order to reach the unknown, and Faustus is an obvious one, and is made several times in the biography.

The Faustus myth, Rickword believed, contained the universal truth that "the desire for more power, more joy, and more entire perfection, in short, for the absolutes of duration and sensation which lure us in Helen's fabled face, is enough to damn a man to suffering in this life with no need for the metaphor of hell".[39] His broodings on this theme led him on, after completing *Rimbaud*, to begin work on a verse play in which the story of Faustus was to be retold in a contemporary setting. The close connection between the two works is demonstrated by the fact that he drafted his play on the unused or half-used pages of an exercise book in which he had made notes for the biography.*

The play begins with Faustus brooding on his frustrations in sinewy couplets which suggest that had Rickword completed it he might have had great success in reviving the poetic drama. Mephistopheles is not summoned up by incantations as in Marlowe's tragedy, but steps out of a mirror, an incarnation of Faustus's pride. At this point the difficulties of transferring a medieval story to the twentieth century become apparent, for how is the contract between them to be made convincing to a modern audience? Rickword sidestepped the problem with a stage direction "Draw up contract", intending to return to it later. After a prose scene set three years later in which two of Faustus's employees inform us that he has become the master of boundless wealth, "the real king of the world", he declares his intention to "reveal" himself to the people. And then the play disintegrates into fragments of speeches in which he denounces the venality of society. Two other incomplete scenes, one of them a conversation between Faustus, Mephistopheles and Dante apparently set in hell, indicate that Rickword planned to introduce both Helen of Troy and Goethe's Margaret, whose mother appears as Faustus's landlady.

There he left this tantalizing fragment, but he did not lose interest in the theme. The poem "Rimbaud in Africa", probably written in March 1925, tells the story of Rimbaud's life in terms of the Faustus legend. A review of a reprint of the Elizabethan Faust books in *The Calendar of Modern Letters* for December 1925, which although unsigned was written by Rickword, discusses the significance of the legend, and reaches the conclusion that "since man naturally hates god, the progeny of the damned conjurer, humanity's stalking-horse and scape-goat, will always in some form or another have a part in our scene".[40] He returned to the subject for the last time in "Theme for The Pseudo-Faustus", published in April 1927, which is largely a re-writing of the opening scene of his play. How far he identified himself

* Passages of the play were written on pages of the exercise book which Rickword subsequently numbered A1-A14. As drafts of *Circus* and *Luxury*, which date from the summer of 1924, were written on page A12, this suggests that the bulk of the play was written in the spring or early summer of that year.

with Faustus, as he had previously identified himself with Rimbaud, is indicated by the fact that the poem appeared in *The Calendar* under the pseudonym "Gabriel Foster" – and it is as "Mr Foster" that Margaret's mother addresses Faustus in the play.

After the publication of *Rimbaud* Rickword made his first prolonged visit to Paris, together with Higgins. It enabled him to stock up with reprints of French novels. A jeweller's shop window in the Place de la Paix inspired "Luxury", a Baudelairean vision with revolutionary undertones:

> The churches' sun-dried clay crumbles at last,
> The Courts of Justice wither like a stink
> And honourable statues melt as fast
> As breakfast garbage down the kitchen sink.

His indignation may have owed something to the fact that by the end of their stay they were both so hard up that they pawned their typewriters, and were obliged to borrow five pounds from a friend of Higgins before they could pay their bills.

On returning to London they rented a flat in Long Acre, close to Covent Garden Market, which provided the subject of the sonnet "Assuagement". Here Rickword wrote his last contributions to *The Times Literary Supplement*, the most important of which were three studies of Metaphysical poets. Reviewing a reprint of *Hero and Leander*, he concentrated on Chapman's neglected and underrated conclusion to Marlowe's poem, and argued Chapman's claim to be ranked with Donne as a pioneer of the Metaphysical school. The other two dealt with Donne himself – a review of a biography, which gave him the opportunity to analyse both Donne's style and his psychology, and an essay on his religious thought, "Donne the Divine". This article, which appeared on Christmas Eve, must have given particular pleasure to Rickword's parents, with whom he probably spent Christmas. The first leading article which he had written for *The Times Literary Supplement* and his longest contribution to the paper, it bears the mark of his Anglo-Catholic upbringing, particularly in the warmth and imaginative sympathy with which he writes of the significance of Christmas for the believer.

Rickword wrote one more review for *The Times Literary Supplement*, which appeared on 29 January 1925. It marked the end of the period of his life which had begun in July 1920 with his first contribution to the *Daily Herald*, when reviewing for other men's papers had been his primary occupation. Henceforward he hoped to be his own master.

VI. The *Calendar of Modern Letters*

IN the autumn of 1924 Douglas Garman turned up again in London. He had recently inherited a small income on his father's death and had decided to leave Cambridge, where he had studied first classics and then modern languages, without taking his degree. The long discussions on his future plans which he held with Rickword and Higgins usually came back to the possibility of running their own literary magazine, an idea which appealed equally to all three. Rickword had no money, and Garman, who had expensive tastes, could guarantee only enough to cover the cost of his first issue. Fortunately his closest friend, Ernest Wishart, another Cambridge man, was the son of a wealthy father. Seeing in Garman a potential dramatist, he had already offered to back a play by him, and by the end of the year Garman had talked him into agreeing to support a magazine instead.

The *Calendar of Modern Letters*, as it was decided to call the new magazine, was very much a family affair. Rickword and Garman were to be the editors; the business manager was Rickword's cousin Cecil, who also proved to be an excellent reviewer of fiction; the not very efficient advertisement manager was Garman's only brother; and Wishart, without whose financial backing it would never have come into existence, was married to his sister Lorna. For the time being Higgins held no official position, but poems, critical essays or reviews by him appeared in fourteen of the magazine's eighteen issues.

By January 1925 three rooms had been rented on the top floor of an eighteenth-century house in Featherstone Buildings, just off Holborn and conveniently opposite a large public house. Rickword and Higgins found their Long Acre flat too cramped for their new responsibilities and moved into Woburn Square, a Bloomsbury district which had come down in the world. Here for about £3 a week they rented a spacious flat.

Looking back on the founding of the *Calendar*, Rickword described Garman, Higgins and himself nearly fifty years later as "a sort of discontented club, discontented with all the established novelists and the literary cliques".[1] They saw their task as a double one, destructive and constructive – as Rickword wrote in his memoirs, "to clear the ground of, not weeds only, but some respectable but overgrown trees that were depriving the more worthy newcomers of the light which they required to develop", and at the same time "to find and bring forward these new plants". The *Calendar* was very much a mouthpiece for the young, nearly half the contributors being under thirty. In the post-war world the generation gap was perhaps wider than it had ever been; the young saw in their elders a guilty generation that had sent them to war, robbed them of their brothers and friends, and left them to face a hopeless future. The younger intellectuals in particular believed that the major literary figures surviving from before the war had either contributed actively to bring it about, peddled panaceas which had proved useless to prevent it, or at best upheld aesthetic standards irrelevant to the post-war world. In the eyes of the editors of the *Calendar* these possessors of inflated reputations needed to be exposed, and this task was undertaken in the "Scrutinies" which began in the first issue.

On one question of policy Rickword, Garman and Higgins were agreed – if the *Calendar* was to attract the best authors it must pay professional rates. This meant three guineas a thousand words, as much as *The Times Literary Supplement* and a guinea more than most of the weeklies. As they discussed possible contributors throughout the winter evenings some names constantly recurred – D.H.Lawrence, James Joyce, Wyndham Lewis, E.M. Forster. If none of these could be described as a newcomer, neither were they part of the literary establishment; the first three were widely regarded as not quite respectable, and Forster in his quiet integrity stood apart from all cliques. Approaches to Lawrence and Lewis proved disappointing; Rickword had hoped to obtain short stories from them, but instead Lawrence offered his nouvelle *The Princess*, which was too long for one issue. Although Rickword disliked serializing works, it was essential to have a well-known name in the first issue, and *The Princess* was accordingly published in three instalments. Lewis was even more troublesome. Invited to submit either a short story or a longer work of fiction for serial publication, he offered instead a rambling critical essay, which he suggested should be published in three instalments of 5000 words; Rickword persuaded him to cut it, and it finally appeared in two instalments of 6000 words. Forster was more reasonable; he dropped in to the office one afternoon for a long chat with Rickword, and later produced a devastating review of Sir Sidney Lee's life of Edward VII for the second issue.

The attempt to recruit Joyce as a contributor ended in a tragi-comic failure. While the first number was being prepared Rickword wrote to his publisher, Sylvia Beach, offering "the hospitality of our pages to Joyce, the greatest power of the present generation".[2] He was granted permission to publish the "Anna Livia Plurabelle" section of *Finnegans Wake*, but when it went to press the printers refused to set up a passage which they considered obscene. When he asked permission to delete this passage Joyce refused to discuss any alteration of his text, and he was obliged to return the manuscript.

A magazine needs others besides star names to keep it going, and Rickword was able to draw on three groups of associates for material.

There were his friends from Oxford days; A.E. Coppard contributed a short story to the first issue, and L.P. Hartley supplied a few reviews. The film critic Iris Barry, who was married to Alan Porter, can also be included in this group. Then there were the trench poets; verse came from Sassoon and Blunden, prose from Nichols, and a great deal of both from Graves. Finally there were Rickword's journalistic associates Turner, who wrote on the drama and contributed poems, and MacCarthy, who submitted an essay on Byron. Help also came from Sidney Schiff, the generous patron of many writers, who not only provided a short story under his pseudonym Stephen Hudson but put Rickword on the track of Edwin Muir. After hearing about him at one of Schiff's Sunday afternoon tea parties, Rickword visited Muir at the cottage near Beaconsfield where he was living and enrolled him as one of the *Calendar*'s most valuable contributors.

The editors scorned publicity, and the first number came into the world almost unheralded. It received one advance notice from the Irish nationalist M.P. and journalist T.P. O'Connor, who edited a popular literary weekly. In his column of literary gossip, "T.P.'s Table Talk", he included an item which gives a glimpse of how the young Rickword struck his contemporaries:

> The next day or two will bring forth a new literary periodical and a new editor. The first is a monthly, which, I understand, will be called the *Calendar of Letters* – there is a pleasant eighteenth-century ring about the name – and the editor is Mr Edgell Rickword. Mr Rickword is one of a group of young poets produced by Oxford in the two or three years following the war – a group which includes Mr Roy Campbell, the South African author of *The Flaming Terrapin*, Mr Richard Hughes and Mr Alan Porter. The common denominator of their diverse talents, I should say, is an impatience with mere rationalism...Mr Rickword himself has a background which includes Flanders as well as Oxford. He was an infantry officer during the war, and lost an eye through wounds. Slight, fair-haired and boyish, his very quiet manner belies a definite and mature attitude towards life and letters.[3]

The first number, which went on sale at the beginning of March, was a strong and well-balanced one. The opening instalment of *The Princess* was followed by three poems by Graves, two of them of some length, an essay on Poe by Garman, one on Barrie by Rickword, translations of a letter from Dostoevsky to his mistress and a Russian account of her, a story by Coppard and a poem by Sassoon. The second half of the magazine, "Comments and Reviews", was ushered in by a policy statement by Rickword. "We lay down no programme as to THE CALENDAR's performance nor prophecy as to its character," he wrote, "since these things cannot interest our readers till they have a tangible existence, and then we shall be ready to join our own criticism with theirs." Disclaiming any intention by the editors to found a sect of readers "with whom we share any particular set of admirations and beliefs", he declared:

> The aim of writing is not to convince someone else (for that can never happen against the will) but to satisfy oneself. If, as well, the reader's pleasure is aroused by one of the many means which literature has to waken such a response, then the reader may make a gift of his assent or dissent to the conventicles which are founded on those wraiths, for the cycle of expression is complete without them.

He went on to give an assurance that

> in reviewing we shall base our statements on the standards of criticism, since it is only then that one can speak plainly without offence, or give praise with meaning. It is difficult to keep these standards in a little space and still to be just to contemporary work which is perhaps immature. It would be best if our readers would remember that, since we can notice only a few of all the books which are published, our choosing a book at all means that we believe it to merit their attention. The only other books we shall mention will be those whose incompetence has not received sufficient attention in other Reviews.[4]

Two books on medieval society were discussed by Bertrand Russell, and Richard Hughes's plays by Turner; the other reviews were all by Higgins, who dealt with Sacheverell Sitwell's poems and a life of Flecker, besides devoting four pages to an unimportant squabble between Lawrence and Norman Douglas, or by Garman, who gave qualified approval to *Those Barren Leaves* and *The Constant Nymph* and declared Arthur Symons's translations of Baudelaire "an unpardonable travesty".[5] The issue ended with two pages of short reviews – regrettably unsigned, as some are of considerable interest.

This number laid down the pattern which, with inevitable variations, later issues were to follow: two pieces of fiction, a number of examples of a poet's work, two or three critical essays, fifteen to twenty pages of reviews. *The Times Literary Supplement* gave it a warm welcome: "This new monthly periodical...is evidently to be devoted to imaginative and critical literature of a high standard. If the taste and distinction of the first number are maintained in subsequent issues, it is to be hoped that the 'Calendar' will gain both the respect it merits and the attention it needs."[6] Over 7000 copies were sold. Prospects for its future seemed bright.

The Times Literary Supplement singled out for praise Rickword's "penetrating and very amusing study of Sir James Barrie", but it is doubtful whether this reaction to his essay was typical. Today, when Barrie is remembered almost exclusively as a psychological oddity and author of *Peter Pan*, it is difficult to appreciate the position which he occupied in 1925 – created a baronet in recognition of his literary achievement, president of the Society of Authors, a former rector of St Andrews University, a future chancellor of Edinburgh University. "To you, it may seem that it wasn't sticking one's neck out to criticize Barrie, but really it was so in those days," Rickword said in 1973. "He was still rather a deity; and even if some people admitted that he was a bit soppy, they still thought him a charming man, so witty and lovely, and 'Have you been to *Mary Rose*?' The tears! People actually wept."[7] Many people found deeply disturbing the disrespect for established authorities displayed in the "Scrutinies", of which this was the first. When Turner suggested that Virginia Woolf should write on Edmund Gosse for the series (did his review of *Rimbaud* still rankle with Rickword?) Sassoon described the idea as an outrage, and plaintively asked his diary "Why do they want to be 'attacking' everyone?"[8]

After the two or three months' strenuous preparation that had preceded the appearance of the first number Rickword felt that he was entitled to a holiday, as the editors had almost enough material in hand to fill the next two issues. He had never been further south than Paris, and felt a desire to swim in the Mediterranean. From Paris he took the train to Avignon; the city delighted him, but as spring was very late that year he was disappointed by the absence of the Provençal sun. At Nîmes, where a programme of bullfights was due to take place in the Roman amphitheatre, he passed an uncomfortable night in a small baggage room under the stairs of the hotel, but as he sat on the terrace next day with an aperitif before lunch he felt the full impact of the southern sun for the first time. After taking the train to Aigues Mortes, he achieved his ambition at the little fishing port of Le Grau-du-Roi, though not for long, as the water was still cold with melting snow from the Alps. He visited Arles, still haunted by the ghost of Van Gogh, and spent a night in Paris, where he picked up a dozen or so books, before returning in time to put some finishing touches to the May issue.

Back in London, he resumed the bohemian life which he had led since the removal of Peggy and the fostering of the children. Before then he had had virtually no experience of a bachelor existence, having passed straight from home and school to the army, from the army to the university, and from the university to fatherhood and marriage. Now, deprived of a home life, he found his social life in the saloon bars of a few public houses in Central London where the atmosphere approximated to that of a French café.

Most famous was the Fitzroy in Charlotte Street, where on the rare occasions when he expressed an opinion he was always listened to with deep respect. A little farther south, on the corner of Charlotte Street and Percy Street, was Kleinfeldt's, named after its proprietor. Handy for those frequenting the British Museum Reading Room was the Plough in Museum Street, which was a favourite with London's Irish colony, among them Liam O'Flaherty, author of *The Informer*, who contributed a short story to the *Calendar*. The atmosphere there was less genial than that at the Fitzroy, however, and at night it tended to become quarrelsome. In later life Rickword though a steady was a moderate drinker, but at this period he seems to have found himself on at least one occasion at Vine Street police station on a drunk and disorderly charge.

In his old age he looked back nostalgically at the restaurants which he had frequented as a young man. "Plebeian eating-houses abounded wonderfully in London in the 1920s, still often with bare floors, benches and scrubbed wooden tables," he recalled in his memoirs.

Chop-houses and cook-shops, select dining-rooms and good pull-ups for carmen, even coffee stalls and potato barrows provided hunting grounds for a bohemian generation, driven there by necessity or by revulsion against the insipidity of the conventional damask. Not that we merely ate to live; disciples of Brillat-Savarin were to be met even in these outlandish haunts, who could achieve a meal of distinction even within the limits of a half-crown table d'hôte. And in our fraternity a continuous grading and re-grading of these establishments went on, a *guide gastronomique* circulating by bush telegraph: "Archie's gone off frightfully" or "Pingo's has changed hands". Looking back, one remembers most vividly the bizarre profusion of these demotic resorts. Beyond the usual run of joints, chops, steaks, there could be had tripe soused or tripe and onions, stewed and jellied eels, pigs' trotters, black puddings, meat-crammed pies, scarlet saveloys, velvety pease pudding. For visual charm there were the vegetable shops and particularly the shellfish stalls, the delicate naked bodies of cockles and winkles, whelks and mussels, nacreous greys and acidic ochres, piled high in little saucers steeped in sharp vinegar. Philip Heseltine always sought for the pleasures not yet dulled by reiteration, and among the minor ones was the discovery of a small gastronomic gem. He had come upon this at a public-house-restaurant in the Fulham Road. Its actual concoction was the secret of the landlady, but in the main it consisted of an amalgam of ripe gorgonzola impregnated with port wine and variously spiced, then spread in a thick creamy layer on thin toast. This was a superb conclusion to a meal, and Heseltine used to enjoy introducing it to a friend.

In February 1926 the *Calendar* completed its first year of publication. The editors had published fiction and poetry by a judicious blend of familiar and little-known names and had made at least one genuine discovery in the short-story writer Dorothy Edwards, the apparent naïvete of whose style concealed the subtlety of the psychology. In the first four issues at least a quarter of the magazine had been written by Rickword, Garman and Higgins; this proportion was drastically reduced in subsequent numbers as a team of critics, some of them previously unknown, became regular contributors – Edwin Muir, H.C. Harwood, John Holms, L.P. Hartley, Cecil Rickword. The composer Cecil Gray and the mathematician J.W.N. Sullivan wrote regularly on musical and scientific topics. Occasional contributions by E.M. Forster, Aldous Huxley and Robert Graves showed them at the top of their form.

Yet at the end of the first year the magazine's circulation had fallen to below 3000. Some readers may have felt that there was too much of certain writers, others may have found the amount of translation from Russian writers excessive. There seem to have been the usual complaints, which received support from *The Times Literary Supplement*, that the verse published was too obscure. Probably the strongest reason for falling sales was a widespread feeling that readers were being given too much critical powder and not enough jam in the form of lighter reading, but whatever the truth, a change of policy was clearly necessary. No issue appeared in March, and from April onwards the *Calendar* became a quarterly; at the same time the price was raised from one and sixpence to half a crown, although the size remained the same as before, varying from eighty to ninety-six pages. Whether this steep increase in price was likely to push up sales without a drastic change in content was another matter.

At the time when this change of policy was under discussion an equally important change took place in Rickword's domestic affairs. He had decided to live with his latest girl-friend, Thomasina, which meant leaving the Woburn Square flat. Because of the magazine's financial difficulties he needed to economize, and living was cheaper in the country; moreover, as the *Calendar* was to appear less frequently the editors did not need to spend so much time in London. After his father's death Garman's mother and younger sisters had moved to Herefordshire, and he suggested that Rickword and he should settle in the same area. They found two empty cottages at Penybont, a village in Radnorshire, and by the middle of February Rickword was installed in one of them with Thomasina. He wrote to Wyndham Lewis: "This place is much better than I expected and I'm very satisfied with the change… so far", adding: "Don't forget to let me know if you want a spell of rural life". Fortunately Lewis did not accept the invitation; life in a small cottage with a man of such volatility might not have been comfortable.

By the standards of even a few years later Penybont was very isolated from the outside world; there was no newsagent in the village, few if any of the inhabitants possessed a radio, and if Rickword wanted to learn the news he had to walk the five or six miles to Llandrindod Wells. It is still surprising that he, as a Socialist, should have been taken by surprise by the general strike, which had been impending since long before he left London; presumably he had become too absorbed in his writing and editorial work to be fully conscious of what was happening in the outside world. When the news did reach him he felt himself as emotionally involved as he had done during the Colchester lock-out and the Oxford bus strike, yet it was over a week before he and Garman decided that they must go to London and see what assistance they could give the strikers.

Travelling was not easy, as the vast majority of the railwaymen had obeyed the strike call, but on 11 May they managed to find a train run by blackleg labour. This took them as far as Crewe, and after spending the night in a waiting room full of drunken strike-breakers they went on to London. They had not been there long when newspapers came out with the announcement that the T.U.C. had called off the strike unconditionally. Both were stunned; they could not understand what had happened, except that something in which they believed had been ignominiously defeated. As it was, there seemed to be nothing they could do except get drunk that night and go back to Wales in the morning.

Rickword's political position during this period is difficult to assess. Unlike those which he later edited, the *Calendar* was not a political journal, although in general its tone was radical; good examples are Forster's essay on Edward VII, J.W.N. Sullivan's criticism of the class bias of eugenics and the review by "Robert Craves" (a misprint or thin camouflage for Graves) of Edward Thompson's book on the Indian Mutiny.[9] When John Gross detected "a recurrent *communisant* strain in the magazine"[10] he was unduly influenced by his knowledge of its editors' later careers. During the *Calendar* period, although they were clearly interested in developments in the Soviet Union, their attitude was far from uncritical. An unsigned note on Trotsky's *Literature and Revolution* remarks that it "tells us a lot about contemporary affairs which is very much to the point", but that "there is much more propagandist comment than real criticism". A short review, also unsigned, of a book on the Cheka neither denounces the Soviet government's use of terror nor attempts to defend it, but refers to the fundamental question raised by the book ("How far are the Marquis of Queensbury rules drawn up by democratic sentiment capable of being imposed on the perpetual warfare of man and man?") without suggesting an answer. The stories by Leonid Leonov, Alexander Nievierov and Isaac Babel which the *Calendar* published give a vivid picture of Russia in revolution, but would certainly not constitute effective Communist propaganda. As evidence of the magazine's alleged Communist tendencies Gross quoted a statement by Garman that "a regeneration of intelligent sensibility may only be possible after a devastating and bloody revolt against the sickly, bourgeois, animal consciousness of our age", but he did not quote the reference in the same essay to "the foggy and mean-spirited equalitarianism which assumes that the common accident of birth entitles all men to an equal consideration"[11] – hardly a Communistic sentiment. What the two passages do suggest, taken in conjunction, is that Garman at this time, like Rickword, was influenced by Wyndham Lewis.

There is no doubt of Rickword's admiration for Lewis. He had written to him twice in January 1925 inviting contributions. When publication of an essay of his was delayed, Rickword wrote to him explaining that "we did not want to waste it in the slack season". In a letter of 23 April 1926 he described Lewis's *The Art of Being Ruled* as "a marvellous piece of navigation or charting of our position", referred to "that unique pleasure which your work gives" and asked, "When are you going to give us another book?" In November he asked Lewis for "another contribution soon", and in April 1927 he suggested that he should write an essay for the "Scrutinies" series. Lewis's writings occupy 97 pages in the *Calendar* – more space than those of any other contributor except Rickword himself – and another nine are devoted to reviews of his books.

Rickword's high opinion of Lewis's writing seems at first glance all the more surprising because he was a Socialist and Lewis an avowed admirer of Fascism. Two explanations of this apparent paradox are possible. It is clear that he admired him primarily for literary reasons; in his review of *The Art of Being Ruled* he praises "the gifts of rhetoric which Mr Lewis possesses, to the permanent enrichment of English literature", while criticizing the muddle-headedness with which his ideas are often formulated. He was also attracted to Lewis's ideas by his disgust at the corruption of post-war society and his conviction that revolutionary changes were necessary. He refers in the same review to "the amorphous, inhuman, *valueless* mess in which liberal-egalitarian-scientifico-humanitarianism has landed us", and praises Lewis's intention of "arresting the degradation of the values on which our civilization seems to depend (threatened now by the barbarians *within*) and of re-asserting the terms on which the life of the intelligence may regain its proper ascendancy over the emotional and economic existence".[12] The phrasing, and even the use of italics, are very like Lewis.

To call Lewis merely "an avowed admirer of Fascism", although true, is misleading. In *The Art of Being Ruled* the enemy is not Communism but liberalism, parliamentary democracy, egalitarianism and humanitarianism. In ironic contrast to Rickword's critical references to Communism in his *Spectator* reviews, Lewis emphatically declares that "in the abstract I believe the sovietic system to be the best", and speaks of Communism and Fascism with equal approval, referring to "the sovietic and fascist power" and calling Fascism "an extreme form of leninist politics". He may have helped to make Rickword's attitude towards Communism more sympathetic, but he certainly never converted him to his own sympathy for Fascism. As Rickword later recalled in a manuscript note, he was "not happy" about Lewis's essay "The New Roman Empire", which proposed the unification of Britain, France and Italy with Mussolini as Emperor; he decided to treat it as a piece of whimsy, however, and it duly appeared in the *Calendar*.

Lewis's position was not one which he could occupy for long; he had to choose between Communism and Fascism. Even in *The Art of Being Ruled* there is an element of racial rhetoric that suggests which he was likely to choose, as when he asserts that the idea of freedom has "made it impossible for the white race to combine and consolidate itself" and has caused "the rapid eclipse of european power".[13] In "The New Roman Empire" he complains that political thinkers discuss "that half-breed, 'the nation', or that shoddy abstraction, 'the class'," while neglecting the "far deeper reality"[14] of race. By September 1927, when the second number of his periodical *The Enemy* was published, he had made his choice. In it he declared that "I now have come to believe that Russian Communism not only should not, but cannot, become the creed of the Western peoples", and praised the extreme right-wing youth movements in France, Germany, Austria, Hungary, Italy and Romania. The same issue contained *Paleface*, an attack on the glorification of the primitive in literature, in which he asserts that the "Aryan world" is menaced by a Communist conspiracy to rally the non-white peoples against it.[15] Just over three years later he wrote a book in praise of Hitler.

Although they soon moved politically in the opposite direction, Rickword and Garman shared many of his ideas in 1925-26 and tended to imitate his rhetoric, as their attacks on liberalism and egalitarianism suggest. His influence can be detected in Rickword's most controversial piece of writing, his "Notes for a Study of Sade", which appeared in the issue of the *Calendar* for February 1926. It is surely more than a coincidence that he compares Sade, as a moralist who forces men to re-examine the motives for their actions, to Bernard Mandeville, and that in his review of *The Art of Being Ruled* he compares it to Mandeville's *The Fable of the Bees*. We seem to hear Lewis's voice when he classes together all forms of humanitarianism, such as "English middle-class Socialism (distinct from proletarian envy-revolts)", as "forms of expression in which the identity can be diffused, almost lost touch with, in a blissful anonymity", or when he suggests that "society must have a positive sadistic tendency if it is to exist in a healthy state, or the surrounding egos, races, or 'lower' forms of life will absorb it for their own purposes". But there is much more in the essay than echoes of Lewis; it is the product of Rickword's war experiences, his study of French literature and his meditations on human psychology and the nature of society, and might have assumed the same form if he had never read Lewis.

Sadism and masochism, he suggests, are permanent characteristics of the human race, which is divided into "the natural givers and the natural takers, those who suffer and bestow, and those who exert and assert", according to which tendency predominates. He deals with this theme ironically, before passing on to apply it to war, in a passage which clearly draws on his own memories.

> War, the greatest of all crowd experiences, probably owes its irrationally prolonged existence to the provision it makes for both tendencies in human emotion. Under the excuse of patriotism, manliness, and courage, the masochist can hug his exquisite bundle of thorns and win decorations for exceptional bravery in the discharge of his temperament. The sadist will not be found where there would seem to be most reason to expect to find him; those, at least, who have any intelligence remove themselves early in the programme to posts of minor or major authority in the Base Camps and bull-rings of the Back Area, where discipline provides them with more docile subjects than the fear-crazy men of the enemy line, made dangerous by despair.[16]*

Before May 1926 Rickword had been a Labour Party supporter, and Garman had no very strong political sympathies. Lewis's Communist leanings seem to have attracted them in that direction, but the decisive factor in their political development was the general strike. An attempt to defend working-class interests by peaceful methods had been betrayed by the cowardice of the trade union leaders, and they found themselves faced with the question whether force was necessary. A review of Trotsky's pamphlet *Where is Britain Going?*, probably by Garman, which appeared in the issue of the *Calendar* for July 1926 is far more sympathetic than the review of his *Literature and Revolution* published a year earlier. Lewis's influence is still evident in "on every side, the slug humanitarianism leaves its slimy trail, obscuring the function of intelligence and atrophying emotion", but the latter part of the review is couched in Marxist terms:

> Whether or not there exists a proletarian party to take advantage of the position remains to be seen, for it is obvious, as Trotsky points out, that for the purposes of revolution a very deep distinction exists between a proletariat and a proletarian party. This is a question of the greatest importance from the point of view of culture. The answer to it will decide whether England – and, if Trotsky is right in his opinion of her importance, whether Europe – is to stay on the road of continually degenerating values, or to create a revolution as vital, potentially, as the inception of Christianity.[17]

* Rickword clearly had in mind the cruelties practised at the notorious "bull-ring" in the Etaples Base, which provoked a major mutiny in 1917.

The author of this review, whether Rickword or Garman, would seem to be well on his way to joining the Communist Party, yet Rickword did not take this step until 1934 and Garman not until 1936. Both must have read the two works of Trotsky's reviewed in the *Calendar*, but these may well have been the only Marxist books (apart from William Morris's writings) with which they were familiar. Rickword told an interviewer in 1980 that "I didn't open Marx until about the end of the 1920s, I suppose".[18] There were few intellectuals in the Communist Party in 1926, and it is doubtful that, had they applied for membership, they would have been accepted. The review of *Where is Britain Going?* defines the party's aim as "the demolition of the existing ideology", and discusses revolution in terms of culture and the "rejuvenescence of values". This idealist approach would certainly not have been acceptable to King Street.

While living at Penybont Rickword had sufficient leisure and freedom from distractions to write his longest poem, "The Happy New Year", which he began not later than March and completed, except for the final polish, in August. The origins of the poem are complex. It can be regarded as an attempt to rival and even to surpass "The Waste Land"; both use natural processes (drought and rain in "The Waste Land", the movements of the sun in "The Happy New Year") and the magical rituals by which men have sought to control them as the framework for a criticism of contemporary society. At the same time there is a suggestion of burlesque of Eliot's poem, as when the appearance of the Lebanon Girls and the Frazer Eight ironically comments on his borrowings from *The Golden Bough*. It is difficult to believe that such lines as

> the wall-eyed city, blinking steel and stone,
> spits back his bounty in the monarch's eye

and the Chorus's sympathetic comment

> O poor old man! Poor good old man!
> To shame the silver cloud-locks thus!

can have been intended seriously.

The theory that the poem originated at least in part as a burlesque is supported by a very curious paragraph in the issue of the *Calendar* for April 1926, which ironically explains that "some of our readers have complained of the conventionality of the verse which we publish, so we have procured at great expense a specimen of a more emancipated technique", and goes on to quote a note by the supposed author:

"Mocking the God" is the first movement of an anthropological theme. By gibing at the tribal fetish, a certain people is afflicted with a long period of semi-darkness and incessant rain. The crops rot, the land becomes water-logged, and complete sterility ensues. This the author

considers an adequate symbol of the contemporary consciousness. He
hopes to conclude with a description of the removal of the curse and
the restoration of fertility, but he has as yet found no adequate symbol,
except the Sir Percival of the Graal Legend, which is too romantic for
his taste. The literary references are intended to enrich the texture of
the verse with imagery, for invention risks being vulgar, and, besides,
the success of several very cultured poems has recently approved the
innovation.[19]

The reference here to Eliot is obvious; indeed, much of the note is more
relevant to *The Waste Land* than to Rickword's poem. Most of the
first twenty-nine lines of "The Happy New Year" are then quoted, with
alterations and additions which make them ridiculous, and are followed
by a further note by the supposed author in a parody of the style of
Gertrude Stein. The existence of a typed copy of this paragraph among
Rickword's papers suggests that he wrote it himself.

Another source of "The Happy New Year" is the Elizabethan translations of Seneca's tragedies, and especially Jasper Heywood's version
of *Thyestes*, from which Rickword took the epigraph to his poem. He
states in his memoirs that he had read these some months before going
to Wales, and found them "quite exciting, with a rather clumsy eloquence
which suited my sensations". His attention had no doubt been drawn
to them by their forthcoming publication in the Tudor Translations
series with an introduction by Eliot, reported in the second number of
the *Calendar*; as this edition did not appear until late in 1927, however,
he may have read the plays either in the original edition of 1581 or in
an earlier reprint. The theme of *Thyestes*, the murder of three boys by
their uncle, who serves their flesh to their father to eat, suggests the
slaughter of the younger generation by its elders in the war; we may
compare Owen's use of the story of Abraham and Isaac in "The Parable
of the Old Man and the Young". Gabriel Pearson comments on the lines

some
fall on pity's sword and heap up
lap-fulls of bowels in ostentatious arms,

which recall the messenger's speech describing the murder of Thyestes'
sons: "Rickword's image relates specifically to the aftermath of the
War, men become fodder for ostentatious charity as they had been
fodder for mass slaughter on the Western Front".[20] Other lines in the
poem are underpinned by memories of the war, for example,

A fog-like poison drifts and whirls
such dreadful faces as the sun shone on
lying in fields, propped against walls,

suggesting the aftermath of a gas attack. Pearson remarks, "The Great
War is never far from Rickword's imaginative centre".

At the end of Act IV of *Thyestes*, after the messenger's speech, the chorus describe how the sun has turned dark with horror at Atreus's crime, and foretell that the stars will fall from heaven, concluding with the lines Rickword quotes in his epigraph, which prophesy the return of chaos. He clearly found this speech, that parallels the Biblical descriptions of Judgment Day, highly evocative. The lines in "The Happy New Year"

> heaven, whence drifts the thin grey ashen rain,
> the burnt-out proclamations of false stars

may have been suggested by Seneca, but they also echo "the soft rain falling of the failing stars" in "Regret for the Passing of the Entire Scheme of Things". Even before reading *Thyestes*, it would seem, Rickword had associated a darkened sun and falling stars with a society in chaos, and the chorus to Act IV may have suggested to him the idea of using the sun's progress from winter to summer to suggest changes within society.

He left among his papers a "programme note" to "The Happy New Year", probably written for the collected edition of 1976, although ultimately he published only the first sentence of it.

> The action spans a solar year. In the first part we follow the Sun almost visually as he falls through the celestial map (of the Ptolemaic system) from the zenith through the astronomical signs, Houses, to the no-where below the Arctic horizon. In the second phase after a sojourn in a formless zone he retraces his steps and sequentially injects his vigour into the earthlings dwindling from his absence. This peregrination is observed with detachment expressed in an ironic commentary by the Sinisters who finally dissociate themselves.

This note facilitates the interpretation of the poem.

After an opening passage which appears to have been largely intended as burlesque, a grim seriousness enters the poem with the lines

> O now is doomsday, now the shut of eve,
> and the small rain comes down,

which are followed by images of poverty: "a dead coal in a rusty grate ...splintered floor-boards and cold empty hearths". In the same speech it is made clear for the first time that the scene is London; the repeated references to London districts and the Thames are characteristics which the poem shares with "The Waste Land". The Sinisters, who now enter, are the unlucky, the unemployed singing in the streets ("the choirs of sorrow"), the homeless, the ex-servicemen still suffering from venereal diseases contracted in wartime; they are also the Left in the political sense. After their appearance the scene is blotted out; the sun has fallen below the horizon, and the world is plunged into darkness. The turning-point comes when in their speeches images of disease, poverty, cold and darkness are replaced by images of childbirth, liberation and music. The Dexters are heard for the first time – heard but not seen, for they are the Sinisters' opposites, the fortunate who have beds to go to and need not leave them till the Sun is well up, cheerful extroverts whose Utopia is "a world well-stocked with mates and meat". As the Sun climbs the fertility imagery of "birth-break" and "mates" is developed in fantasies of "cornucopias swollen huge with seed" and "mountains of incredible spawn".

In the *Collected Poems* of 1947 "The Happy New Year" is described as a masque. Rickword was well aware, as he made clear in his review in the *Calendar* of Enid Welsford's *The Court Masque*, that the genre developed from "a rough, licentious ritual", and that "the impulse behind even the elaborated form was always to celebrate, or to induce, fertility and felicity".[21] The masque element in the poem first becomes apparent when fertility rituals ushering in spring, from Gardens of Adonis to the Green Man, are described by the Presenter and mimed by the dancers. The Sun enters London in triumph, and Eden is restored by the lovers in the parks, as free from any sense of sin as Adam was before the fall. The Dexters at last appear on the scene with a bawdy song, and the Chorus compares the Sun himself to a monstrous phallus. We are nearer here to Aristophanic comedy, itself close to its origins in agricultural magic, than to courtly masque.

"The Happy New Year" was begun a few weeks before the general strike, and completed about three months after its defeat. The optimistic final scene is a gesture of defiance to that defeat, and affirms Rickword's faith in the ultimate triumph of the strikers' cause. Even the ironic Sinisters hail a world made new, and the masque, like most masques, reaches its climax in a general dance. The Presenter now sees the Sun as "the heavenly ploughman" who

> now plods through cloud-barred fields
> slanting a last mild smile
> on the town's thick-sown furrows
> ripening to harvest,
> whence the dexterous couples
> hitched fast by votive bonds
> must draw Time's toppling wain.

Here is implicit a vision of universal plenty, but Rickword was not satisfied; in the 1947 edition he added at the end of this speech the line, "to all-men's Harvest Home", which made explicit his conviction that earth's plenty must be shared by all. We need not take this Utopian vision too solemnly, as the pun on "hitched" (both "attached to the cart" and "married") makes clear, but that does not mean that it is not to be taken seriously; we are reminded of the masque in *The Tempest*, where the songs of Juno and Ceres similarly link marriage with harvest. Sexual and social themes are again combined in the Chorus's comment:

> Like begets like, immortal in each kind;
> through perishing units' union, death's defeat.

On the surface we have merely a celebration of the role of human fertility in overcoming death; the individual perishes, the race survives. But in 1926 "union" would have suggested a trade union; a second complementary meaning emerges: the solitary individual is helpless, yet through unity with his fellows he can defeat the death-forces in society.

We again recall *The Tempest* in the Presenter's final speech, which in its abrupt change of tone after the celebration of fertility and the masquers' dance recalls Prospero's "Our revels now are ended":

> I see others who walk the earth to-night, homeless
> throughout the city, pacing day's void suburbs
> by unmade roads, raw gardens, blank-eyed lamps,
> cinders and tin-cans and blown evening papers,
> among refuse-pits and sewer-mouths,
> wandering fires and voices of the swamp;
> passing deliberately into the night
> through the infinite extension of this landscape,
> partnered with only thoughts
> that march beside them like the sky's young daughters.

We are back in the world of the Sinisters, the homeless who "crowd midnight pavements", and who have agreed to remain silent only until the short final dance is done. Now they return to remind us that a world of plenty is still only a dream, and that they inhabit a nightmare world which blends the shabby suburbs of Rimbaud's "Ouvriers" with Bunyan's Valley of the Shadow of Death. In his later years this ending seemed too negative to Rickword, and he rewrote the last two lines for the 1976 edition to read

> with thoughts like pilgrims' staves they picked their way
> to a lucid zone, whence fresh horizons blazed.

The echo of *The Pilgrim's Progress* in the original presumably gave him the hint for this transformation; Bunyan's hero, walking the earth homeless by his own choice, passed beyond the Valley of the Shadow on his way to the Celestial City.

In the autumn of 1926 Garman decided to visit the Soviet Union, in his own words, to "study the effect of revolution on culture". Although Higgins replaced him as assistant editor, this change was bound to involve more work for Rickword, and in October he returned with

Thomasina to London, where he rented a furnished bed-sitting room in Pimlico. Garman sailed early in November and found employment in Leningrad teaching English. His departure intensified the problem of finding enough contributors to fill each issue. It was an ominous sign that already the issue for February 1926 had contained long articles by Rickword and Higgins and a story by Garman, and that in the subsequent issue the three of them supplied the poetry. Whereas Rickword had published his own verse in only one of the first twelve issues, he included it in three of the last six, less from vanity, it is safe to assume, than from necessity. Some new contributors came forward during 1926, including T.F. Powys and H.L. Kahan who contributed stories and the poets Hart Crane and Allen Tate. At the beginning of 1927 Roy Campbell returned after two and a half years in South Africa: he contributed poems and reviews, and was probably responsible for the publication of a story by his friend William Plomer. Even so, Rickword was obliged to disguise the extent to which he was writing the magazine himself by using pseudonyms; two satirical essays by "Jasper Bildje", and a poem attributed to "Gabriel Foster" were published.

Circulation continued to fall, and was now only a thousand or so. This situation could not continue indefinitely: it was decided to end the *Calendar* with the issue for July 1927. In his memoirs Rickword described the reasons for this decision:

> Its demise can be attributed not so much, as many people thought, to financial reasons as to the lack of new young writers. We couldn't get work of the quality that would have justified us carrying on. The paucity was due to the tremendous number of young men killed in the catastrophe of World War I. Of course, we could have had the established writers such as Shaw and Wells, but these we did not want.

The last issue closed with a statement by Rickword, to which he gave a title from Donne: "A Valediction Forbidding Mourning".

> We have decided to scuttle the ship, rather than to have the leaks periodically stopped by a generous patron, because the present literary situation requires to be met by a different organization, which we are not now in a position to form. Could such an organization be formed, we should find means to bring it into play. Our conception of the nature of a literary review does not, however, encourage us to expect an immediate metamorphosis, for such a combination as we envisage is dependent on the happy meeting of many contingencies...There is sometimes a moment in the creation of a work of art when a new conception interposes itself and makes further revision impossible. A review has quite different functions from a work of art, but the parallel may serve to explain the unwillingness of those most closely associated with The *Calendar* to continue it in its present form.[22]

The nature of the organization envisaged was never explained, but it seems clear that the "new conception" referred to is the change in the editors' political outlook over the previous year. Arnold Rattenbury has written of the authors dealt with in "Scrutinies":

> The traditions they represented were increasingly seen to be those of a largely moribund literature, and increasingly the issue was posed as to whether this was not because the whole of the society producing it was moribund. The final number of The *Calendar* came to the conclusion that in fact this was the case, and that the proper preoccupation of writers must now be social change. The questions had been literary, the answer political.[23]

Although this may be an over-simplification, there is no doubt that Rickword already saw cultural values as determined by social relationships, and believed that a regeneration of literature could not be achieved without a social revolution. He seems to have envisaged a new periodical as the centre of an organization of writers and readers dedicated to both aims, and in the next magazine which he was to edit, *Left Review*, he attempted to create such an organization.

The *Calendar*'s achievements were considerable. It published fiction by an impressive array of talent: Lawrence, Coppard, William Gerhardi, Luigi Pirandello, Iris Barry, Dorothy Edwards, Leonid Leonov, Liam O'Flaherty, Alexander Nievierov, T.F. Powys, H.L. Kahan, Alexei Remizov, Isaac Babel, William Plomer. The poetry was more uneven. Rickword was at the height of his powers, and the fifteen poems by him which appeared in the *Calendar* included such outstanding works as "Introduction" (later renamed "In Sight of Chaos"), "Birthday Ruminations", "Luxury", "The Deluge" and "Theme for *The Pseudo-Faustus*". Garman's and Higgins's poems, on the other hand, display potential rather than achievement. *The Times Literary Supplement* commented that "all three write difficult, intellectual poetry, and, in the manner of selecting from their impressions the experience of the senses, show the influence of Rimbaud"[24]; the resemblances between their work, however, probably arose rather from imitation of Rickword by admiring friends. Apart from Rickword's, the outstanding poetic contributions to the *Calendar* came from Edwin Muir, then little known, Robert Graves, Richard Church and the Americans John Crowe Ransom, Hart Crane and Allen Tate; Sassoon's, Blunden's and Campbell's poems are only mediocre examples of their work, and the two poems by Lawrence are weak.

A striking feature of the *Calendar* was its editors' interest in European literature. Although they published only two translations from the French – a selection from Baudelaire's *Journaux Intimes*, translated by Rickword, and a witty parody of Anatole France by Louis Rougier –

Samuel Hoare contributed essays on Rimbaud and Valéry and a long
review-article on Gide and Proust, and Rickword wrote shorter articles
or reviews on Villiers de l'Isle Adam, Lautréamont, Rimbaud and
André Breton's *Manifeste du surréalisme*. On Surrealism he commented:

> It ignores altogether the constructive effort in poetry, the organisation
> of the *whole* into something significant. It is the lack of this organisation
> which makes so tedious the reading of M. Breton's prose poems *Poisson
> Soluble*. The concatenation of imagery is sometimes stimulating, but it
> leads nowhere. The poem and the day-dream are not identical, though
> they make use of the same mental processes.[25]

In later years he regretted this abrupt dismissal of Surrealism, describing
his attitude in his memoirs as "positively frumpish". Italian literature
was represented in the *Calendar* only by two short stories by Pirandello,
and German by one by Rudolf Kassner, but a great deal of space was
devoted to Russian literature. It serialized Mme. Dostoevsky's
memoirs, and published the first English translation of *The Wood
Demon* at a time when Chekhov was still little-known in England; in
July 1925 it was able to report that "*The Cherry Orchard* has at last
been put on the English stage"[26] twenty-two years after it was written.
The *Calendar* took a great interest in lesser-known modern Russian
writers, devoting seven pages to a review of D.S. Mirsky's *Contemporary Russian Literature, 1881-1925*, and was a pioneer in publishing
translations of post-revolutionary writers such as Leonov, Nievierov
and Babel.

But it is especially for its criticism that the *Calendar* is remembered.
A brilliant group of critics had formed around the editors, developing
a distinctive approach and style in the course of discussions at which
they "got an arrived-at consensus".[27] Their stringent method of analysis
can be seen at its best in the "Scrutinies" series – Rickword on Barrie,
Garman on de la Mare, Higgins on Masefield, Muir on Bennett, Cecil
Rickword on Shaw, Holms on Wells. To these may be added a number
of occasional contributors, including, if the word "criticism" is interpreted in a broad sense, Samuel Hoare on French literature, Huxley on
Breughel, Arthur Waley on Japanese literature, Forster on anonymity,
Richard Church on Wells and Yeats, Lawrence on art and morality,
Graves on swearing and anthologies, Gordon Craig on the Japanese
puppet drama and Alec Brown on C.M. Doughty. Rickword's own
contributions, concerned mainly with poetry, illuminate his own practice. In a study of eighteenth-century verse, for example, he insists that

> the axiom that in a good style all must be congruous...is valueless
> without its completive axiom – that an element of strangeness is neces-
> sary to beauty. The only method of reconciling these two claims is the

use of the conceit, or, more generally, the metaphor, wherein the maximum amount of apparent incongruity may be resolved instantaneously.[28]

Here he outlines what he put into practice in *Invocations to Angels*.

A more important study is "The Re-Creation of Poetry", which has been described as "an essay of generalization as important as any of those written by Eliot or Leavis".[29] Rickword protests against the limitation of poetry to certain themes or emotions; he asserts the poet's right to deal with all types of experience, including those "negative" emotions which find expression in satire. That he particularly had the Georgians in mind is evident from his reference to "the contemporary preponderance of 'nature' themes and imagery drawn from the back-garden of the week-end cottage",[30] and is confirmed by his later comment: "I meant that the poetry of my contemporaries was kind and nice and sweet, and that there was no need to confine poetry to the expression of such feelings...When you think of Drinkwater or Noyes, that sort of people! You see there was never anything harsh or discordant in what they wrote".[31]* His references in this essay to Swift, Pope and Charles Churchill as masters of the type of poetry he had in mind are symptomatic of the interest in English satirical verse which he shared with the other editors. In a review of a history of English satire Higgins protested against the author's dismissal of satire as "a relatively low form of literature", declaring it "an integral part of the literature of contemplation".[32] Garman reviewed approvingly a selection from Skelton's poems, and an unsigned review of John Marston's *The Scourge of Villanie* quoted at some length his description of Friscus,[33]

> that neat gentleman
> That new discarded Academian,
> Who, for he could cry *Ergo* in the school,
> Straightway with his huge judgment dares controle
> Whatso'er he views.

If, as seems likely, Friscus contributed to the making of Twittingpan, this would suggest that the review is by Rickword.

The most important of his reviews of contemporary poets is that of Eliot's *Poems, 1909-1925*, in which it has been suggested that he "made amends" for his earlier criticism of "The Waste Land".[34] This is misleading. He opens with a generous compliment to Eliot:

> If there were to be held a Congress of the Younger Poets, and if it were desired to make some kind of show of recognition to the poet who has most effectively upheld the reality of the art in an age of preposterous

---

* In fairness to the Georgians, it should be pointed out that Noyes was never one of them, and that Rickword had learned much about the expression of negative emotions from Sassoon, who was.

poeticising, it is impossible to think of any serious rival to the name of
T.S. Eliot... 'That Mr T.S. Eliot is the poet who has approached most
nearly the solution of those problems which have stood in the way of
our free poetic expression,' and 'that the contemporary sensibility, which
otherwise must have suffered dumbly, often becomes articulate in his
verse,' are resolutions which express a sort of legal minimum to which
individual judgments must subscribe.

He pays tribute to Eliot's mastery of technique, which enabled him "to
get closer than any other poet to the physiology of our sensations (a
poet does not speak merely for himself), to explore and make palpable
the more intimate distresses of a generation for whom all the romantic
escapes have been blocked", and suggests that "Mr Eliot's sense of
rhythm will, perhaps, in the end, be found his most lasting innovation".
He does not retract a word of his analysis of "The Waste Land", but
rather develops it:

> His success is intermittent; after a short passage of exquisite verse he
> may bilk us with a foreign quotation, an anthropological ghost, or a
> mutilated quotation... Mr Eliot cannot be acquitted of an occasional
> cheapness, nor of a somewhat complacent pedantry... It is the danger
> of the aesthetic of "The Waste Land" that it tempts the poet to think
> the undeveloped theme a positive triumph and obscurity more precious
> than commonplace.[35]*

In his treatment of other contemporaries Rickword repeatedly
emphasized the need for a poetry which was relevant to the contemporary world and written in a living language. He praised Carl Sandburg
for having "accepted his environment as material for his poetry – the
things that surround him for imagery and the names by which people
call them for the texture of his verse". No English poet received such
a high compliment. "Any movement towards poetic creation contains
two elements," he pointed out, "a reaction against the unintellectual
use of a debased poetic idiom, an effort to re-define the content of
words, and the creation of a new idiom", and in Richard Hughes's
verse there was "more evidence of the first of these processes being at
work than the second".[36] While recognizing the "strain of individuality" in Gordon Bottomley's work, he deplored his "desire to be poetic"
and his failure to "write sustainedly without reliance on literary models",
and Laurence Binyon, another traditional poet for whom he showed a
certain respect, was found wanting for similar reasons: "There is no

* The original text contained a cryptic statement, which Rickword removed from *Essays
and Opinions*, that Eliot's French poems "remind us of Dryden's prefaces (vide Swift)"
(*Calendar* II, p.279). In his own copy of *Towards Standards of Criticism* (1933, p.102),
where the review is reprinted, Rickword wrote the lines referred to:

> Though merely writ at first for filling,
> To raise the volume's price a shilling.

sign of his having apprehended any non-literary experience, no sign of contemporary speech in his idiom, or of contemporary life in his imagery". On *The Torch-Bearers*, the attempt by Alfred Noyes (a poet for whom he showed no respect whatever) to create a scientific epic, he commented: "If 'science' had really meant anything, poetically, to Mr Noyes, it would have altered his universe; would have created metaphors. As it is, he sails his pretentious kite with rags of literature and superstition in its tail." From these two poets' work he drew the conclusion that "a poem which was never modern will not pass into that curious state of suspended animation by means of which the poems we call classic are preserved active to the palate".[37]

A few of Rickword's other contributions to the *Calendar* deserve mention. His essays "The Apology for Yahoos" and "Some Aspects of Yahoo Religion" pungently satirized British attitudes towards sex, sport and literature, in a manner reminiscent of Samuel Butler rather than of Swift. And two of his unsigned contributions to the "Notes and Reviews" section upheld the dignity of the arts against philistine attacks; in one he rebuked the "scurrilous vulgarity" of the press campaign against Epstein's "Rima", in the other he replied to Arnold Bennett's description of poets as "parasites on society".[38] The latter, which appeared in the final issue, formed a fitting epilogue for a magazine which had consistently striven to maintain the highest standards.

VII. *Scrutinies* and Poetry

BETWEEN the wars Rickword's life fell into a pattern: migration to the country in the hope of living more cheaply and writing without interruption, followed within a few weeks or months by a return to London. After Garman returned from the Soviet Union in the spring of 1927 he and Rickword agreed to take a house in the country near London and to collaborate in translating a new biography of Baudelaire, whom both revered. They found an empty farmhouse near Great Waltham, in Essex, large enough to house the two of them together with Thomasina and Garman's wife Jean, and moved in at about the end of May. This *ménage à quatre* lasted until the autumn, when the Garmans left, having inherited some money. Rickword's relationship with Thomasina broke down at about the same time, and he was left alone in the house as winter drew on; at one point he was cut off by a heavy snowstorm and slept in front of a roaring log fire surrounded by a barricade of mattresses. The lease expired early in 1928 and he went back to London, where he found lodgings in Bloomsbury.

His period of solitude had given him time to reflect on future plans. He had decided to work full-time in publishing. Although the *Calendar* appeared a failure, it was the starting-point of several developments, one of which was the establishment in the spring of 1927 of a publishing house by Ernest Wishart, with the aim, as Garman later told Jack Lindsay, of "bringing out all the good literature that was being rejected by commercial firms".[1] Wishart & Company was in many respects a continuation of the *Calendar* by the same personnel; both Rickword and Garman did editorial work for it, and Cecil Rickword acted as its business manager, as he had previously done for the *Calendar*. Its early publications included Garman's only collection of poems, *The Jaded Hero*, and two books by Dorothy Edwards, who had been one of the *Calendar*'s discoveries. If a plan of Rickword's had succeeded, another of the new company's publications would have been the English edition of *White Buildings*, Hart Crane's first collection of poems. In response to Rickword's suggestion that Wishart should distribute the book in Britain, Crane wrote on 7 January 1927:

> Probably no one should be "thanked" for taking an interest in poetry, but your kindness and interest in what little I've so far accomplished are much appreciated. It is re-assuring to me – especially from the fact that a couple of years ago I found so much in your Rimbaud volume which was sympathetic and critically stimulating.[2]

Crane's American publishers were unable to supply sheets, however, and the idea came to nothing.

In the spring of 1928 Wishart brought out Rickword and Garman's translation of François Porché's *Charles Baudelaire*, which was attributed to "John Mavin", a pseudonym formed by combining Rickword's first Christian name with Garman's second. The book was favourably reviewed by *The Times Literary Supplement*, which praised the translators' "fluent style".[3] The other book of Rickword's which Wishart published in the spring of 1928 met with a less friendly reception. *Scrutinies by Various Writers*, which he edited, reprinted his study of Barrie and five of the six other "Scrutinies" which had appeared in the *Calendar*: Garman on Walter de la Mare, Higgins on John Masefield and "Ancients and Moderns" (a dialogue on the condition of poetry), Muir on Arnold Bennett and Holms on H.G. Wells. To these were added essays by Dorothy Edwards on G.K. Chesterton, D.H. Lawrence on John Galsworthy, Robert Graves on Rudyard Kipling, Thomas McGreevy on George Moore, W.J. Turner on Bernard Shaw (for some reason this replaced Cecil Rickword's "Scrutiny" on Shaw which had appeared in the *Calendar*) and Roy Campbell on contemporary poetry, with a foreword by Rickword. This collection was very much an offshoot of the *Calendar*, for of the six essays not reprinted from its pages only one (that by McGreevy) was by an author who had not contributed to it.

The public had been given warning of what the tone of *Scrutinies* would be by a preliminary advertisement, which described it as a volume of "unsympathetic studies of Our Elders by some of their juniors". In his foreword Rickword led his fleet into action with all his guns blazing. After boldly claiming that "by this time, many of the revaluations it suggests are shared by most intelligent people", he declared that reputations established before the war "stood like an avenue of cyclopean statues leading to a ruined temple". Warning critics not to describe the book as "the merely inevitable reaction", he maintained that "a reaction is never inevitable; it is only necessitated by the incompetence of a previous period of criticism". In conclusion, he gave notice that "it is proposed to compile a second, and if necessary a third, volume in which later developments may be considered with similar freedom".[4]

If the book was intended to be provoking, it succeeded. A week after it was published the *Spectator* rushed in to denounce it as "a ludicrous volume", and declared: "It is difficult to take this volume quite seriously. Undiluted abuse, often of the most puerile sort, is not criticism, and it contains little else." *The Times Literary Supplement* adopted a lofty moral tone. "The editor of this collection of flings at established literary reputations peremptorily warns critics not to call them 'the merely inevitable reaction'," it said. "We should not have been so pessimistic. We are in no danger of thinking that it is inevitable, even for young men in a hurry, to adopt the standard of literary courtesy set up in this volume." The *New Statesman* was patronizing but tolerant, asserting that "a chill as of some haunt of dissenters pervades this miscellany", directed against "the Bishops of the literary Establishment", and that "the atmosphere is one of vague depression". It nevertheless felt that "this unequal symposium has good moments" and that a second volume would be welcome. In the *Observer* F.L. Lucas (whom Rickword had described as a "man of learning, who, with the affectation of familiarity, flatters the common audience by discrediting the apparatus of critical thought") called *Scrutinies* a "papery wasp's nest", "not very entertaining" and pervaded by a "tone of frenzy", and decided that apart from Muir's and Graves's contributions "the rest of the book will damage no one but its authors".[5]

The critics' reactions are most remarkable for the way in which they contradict one another. It is difficult to reconcile Lucas's "tone of frenzy" with the *New Statesman*'s "vague depression". Lawrence's attack on Galsworthy was described by the *Spectator* as "revolting in taste and indecent in expression", by the *Observer* as a "pitiful piece of scurrility", and by the *New Statesman*, which singled it out for praise, as "hard-hitting, well-aimed and well-merited". The critics' differences can in part be accounted for by the diversity of the essays in the book, which apart from their critical stance have little in common. The irony of Rickword's dissection of Barrie is very different from the knockabout humour which Graves finds appropriate for Kipling, and both are remote from the shrillness of Lawrence's contribution, the only one to which the word "frenzy" could conceivably be applied. The *Spectator*'s phrase "undiluted abuse" is equally inappropriate; Holms's essay on Wells, for example, is admirably balanced, and even Lawrence recognizes the elements of greatness in *The Man of Property*.

What seems to have infuriated most of the reviewers was the Scrutineers' irreverent attitude towards all established institutions, literary, political or social. They continued the revolt of the young against the older generation which had been one of the driving forces behind the *Calendar*. The bitterness of the ex-servicemen is discernible in Rickword's suggestion that the writers discussed had profited from the elimination of "half a generation of potential rivals and critics"; in his comment on Barrie's address on Courage that "those who have had to use this quality in situations of physical danger will appreciate how different their feelings were from the feelings which Barrie's approbation foists on them"; and in Graves's description of Kipling as "one of the prophets of the war with Germany who helped to make it possible". Graves spoke disrespectfully of the Empire only three years after the British Empire Exhibition at Wembley, and Muir and Lawrence even went so far as to speak irreverently of property, an institution in which many, in Muir's phrase, "believed religiously".[6] By editing this subversive collection Rickword marked himself in the eyes of the Establishment as unsound, and it took him many years to live it down.

One man who read *Scrutinies*, and especially Lawrence's essay, with excitement soon after its publication was Jack Lindsay, who described it as "the only intelligent book of criticism published for years".[7] Lindsay, the fourth Australian, after Worth, Turner and Higgins, who was profoundly to influence Rickword's life, came of a distinguished literary and artistic family. His father was the novelist and black-and-white artist Norman Lindsay; his father's three brothers were also artists; the cartoonist Will Dyson was his uncle by marriage; and his two younger brothers, Philip and Raymond, became a historical novelist and a painter respectively. Although Lindsay had distinguished himself as a classical scholar at the University of Queensland, and the classics remained his first love, he could have said, like Bacon, "I have taken all knowledge to be my province". In his own words, his aim was to "conquer all the problems of culture", and he combined this passion for knowledge and a determination to synthesize his knowledge into a system with an inexhaustible energy. After meeting him, Rickword found that "the frequent answer to my inquiry about such and such a book that he was writing was, 'Oh, I got that off a couple of weeks ago'." The 150 books which he published between 1923 and 1981 included poetry, verse plays, novels on historical and contemporary themes, short stories, stories for boys, biographies, history, literary criticism, art history, works on philosophy, science and archaeology, autobiography, and verse and prose translations from Greek, Latin, Russian, Czech and Polish writers. During the same period he edited four magazines and eighteen books, contributed many stories and essays to periodicals, and wrote plays, film scripts and a study of English poetry which "extended into many million words",[8] though only a few chapters have been published.

In 1928 most of this lay in the future. He had arrived in England two years before, leaving a wife behind him in Australia, and had founded the Fanfrolico Press (a name chosen to suggest "a Rabelaisian Utopia"[9]) to publish de luxe illustrated books, beginning with his own translations of Aristophanes, Petronius and Propertius. The manager of the business, P.R. Stephensen, was an Australian of Communist views who made some of the first English translations of Lenin, Blok and Mayakovsky. Lindsay was spending three days a week in London attending to the work of the Press and the rest of the time at a cottage in Essex which he shared with his mistress, a neurotic woman separated from her husband who called herself Elza de Locre. Soon after his move to Essex, however, he met Betty May, a well-known figure in the literary and artistic Bohemia of the time, at the Plough in Museum Street. On the following evening they became lovers, and for several months he found himself with a mistress in town and another in the country. Though he told Betty about Elza, he left Elza in ignorance of Betty's existence.

Lindsay and Stephensen together edited the *London Aphrodite*, six numbers of which appeared between August 1928 and July 1929. The tone of the magazine was suggested by its title, which parodied that of Squire's *London Mercury*. As at this time Lindsay was a Nietzschean and Stephensen a Marxist it had no very consistent policy, except to preach beauty and the joy of life and to outrage reactionaries and modernists alike, but the result was certainly lively and amusing. It formed a connecting link between the *Calendar* and *Left Review*, in that its contributors included several who had appeared in the *Calendar* and a number who were to appear in the second volume of *Scrutinies* and *Left Review*. It resembled both magazines in its internationalism, publishing translations from Laforgue, Capek, Blok and Esenin, whilst Stephensen's contributions, which were far to the left of anything published in the *Calendar*, anticipated the Marxism of *Left Review*.

One evening in the summer of 1928 Lindsay, who had wanted to meet Rickword ever since he had read *Scrutinies*, was introduced to him in the bar of the Fitzroy. He went back to where Betty was sitting and told her "It's Edgell Rickword, the person I most wanted to meet in England",[10] a description which naturally aroused her interest in Rickword. As a result of their meeting Lindsay was introduced to Garman and Higgins and Rickword to Stephensen, and something of an alliance was formed between the Scrutineers and the Fanfrolicers, with Rickword, Garman and Higgins contributing to the *London Aphrodite* and Lindsay to the second series of *Scrutinies*, Rickword writing for the Fanfrolico Press and Stephensen publishing his short stories.

Lindsay's admiration for Rickword increased when his third book of 1928, *Invocations to Angels and The Happy New Year*, was published by Wishart in December. It was seven years since *Behind the Eyes* had appeared, and in the interim he had often considered bringing out another collection. In the spring of 1924, with *Rimbaud* off his hands, he had gone so far as to draw up a list of poems to be included, thirteen of which were to appear in *Invocations to Angels*, often under different titles from those which they are given in the list: "Adolescence Re-visited" ("Farewell to Fancy"), "Toilet", "Sir Orang Haut-ton at Vespers", "Race Day", "Poet's Epitaph" ("Necropolis"), "Phenomenon in Absence" ("Absences (i)"), "Transparency", "Terminology", "Ceremony" ("Earth and Age"), "Cascade", "Beyond Good and Evil", "Regrets for Culs-de-Sac" ("Regrets for Certain Blind Alleys") and "Moonrise" ("Moonrise over Battlefield"), which was queried. Another of the poems on the list, "Votre âme" ("Strange Party"), was reserved for Rickword's third collection, *Twittingpan and Some Others*; six others – "From Verlaine", "Maiden Modesty", "Girls", "To a Nature Poet", "Dawn of Meaning through Emotion" and "The Spirit Craves the Immortal" – were never published by him but survive in manuscript form; and two more, "Assonances" and "Ideals", both of which were queried, seem to have disappeared. At a rather later date two other poems were added to the list, "Les Martyrs", which was to appear in *Twittingpan*, and "Substitutes", another missing poem.* He may have dropped the idea of publishing this collection because his energies were diverted, first to his Faustus play, then to his stay in Paris and finally to the planning of the *Calendar*, but it is more likely that even when drawing up the list he was already dissatisfied with some of the poems which it contained. His poetic theory and practice were rapidly changing, and such a sentimental piece of Romanticism as "The Spirit Craves the Immortal" would have looked very incongruous beside the urbane wit of "Farewell to Fancy" and "Sir Orang Haut-ton at Vespers".

Rickword's development from the youthful poet and lover of 1921 to the embittered ironist of 1928 can be traced in *Invocations to Angels*. The earliest poems, written between the autumn of 1921 and the end of 1923 – "Terminology", "Transparency", "Earth and Age", "The Cascade", "Annihilation", "Beyond Good and Evil", "Absences (i)" and probably "To the Sun and Another Dancer"† – are marked by Metaphysical wit, a rich play of fancy, healthy sensuality and sheer joy in the potentialities of language, and parade a literary dandyism which makes them akin to the early poems of the Sitwells and to Eliot's quatrain poems. They are set in the same landscape of forests, mountains and mysterious pools as the poems in *Behind the Eyes*, a landscape populated by a strange fauna. Many of the poets of Rickword's generation shared a fondness for mythical beasts; poems by his literary associates include "Leviathan" by Peter Quennell, "Unicorn Mad" by Richard Hughes and "Herodotean Phoenix" by Alan Porter. Rickword himself had introduced a hippogriff and a wyvern into "The Soldier Addresses his Body", Leviathan into "Cosmogony" and a unicorn and a phoenix into "Beauty Invades the Sorrowful Heart"; now we encounter "Ecstasy that lofty unicorn" in "Terminology" and the Phoenix which

---

* This list, which is among the Rickword manuscripts in the British Library (Additional Manuscript 54200A, p.55), is attributed to the spring of 1924 because it does not include "Circus", "Luxury", "Memory" and "Assuagement", all of which can confidently be dated in the summer or autumn of that year. "From Verlaine" is probably a translation of "Il pleut doucement sur la ville" which Rickword made at Chipstead in 1922, rather than the poem which appeared under the same title in *Twittingpan*.

† There is no external evidence on the date of this poem, of which no manuscript survives and which was never printed before it appeared in *Invocations to Angels*. Although it is not included in the 1924 list, internal evidence suggests that it belongs to this period.

> burns on Pain's rich tree
> in praise and prayer and frankincense

in "The Cascade". Even less unusual animals assume something of the
same mythical quality, as when speech

> bids *leopard* from the accustomed haze
> break and like fire glide down his leafy ways;
> or drawing softly back the sea's rich veil
> reveals domestic the grave monarch *whale*   ("Terminology")

or when

> From his lair the leopard roams
> down the rows of ordered homes
> and the ancient serpent winds
> softly, through the lowered blind.   ("Transparency")

This leopard, which seems to belong to the same genus as Blake's tyger,
reappears a few lines later as a personification of Joy – a key word in
these poems.

Another group of poems – "Toilet", "Race Day", "Sir Orang Haut-
ton at Vespers", "Invocations to Angels", "Regret for Certain Blind
Alleys", "Moonrise over Battlefield", "Farewell to Fancy" – probably
belongs to 1923 and the early months of 1924. They overlap in date
with the first group, with which they share certain properties (the reflecting lakes in the last verse of "Invocation to Angels", for example, recall
those in "Annihilation" and "Beyond Good and Evil"), but they display
an increased sophistication and a greater use of realistic detail. Rickword had deleted a verse which appears in an early draft of "Transparency":

> Lilith pale in widow's weeds,
> Brother Cain in heavy tweed,
> Ragtime-singing Antient Pistol –
> These may dim not light that crystal

as incongruous with the general tone of the poem, but in the later group
suburbs, trams, pubs and building sites do not seem out of place. In
"Race Day" a reference to Leda and the swan is closely followed by
the line "a kike conversing with a tart". The tone of these poems, if
ironic, is still genial, but there is an awareness of the more sordid aspects
of relationships between the sexes, "the crowd's foul pleasure-litter".

Peggy's madness was for Rickword as traumatic an experience as
the Western Front had been. In "Absences (ii)" and "Absence (iii)" he
says goodbye to the familiar woodland pool of the earlier poems and
to the Joy of which it had been a symbol:

Now is Joy's own image spilled
and the landscape in eclipse
has the crumpled emptiness
. of a just discarded dress.

All the scene that Self had willed
his mirror, so to ruin slips.
No lake, no glass will now return
the form with which, lonely, I burn.

In his loneliness and frustration he resorted to prostitutes, which no
doubt is what Jack Lindsay meant when he said that Rickword "in a
sense was trying to live out a Baudelairean life".[11] "Circus" (originally
called "Piccadilly Circus, Nightfall") probably dates from the early
summer of 1924; one draft was written on the back of a letter dated
27 May 1924, informing him that his bank account was overdrawn by
£7 8s. 9d. A group of poems probably written rather later – "Poet to
Punk", "Don Juan Queasy" (originally called "Seduction") and
"Chronique Scandaleuse" – deals with prostitution or irregular sexual
relationships. It is difficult to imagine a greater contrast than that
between the tenderness of "Absences" and the brutal cynicism of "Noc-
turne téléphonique", the unpublished poem which, with its harshest
crudities removed, provided the basis for "The Deluge". Other poems
of the same period, notably "Luxury", are obsessed with the corruption
of society, and the two themes meet in "The Deluge", in which Rickword, anticipating the use of the flood myth as a symbol of social
upheaval by Hugh MacDiarmid in "Prayer for a Second Flood" and
by Cecil Day Lewis in "Noah and the Waters", imagines himself and
a prostitute as the only survivors. It is in these poems, in which the
prostitute appears as the most admirable because the most honest
member of a society held together only by the cash-nexus, that he comes
closest to his master Baudelaire. The French poet's influence can be
discerned in the strictness of the forms through which this anarchic
message is conveyed, the lyrical stanzas of the earlier poems being
replaced by heroic quatrains (the cadences of "Poet to Punk" ironically
echo those of Gray's "Elegy") or the Petrarchan sonnet.

In an essay published in the *Calendar* in January 1926 Edwin Muir
suggested that for the first time English poetry had become a poetry of
the town rather than of the country, and that it reflected "the peculiar
set of impersonal feelings which all town-bred people carry about with
them, without guessing it, from their birth, the feelings which seem to
make them a part of the crowd and yet keep them outside it".[12] It was
in 1924 that Rickword's poetry turned to urban rather than rural set-
tings. The process begins in the Faustus play, with its "rows of gnawing
roofs", its hurrying crowds and Faustus's contemptuous rejection of

his landlady's suggestion that he should "take a spell / Somewhere in the country". The two worlds are contrasted in "Assuagement", the "kind-bosomed fields" and "ancient pools" set against the "angry city" with its "streets of pain and theatres of despair". The adjective "kind-bosomed" suggests that Rickword associated the country with Peggy, the farmer's daughter, and that in his wanderings to Penybont or Great Waltham he was seeking in vain the lost Eden of Chipstead. At the climax of "The Happy New Year", very much an urban poem, where social and sexual problems are resolved in a world of plenty, the city is seen in rural terms:

> the town's thick-sown furrows
> ripening to harvest,

but the final speech returns to the sordid suburbs.

In the last group of poems in *Invocations to Angels* he comes very near to despair; as he remarked in 1976, "some of the later and longer poems in *Invocations* have a distinct inclination towards nihilism".[13] This mood is already apparent in "In Sight of Chaos", published in the *Calendar* in May 1925, which is concerned with time and mortality, themes which he also handles in "Necropolis" and "Birthday Ruminations". It retains much of the sophisticated wit of the earlier work, as in the comparison of the sea to a cat

> rubbing the edge of things
> and purring on the limits of destruction

or in the lines on the adultery of Ares and Aphrodite; there is even a mythical beast, the Kraken. Yet it ends in something near hysteria. There are pools and leopards of gold beside them in "Prelude, Dream and Divagation", but the moonlit landscape is not one of joy but of "endless avenues of unavailing woe". The "inclination towards nihilism" reaches its climax in "Theme for The Pseudo-Faustus", published in April 1927 and probably written not long before. This poem is largely a rewriting of the first scene of the Faustus play, from which it borrows many lines, often with little or no change, but its mood is very different. Faustus's triumphant cry in the play:

> The early men were not so young as I,
> At every breath ten generations die
> And the first impact of the god's full gaze
> A stronger Adam from this flesh shall raise

is echoed in the poem, but is immediately followed by the reflection that

> our brief dawn-crow is muffled in the wet
> blanket of history; like a leching frog
> caught in mid-rapture under the world's vast turd

> we jerk exhausted limbs in endless folds;
> and stifling, spitting, furiously frustrated,
> perish, not budging, with intense exertion.

It is not surprising that Rickword took refuge from this mood in satire.

Lindsay hailed the book as evidence that Rickword was a greater poet than Eliot. "Here indeed is stated a dissatisfaction with the death that christian industrialism has forced upon all human integrities," he wrote,

> but the statement does not rest there. It does not accept hopelessness as Eliot's does. Behind it moves a lyrical challenge, a continually applied contrast of delight. This is because the attack is made by the whole man, who delights even in the spectacle of his own despair...The poetic statement cannot remain here; but made from this angle it stimulates resistance and is a legitimate part of the poetic schema.*

Peter Quennell's tribute was equally warm but more conventionally expressed:

> His literary ancestors – Rimbaud, of course, Laforgue and Corbière as well as the English metaphysical poets – have taught him the function of "wit" in poetry, the manifold advantages of simplicity, crudity, directness...He is one of the very few modern poets with whom the student of poetry need cultivate a more than nodding acquaintance; his volume is one of the few which a critic should go to the trouble of purchasing and keeping on his shelves.

Other critics were less enthusiastic. The Irish poet Austin Clarke wrote:

> Neatness of form contrasting with a bewilderment of images, hard driven by metaphysical needs of expression, marks Mr Edgell Rickword's present stage of finding himself...His continual search for incongruities to surprise us leads him to mistake the first ferment of the imagination, in which useless matter is thrown up, for modernism.

Most of the critics were torn between respect for Rickword's poetic achievement and uneasiness at the book's pessimistic tone. The review in *The Times Literary Supplement*, after deploring the prevalence of "the poetry of disillusion and dreariness", continued: "Mr Rickword, whose culture, imagination and sympathy command attention, is one of those who fall short of the excellence shadowed forth in their best passages by reason of a preoccupation with one kind of sentiment... All is subdued to the scholarship of irony and surrender". Humbert Wolfe, a very minor versifier whose "ingrained banality of style" Rickword had exposed in the *Calendar*, expressed a similar view less pompously:

* This was published in July 1929, before Eliot had published *Ash Wednesday*.

Few living poets have a more certain control of technique, and he accepts nothing secondhand either in thought or manner. But he suffers, as Mr Huxley appears to suffer, from some obscure malaise, which makes him again and again destroy his own achievements. Something hurts, and he is for ever biting on the aching tooth...Poetry as good as Mr Rickword could write will not be written as long as he yields to the bitter temptation of the spirit that denies.*

But the most impressive statement of this position came from Dilys Powell, who like Lindsay compared Rickword with Eliot. "The rhyming apostles of despair are so numerous lately," she wrote,

> that the callous reader is tempted, now and again, to question the sincerity of the current charnel verse...From the ranks of the disillusionists one or two figures stand out in an indisputable sincerity. Mr T.S. Eliot is one, and Mr Edgell Rickword with his new book has shown himself another. He has, indeed, a good deal in common with Mr Eliot, but his verse is denser, much more tightly packed with images, while it lacks the terrible sharpness of *The Waste Land*. Nor has it the religious feeling of Mr Eliot's later work; indeed, there is less to redeem Mr Rickword's world from decay than there is to recover Mr Eliot's from its whimpering end...I find Mr Rickword's visions of chaos singularly impressive. His poetry is obviously morbid; I should not put it on a level with creative work that has a less restricted field; but I do think that it is important intrinsically as well as for its place in modernist poetry.[14]

Whatever the critics might say, *Invocations to Angels* found fervent admirers among the younger poets, inside and outside the universities. Rickword described in his memoirs his meeting with one of them, probably in the summer of 1929.

> One afternoon as I was strolling down the Fulham Road I was astonished to find beside me a young Apollo with golden hair, who had appeared from nowhere and who addressed me with a certain veneration in his tone of voice. I learnt that this was Stephen Spender, and that he had come to give me a copy of the early poems which he had printed on his own small press with the help of Auden.† And so I led him into conversation on life in Oxford, from which he had recently come down. After Auden he was sure that Clere Parsons was the most interesting poet of his circle, and I was delighted to hear that Parsons was the propagator of my verse amongst those – and there were many – who looked up to him as the founder of the school. His early death a few months later was a great disappointment to all those who had a sense of his specifically individual and melodious talent.

* It is ironic that Wolfe, ignorant of the existence of Rickword's Faustus play, should accuse him of listening too much to Mephistopheles.

† It is uncertain whether the book which he gave Rickword was a selection from Auden's early verse, of which he had printed about thirty copies, or a pamphlet of his own poems, *Nine Experiments*.

It is certainly difficult to read Parsons's reflections on the nature of language in "Some Melody of Words Continues On" and "Interruption" without being reminded of "Terminology". Spender himself, in a letter to Rickword, confirmed in 1973 that while at Oxford he had been greatly influenced by his poems, and suggested that his own early poem "In 1929" had "exactly the rhythm and something of the strangeness" of Rickword's "In Sight of Chaos".

At Cambridge Rickword's admirers included William Empson, who described their encounters nearly fifty years later.

> There was a time, around 1929, when Edgell Rickword was the Sage of the Fitzroy Tavern in Charlotte Street, much jostled by other sages, and very unassertive, indeed he could hardly be got to speak, and then hardly above a whisper, but he was the real one, if you happened to know. John Davenport knew, and advised a few other Cambridge students, including myself; we felt that a visit to London had to include looking for him there. I remember straining my ears, and of course I often succeeded in hearing him, but I cannot remember anything he said. This is the less odd because what he said was remarkable for its studied moderation, and respected for that, even by us.[15]

Outside the universities one of his admirers was Roy Fuller, then still in his teens; although they were not to meet until some years later, Fuller has described him as "poetic hero of my youth and ever after".[16]

Another poet whom Rickword met soon after the publication of *Invocations to Angels* was Hart Crane, who was visiting England. He described their meeting in an essay called "Poets' Fare", which he had printed in 1975 and circulated among his friends as a New Year card, and which is worth quoting in full.

> It was on New Year's Day 1929, or thereabout, that I met Hart Crane for the first time. He had been in England a couple of weeks, and had met Paul Robeson and eaten Christmas pudding with Robert Graves and Laura Riding and was rather miserable. The damp raw London cold "was like a knife in the throat", he said.
>
> I had published some of his elegant, elusive poems in the *Calendar* in 1926 and 7, and had heard from Graves that he intended to look me up. So when Crane's call came through I was ready with some suggestions. He did not care where we went so long as it did not remind him of the gilt and marble palace in which he dossed, which was as icy as a cellar. But he had enjoyed the plebeian sociability of the dockland pubs in Limehouse, though they were not so sinister as he hoped to find them, having seen cinema versions with Chinese opium-dens and dark alleys where stranglers lurked. And of course we had both been anguished by Lilian Gish in "Broken Blossoms".
>
> So we agreed to meet that afternoon in a definitely plebeian locality. When he turned up at my office we went into the Tube and booked to

the Angel. As the pubs had closed for the afternoon I led him along Upper Street, until near Agricultural Hall we came to my familiar feeding-den, a *Pull-Up for Car-men* which had been a stand-by for generations of casual labourers.

Soon we were sitting in a comfortable "pew", formed by two high-backed settles (so convenient for talking) facing my recommended ration of two large kippers, two thick slices of buttered toast and a huge mug of tea. The tea was too sweet for our taste, but when stiffly laced with rum from a hip-flask, from Crane's hip, it had the aroma of a real Caribbean drink, such as he had been extolling to me, and it blended most happily with the musky kipper flesh.

Crane's imagination was absorbed by the sea. He began with a rhapsody on the *Bateau Ivre* of Rimbaud and the richness of his imagination, though he had never seen the sea when he wrote the poem. It fulfilled and even transcended the gorgeous seascapes which had fostered Crane's own creative moods in his sojourn on the Isle of Pines off Cuba, and I remembered the opening of his *O Carib Isle*:

> The tarantula rattling at the lily's foot
> Across the feet of the dead, laid in white sand
> Near the coral beach...

Then the talk shifted to *Moby Dick* which Crane told me he had read at least three times and found it each time more superb. And he told me how glad he had been when I printed his poem *At Melville's Tomb*. "I worship him. It's a good poem and Melville was a great American, yet not a magazine in America would take it."

Crane's threnody has a haunting close, which I listened to with a chill of apprehension, as well I might have done had I foreseen what was to come:

> Compass, quadrant and sextant contrive
> No farther tides...High in the azure steeps
> Monody shall not wake the mariner.
> This fabulous shadow only the sea keeps.

Ominous prophetic lines! For only a year or so later Hart Crane plunged tragically from a ship at sea and no trace of his passing was ever found.*

Towards the end of 1928 Rickword met Edward Hayter Preston. Preston, a journalist, had edited the *Cerebralist*, which in 1913 had published poems and prose by the Imagists Ezra Pound, Richard Aldington and F.S. Flint, and was himself the author of two books of prose poems, *Windmills* and *The House of Vanities*. Rickword recalled him in his memoirs as "an all-round fellow driven hard by the necessity of keeping the family going", and commented: "He was the last of the pre-war generation, and combined the best of the Romantic period with a political awareness of European affairs. He was one of the first

---

* Crane in fact committed suicide on 27 April 1932.

to understand, and to make clear in his feature articles, the growing menace of Hitlerian Nazism." Paul Allen, who knew both Preston and Rickword well in the 1950s, has described him* as "a kind of bluff visionary with a Dr Johnson-like Leicester background" and "a really imaginative man who made astonishing statements which Edgell liked to correct and challenge with the kindest irony".

At about the same time that he met Rickword Preston, who had been supporting himself by freelance journalism, was appointed literary editor of the *Sunday Referee*, a popular paper devoting much of its space to theatrical news. The transformation which he brought about was remarkable – it is difficult to imagine any Sunday paper today, popular or "quality", filling two entire columns with a new verse translation of the *Pervigilium Veneris*, as the *Sunday Referee* did in 1930. It was in its poetry column that Dylan Thomas's verse first appeared three years later. Always ready to give a hard-up poet a hand, Preston invited Aldington to contribute the main literary article each week, and frequently gave Rickword a book to review, usually a collection of verse or a critical study.

His contributions, twenty-five of which appeared between January 1929 and November 1931, are models of what a short review should be, and abound in memorable phrases.

> That none of Swift's major poems is included in the *Oxford Book of English Verse*, that semi-official standard for poetic gold, is evidence of a contemporary depravity of taste no less pronounced than that of the mid-eighteenth century.

> It is absurd to imply, as some of the antagonists of modernism do, that the simple and changeless things of life, trees and cows and the countryside generally, are in some unexplained way more "human", and so a proper subject matter for verse, than the creations of the human intellect and the mad confusion of civilization.

> Since Crabbe, there has been hardly a poet who could versify the details of everyday life without staggering in turn from violence to bathos.

> The anthology habit, that most effective means of swamping real talent under mediocrity's numerical advantages...

> Mr Roy Campbell is the finest rhetorician writing now; I mean, he is a poet who includes a rhetorician, not that awful thing a rhetorician who is not a poet.

> The translations least offensive to the creator of the poem are those which are, at any rate, good poems in the translator's own language.

> Mr Henderson is not afraid to be prosaic, and that is a good omen in a first book of poems. We must distrust the young writer who is poetic at any price.[17]

* In a letter to the author.

A review of particular interest is that of E.M.W. Tillyard's *Milton*, Rickword's first study of a poet who was to inspire some of his finest writing. In it he stressed two points, Milton's humanism, and his continued relevance.

> For a couple of centuries the flesh-hating Puritan and dogmatic theologian who made God Almighty talk like a School Divine have hidden the humanist, the man of the Renaissance and student of oriental, non-Christian mysticism which were no less important elements in a complex character... Remote as Milton's theological symbolism may seem to us, it represents a conflict of idealism, passion and experience which is essentially the same as that which lies beneath much of the frustration and seeming-scepticism of to-day.[18]

These were points which he was to develop more fully later.

An essay written a little earlier shows his developing concern with the relationship between poetry and society. The first book published by the Fanfrolico Press had been Jack Lindsay's translation of Aristophanes' *Lysistrata*, a handsome volume with illustrations by Norman Lindsay. Jack Lindsay now proposed to publish his own translation of the *Ecclesiazusai* (*Women in Parliament*) in the same format, and invited Rickword to contribute an introduction. He willingly accepted, and produced his first important critical essay since the disappearance of the *Calendar*. Lindsay no doubt supplied much of the classical scholarship, as well as the translations of passages from dramatists contemporary with Aristophanes, but it is Rickword's mind, in many of its aspects, of which we are conscious throughout. The theme of the play, in which the women of Athens introduce a system of communism, sexual as well as economic, gave him the opportunity to discuss many topics – sexual relationships, the role of women in politics, popular fantasies of a world of plenty, the decline of popular art. It is, perhaps, the first of his writings in which we can detect a movement in his thinking towards Marxism. Many of his contributions to the *Calendar* could not have been written by a Marxist; the foreword to *Women in Parliament* could. But Rickword's Marxism, unlike some varieties, was a joyous, humanistic, libertarian creed; he never departed from the principles laid down in this essay:

> The restriction of other people's pleasure on grounds of high moral principle was a species of perversion [Aristophanes'] world was mercifully spared. But unfortunately the good-humoured type of man or woman is not one that hankers after political influence: the machinery of government generally falls to the earnest busy-bodies... Why, after all, should not politics be poetic and humour grease the easy yoke? Why do men, without a qualm, entrust their bodily well-being, their only pledge for the delight that is their birthright, to those acquisitive or censorious individuals who make up the major part of the politicians of the world?"[19]

A discussion of Aristophanes over a bottle in Rickword's rooms one night provoked a remark which had a lasting effect on Lindsay, as he recalled in his autobiography.

> Trying to formulate what I felt about the poet's allegiance to life (which in Fanfroliconean terms meant Girls and Wine), I said something about Aristophanes not really caring what happened to Athens. I meant that his care for Athens was poetically his care for the freedoms that begat poetry, not for the city in an abstract political sense; but Edgell said gravely, "I think he cared a great deal", and suddenly I felt that the opposition I was making between the city of poetry and the city of political actuality was a false one.[20]

Shortly after this incident, Lindsay was startled when Betty said to him, "Do you mind if I go and live with Edgell? Do you say I mustn't?"[21] He had not noticed that Edgell was particularly interested in her; indeed, it is impossible to say which of the two had taken the initiative, as Rickword in his memoirs remained discreetly silent on the point. Lindsay's Fanfroliconean principles allowed him no alternative but to assure her that she was free to do as she wished and he had no claim on her; if anything, he was probably relieved to be free of the strain which concealing the affaire from Elza imposed upon him. The break made no difference to his friendship with either Rickword or Betty.

Betty, who was to share Rickword's life for the next three years, was a few years his senior. She was born in the East End, one of a family of four children who had been deserted by their drunken father. After vainly struggling to support them, their mother sent Betty and her eldest brother to their father, who was living with a brothel-keeper. He was sentenced to a term of imprisonment soon afterwards, and Betty lived for two years with an uncle and aunt on a barge. She was a natural dancer, and picked up a few pennies by dancing for the amusement of sailors. She was next sent to live with another aunt in a Somerset village, where for the first time she went to school. When she was in her teens the schoolmaster fell in love with her, and to avoid a scandal her aunt gave her a few pounds and packed her off to London. Her two great assets, her beauty and her untrained talent as a singer and dancer, enabled her to earn her living as an artists' model and an entertainer in night clubs. A white slaver lured her to Bordeaux with offers of work as a dancer; when she discovered his real purpose she left him and attached herself to the leader of an apache gang, who took her to Paris. A fight with another woman member of the gang earned her the nick-name of "the tiger-woman", which stuck to her. The gang was broken up by the police, and she fled back to London.

After her return she moved in the pre-war cultural Bohemia which centred on the Café Royal. Her circle of acquaintances included the artists Jacob Epstein, Augustus John, William Orpen and Nina Hamnett, several of whom used her as a model; the writers Rupert Brooke, Ronald Firbank, Anna Wickham, Nancy Cunard, Roger Fry and Clive Bell; and the musicians Philip Heseltine and Cecil Gray. Her beauty attracted middle-class admirers, to one of whom, a barrister, she became engaged. He tried to teach her to behave like a lady by sending her to live with his father, a Cornish rector, but after three months boredom drove her back to London, where she became engaged to another admirer. On the eve of their wedding, however, she decided that she preferred her third suitor, a medical student, and married him instead. On the honeymoon he taught her to take cocaine. When war broke out he joined the army, and after he was killed in France she married an Australian major, who cured her of the drug habit. She later divorced him for infidelity, and after the war married an Oxford undergraduate, whose friends included Bertram Higgins and Alan Porter. A weakling addicted to drugs and fascinated by magic, he joined Aleister Crowley's community at Cefalú, in Sicily, together with the reluctant Betty, who had too much common sense to be taken in by Crowley. Less than three months later he died of enteric, and she returned to England. Her fourth husband was a sporting journalist, but her boredom in the country and her daily conflicts with his possessive mother soon brought that marriage to an end. Shortly before meeting Lindsay she had told her life-story to a journalist, Gilbert Armitage, who wrote it up for her, and it was published in 1929 under the name *Tiger-Woman*, earning her £500.

After joining her early in 1929 Rickword resumed his search for Eden, and rented a small furnished cottage in Sussex for a month, where Lindsay visited them for a weekend. "Betty looked so like a hardworking gipsy in the rough conditions," he recalled, "that the place survives in memory rather as a caravan camping-site, smudged with the floating smoke-wreaths of a rich wood-fire, while the crackle of broken-up twigs punctuates the conversation and Betty flinging back the hair from her sweaty face bares her housewifely elbows."[22]* But she was quickly bored by the country, as her first fiancé and her fourth husband had discovered, and after a short stay in suburban Woodford they moved back to Central London, where for ten shillings a week they rented a room over a greengrocer's shop. They soon found that the greenstuff sheltered large quantities of lice, which attacked them both, but fortunately Rickword's wartime experience had taught him how to deal with this pest. The incident inspired his poem "The Poor Astrologer's Gift to his Sweetheart", a brilliant exercise in the manner of the Metaphysicals.

* In his memoirs Rickword states that the cottage was in Kent, but Lindsay remembered that it was near Lewes, where they played shove-ha'penny in a pub before going on to the cottage by bus.

Hoping to raise some money for a move to cleaner quarters, he hinted to Lindsay that he might be paid for his foreword to *Women in Parliament*, and at the same time offered him "The Poor Astrologer" for the *London Aphrodite*. Lindsay eagerly accepted it, and made out a cheque which enabled Rickword and Betty to move to the Fulham Road area. Here they had their home for over two years, first in a single large room opening on to a neglected garden, then in a furnished flat with a living room, bedroom and kitchen. He remembered the area with affection, as a leafy neighbourhood where a barrel organ played at regular intervals and on Sundays a crumpet man came round ringing a bell and carrying a tray of crumpets on his head. There were three public houses, each with a character of its own – a corner pub which served good meals; the Finches, where Red Biddy was much in demand among the older drinkers; and a quieter pub frequented by the local Bohemian community, where Rickword spent more time than in either of the others.

He met some characters in one or other of the local pubs – a writer of cheap detective stories and his tiny wife, known as "the Bug", who when money ran short would lock him in his room with an unlimited supply of cigarettes but no food or drink until he had finished that week's story; a decayed Shakespearian actor with an endless flow of theatrical anecdotes; a young American sculptress who presented him with a bronze bust of himself. But by far the queerest fish swimming in these waters was a young New Zealander of Polish origin who styled himself Geoffrey Wladislas Vaile Potocki, Count de Montalk. He lived in a dream of the middle ages, and was a fantastic snob and violent anti-Semite. His eccentricities increased as time passed; he grew his hair long, took to wearing a red beret and an ankle-length red robe, and styled himself His Majesty Wladyslaw the Fifth, by the Grace of God King of Poland, Hungary and Bohemia, Grand Duke of Lithuania, Silesia and the Ukraine, Hospodar of Moldavia etc. etc. etc., High Priest of the Sun. In 1929 his madness had not yet gone to these lengths, and Rickword often went for a walk with him to hear what extraordinary opinions he would utter next.

Women in Parliament appeared in June in a limited edition of 500 copies. Jack Lindsay's faithful and vigorous translation, Norman Lindsay's full-blooded illustrations and Rickword's foreword together formed a salvo of defiance to the Home Secretary, Sir William Joynson-Hicks, against whom the Fanfrolicers and their allies were conducting a guerrilla campaign. In him they saw a mean-minded, sanctimonious, intolerant, philistine bigot; he personified everything that Rickword most disliked. In religion he was a fanatical Evangelical, but his brand of Christianity taught him to hate rather than love his neighbour. After entering Parliament in 1908 he became notorious for jingoism, anti-

Semitism and the fervour with which during the Ulster crisis he preached civil war. The Russian Revolution drove him to frenzy; henceforward he saw Bolshevism everywhere, whether in British trade unionism, Indian nationalism or modern art and literature. When General Dyer shot down 379 unarmed Indians at Amritsar, it was Joynson-Hicks who defended him in the Commons. He loudly declared his admiration for Mussolini and longed to play a similar role in England. His appointment as Home Secretary in 1924 gave him an opportunity. He declared war on Communists, pornographers, homosexuals, aliens (all of whom he suspected of being immoral, and probably Communists as well) and people who dared enjoy themselves, whether by holding hands in Hyde Park or by drinking after hours. In 1925 twelve leading Communists were imprisoned, nominally for sedition (though none of them had said or written anything comparable in violence with the Home Secretary's speeches on the Ulster question), in reality to keep them out of the way during the coming general strike. It is not difficult to imagine Rickword's reaction to all this. As a man passionate about individual freedom he deplored "the state of childish obedience to which this renowned nation has sunk", and compared England to "a gigantic nursery where already nearly all our toys are put away at ten o'clock, and some of them long before that".[23]

Joynson-Hicks's greatest pride was his campaign against pornography, by which he understood all books dealing with sexual matters in an adult manner. Although he did not originate this campaign (*The Rainbow* had been suppressed as far back as 1915, and copies of *Ulysses* had been seized by customs officers in 1923), he intensified it alarmingly in 1928-29. Two novels, *The Well of Loneliness*, which dealt with lesbianism, and *Sleeveless Errand*, which contained the word "buggers", were banned; copies of *Lady Chatterley's Lover* were burnt by the customs; and a typescript of Lawrence's *Pansies* was seized in the post. Joynson-Hicks was cheered on by the chairman of the London Public Morality Council, who demanded the suppression of "books dealing with birth control, translations such as *The Decameron* and books of a pseudo-sociological or scientific nature",[24] and by the popular press which, then as now, revelled in the opportunity to be simultaneously prurient and moral. James Douglas, editor of the *Sunday Express*, who had been largely responsible for the suppression of *The Rainbow* and *The Well of Loneliness*, was particularly noisy.

The Fanfrolicers became involved when Lindsay suggested that his press should publish a book of reproductions of Lawrence's paintings. Lawrence gave his approval, but Lindsay, who received many threatening letters, backed out, fearing a prosecution which would ruin his press. Instead he encouraged Stephensen to found the Mandrake Press, which published the reproductions in June 1929. An exhibition of the paintings opened in London at the same time and was raided by the police, who seized thirteen pictures in which nudes were depicted with pubic hair, together with copies of the book and some drawings by William Blake. At the subsequent hearing the magistrate refused to admit the evidence of leading painters and art critics who were prepared to testify to the paintings' artistic merits, on the ground that "the most beautiful picture in the universe might be obscene",[25] but a compromise was reached whereby the paintings were returned, on the understanding that they would not be exhibited again, and the seized copies of the book were destroyed. No action was taken against Blake, whose address the police sought in vain to discover.

Although by the time this judgment was given the Baldwin Government had been defeated in the 1929 general election, and Joynson-Hicks had been kicked upstairs to the Lords as Viscount Brentford, his spirit continued to dominate British justice. Against the whole system of censorship Stephensen launched a series of satirical pamphlets, including *The Sink of Solitude*, directed against Douglas, and *Policeman of the Lord*, an attack on Joynson-Hicks, and Rickword supported him with his Swiftian satire "The Handmaid of Religion", which commented with grave irony on some unusually fatuous remarks by Joynson-Hicks and the Archbishop of Westminster, Cardinal Bourne. When the former, perhaps with the Fanfrolico Press editions of the classics in mind, put forward the theory that "nothing contributed more to the degradation of the Roman Empire than the stream of pernicious literature which flowed like an open sewer through that great city", it was difficult for anyone to take him seriously after reading Rickword's paraphrase of his words:

> Neither barbarians nor malaria
> destroyed Rome's grip on her vast area,
> but naughty novels sold in shops
> unhindered by censorious cops.

But there was more to the poem than high-spirited fun. With his Anglo-Catholic background and his wide reading, Rickword was as familiar with the mainstream of Christian thought as his opponent, perhaps more so, and could justly rebuke him in Christian terms:

> though our moralists annex
> all blame to the one sin of sex,
> Churchmen, when manners were more genial,
> found fleshly lapses almost venial;
> at least when measured side by side
> with sins of spiritual pride.

Clearly the development of his poetry had entered a new phase. A verse satirist had been born.

One product of his association with Stephensen was the publication by the Mandrake Press in October 1929 of a collection of his stories, *Love One Another*. Only two of the seven "tales" are conventional short stories of everyday life, the title story and "The Dance", a psychological study. The other five consist of his first two published prose works, "The Cow" and "The Bull"; "Pioneers, O Pioneers!", which had appeared in the *Calendar*; "Orders to View", his imitation of Rimbaud's *Ouvriers*; and "Undine: The Last Adventure of the Chevalier Errant", a rather laboured fantasy containing a strong satirical element. The book aroused little interest, and the only review, by Gerald Gould, was unenthusiastic. "Mr Rickword," he wrote,

> has irony and force and command of phrase; at least one of his tales – "The Dance" – is very good indeed; but he does seem sometimes, as in his first story, "The Cow", to be indulging in an artificial brutality which defeats its own end. It is hard to take any interest in a young man who, in such a quick succession of moods, loves a girl rapturously, loathes her disgustedly, and sticks a knife into her efficiently.[26]

Rickword took the hint, and did not attempt prose fiction again.

As his second book for the Mandrake Press it was suggested that he should translate the *Histoire Amoureuse des Gaules*, a seventeenth-century erotic work by Roger de Rabutin, Comte de Bussy. But October 1929, the month in which *Love One Another* was published, was also the month of the Wall Street crash which ushered in the Great Slump. The market for limited and de luxe editions collapsed; the Mandrake Press was declared bankrupt in November 1930, and the Fanfrolico Press suffered a similar fate. Stephensen went back to Australia. Elza learned of the Betty episode and took advantage of it to subject Lindsay to psychological blackmail and to impose her domination upon him, from which he was released only by his conscription into the army in 1941. During the years between she forced him to live in her native West Country, remote from his friends, and became abusive when she discovered that he was corresponding with them. In consequence Rickword after 1930 lost the intellectual stimulus of Lindsay's friendship for several years.

1930 proved an uneventful year; he did editorial work for Wishart, reviewed for the *Sunday Referee* and enjoyed his domesticity with Betty in Fulham. The one disturbing incident was the publication in June of *The Apes of God*, Wyndham Lewis's *roman à clef* in which many of the leading figures of the literary world appeared under thin disguises – the Sitwells, Lytton Strachey, Sidney Schiff and many now forgotten. Rickword was introduced as Hedgepinshot Mandeville Pickwort, a young Oxford-bred "half-mid-European" man, "a small bleached colourless blond", who smoked a pipe and "was dressed in a spotted

and baggy undergraduate get-up". Pickwort, we are told, "was a poet
and a picker up of words as he went", who "carried on the 'decadent'
tradition upon a tide of pallid very low-volted reactions, for what it
was worth". He is said to be editing an anthology of *Verse of the
Under-Thirties*, together with his friend Siegfried Victor, a tall and
handsome young man who has been in Moscow and is obviously meant
for Garman. They are accompanied by four friends who cannot be
identified, though Bertram Brown, who "had a brutal bridling little
pen – but he was under the influence of Pickwort, which was a pity",[27]
may be intended for Higgins. The portrait of Pickwort is obviously
hostile in tone, but the satire, if that is what it is meant to be, is blurred.
The description of him as "half-mid-European", for example, was presumably intended to appeal to anti-Semitic prejudice by suggesting that
Rickword was a Jew, but as there was nothing Jewish about him the
suggestion seems pointless. Again, it is not clear whether the name
"Mandeville" was meant to suggest that he was a liar, like the author
of *The Travels of Sir John Mandeville*, or to refer to his admiration for
the author of *The Fable of the Bees*. No one has ever discovered what
offence he had given Lewis. Possibly Lewis had been injured by the
fact that Rickword had ceased to accept him as his political guru, but
merely to have been his friend was enough to expose one to his suspicions; many of those lampooned in the book had been his friends,
patrons or benefactors. Rickword treated this attempt at satire with
contempt, but he did not forget it.

VIII. *Scrutinies* and Satire

IN 1931-2, as in 1928, Rickword published a volume of "Scrutinies", a collection of poems and a translated biography of a French poet. In *Scrutinies, Volume I* a group of writers who had established their reputations before the war, and some of whom, as Rickword observed in the foreword to the second volume, had been "national figures...each expressing the 'conscience' of some numerically important group", were considered by critics some twenty or thirty years younger than themselves. The second collection, which appeared in February 1931, dealt with writers who had achieved fame since the war and whose reputations had not yet been "hallowed by long years of habitual praise"[1] – Eliot, Aldous Huxley, Joyce, Lawrence, Wyndham Lewis, the Sitwells, Lytton Strachey and Virginia Woolf. For various reasons most of the contributors to the first collection were unavailable. Lawrence had died; Dorothy Edwards had committed suicide; Graves had settled in Majorca and Campbell in Provence; Garman was visiting his brother in Brazil; Holms was living with the American heiress Peggy Guggenheim, and resisted all invitations to write. The only contributors to *Scrutinies I* who reappeared in its successor were Rickword and Higgins, whose essay on Eliot's criticism marked the end of their long collaboration. When it appeared he had already sailed for Australia, where he was to sink into obscurity, except for a small circle of admirers who venerated him as a greater poet than Eliot.

Among Rickword's new team were three former contributors to the *Calendar*, Alec Brown, Mary Butts and Peter Quennell, who wrote on Eliot's poetry, Huxley and Lawrence's later novels respectively. Jack Lindsay dealt with Joyce, and Brian Penton, his assistant at the Fanfrolico Press, produced a Fanfroliconean essay on the novel in which he proclaimed "man's only greatness, the godlike pursuits of lechery and booze".[2] The other new contributors were Sherard Vines on the Sitwells, Christopher Saltmarshe on Strachey, William Empson on Virginia Woolf, Gilbert Armitage on poetry and society, Montagu Slater on twentieth-century painting and Constant Lambert on contemporary music. They represented a younger generation than the writers in *Scrutinies I*, and were most of them considerably younger than those whom they criticized. Thus Lawrence, who in the first collection had savagely attacked Galsworthy, was himself reprimanded in the second by Quennell, who was twenty years his junior. Whereas those whose tastes had been formed before the war still regarded Eliot, Joyce, Lawrence and the Sitwells with some suspicion, and Rickword and his contemporaries had had to fight in their defence, to the new Scrutineers these writers were the literary establishment, towards whom irreverence was permissible and even obligatory. As one reviewer observed, " 'if only' is one of the keynotes of the whole chorus";[3] each critic, while taking his subject's greatness for granted, complained that he had disappointed his admirers' expectations. The one exception was Saltmarshe's essay on Strachey, which, like Rickword's on Barrie in the first collection, demonstrated how a very minor talent could fool his contemporaries into rating him far above his merits.

Rickword himself contributed a foreword and an essay on Wyndham Lewis. In the former he replied to the "angry screech" and the "dignified rebuke of our 'low standard of literary courtesy' " with which the *Spectator* and *The Times Literary Supplement* had greeted the first collection, remarking: "To a paralytic, I suppose, any man who walks with ordinary freedom must seem to be executing a violent and gratuitously offensive gesture". His essay on Lewis is if anything overgenerous, but he makes it clear that his admiration is no longer so high as it was in the days of the *Calendar*. On *The Art of Being Ruled* he comments:

> At the time, I thought it might be a *Culture and Anarchy* for our generation, thinking that the rather thick and muddled prophetics would be cleared up in subsequent pronouncements. This has not yet occurred, and the trend of Lewis's later writings does not encourage one to think that it ever will.

He then proceeds, with unfailing courtesy, to demolish any claim to be a systematic thinker which Lewis might possess, and leaves us with the picture of "the most forceful and resourceful prose-writer of his generation" recklessly expending his energy, like "a powerful man tormented by gnats".[4]

Scrutinies II did not provoke such strong reactions as its predecessor had done. Although *The Times Literary Supplement* considered that "the standard of literary courtesy is still highly variable", it recognized that the book contained "genuinely creative criticism", and handed out prizes for the three best essays to Alec Brown, Mary Butts and Jack Lindsay, with a consolation prize for Rickword as runner-up. The *Spectator*, so indignant about the previous volume, praised this one as "a workmanlike collection of essays", and singled out Rickword's as "a model of what criticism should be, tempered, just, appreciative where merited". The *New Statesman* prophesied that "if later volumes are as alert and vigorous as this one, they are likely to play a part in the formation of taste".[5] Rickword had suggested in his foreword that further collections might appear, but in fact *Scrutinies II* was the last of the series.

He suffered a serious blow when in April his cousin Cecil was killed in a road accident, at the age of thirty-one. Since childhood he had been closer to Cecil than to his brothers and sisters, partly because they were almost the same age, partly because of their common intellectual interests. Cecil Rickword combined the practical ability as an organizer which his work for the *Calendar* and Wishart & Co. had demonstrated with exceptional sensitivity as a critic. His essay *A Note on Fiction*, which F.R. Leavis described as "an incomparable aid to the intelligent criticism of novels",[6] has established itself as a classic document of twentieth-century criticism, but the essay on Shaw and the reviews which he contributed to the *Calendar* are of almost equal value. His death left an emotional gap in Rickword's life and involved him in practical difficulties, as he was obliged to devote more time to the running of Wishart's.

His third collection of poems, *Twittingpan and Some Others*, which was published in September, differs radically from its predecessors in that the three longest poems and the majority of the shorter ones are satirical in tone. As he himself had written, "the sense of irony returns as the poetic impulse diminishes".[7] In later years he described his turning towards satire as an attempt to counter the inclination towards nihilism discernible in the later poems in *Invocations to Angels*,[8] but this is not the whole truth. His interest in satire is already apparent in "The Re-Creation of Poetry" and other contributions to the *Calendar*, and the satirical lyrics in *Twittingpan*, such as "Provincial Nightpiece" and "Ode to a Train-de-luxe", have much in common with such poems in *Invocations to Angels* as "Farewell to Fancy" and "Sir Orang Hautton at Vespers", which may date from as early as 1923. Even the more formal satire of "The Encounter"* may have originated in the mid-1920s rather than the early 1930s.

In this poem, modelled on the ninth satire in Horace's first book, he consciously worked within a tradition of Horatian satire which runs from Donne, through Rochester, Oldham, Swift and Pope, to Byron. That does not mean that he imitated any of his predecessors; all "The Encounter" has in common with Horace's poem and those of Donne and Oldham on the same theme is that it opens with the poet's meeting with a bore, describes their conversation as they walk through the streets and closes with their parting. Aware that he was laying himself open to comparison with his predecessors, he repeatedly rewrote and revised it; there are four drafts among the manuscripts in the British Library, and these do not necessarily include all the discarded versions. In the process of revision he omitted some lines which are worth pre-

---

* In *Twittingpan and Some Others* this poem is entitled "Twittingpan or The Encounter", which was shortened to "The Encounter" in the 1947 and later collected editions. To avoid ambiguity, the book is here referred to as *Twittingpan* and the poem as "The Encounter".

serving, such as Twittingpan's rhapsody on passing a sanitary engineer's:

> See where in Shanks's shop serenely shine
> Toilet utensils with a thrilling line,
> Their virgin whiteness and seductive curve
> The sublimation of the need they serve.
> What mondaine famed for elegance and wit
> Need blush to sit there when she wants to think?

Internal evidence suggests that the poem was begun several years before it reached its final form. It refers to the Tokyo earthquake of 1923, to J.B.S. Haldane's *Daedalus*, published in 1924, and to Erik Satie's ballet *Parade*, first performed in London in 1919 and revived in 1926. The reference to Epstein's sculptures as a subject of controversy, topical at any time between the wars, would have been especially so in 1925, when Rickword denounced in the *Calendar* the press campaign against "Rima". When he speaks of Twittingpan "on some Red-film show-day expounding *tonal montage*" he clearly has in mind the activities of the Film Society, founded in 1925, which showed banned Soviet films such as Eisenstein's *Battleship Potemkin*, and one draft of the poem does mention the Film Society in this connection. There is a curious textual variant in the poem as printed in 1932 in the anthology *Whips and Scorpions*, where instead of "He had championed Epstein, Gertrude, and *Parade*" we find "Epstein, Joyce, and Coward". This seems to represent an earlier reading than that in *Twittingpan*; Noel Coward had caused a scandal with *The Vortex* in 1924 and *Fallen Angels* in 1925, but by 1931 had achieved respectability with *Cavalcade*. On the other hand, the final version incorporates in modified form the couplet

> Eked out, like Eliot's later works,
> With sanctimonious quips and quirks,

which originally appeared in "The Handmaid of Religion" as printed in 1929, and other details which must be of late date are references to Sir James Jeans's *The Mysterious Universe*, published in 1930, and to Haldane as a professor and to Bertrand Russell as a lord, titles which they obtained in 1930 and 1931 respectively. It would therefore appear that "The Encounter" was begun not later than 1926 and was drastically revised or rewritten in 1930 or 1931.

Twittingpan is an affected intellectual dilettante, homosexual, snob and name-dropper, who not only claims to be an authority on literature, art, music, the film and the ballet but also shows off his scientific knowledge, which, it is made clear, he has acquired from the half-understood popularizations of Jeans and Haldane. In the final section of the poem Rickword takes a very effective revenge on Wyndham Lewis for the satirical portrait of himself in *The Apes of God*, not by attacking him, but by putting a panegyric on him into the mouth of Twittingpan, who possesses most of the qualities which Lewis found most objectionable. He is essentially an amateur, and as Rickword remarked in *Scrutinies II*, "the competition of the wealthy amateur with the genuine artist" was one of Lewis's favourite complaints. He has championed Gertrude Stein and (in one version) Joyce, two of Lewis's pet aversions. He links Lewis with the sentimental Middleton Murry as objects of his worship – not an association which Lewis would have relished. Above all, he is homosexual, and whenever Lewis discusses homosexuality (which he frequently does, at enormous length) he seems in danger of overstepping the bounds of reason. Rickword had already satirized in *Scrutinies II* the obsessions which Lewis's disciples were expected to share with him:

> At a gathering of Enemy supporters I imagine a drowsy summer hum like that which comes through the open windows of the village school. The pupils will hoot whenever the word *Time*, pronounced with a hint as to its sinister significance, falls on their ears; they will eschew the "gonadal ecstasies of sex" and espouse "all the male chastity of thought"; they will assert that they are "on the side of the intellect", and sing in chorus "I am for the physical world".[9]

This passage, funny enough in itself, becomes hilarious when paraphrased in homosexual and masochistic terms by Twittingpan:

> Don't you think Wyndham Lewis too divine?
> That brute male strength he shows in every line!
> I swear if he'd flogged me in his last book but one,
> as some kind person informed me he has done,
> I'd have forgiven him for the love of art.
> And you, too, ought to take his works to heart
> as I have done, for torn by inner strife,
> I've made him mentor of my mental life.
> You cannot imagine what a change that worked.
> I who was all emotion, and always shirked
> the cold chaste isolation of male mind,
> now thrust in front of all I had kept behind.
> I'd lived in Time and Motion and Sensation,
> then smashed my watch and burned the Bloomsbury *Nation*.

There the feud ended. Nothing was left for Lewis to say, and Rickword had no desire to pursue it further.

"Hints for Making a Gentleman", the third of the longer satires in the book (after "The Handmaid of Religion", already described), is the most powerful and Swiftian of the three. Where the other two are comparatively light-hearted in tone, here Rickword gives full vent to his distaste for the bourgeoisie, its institutions (public schools, the Army and the City), its ideology and its morality. His debt to Swift is apparent, not only in his choice of metre, but in the ironic approval expressed throughout for the objects of his satire, until he reaches his final punch-line:

> for as his body muckward sinks
> he still lacks sense to tell he stinks.

Like "The Encounter", this poem was the product of much revision; four drafts survive, one of which contains some pointed lines omitted from the printed version:

> He sees his sons and daughters praise
> His own ideas in different ways,
> For though they laugh at them, he knows
> They'll like his money when he goes.

Reading this poem, more than any other in the book, we are conscious that the author is on his way to Communism.

It would be a mistake, however, to imagine that his journey there followed a straight path with no deviations. He later described another poem in this collection, "Apostate Humanitarian", as "essentially reactionary", and summed up its message as "if you say 'To Hell with everything!' 'Stamp on everybody!' then the Gods will come back".[10] The "reactionary" nature of the poem is disguised in the later collections by the omission of the dedication to Geoffrey Potocki de Montalk, and by an alteration in the first line of the last verse, which in the original reads:

> then with democracy's collapse
> swift forms replenish our tired earth
> of bouncing goddesses and mirth-
> mad gods with wine-and-oil smeared chaps.

It would seem that when these lines were written, somewhere between 1929 and 1931, Rickword had not entirely shaken off Wyndham Lewis's influence, and perhaps was taking even Potocki's ideas more seriously than in later years he was prepared to admit.

But, unlike Swift, he was too kind-hearted to indulge in personal satire. The poem "An Old Rhyme Re-rhymed", for example, which was directed against Eliot's entry into the Church, was originally entitled "Poor Tom's a-cold" and carried the dedication: "For T.S.E., fellow-plagiary". "I thought I ought to cut it out for decency's sake," he explained in 1973. "'Tom's a-cold'. Now that was a very ungentle-manly thing to do, when I come to think of it. Poor Eliot suffered.

Ought one to behave like that to a person? Would it hurt him?"[11]*
"The Contemporary Muse" also underwent some changes. The copy
sent to the printer lacked the last four lines, which were tacked on at
the last moment. Rickword considered extending it into a longer satire
on contemporary poets, and added these lines:

> Play up, my dear, play up and play the game –
> Scratch backs, that is, and they may do the same
> for you, when dead. Praise Wolfe for rhyme and wit;
> Blunden for observation, a sure hit
> though you can't tell a starling from a tit.
> What curse has sterilised the laurelled Shanks
> whose hawthorn wreath has withered as the Bank's
> security for an overdraft of fame –
> and his fellow-champion's case is much the same.†

Another stray couplet written on the back of a draft of "The Encounter"
seems to have been intended for the same poem:

> Graves in his island paradise might prove
> the literary world well lost for love,

but Rickword abandoned the idea of making his satire personal and
crossed out all but four of the lines which he had added to the printer's
copy.

   Twittingpan produced less response from the critics than *Invocations
to Angels*. *The Times Literary Supplement*, while praising its "pointed,
effective satire" and "neatly turned" verse, felt that in the shorter poems
"a vein of acrimony persists, precluding any warmth of sentiment...
There is more 'cold thought' than feeling in these verses; but they have
plenty of vigour – still vigour though 'frozen'." As with the previous
collection, the most interesting criticism came from Dilys Powell, who
wrote:

> Mr Edgell Rickword grows yearly more disgusted with a world which,
> as he sees it, is almost entirely composed of falsehood and stupidity; by
> far the gloomiest of living poets, he is disillusioned even with disillusion-
> ment. He is the Swift of our age, both in his disgust and in the terms in
> which he expresses it; one dare not wish his poetry less savage for fear
> it should lose its edge...This book is rich in the perverse way in which
> Donne is rich; I do not recommend it to the squeamish.[12]

It is a perceptive judgment, though it surely underestimates the element
of sheer fun in "The Encounter" and "The Handmaid of Religion".

* The use of "ungentlemanly" comes rather incongruously from the author of "Hints
for Making a Gentleman".

† The "hawthorn wreath" is the Hawthornden Prize, awarded in 1919 to Edward Shanks
and in 1920 to his fellow-member of the Squirearchy John Freeman.

Twittingpan was Rickword's last book consisting entirely of previously uncollected verse. After 1931, although he lived another fifty years, he published only eleven more poems. His virtual abandonment of poetry has been widely attributed to his conversion to Communism – by Julian Symons, for example, who wrote: "What a lot of good poems were stillborn, how much perceptive criticism we lost, when Edgell Rickword joined and (so far as I know) remained faithful to the Communist Party". David Holbrook attributed his "paralysed silence" to "total and catastrophic subjection of the free mind to a herd cause". Some on the left have adopted a fundamentally similar view, assuming that he sacrificed his art to his beliefs. Laurence Coupe referred to "his renunciation of poetic speech", and commented: "To assume the primacy of poetic 'praxis' over political is...to surrender to the idealism that Rickword has consistently opposed – an idealism that would ultimately prefer art to life". A more subtle variant of this theory is found in Jack Beeching's review of the 1947 *Collected Poems*, which argued that they are a record of a personal conflict which "began in the trenches of 1918 and ended in the slump" with Rickword's acceptance of Communism. Beeching attached particular importance to "The Happy New Year", of which he wrote:

> It is significant that the masque which ends the book is an invocation to the sun, the sceptical solitary's vindication of unity with his fellows:
>
> > Like begets like, immortal in each kind;
> > through perishing units' union, death's defeat.
>
> The individual transformation from loathing of contemporary sterility to confidence in the life-giving powers contained within the integument of a decaying society:
>
> > whence the dextrous couples
> > hitched fast by votive bonds
> > shall draw Time's toppling wain
> > to all-men's Harvest Home
>
> is at once the perfected consummation of a personal development and a resolving of the conflict which initially provoked the cycle of poems. There was no more to be written because the last word had been said.[13]

The weakness of all these theories is that they ignore Rickword's own statements, dates or both. His abandonment of verse in 1931 can hardly be attributed to his entry in 1934 into the Communist Party. Coupe in 1981 referred regretfully to "the loss to English poetry involved in his decision", yet in an interview published eight years earlier, in reply to the question "Why did you decide to stop writing poetry?", Rickword had said "I didn't decide".[14] Beeching seems to have been misled by the position of "The Happy New Year" at the end of the 1947 collection into imagining that it was the latest poem in the book, whereas in fact it was written in 1926, and the Utopian reference to "all-men's Harvest Home" was an addition made twenty years later.

Rickword himself was caustic about the theory that his Communism killed his poetry. "I hadn't any impulse to write poems," he said in an interview in 1975.

> I would have quite liked to, but I was getting into rather a different mood, less subjective I suppose, and I think poetry must have much of the subjective in it. I had stopped writing poetry well before I became a party member, so all that stuff about how being a communist killed me off as a poet is nonsense. And very impertinent too, I think. I don't see why these people should think they know what went on in my mind better than I do...I don't think I tried very hard, because for some time I had had the news that it had ceased. I simply wasn't in a mind to write poems. But my acquaintance with Marxism didn't act as a psychological brake on my writing life. Lyric poets tend to finish early, you know... Some writers felt that they could only come to terms with their work if they were politically committed. It's a sense of revelation almost. That being committed makes you a poet, or even becomes a very worthy subject for poetry. And I believe that I tried to think like that, but then nothing happened. I didn't flog it. You can't force a poem.[15]

Rickword's other statements on the subject suggest two possible explanations for his silence, one psychological, one social. "One had given up dreaming, I suppose. I think dreaming is a very important factor in getting the imagery of poetry, the atmosphere. One tends to become so logical over 25 or 26".[16] "I wrote very little poetry after 1930; people are puzzled about this, but I don't think it should be puzzling. Lots of poets have written for about ten years, and then stopped." "Why did Peter Quennell not write more poetry, or William Empson? It was a very bad time, you see. We haven't talked about the Depression, the sense then – as in *Journey to the End of the Night* by Céline – of the ghastly degradation of existence."[17] There are clues here that need to be followed up.

Of the 98 poems which Rickword published (counting the three parts of "Absences" and the two of "Poet to Punk" as separate poems) 43 appeared and at least four more were written before the end of 1923. In other words, nearly half of his published poems were written between his twentieth and his twenty-fifth birthdays, and in addition a considerable section of his unpublished work certainly dates from this period. ("One tends to become so logical over 25...") Behind these poems we can sense the trauma of the Western Front, the stimulus of his Oxford friendships and his love for Peggy, although there seems to have been some flagging of inspiration in 1923 as his marriage came under strain. The new trauma of Peggy's madness, the intellectual excitement of his work on the *Calendar* and the general strike all contributed to make 1924-6 an extremely fruitful period; not only did it produce some of his strongest and most mature lyrics, but he also attempted work on a more ambitious scale, unsuccessfully in his Faustus play, successfully in "The Happy New Year". After the new shock of the betrayal of the general strike the impulse slackened; from the mood of nihilism and despair which this event induced he took refuge first in satire, then in silence.

His beloved Rimbaud gave up writing verse before his twentieth birthday. Marvell, another poet whom Rickword admired, probably wrote all the lyrics upon which his reputation rests before he was 35, and afterwards produced mainly political and satirical verse. Housman wrote the greater part of *A Shropshire Lad* at the age of 35, while in a state of "continuous excitement" in the early months of 1895, and did not bring out another collection until 1922; its publication was hastened by another burst of poetic activity in the April of that year, when he wrote about ten poems. Rickword, like Housman, was reluctant to rush into print: he set himself the highest standards of craftsmanship. He omitted from his collections poems which had already appeared in periodicals, dropped from his later collections poems included in his earlier ones, changed his mind about poems which he had decided to publish and never printed some poems which are little if at all inferior to others which appear in his collections. He was familiar with the example of Wordsworth's later work: he would not attempt to produce poetry by an act of will after he realized that the poetic impulse had failed. "You can't force a poem."

He associated the failure of the impulse not with his conversion to Communism but with a rather earlier event – the Great Slump. He was by no means the only poet of the 1920s who ceased to write verse at that time. Edith Sitwell wrote only two poems between 1929 and 1939, and Aldous Huxley, whose poems had much in common with Rickword's, wrote only prose in the 1930s. Several of Rickword's friends and acquaintances repeated the same pattern. Peter Quennell, the youthful prodigy who contributed poems to *Georgian Poetry* at seventeen and to the *Calendar* at twenty, was regarded as a rising hope of English poetry (Harold Monro in 1929 referred to him in the same breath as Eliot, Pound and the Sitwells), yet after 1930 he concentrated on biography and criticism. Richard Hughes, who published his collected poems in 1926, wrote mainly prose fiction after *A High Wind in Jamaica* became a best-seller three years later; one of his last published poems, which appeared in 1931, was appropriately called "Death of the Spirit of a Young Poet". When Alan Porter, of whom great things had been expected, published *The Signature of Pain* in 1930 it contained poems welcoming its belated arrival from Hughes, Blunden and three other poets, yet it proved not only his first but his last collection. Douglas Garman published his one collection, *The Jaded Hero*, in 1927, and afterwards wrote only a handful of poems. Jack Lindsay has commented: "With the Great Slump, there was an almost clean break in the intellectual scene. A different political and a different cultural situation arrived."[18] Rickword's abandonment of poetry was not unique; it has been consistently misread mainly by those who seize on it to make a political point.

During the years that followed he must often have been reminded of Ulysses' warning to Achilles:

> Perseverance, dear my lord,
> Keeps honour bright. To have done, is to hang
> Quite out of fashion.

After the publication of *Invocations to Angels* he enjoyed a high reputation; in an essay written in 1930 Basil Bunting maintained that after "our really great poets", Pound, Eliot and Yeats, the three outstanding English poets were Auden, Quennell and Rickword.[19] But because he failed to keep his name before the public by producing new poems and new collections, his poetic achievement came to be neglected and almost forgotten, as his treatment by anthologists demonstrates.

In 1932 he was represented in *Younger Poets of To-day*, edited by J.C. Squire, which was reprinted two years later as *Third Selections from Modern Poets*. His relations with Squire are a curious story. In the early 1920s, when Squire printed four of his poems and his essay on Beddoes in the *London Mercury*, he was regarded as a junior member of the Squirearchy because of his association with Turner; in his satire "The Jolly Old Squire or Way-Down in Georgia", published in 1922, Osbert Sitwell included him among Squire's hangers-on. When in 1924 Squire published *Second Selections from Modern Poets*, which was confined to the work of poets under fifty, Rickword seemed an obvious candidate for inclusion, but the ultra-conservative editor had by then developed doubts about his undesirable Modernist tendencies and excluded him from the anthology. By 1932 he had overcome his doubts sufficiently to represent him in *Younger Poets of To-day* by "Regret for the Passing of the Entire Scheme of Things", which had appeared in the *London Mercury* as long ago as 1921, but not by any of his more mature work.*

Another anthology published in 1932, *Whips and Scorpions*, a collection of twentieth-century satirical verse edited by Sherard Vines, is of particular interest, as Rickword seems to have had a hand in compiling it. Not only was it published by Wishart, but fourteen of the thirty-five

---

* This poem was also included in *The Mercury Book of Verse: Being a Selection of Poems published in The London Mercury, 1919-1930* (1931).

poets represented had contributed to the *Calendar* or to *Scrutinies*, and
two others had been friends of his since their Oxford days. The collection,
in which most of the poems poke fun at war, religion, the bourgeoisie,
the literary world or the United States with an irreverent facetiousness
remote from the gravity of true satire, demonstrates how far he towered
above his contemporaries as a verse satirist. After reading some of the
contributions of Aldington, Turner and Osbert Sitwell, whose free verse
degenerates into chopped prose, or Auden's shapeless and puerile
"Birthday Ode", one turns to "The Encounter" or "The Handmaid of
Religion", in which Rickword displays his command of form, his ability
to concentrate on his target and his respect for the great tradition within
which he worked.

The only other anthologies of the 1930s in which his work was
represented were *A Treasury of Modern Poetry* (1936), edited by R.L.
Mégroz, which reprinted five poems from *Invocations to Angels*; *Poems
of Twenty Years* (1938), edited by Maurice Wollmann, which included
"Intimacy"; and *Poems for Spain* (1939), edited by Stephen Spender
and John Lehmann, which contained "To the Wife of Any Non-Intervention Statesman". Nothing of his is to be found in Yeats's *Oxford
Book of Modern Verse* (1936) or, more surprisingly, in *A New Book
of Modern Verse 1920-1940* (1941). His exclusion from this collection
cannot be attributed to ignorance of his work (of the two editors,
L.A.G. Strong was an Oxford contemporary of his and C. Day Lewis
had contributed to *Left Review* while Rickword edited it) or to political
prejudice, for at least eight of the poets represented were or had been
Communist Party members.

Through his friend Hayter Preston, who put him in touch with a
young publisher named Humphrey Toulmin, he received a commission
to translate a new French life of Verlaine by Marcel Coulon, for which
he was paid £50. This book, which appeared in June 1932 under the
title of *Poet Under Saturn: The Tragedy of Verlaine*, completed the
trilogy which he had written or translated on the three French poets
whom he most admired – Baudelaire, Verlaine and Rimbaud. His long
introduction to Coulon's book gives a lively and amusing account of
Verlaine's various visits to England, and contains passages in which
we may detect a touch of autobiography, as when he refers to Verlaine's
poetry of contrition as "comprehensible to all who have been brought
up under the Christian ideology", or quotes with appreciation his
description of London as "prudish, with every kind of vice flaunting
its presence; everlastingly drunk, in spite of the ridiculous laws against
drunkenness".[20]

IX. The Road to Communism

BY the autumn of 1931 the slump was hitting the book trade badly. Publishers became more cautious about commissioning new books, unless they could anticipate substantial sales. After completing *Poet Under Saturn* Rickword found it impossible to obtain another commission, and fell back on his old plan – migration to the country, where he could live cheaply and write in peace. In October he and Betty rented a furnished house a few miles from Maidenhead, with a large garden, chickens and ducks which supplied them with vegetables and eggs. Shortly after moving in they listened to their battery-operated radio announcing the results of the general election, an event which was to exercise a decisive influence on Rickword's future life.* When their lease expired they returned to London, settling temporarily in a sleazy boarding house in Torrington Square, but in January 1932 they found another house to let in the Maidenhead area, at a rent of only £1 a week. As his only reliable source of income was his disability pension of about £3 10s. a week, this opportunity was too good to miss.

Soon after they moved in he made his only appearance at the Old Bailey, as a witness on behalf of his friend Geoffrey Potocki. Several months earlier Potocki had taken five of his poems to a printer and asked to have fifty copies printed for private circulation among his friends. On reading them through the printer found that they contained erotic passages which, in those days when the spirit of Joynson-Hicks still presided, might have been considered obscene, and to protect himself he showed the manuscript to the police. If Potocki had agreed to be dealt with summarily when he appeared before a magistrate, he would probably have been bound over or sentenced to a trivial fine; instead, unable to resist an opportunity to show off, he opted for trial by jury, and on 8 February he appeared at the Central Criminal Court before Sir Ernest Wild, the formidable Recorder of London. He was provided with a defence barrister by the generosity of Ernest Wishart,

* The chronology of this period of Rickword's life, as recorded in his memoirs, is very confused. He states that he was still living in Fulham when he learned of Philip Heseltine's death (in December 1930); that he moved to the country after *Poet Under Saturn* (published in June 1932) had gone to press; that his cousin Cecil (killed in April 1931) helped to make his new home habitable; that he had settled in "by the last months of 1929"; and that soon after moving in he listened to the election results, which were "disastrous for the Labour Party". The only way of reconciling these statements is to assume that he moved to Maidenhead in October 1931; that he has confused the elections of May 1929, which Labour won, with those of 27 October 1931; and that Cecil's assistance was given on another of the seven occasions between the spring of 1927 and that of 1931 when he changed his address.

who, although his own firm was not involved, was concerned with the freedom of the press; almost certainly he made this gesture at the suggestion of Rickword, whose friend Potocki was. The accused made no attempt to ingratiate himself with the judge and jury by having his hair cut and wearing a dark suit, but presented his normal appearance in the dock – flowing hair, a red cape, a white scarf and sandals. Counsel for the prosecution when presenting his case mentioned the sinister fact that a copy of the banned *Well of Loneliness* had been found in Potocki's room in Hammersmith, as well as two books of verse by the accused entitled *Lordly Love Songs* and *Surprising Songs*. After Potocki had given evidence that the poems were a literary experiment for publication among his literary friends, a remarkable dialogue took place between the Recorder and the accused.

> RECORDER: You call that poetry?
> POTOCKI: Yes.
> RECORDER: That is how a poet writes? How did you become a poet?
> POTOCKI: My lord, it is the choice of the gods.
> RECORDER: What gods?
> POTOCKI: A man cannot call himself a poet if he is not a poet.

Fortunately the Recorder, finding himself out of his depth, did not pursue the matter. It is improbable that an explanation by the accused that he was a polytheist would have improved his standing with the court.

Rickword was then called to testify to the literary value of the five poems. According to Potocki,

> he was dressed in a sombre brown overcoat (if I remember rightly he kept his hands in the pockets of it most of the time) but as he swayed backwards and forwards with a slight movement very characteristic of him, against the background of a meretricious fake-classical oak pillar, he looked very imposing in a whimsical way of his own.

When counsel for the prosecution said "Mr Rickword, you are a poet, I understand?" he promptly replied "Yes" without any false modesty. "How long have you been a poet?" was the next question. He gazed into space, swaying slightly, and after a moment's consideration answered "about fifteen years" – a reply which caused some surprise in court, as he looked considerably younger than his thirty-three years. On two of his poems, a translation of Rabelais's *Chanson de la Braguette* and a parody of Verlaine's *Taille High Life*, he gave evidence that they were very good versions of the originals, but he preferred not to express an opinion on Potocki's own poems, cautiously stating that "They're not my style". Counsel for the defence appealed to the jury not to be prejudiced against the defendant because he was a poet,

admitting that "in England it is customary to regard poets with contempt unless they are dead". "Rather like politicians," the Recorder
remarked, which raised a laugh.

In his summing-up Sir Ernest did not leave the jury in any doubt
about the verdict he expected from them. "A man must not say he is
a poet and be filthy," he declared. "He has to obey the law the same
as ordinary citizens, and the sooner the highbrow school learns that,
the better for the morality of the country." When the jury had duly
found the defendant guilty, he commented that no decent-minded jury
could have come to any other decision than that the accused had attempted to deprave our literature, and expressed his determination that as
far as possible literature should be protected against "offal of this kind".
Turning to the prisoner, he asked what punishment he thought he
deserved, to which Potocki replied: "I think I deserve to be sentenced
to several years in Buckingham Palace".[1] Sir Ernest, unaware of his
obsession with monarchy, was deeply shocked, and immediately sentenced him to six months in the second division.

Potocki served his time in Wormwood Scrubs, where he proved to
be one of the most unconventional prisoners that it had ever received.
On the night of his arrival he had a conversation with two other prisoners in which "I not only upheld the Divine Right of Kings, but
announced that it was my own intention ultimately to become a King".
He surprised the prison chaplain by telling him that he was a pagan
and asking to be supplied with a Shakespeare instead of the usual Bible,
a request that was not granted. During his imprisonment he showed
his familiarity with Rickword's poems in unusual circumstances. "To
see the prisoners in grey walking round and round the exercise ring,"
he afterwards wrote, "reminded me of a *danse macabre* – the very
opposite of that Dance of Life as which Havelock Ellis so rightly sees
the Cosmos. I wrote on my bench in the Brush Shop, in order to remind
me of that Dance of Life, Edgell Rickword's line, 'Fantastic ceremonial
floods the world'."[2] This quotation from "The Happy New Year" was
not appreciated by the authorities, and Potocki was ordered to rub it
out.

Rickword and his friends took an interest in the case, less from sympathy with Potocki, who had brought most of his misfortunes upon
himself, than because of the issues which it raised. Wishart & Co. had
started a series of pamphlets on topical issues, for which Gilbert Armitage wrote a study of the case called *Banned in England. An Examination
of the Law Relating to Obscene Publications*. After Potocki was
released Rickword wrote him a friendly letter commissioning a pamphlet for the series on his prison experiences. In the pamphlet, which
was called *Snobbery with Violence. A Poet in Gaol*, Potocki gave a
vivid description of the degradation of prison life, and paid Rickword

the compliment of quoting his lines

> The arts, perhaps, are more obscene
> than Jix or Bourne can even mean

as the epigraph to one of his chapters. Penal reform was a cause on which Rickword had felt deeply ever since, eleven years before, he had described prison life as "a system of deliberate brutality which could only be realised in a thoroughly detestable state of society".[3]

Once again Betty was to demonstrate that rural life did not suit her. She had established friendly relations with the elderly landlady of the local pub, but otherwise she could find little congenial company. In his memoirs Rickword described the widening rift between them:

> Betty's social talents had little opportunity to express themselves in the atmosphere and routine to which we had reduced ourselves. Our conversation became less spontaneous. There would be long gaps while we both struggled to find a topic on which to suspend the thread of conversation. As the summer wore on Betty began to say that she thought she would like to go back to London, rather than face another winter in this rather lonely countryside, as it became when the weather was severe. She spoke of a friend who, she thought, would certainly let her have a room.

Rickword suspected that one reason for the rift was that Betty had become interested in another man. Whether this was so or not, it was certainly about this time that another woman entered his own life – Nancy Cunard.

Nancy, who was two years his senior, had had as eventful a career as Betty, although their social backgrounds were very different. Her father, the grandson of the founder of the Cunard Steamship Line, was a foxhunting baronet with a medieval mansion in Leicestershire, whose only deviation from the conventions of his caste was his passion for making ornamental ironwork; her mother, a wealthy American, combined social ambitions with some artistic interests. The two proved incompatible, and when Nancy was fifteen Lady Cunard left her husband and set up her own establishment in London. This upheaval seems to have had a traumatic effect on Nancy, who developed an intense dislike of her mother. Eager to escape from Lady Cunard's house, she married an officer in 1916; the marriage did not last, and she transferred her affections to another young officer, who was killed in action soon after. She and her husband separated after the war and were later divorced. A serious illness and a series of operations, including a hysterectomy in the winter of 1920-21, further complicated her emotional life. Meanwhile she was beginning to establish a small reputation as a poet; her poems had appeared in the first issue of the Sitwells' anthology *Wheels*, which took its title from one of them, and her first collection, published in 1921, received a favourable review from Rickword, who detected in it "the pulse of an original mind".[4] From 1923 onwards she lived mainly in Paris, where she was closely associated with the Surrealist group; perhaps the most passionate of her many love affairs was that with the Surrealist poet Louis Aragon, which lasted for two years. It was under his influence that she acquired the sympathy with Communism which she retained, although she never joined either the French or the British party; indeed, Rickword believed that if she had applied she would have been rejected. In 1928 she founded the Hours Press, which published works by Aragon, Norman Douglas, George Moore, Richard Aldington, Arthur Symons, Samuel Beckett, Roy Campbell, Robert Graves, Laura Riding, Ezra Pound and Havelock Ellis. The *affaire* with Aragon ended in the same year, after he had made an unsuccessful attempt at suicide.

Her next *affaire*, with a black American pianist named Henry Crowder, transformed her life. Lady Cunard's horrified reaction led to a final breach between mother and daughter. In a pamphlet called *Black Man and White Ladyship* she violently attacked her mother's racial prejudice as symptomatic of a worldwide evil and argued the right of the black race to equality. Rickword's feelings on reading it were mixed; he thought it both scurrilous and hysterical, yet he had to admit that it had opened his eyes to injustices of which previously he had been only partly conscious. For Nancy the pamphlet was only the first shot in the war against racialism to which she committed herself, for she decided to produce a comprehensive anthology on all aspects of Negro life, history, politics and culture. In search of material she visited New York in 1931, staying in Harlem, and greatly embarrassed Crowder by insisting on being seen with him everywhere, in defiance of the colour bar.

Her first meeting with Rickword took place in April 1932, when she came to London before making a second visit to America. She stayed at the same hotel in Greek Street, Soho, as he and Betty, who had come up to London on business. The three struck up a conversation over a drink in the lounge and afterwards had dinner together. Nancy's path and Betty's had already crossed before the war, when both had frequented the Café Royal as members of Augustus John's circle, and she and Rickword had friends in common, among them Wyndham Lewis, with whom she had had a brief and tempestuous *affaire* in Venice, and Robert Nichols, who had showered her with sonnets. Soon after dinner Betty went to bed, leaving them to continue their conversation, which inevitably turned to the colour question. Rickword mentioned that he worked in publishing; he promised to persuade Wishart to include some publications on the subject in his list – an offer of which Nancy made a mental note. Both had been drinking, and when at last they went upstairs Rickword was so drowsy that he unconsciously accompanied her into her bedroom, which was on the same landing as his own, and immediately fell asleep in a chair beside her bed. After a while Betty burst into the room, seized him by the hair and dragged him to his feet, while Nancy slept on, quite unconscious of the disturbance. He meekly accompanied Betty to their room, and next morning explained why he had not followed her to bed. "So you had a serious talk on the colour question?" was her only comment. "I thought so. You didn't half look a fool, flopped in that chair with your mouth open."

They had already reached an understanding that they would separate, and this incident determined that their parting would be sooner rather than later. Betty went to stay with a married couple in Norfolk, and for some time they communicated only by telephone. The four met in London in the autumn, and on impulse took weekend tickets to Dieppe, crossed from Newhaven in a gale and enjoyed such a bibulous evening that they attracted the attention of the gendarmerie. After returning to London Rickword and Betty spent their last evening together at the Greek Street hotel, making a pathetic attempt to talk as if everything were still the same, and went their ways in the morning without animosity, Betty to Norfolk, Rickword to lodgings near Chalk Farm station.

Throughout 1932, fully occupied with his work for Wishart's, he published no original writing except his introduction to *Poet Under Saturn*, but one of his major critical essays appeared early in 1933. His review in the *New Statesman* of a new cheap edition of *The Cambridge History of English Literature*, entitled "Dictionnaire des Idées Reçues", clearly illustrates the revolution in critical standards which had taken place since the war, and to which he had contributed so much. "The volumes of the *History* were issued during the years 1907-16," he wrote,

so if we suppose the contributors to have been aged on an average forty their sensibilities and opinions would have been formed about twenty years earlier... One may recognize many of the symptoms of a romantic convention in its decline: a peculiar irresolute sensuality tending to dissipate itself in day-dreams and generally dignified with the name of idealism, a shrinking from the acceptance of the intellectual factor as vital to literature, a pouting disapprobation of satire, a lack of conviction as the essentiality of form... The notion of the poet as a slightly superior sort of hiker is persistent as a serious canon of criticism, and the conception of nature so brilliantly created by the romantics, and by Wordsworth in particular, is endowed with the prestige of an incontrovertible standard however vaguely applied... Of "Eloisa to Abelard" (the critic) grumbles, "It may be doubted whether, in Pope's fervid tones, we are listening to the voice of nature and passion and not rather to a piece of superb declamation". What is peculiar here is the assumption that the voice of nature and passion is somehow preferable to a piece of superb declamation, that literary art is not quite nice. Even a don, one would think, should have recognised the voice of nature and passion

on his college roof some moonlight night, and human passion, in the
natural state, is not much more articulate than feline, nor a poet's than
a stockbroker's.[5]

This review, the last which he wrote for the *New Statesman*, marks the
end of the period in which his criticism was primarily literary. In his
later writing, although his sensitivity to literature did not decline, social
and political criteria became increasingly important.

The value of his contribution to the critical revolution was fully
recognized by the Cambridge lecturer F.R. Leavis, who showed his
admiration by using the critical essays in the *Calendar of Modern Letters*
for teaching purposes and by selecting the name *Scrutiny* for his critical
quarterly, the first issue of which appeared in May 1932. The choice
of name he himself described in 1963 as "a salute and a gesture of
acknowledgement – an assertion of a kind of continuity of life with
the *Calendar*".[6] The manifesto with which the first issue opened cited
the fact that 'The *Calendar of Letters*, which deserved the whole-hearted
support of the educated, lasted less than three years" as evidence of
"the general dissolution of standards",[7] and later issues contained a
series of "Evaluations" of contemporary thinkers and another of "Revaluations" of writers of the past which were obviously based upon
the "Scrutinies". If the firm of Wishart & Co. was the first offshoot of
the *Calendar* and the two volumes of *Scrutinies* the second, *Scrutiny*
was the third.

Another tribute to the *Calendar* was *Towards Standards of Criticism*,
a selection from its critical articles and reviews edited by Leavis which
Wishart published in May 1933. From among "the really distinguished
critics, each one better than any that finds frequent employment in
existing periodicals",[8] writing for the *Calendar*, Leavis selected work
by Garman, Higgins, Hoare, Holms, Muir, Quennell and the two
Rickwords, but it is Rickword himself who is most fully represented.
The book further enhanced his reputation and that of the *Calendar*.
The Times Literary Supplement commented that "one can imagine no
better corrective than these lively studies to the loose, impressionistic
mode of criticism which is so prevalent". In another review I.M. Parsons
defined the task of critics as "to be intelligent without becoming
academic, and profound without obscurity, to present a solid front
without suspicion of coterie, and be confident without inviting the
charge of priggishness", and added: "The *Calendar* set itself this standard, and paid the price".[9]

The "continuity of life" between the *Calendar* and *Scrutiny* is most
apparent in the field of criticism, where the latter maintained the standards which the former had set. The same cannot be said of poetry and
fiction. The first issue of *Scrutiny* stated that it would publish original

compositions, but pessimistically added: "Since, however, more people are able to write good criticism than good verse or short stories, we commit ourselves to no large or constant proportion of creative work". In fact, the only verse and fiction which it published in its first year of existence were poems by Ronald Bottrall, C.H. Peacock and Selden Rodman and an extract from a novel by Peacock – hardly names which stand comparison with those of the contributors to the *Calendar*. On the other hand, *Scrutiny* devoted far more space to political or social questions. Discussions of such subjects in the *Calendar* had been confined mainly to Wyndham Lewis's contributions; the first issue of *Scrutiny*, however, announced that it would not be "a purely literary review" but would be "seriously preoccupied with the movement of modern civilization".[10] The first three issues contained articles on the political situation, Bentham, war poetry, advertising and various aspects of education, whilst the reviews largely dealt with books on political, social and educational questions. Leavis and his colleagues were not more politically-minded than Rickword and Garman; what had intervened between the *Calendar* and *Scrutiny* was the world economic crisis, which had forced every thinking person to reconsider the nature of society.

In the early days of *Scrutiny* an alliance or at least a fruitful dialogue between the Leavisites and the Marxists seemed possible. Contributors included Communists and Communist sympathizers such as Rickword, whose review of Eliot's *Selected Essays* appeared in the issue for March 1933, Garman, A.L. Morton and Montagu Slater, and other contributors showed themselves not unsympathetic to Marxism, among them Herbert Butterfield, whose study of the Marxist philosophy of history was published in the same issue, and L.C. Knights, whose *Drama and Society in the Age of Jonson* was a near-Marxist contribution to literary history more valuable than any produced by the Marxists in the 1930s. There was even a moment in 1933 when it seemed not impossible that Leavis himself might embrace Marxism. In the issue for December 1932 he claimed that the magazine presented an alternative to both Marxism and Eliot's Anglo-Catholicism and Royalism, but in the following issue he adopted a more positive attitude. "I agree with the Marxist," he wrote, "to the extent of believing some form of economic communism to be inevitable and desirable, in the sense that it is to this that a power-economy of its very nature points, and only by a deliberate and intelligent working towards it can civilization be saved from disaster".[11] In his introduction to *Towards Standards of Criticism* he asked: "Can the intelligent and courageous justify to themselves any but a concern, a direct concern, with fundamentals, with the task of social regeneration? – social regeneration, which means, in the first place, revolution, economic and political?" He went on to take up

Rickword's suggestion in his "Valediction" to the *Calendar* that "the present literary situation requires to be met by a different organization", and hinted that "a campaign for standards in literary criticism, together with the relevant attention to contemporary civilization in general, could be effectively associated with a movement in the educational field".[12] A meeting was actually held in Cambridge in the summer of 1933 which discussed whether *Scrutiny* should become the centre of a movement with its own political programme, but decided against it. Instead it developed into a purely critical journal, the alliance between Leavisites and Marxists broke down, and Rickword, whose first contribution to *Scrutiny* was also his last, was forced to resume his search for a literary journal which would also be a centre for political organization.

In the spring of 1933 Nancy Cunard reappeared in London. Her second visit to America in the previous spring and summer had been even more eventful than her first. The press had published sensational and inaccurate stories about her relationship with Crowder (according to one paper, she had come to New York in pursuit of Paul Robeson) and her attack on her mother, and she received many threatening or obscene letters from racialists. She fought back courageously, and seized on the opportunity to draw attention to the case of the Scottsboro boys, eight black youths who had been sentenced to death in Alabama on a trumped-up charge of rape. After visiting Cuba and Jamaica she returned to France, where she finished putting together the mass of material which she had accumulated for her anthology, originally entitled *Colour* and now renamed *Negro*. As she could not bear to omit anything, it ended up as an enormous work which London publishers proved understandably reluctant to handle, even though she was prepared to cover the costs herself. After Jonathan Cape, Victor Gollancz and other publishers had rejected it, she turned in desperation to Rickword, remembering the promise which he had made her. He not only persuaded Wishart & Co. to publish *Negro* at her expense, but himself contributed an essay on slavery and assisted her with the technical details of preparing the book for publication, often staying up all night to work with her on the proof-reading or other tasks.

Other nights were spent more agreeably, for they soon became lovers. Nancy Cunard was a woman with an intense power over men. Aldous Huxley, who once walked up and down the street beneath her window all night, was obsessed with her, until he wrote her out of his system by introducing her into *Antic Hay* as Myra Viveash. She was strikingly beautiful (a man once called her "incomparably bewitching", another woman "the most beautiful woman I've ever seen"), tall and very slim (she has variously been described as "slim to the point of evanescence", "rail-thin" and "emaciated"), with a small head held erect, eyes which

some saw as "arctic blue" and others as like green jade, short fair hair,
a very white skin, long legs and slender arms and hands, moving with
a distinctive walk – a "delicate dance", "floating… with a little spring
at every step" and "slightly tripping… like a water wagtail's".[13] No
slave to fashion, she dressed well but always in a style of her own
choice. From wrist to elbow her arms were encircled with African ivory
bracelets which she constantly polished, and which were painful when,
playfully or angrily, she boxed a friend's ears or slapped his face. Her
manners were exquisite, even when, as frequently happened, she was
drunk, but when some cruelty or injustice provoked her to anger her
language became violent. She would have felt at home with Clodia and
Sempronia, those patrician ladies of the late Republic who dabbled in
revolutionary politics, and might have inspired Catullus to write greater
poetry than poor Nichols's sonnets.

Rickword knew too much about her to expect fidelity, and did not
consider himself obliged to remain consistently faithful himself. They
took a large studio flat, but when Crowder arrived in London at her
invitation Rickword was unceremoniously bundled out. He did not
particularly resent this, and established friendly relations with Crowder,
whom he found a very acute observer. Crowder, however, was not
prepared either to resume his sexual relationship with her or to play
the political role as a champion of black rights for which she had cast
him, and she returned to Rickword. She rented an attic flat in Percy
Street, in the heart of Fitzrovia, decorated it with Crowder's assistance,
and furnished it with paintings presented to her by some of her many
artistic friends, and with African sculptures, some of them disconcert-
ingly phallic. At first all went well; Crowder had found himself a black
girl friend, and Rickword and Nancy were wholeheartedly engaged in
getting *Negro* into its final shape. By the autumn the bulk of the work
had been done, and both could turn their minds to other things. After
a while he noticed that increasingly often she evaded meeting him in
the evenings, and he resigned himself to looking for another companion.
He found her in Doris Back, a married woman living apart from her
husband, whom he met about this time. "As she was unattached," he
recalled in his memoirs, "I did a little modest wooing."

Negro at last appeared on 15 February 1934, with a dedication to
Crowder, who had inspired it but taken little interest in it, and an
acknowledgement of the help given by Rickword and Nancy's French
lover Raymond Michelet, who between them had done much of the
hard work. The contents of the book, which contained 855 pages and
contributions by about 150 writers, were an extraordinary ragbag –
essays on slavery and slave revolts, lynching, the Scottsboro case, jazz,
Negro music and songs, the West Indies, the colour bar in England,
Pushkin (who was of black descent), ancient African civilizations,

colonial exploitation in modern Africa, the South African pass laws and a host of other subjects, poems by black poets, poems on black themes by white poets, pages of Negro music from Africa and the Americas, and photographs and drawings of African works of art (including Nancy's bracelets). The contributors included William Carlos Williams, Theodore Dreiser, Langston Hughes, William Plomer, Ezra Pound, Norman Douglas, Jomo Kenyatta, the French Surrealist Group and anyone else whom Nancy had been able to rope in. Rickword's scholarly essay, "Slavery Papers", mainly consisted of extracts from the evidence on the slave trade and the treatment of slaves in the British colonies laid before the House of Commons in 1790-91, which were left to speak for themselves with a minimum of comment. The same cannot be said for Nancy's contributions, which were neither scholarly nor objective; on the strength of a visit lasting less than three weeks she wrote a long article on Jamaica, and she inserted editorial notes denouncing as "reactionary" and "treacherous" black leaders and organizations disapproved of by the American Communist Party.

The reception of *Negro* was generally unenthusiastic, although the *Daily Worker* said that "the total effect is revealing, impressive", and called it "a book of enduring value". *The Times Literary Supplement* ignored it, and in the *New Statesman* Lord Olivier, the pioneer Fabian and authority on colonial questions, submitted it to a devastating analysis. After proving that Nancy's essay on Jamaica was grotesquely inaccurate and protesting against her attacks on non-Communist black leaders, he reached the conclusion that "when Miss Cunard writes the manifest nonsense and displays the one-sidedness which cannot but appal any instructed sympathisers she prejudices the whole case of her clients".[14]

But before the book appeared she had already found another good cause to support. The Scottish contingent of the national hunger march of the unemployed left Glasgow on 22 January, the Tyneside contingent set out on 1 February, and by the middle of the month other contingents from all over England and Wales were on the road to London. On 14 February she sent Michelet, together with his copy of *Negro*, a note in which she announced that she was joining the hunger marchers, but it was probably not until 23 February, when they began entering London, that she actually set out, after swearing Crowder to secrecy. She wore a man's overcoat, an airman's helmet and several scarves (partly for warmth, she explained, and partly for disguise), and carried a small film camera. Having joined the marchers, she demonstrated her solidarity with the unemployed by picking up one of them and bringing him back to her flat.

After spending a pleasant evening with Mrs Back, Rickword was escorting her to her lodgings when she discovered that her key was not in her handbag. They knocked on the door, but the landlady had gone to bed. He therefore took her to Percy Street, and as they had already eaten and drunk they went straight to bed and quickly fell asleep. Suddenly he was awakened by the sound of the door opening and the entry of Nancy and a young man, who said threateningly "Get up". He had no sooner got out of bed than Nancy broke a plate on his head, and the hunger marcher knocked him down with a punch on the jaw. Fortunately the flat contained two bedrooms; the intruders withdrew, and as the door had no key he jammed it with a chair under the knob. In the morning he and his companion left early before the others were up. Towards noon Nancy's hunger marcher turned up at Wishart's office in the Adelphi, carrying Rickword's belongings in a suitcase, and obviously embarrassed over his behaviour the night before. Rickword laughed it off over a drink, however, and they parted on friendly terms. When the office closed he met Mrs Back, and they went together to the new lodgings which she had found for them both.

She was born in 1899, the daughter of Frederic Russell Quilter, a civil engineer, and his Irish wife, a member of the Despard family, and was christened Doris Russell. She intensely disliked the name Doris, and was invariably known as "Jonny" – no one seems to know why, but all her surviving friends agree that the male name suited her. After leaving school she worked as a clerk in the Bank of England until 1926, when she married a doctor, Gilbert Back. But suburban domestic bliss was not for her; she soon left him, and for some years lived a bohemian life in London, Paris, Venice and Spain. Tall and dark, with raven-black hair and something of the gipsy or the witch in her appearance, she retained her striking good looks well into middle age, with a little help from hair-dye. Her beauty attracted many admirers, among them artists eager to draw her; one in Paris called her "la belle Irlandaise", another in Venice "la sublime Jonny". A very feminine woman, whose creative energies were expressed in dressmaking and cookery, she nonetheless had many masculine characteristics that complemented the feminine sensibility concealed beneath Rickword's manliness. Energetic, resourceful, uncalculating and utterly without self-pity, she was always prepared to solve Rickword's financial problems for him by starting some small business which rarely succeeded. She could down pint for pint with him, spoke abruptly like an officer's wife and swore like a trooper, yet when necessary she could act the lady to perfection. ("Where are my fucking gloves? I've got to go to tea with the bloody vicar," she was once heard to say.) Above all, she was fiercely loyal to "my poet", whom she deeply admired even while launching violent tirades at him when his phlegmatic silence infuriated her. Living with her, a friend has said, "was a little like dwelling on the lower slopes of a volcano",* yet there was a quality of passion in their relationship that kept him going. "An inspiration to meet" was the verdict of a young man who knew her when she was in her fifties,† but the highest tribute ever paid her was the fact that Rickword remained in love with her throughout their thirty years together.

In February 1934 he began living with Jonny; he also joined the Communist Party. He had been moving in that direction at least since 1930, and probably since the general strike, but now the world situation forced him to a firm commitment. His intellectual development, typical of many of his generation, he summed up in a review of Alick West's *One Man in His Time*, which in describing West's book is clearly auto-biographical:

> The armistice of 1918 meant return to the relative freedom of a well-to-do middle class environment, whose associations and social values were supposedly held in common...The twenties were a time of great intellectual excitement, philosophies competing for allegiance abounded and old frontiers in the arts were dissolving...It seemed that final decisions might be deferred indefinitely. But by the end of the decade the underlying social malaise had erupted. The developing economic depression and rise of German fascism were alarmingly evident...The success of the first Soviet five-year plan appeared to be an irrefutable assurance of the superiority of socialist co-operation to competitive capitalism..."[15]

Under the impact of the depression Rickword began to study Marxism from about 1929 onwards. He read widely – *The Communist Manifesto*, the historical chapters of *Capital*, compilations of the comments of Marx and Engels on literature, English and French popularizations such as those of John Strachey – but his studies did not go very deep. Neither the philosophical nor the economic aspects of Marxism greatly interested him; Jack Lindsay believed that a firmer grasp of dialectical materialism would have provided him with the inspiration to continue writing poetry. The nature of his humanistic Marxism is perhaps best defined in two remarks which he made many years later: "I am convinced of the political responsibilities of the writer. But I would interpret 'political' in the widest sense, as being a concern with the fate of human beings, in general and in particular." "I am a Marxist in the sense that I try to relate public happenings to the tissue of cause and effect which he (i.e. Marx) divined in the interplay of material and economic forces."[16] His friend Eric Homberger got to the root of the matter when he wrote: "Marxism provided a basis for thinking that a redeployment of social resources would lead to a better form of society, a better way

* Jack Beeching, in a letter.

† Paul Allen, in a letter. My picture of Jonny is largely derived from accounts sent to me by Mr Beeching and Mr Allen.

of life. In that aspiration for a more completely realized and fulfilled life we see the essential community between the *Calendar of Modern Letters*...and the *Left Review*."[17]

But why was it that in February 1934 he made his decision? Personal factors, such as his daily contact with Nancy, with her strong Communist sympathies, and his study of colonialism and racialism while working on *Negro*, no doubt played a part, but political and social developments at home and abroad were more important. Official figures published in January and February showed that there were 10,702,000 registered unemployed in the United States, 4,058,000 in Germany and 2,389,068 in Britain, and the unemployment question was kept in the public mind throughout February by the advance of the hunger marchers on London, culminating in a mass demonstration in Hyde Park on 25 February, in which it was estimated that 100,000 people took part. In glaring contrast to the economic failure of capitalism were reports from the Soviet Union. The seventeenth Communist Party congress, the "congress of victors", held in January and February, celebrated the completion of the First Five-Year Plan in four years and the abolition of unemployment, and approved the Second Plan, which forecast a 214% increase in industrial production in the five years 1933-37.

Meanwhile the advance of Fascism continued, bringing nearer the threat of war. The news from Germany was of the shooting of political prisoners "while trying to escape", of the arrest of Protestant pastors who resisted Nazi control of the Evangelical Church, of growing tension between the Government and the Catholic Church. *The Times* on 27 February reviewed *Germany, Prepare for War*, by Professor Ewald Banse, which advocated German annexation of Holland, Flanders, Austria and much of Eastern Europe. In France Fascist mobs on 6 February threatened to storm the Palais Bourbon and lynch the deputies and were routed only after the police opened fire. A general strike on 12 February in protest against the attempted Fascist coup was supported by 75% of manual and white-collar workers, and in Paris 150,000 Socialists and Communists demonstrated side by side. In Austria on the same day a coup by the clerical-Fascist Chancellor Dollfuss, which was resisted by the Social Democratic workers, launched a four-day civil war; heavy artillery reduced Vienna's working-class flats to ruins, and before the firing ended hangings of those guilty of defending the constitution had already begun. Sir Oswald Mosley's Blackshirts in Britain and General O'Duffy's Blueshirts in Ireland were growing in strength and did not lack friends in high places. The *Daily Mail* published on 15 January an article by its proprietor Lord Rothermere, entitled "Hurrah for the Blackshirts", and his *Evening News* also proclaimed its support. Sections of the Conservative press expressed approval of Dollfuss's methods of dealing with Socialists.

Rickword later said that the Paris riots of 6 February were the decisive event that helped him to make up his mind. Paris to him was the capital of civilization, and now the barbarians were threatening to take it by storm. He hated unemployment, Fascism and war alike as outrages; his feelings on the National Government's treatment of the unemployed are apparent in the preface which he wrote to *Disallowed*.[18] It was the Communists, he saw, who had taken action on the unemployment issue by organizing the hunger march, despite the opposition of the Labour Party leadership, and thereby had so stirred the public conscience that the Government was forced in April to restore the cuts in unemployment benefit made in 1931. It was the Communist Party which was most active in exposing the nature of the Nazi regime, in opposing Fascism at home and in warning of the danger of war. "The Communist Party seemed to be the only one that was actually *doing* something," he explained in 1975. "And that was why I joined."[19]

X. *Left Review*

RICKWORD'S Communist Party membership lost him a number of friends, notably Roy Campbell who, despite his macho stance, tended to follow the opinions of those under whose influence he was at the time. When he was close to Rickword he held radical views which found expression in powerful poems such as "The Serf" and "The Zulu Girl"; after 1927, when he was associated with Wyndham Lewis, he moved ever farther to the right; and in 1935 his wife persuaded him to enter the Catholic Church. Both he and Rickword felt a certain regret at the breach between them. "He was very good fun, by no means a fool," Rickword recalled in 1975. "I don't know much about communism," Campbell wrote at the time of his conversion, "but I have seen that many valiant and generous men take up that form of imitation-christianity. But they are not happy."[1] He may well have had Rickword in mind.

Campbell was not the only one of Rickword's literary associates who adopted a Fascist or near-Fascist position at this time. "Only an imbecile could not be changed by such an atmosphere – but not necessarily towards the Left," he later said. "Numbers of my [intellectual] acquaintances spoke quite openly of the need to crush any further encroachments by the working-class!"[2] J.C. Squire, who had begun his political career in a Marxist party, the Social Democratic Federation, and had published a collection of satirical anti-war poems in 1916, afterwards moved on via Fabianism and Liberalism to an admiration of Mussolini, whom he described as "a nice Napoleon", and in 1934 became chairman of the extreme right-wing January Club. In the previous year he had been rewarded for his trajectory with a knighthood. Wyndham Lewis praised Hitler for several years from 1931 and contributed to the first number of Mosley's *British Union Quarterly* in 1937, together with Campbell, Ezra Pound and Vidkun Quisling, although after visiting Germany later in the same year he retracted his pro-Nazi views.

As might be expected, the virulently anti-Semitic Potocki became an enthusiastic Fascist, and in 1936 founded his *Right Review* as a counter-blast to *Left Review*, which Rickword was then editing. The two met for the last time when Rickword was walking along the Strand in an anti-Fascist demonstration, and saw Potocki on the pavement in his red medieval robe, with his younger and shorter brother Cedric beside him in a blue version of the same costume, both with their right arms raised in the Fascist salute. After his return to Australia P.R. Stephensen, who had once been a Communist, became a leading member of the

Australia First organization, which advocated Australian neutrality in the Second World War and adopted a pro-German and pro-Japanese attitude, with the result that he was interned. An even more surprising convert was the gentle nature-lover Edmund Blunden. Hoping to avert war by promoting friendship between Britain and Germany, as late as July 1939 he could write of his visits to Nazi Germany:

> The prevailing sense I had, and it does not fade, was of a great clearness and freshness of life, a pervading revival of national dignity and personal unselfishness; something like the quality that Wordsworth once knew in France and expresses in a famous passage of *The Prelude*.

As Rickword ruefully put it in later years, "some of my best friends were fascists".[3]

If he lost some friends, he gained many more. Early in 1934 he was present when about fifteen left-wing writers met in a room over the Fitzroy and decided to form a British section of the International Union of Revolutionary Writers, generally known as the Writers' International. Among those present, according to his later recollections, were Hugh MacDiarmid, Tom Wintringham, Ralph Fox, John Strachey, Amabel Williams-Ellis, Sylvia Townsend Warner, Montagu Slater, Alec Brown and A.L. Lloyd. A conference which met at the Conway Hall on 20 February formally established the British Section of the Writers' International, elected an executive committee consisting of Strachey, Fox and Michael Davidson, with Wintringham as secretary and Rickword as treasurer, and adopted a rather verbose statement of aims. This document, after denouncing "the decadence of the past twenty years of English literature and the theatre", which, it declared, marked "the collapse of a culture, accompanying the collapse of an economic system", extended an invitation to join the association to middle-class writers who "consider that the best in the civilization of the past can only be preserved and further developed by joining in the struggle of the working class for a new socialist society", to working-class writers who "desire to express in their work, more effectively than in the past, the struggle of their class", and to all writers "who will use their pens and their influence against imperialist war and in defence of the Soviet Union".[4]

Of those named by Rickword as present at the Fitzroy meeting only Wintringham, Fox and Slater were certainly members of the Communist Party at that time. MacDiarmid, Sylvia Townsend Warner and Rickword himself were soon to join it, however, whilst Strachey supported its policies and his sister Amabel usually followed his lead. There is no doubt that the founding of the British Section of the Writers' International, which had its headquarters in Moscow and consistently conformed to the party line, was organized by the Communist Party

and that the driving force behind it was Wintringham. Born in the same
year as Rickword, he was the son of a Nonconformist solicitor, and
during the war served in the Royal Flying Corps. He studied at Oxford
at the same time as Rickword, although they do not seem to have met,
and joined the Communist Party on its formation. In 1920-21 he spent
six months in Russia, where he was deeply impressed by the idealism
and dedication of the young Bolsheviks, and met the dying John Reed.
As one of the twelve Communists imprisoned for sedition in 1925 he
was unable to practise his profession as a lawyer, and instead devoted
himself to journalism, writing vigorous prose, mainly on military topics,
and verse which occasionally rose above mediocrity.

At the time when Rickword joined the Communist Party the international Communist movement was in some confusion. In 1928, when
economists were prophesying that the current boom would continue
indefinitely, the Communist International warned that after the post-war
revolutionary period and the subsequent period of temporary stabiliza-
tion the world was entering a third period of economic crises, wars and
revolutions. From this analysis it inferred that it was essential to win the
proletariat away from the influence of the Social Democratic parties, and
for the next five years the world's Communist parties pursued ultra-left
policies of the type which Lenin had described as "an infantile disorder",
denouncing Social Democrats as "Social Fascists" and even as an enemy
more dangerous than Fascism itself. The consequences were disastrous,
for in Germany the mutual hostility of Communists and Social Democrats
facilitated Hitler's rise and the destruction of the Communist Party. The
British party isolated itself from its allies in the trade union movement
and the left wing of the Labour Party, and by the end of 1930 had dwindled
to an insignificant sect of some 2,500 members. Even after the victory
of Nazism the Comintern refused to admit that its policies were bankrupt,
and rejected an offer by the Second International to negotiate on joint
action against Fascism. The Paris riots of 6 February 1934 forced the
world Communist movement to face facts. Under pressure from their
own members, the French Communist leaders agreed to support the
Socialist-led general strike and demonstrations of 12 February.
Although both the Comintern and the Communist parties found it
difficult to adjust their way of thinking to the new situation; after much
manoeuvring a formal agreement on unity of action between the French
Communist and Socialist parties was signed in July, and in 1935 the
alliance was broadened to include the Radicals. The change of policy
on an international scale was completed when the Seventh World Congress of the Comintern approved the policy of the Popular Front, which
envisaged the formation of the broadest possible alliance against Fascism,
including non-Socialists as well as Socialists.

The position of those intellectuals who, like Rickword, had joined the British party in increasing numbers since the Depression, and especially since the establishment of the Nazi regime, was transformed by this change of policy. In the 1920s the proportion of intellectuals in its membership had been far smaller than in the French and German parties, and most of those who had been members since its foundation had degenerated into professional apologists for Moscow, able to provide a plausible justification for every twist and turn in the party line. A few graduates with more independent minds had joined the party in the 1920s, but in general intellectuals had been viewed with mistrust, especially during the "third period". The best-known of the party's theoreticians, R. Palme Dutt, noted with satisfaction in 1932 that a proposal for the formation of specialized groups of intellectuals inside the party had been "nipped in the bud", and asserted that an intellectual who became a Communist should *"forget that he is an intellectual* (except in moments of necessary self-criticism) *and remember only that he is a Communist."*[5] This attitude explains why a British section of the Writers' International was not formed until 1934, although similar bodies had been established in Germany in 1928, in the United States in 1929 and in France in 1932. With the adoption of the Popular Front policy all this was changed; the party headquarters in King Street realized that if it was to co-operate with middle-class Liberals and aristocratic Conservatives who were opposed to Fascism, it could hardly cold-shoulder the intellectuals in its own ranks, and that they might even be able to make a useful contribution to the party's activities.

Such an organization as the British Section of the Writers' International obviously needed a magazine of its own, and a quarterly called *Viewpoint* appeared in April. The first issue was also the last, for it was decided to replace it by a monthly with a more aggressive title, and in October *Left Review*, launched on a capital of £27, was published from Collet's Bookshop (formerly Fred Henderson's "Bomb Shop") at 66 Charing Cross Road. For the first fifteen issues the editorial board consisted of Montagu Slater, Amabel Williams-Ellis and Tom Wintringham. Alick West was added in April 1935. In the issue for January 1936, however, it was announced that they had found that, in view of the magazine's increasing scope and the pressure of their other work, "it would be more efficient to concentrate editorial duties", and that Rickword had taken over the editorship. Although it was also stated that "the editorial board is being enlarged to extend the influence of the Review", no details were given of the new board's membership; Donald Kitchin was named as the assistant editor in the issues from February to May and Derek Kahn from June onwards, with Kitchin as manager, and a leaflet issued in June 1937 also named Stephen Spender, Cecil Day Lewis and Randall Swingler as members. Whatever their role, there is no doubt that for the eighteen months that he held the editorship Rickword was mainly responsible for the magazine's contents.

Ever since the demise of the *Calendar* he had been thinking in terms of a magazine which would be at the centre of a movement with both literary and political aims, and in *Left Review* he had found it. Nominally the organization, the British Section of the Writers' International, predated the magazine, but in practice *Left Review* tended to create its own organization; in April 1935, for example, a contributors' conference was held at Conway Hall under the chairmanship of Ralph Fox, who reported that its circulation had reached about 3,000. The British Section of the International was most useful in the opportunities it offered for maintaining contact with writers from abroad. Mrs Williams-Ellis attended the first conference of the Union of Soviet Writers in August 1934, and reported on it at length in the second issue of *Left Review*. The same issue announced the establishment of a fund for the relief of imprisoned German writers and their families in memory of Erich Mühsam, the revolutionary poet murdered in a concentration camp and asked for contributions to be sent to Rickword as its treasurer.

The British Section of the Writers' International, a product of the transition from the "third period" to the Popular Front, lasted less than eighteen months. An International Congress of Writers for the Defence of Culture, convened by a committee of French writers which included André Gide, Henri Barbusse, Romain Rolland and André Malraux, met in Paris in June 1935, and brought together representatives from 38 countries. The English delegation included not only Fox, Strachey and Mrs Williams-Ellis but also E.M. Forster and Aldous Huxley. The congress concluded its deliberations by setting up an International Association of Writers for the Defence of Culture, with a central committee on which Gide, Rolland, Thomas and Heinrich Mann, Forster and Huxley sat side by side with the Communists Maxim Gorky and Barbusse. The Writers' International and its national sections subsequently dissolved themselves and merged with the new organization.

Left Review was itself very much a Popular Front publication, in that it brought together anti-Fascists of all shades, from Communists to Liberals. Its regular contributors fell into five main groups. There was the small nucleus of Communists who had joined the party before the Depression, Wintringham, Ralph Fox, Montagu Slater and A.L. Morton. Fox, a Yorkshireman, had been a contemporary of Rickword and Wintringham at Oxford, and visited Russia in 1922 with the Friends' Relief Mission, acquiring an interest in Asian society which was later to inform his biography of Genghis Khan. He became a Communist in 1926, and thereafter devoted to journalism and propaganda gifts which might have won him a high reputation as a novelist, historian or critic. Slater, the son of a Methodist tailor, won a scholarship to

Oxford, worked as a journalist and joined the Communist Party, probably in 1927. He and Rickword already knew each other, for he had contributed an essay on modern art to *Scrutinies II*. A little man of enormous energy, he had written two novels and much unpublished verse, and was to write six more novels, prose and verse plays, film and television scripts, pageants and the libretto for Benjamin Britten's *Peter Grimes*, which remains his best-known work. Morton, a farmer's son from Suffolk and the only Cambridge graduate among the four, had worked as a teacher, contributed poems to the *London Aphrodite* and kept a second-hand bookshop before joining the staff of the *Daily Worker*. He shared with Rickword a tongue-tied shyness in company and a deep love of England, and especially the Eastern counties, its literature and its radical tradition.

The second group of contributors had recently joined or were soon to join the Communist Party, or fully supported it without joining it. Besides Rickword himself, they included Garman, Nancy Cunard, John Strachey, Mrs Williams-Ellis, Alec Brown, F.D. Klingender, Alick West, Sylvia Townsend Warner, Valentine Ackland and Randall Swingler, whilst Jack Lindsay was to join their number in 1936. Among these Rickword formed a particular friendship with Sylvia Townsend Warner. The daughter of a housemaster at Harrow, an authority on Tudor church music, sharing a cottage in Dorset with her intimate woman companion Valentine Ackland and a cat called Tom, dividing her time between the cultivation of her garden and the writing of poems, novels and short stories rich in wit and fantasy, she did not conform to the popular conception of a Communist, yet she was as resolute in her convictions as Rickword himself. A third group, which included Storm Jameson, Naomi Mitchison, Winifred Holtby, Phyllis Bentley, Hamilton Fyfe, Eric Gill, Herbert Read and George Barker, was more heterogeneous. Jameson and Fyfe were Labour Party members, Gill a Catholic, Read moving towards Anarchism, but they were all prepared to join with Communists in a common front against Fascism.

Inevitably, *Left Review* attracted the group of younger writers which revolved around W.H. Auden. Among them only Edward Upward was a Communist in 1934, although Cecil Day Lewis became one in 1936 and Stephen Spender held a party card for a short period in 1937, but all of them professed left-wing sympathies. They also possessed a gift for making themselves visible and stayed in the public eye. They proved a valuable acquisition for the Popular Front campaign. The editors of *Left Review* were therefore pleased to print poems by Auden, who sent them the opening chorus of *The Dog Beneath the Skin*, Day Lewis, Rex Warner and John Lehmann and prose by Day Lewis, Upward, Lehmann and Spender, and devoted considerable space to reviews of their writings. At times the critics, who included Rickword, seem to be wrestling with them for the good of their souls, at others they give an impression of growing impatience at their inability to advance beyond vaguely revolutionary phrasemongering or "a well-intentioned liberalism".[6] These differences did not prevent Rickword from extending an invitation to Day Lewis and Spender to become regular contributors, which they accepted.

The least-known contributors to *Left Review*, though not necessarily the least important, were the proletarian writers. The concept of proletarian literature, which may be defined as literature about working-class life written by members of that class from their distinctive point of view, had been the subject of heated controversy in the Soviet Union, and had been much discussed in Germany, the United States and elsewhere. In Britain, although occasional proletarian novels had been published, including Robert Tressell's classic *The Ragged Trousered Philanthropists* (1914) and Harold Heslop's *The Gate of a Strange Field* (1929), little attention had been paid to the idea, and the British Section of the Writers' International made the development of a proletarian literature one of its primary aims. "That was basically the thing we most wanted to do," Rickword said in 1975.

> We didn't want to fill the pages with our own stuff. And we hoped that through the party and also the W.E.A., the Workers' Musical Association and the one or two drama groups – that sort of thing – working people would get to hear of us and send us their work. It seemed reasonable to imagine that there must be a good deal of work painfully written out on old school sheets, old school books, exercise books.[7]

Left Review attempted to promote proletarian literature by publishing stories, reportage, poems and extracts from novels or plays submitted by working-class writers, and by offering prizes for the best piece of writing on a set theme, such as a shift at work or a strike. The results in some respects were gratifying, over forty entries being received for one competition. Those whose stories or competition entries were printed included engineering workers, clothing workers, miners, seamen, agricultural workers, a clerk, a hotel porter and a waitress – evidence of the wide – if sparse – public which *Left Review* reached. Some of the material printed in the earlier issues was extremely naïve, and concentrated so exclusively on the sufferings of the working class that the effect was merely depressing; indeed, Wintringham complained that "our post, several times a week, brings us a story ending with a suicide".[8] Other stories, however, by unknown as well as by previously published authors, had a strength, directness and honesty derived from the fact that they wrote from personal experience, felt deeply about their subject and were able to convey the quality of their experience and their feelings. Among the authors only James Hanley, a former seaman and railway worker, and Ralph Bates, a former engineering worker, docker and fisherman, were well-known before *Left Review* appeared, but several others were sooner or later to achieve recognition – the Welsh poet Idris Davies, a miner turned teacher; A.L. Lloyd, who had laid the foundations of his encyclopedic knowledge of folk song while working on Australian sheep stations and was to extend it while sailing on a whaler; the north-country seaman and short-story writer George Garrett; and a whole group of Jewish workers from London, such as Willy Goldman, author of *East End My Cradle*. Rickword commented:

> The real triumphs of the socially conscious literature of the time were not individual achievements…The real triumph was the drawing into the cultural ambit of a significant number of men and women who were barricaded out from participation in what was regarded as a middle-class preserve. Our aim was a political one, to eradicate Fascism, and this could only be done by the fullest co-operation of the masses. Fascism in Germany had succeeded in giving them the fake dignity of a uniform and a death-wish. We hoped they would find their way to self-expression and life-wish.[9]

There were other aspects of *Left Review*, even before Rickword took over the editorship, with which he could identify and for which he may have been partly responsible. Freedom of the press was one. The first issue contained a protest against the Government's Incitement to Disaffection Bill which was also an impassioned defence of all forms of freedom of expression. "Writers have only too good reason to know that the censorship under a dozen old laws is so effective that two of the most interesting novels of our generation have still to be published abroad," it stated.

> There is open censorship of plays and films and it is used not to suppress vulgarity but to check thought, whether on politics or morals. It is only two years since the London police were able to get a conviction against a poet for the crime of offering poems in manuscript to a printer. The poems were not published except (technically) to printer and police: but the poet was imprisoned…[10]

The references to *Ulysses* and *Lady Chatterley's Lover* and to the Potocki case strongly suggest that this statement was written by Rickword. Later issues protested against the banning as "obscene" of James Hanley's novel *Boy* and a scientific work, *The Sexual Impulse*, the refusal of bill-posting firms to display a Communist Party poster calling for action against the Italian invasion of Abyssinia, and the film censor's refusal to grant a certificate to an anti-war film.

Another feature of *Left Review*, in the healthiest traditions of English radicalism, was its disrespect for the monarchy. What Rickword described as "the super-exploitation of the Royal Family" was in full swing at the time. The Duke of Kent's marriage in 1934 was made the subject of what Hamilton Fyfe called "several weeks' loud and repetitive newspaper drum-beating", and was followed in May 1935 by the celebration of George V's Silver Jubilee, against which *Left Review* published a dignified protest, pointing out that the events of the past 25 years – the First World War and mass unemployment – "have been of a character which forbids rejoicing".[11] The signatories included not only Rickword and other regular contributors, but also G.D.H. and Margaret Cole, the young poet Gavin Ewart, the novelist Walter Greenwood and Bertram Higgins, whose name here appeared in association with those of Rickword and Garman for the last time. The same issue also contained a satirical poem by Garman and reprinted Landor's even more biting lines on the first four Georges, as a reminder that English poets had not always been subservient to the monarchy.

There were features of *Left Review* in its early days with which Rickword may have been less sympathetic. Discussion on the statement of aims adopted by the British Section of the Writers' International ran through several issues, producing more heat than light. Alec Brown asserted, with all the emphasis of capitals, that LITERARY ENGLISH FROM CAXTON TO US IS AN ARTIFICIAL JARGON OF THE RULING CLASS; WRITTEN ENGLISH BEGINS WITH US, to which Montagu Slater retorted "Fortunately it doesn't". Sherard Vines expressed the hope that "defence of the Soviet Union" did not mean "one's Soviet right or wrong". The phrase "the decadence of the past twenty years of English literature" proved particularly controversial. Slater considered that the decadence went back not twenty but 150 years, and Wintringham detected the beginnings of it in Blake. Vines suggested that talk of "the collapse of a culture" was wishful thinking, and the Scottish novelist Lewis Grassic Gibbon dismissed the whole idea as "bolshevik blah".[12] The fact that Rickword took no part in the controversy suggests that he regarded it as futile.

Although *Left Review* published some verse in nearly every issue, he did not contribute any until it had been appearing for over three years. Several of the regular contributors felt a need to assert their Communist faith in poetic form, with unfortunate results. Day Lewis, Wintringham, Sylvia Townsend Warner, Richard Goodman, Rex Warner, Valentine Ackland and John Lehmann all contributed forcible-feeble sloganizing poems; the one poem of this type which is an artistic success is A.L. Morton's "So I Became...", an autobiographical statement which avoids stock rhetoric.[13] Rickword was more than ever determined not to attempt to write poetry when his imagination was not at work.

What he did contribute to the first fifteen issues was an essay and five reviews. *Straws for the Wary*, the first piece of writing which he published after joining the Communist Party, has something of the character of a personal testament. When, to illustrate his point that "the emotional foundations of Fascism...are predominantly adolescent", he remarks that "dressing-up, the gang-spirit, the devotion to the Leader, were an important part of existence up till the age of fourteen" he is obviously recalling his boyhood exploits with Town and Brand. There is more autobiography in his statement that "the conviction of the advance of reason and of the progress of social reform had been severely checked by the forced participation of many of the intelligentsia in the War". Much of the essay is an embittered protest against *la trahison des clercs*, the flight from reason of writers whom he had once respected: Eliot, who "poultices his poetic malaise with dreams of a world of catholic, classic tradition which would restore the human dignity the loss of which he has consistently exploited as the subject matter of his poems"; Lawrence, whom he had sought as a contributor to the *Calendar*, and who "tried to depict the 'primitive' sort of life in which he would have been able to function naturally"; Huxley, another contributor to the *Calendar*, "who from his novels one would judge to have passed his life without much contact with the variety of human beings". Some intellectuals had openly embraced Fascism, such as Squire, "an ex-Fabian, recently rewarded with a knighthood for his long services in keeping any taint of serious living interest out of the very extensive literary domains which have come under his sway". The whole essay, which ends with an impassioned appeal to resist Fascism and war, "not only in their more obvious physical manifestations, but in the subtler emotional forms they take in literature, philosophy and art", is in effect a summary of Rickword's emotional journey since the ending of the *Calendar*.[14]

His other contributions to *Left Review* in 1934-35 throw more light on that journey. In his review of *We Did Not Fight*, a collection of essays by opponents of the Great War, he makes clear the decisive part played by hatred of war in his conversion to Marxism. "Where then, seventeen years after the end of the Great War, and on the verge of a greater one, is that moral integrity to be found which is an essential part of the full life for the worker and the intellectual?" he asks. "It can only arise out of a harmony between knowledge and action. The advance in knowledge necessitates the transformation of pacifism into offensive action against the causes of war."[15] His review of Spender's *The Destructive Element* deals sympathetically with the doubts of an intellectual hesitating on the brink of Communism, as he himself had done for some years. In his comments on Upton Sinclair's *Mammonart* and Philip Henderson's *Literature* he warned against a temptation to which intellectual converts to Marxism sometimes yielded, the inverted snobbery which made Sinclair reject Shakespeare and Balzac and Henderson sneer at Byron and Darwin.

When rebuking such philistinism, one suspects, he also had in mind some of the opinions expressed in the recent controversy in *Left Review*.

To balance these negative criticisms, he declared a positive ideal in his review of the Nonesuch Press edition of Swift's selected writings: "Swift, both for his matter and for the simple tremendous strength of his style, should be a master for every revolutionary writer".[16] Wishart & Co. had announced in 1934 a forthcoming selection from Swift's poems edited by Rickword; it was probably the discovery that the Nonesuch Press was about to publish a fuller selection that led to the abandonment of this project. Of this edition nothing has survived except a typed statement explaining the principles on which the contents had been selected and some almost illegible notes, probably for the preface. One passage brings out, in its application to Swift of the unexpected adjective "lovable", Rickword's deep attachment to him:

> What a lovable figure, but one lovable only by the pure in heart – hence the rancour of a split intelligence like Thackeray – but the testimony of the best men of his day – vide his correspondence – love of Swift almost a touchstone – hence the semi-failure of the Addison abortive friendship (whose weakness was spotted by Pope) and the success of Coleridge.

Rickword's intense admiration for a Tory High Churchman has surprised some critics who do not share his wide knowledge of history and of Swift's writings. He knew that the new Tory Party which emerged in the 1690s under the leadership of the former left-wing Whig Robert Harley was hostile to standing armies, foreign alliances and wars fought for trade and colonies, which enriched City stockjobbers at the taxpayers' expense; that when in opposition it struggled against political corruption and for more frequent elections; that much of the most effective political satire and social protest of the eighteenth century came from Tories such as Pope, Gay, Johnson and Goldsmith; and that when the Tory Party died out in the 1760s many of its supporters found no inconsistency in transferring their support to the Wilkesites and the cause of radical reform. He also knew that Swift carried the radical element in Toryism farther than most of his contemporaries, as in his defence of the Irish people. His incisive prose and verse style, his courage and above all his moral integrity made him a master for Rickword, despite the differences in their ideologies.

1936, the year in which *Left Review* began to appear under Rickword's editorship, was of major importance in the history of the Communist Party. In the early months Mussolini's aggression triumphed in Abyssinia; and in March German troops occupied the demilitarized Rhineland, in defiance of the Treaty of Versailles. Other developments were more promising. The Spanish elections in February resulted in a victory for the Popular Front and the formation of a Liberal Government, supported from outside by the Socialists and Communists. The French elections in May resulted in a Popular Front victory; the Socialists became the largest group in the Chamber, the Communists greatly increased their vote and their representation, and the new Government was headed by the Socialist leader, Léon Blum. Throughout Europe the Left began to hope that the tide had turned at last. Then on 18 July came the military uprising in Spain, openly backed almost from the first by Germany and Italy. In November, when Madrid seemed about to fall, the International Brigade helped defend the city. The civil war had become an international war, in which the Left saw forces of freedom, progress and social justice aligned against Fascism. There were battles, too, on the streets of London. On 4 October when Mosley's Blackshirts attempted to stage a provocative march through the largely Jewish districts of Whitechapel and Stepney, they found the road barred by thousands of East Enders, and the attempts of the police to force a way through for them were unsuccessful. A week later the Fascists took their revenge by beating up Jews and smashing the windows of Jewish shops in the Mile End Road. On 7 November 2,000 hunger marchers converged on London, welcomed by a mass demonstration in Hyde Park. All these events attracted new recruits to the Communist Party, whose membership increased from 7,700 in July 1935 to 12,250 in May 1937.

Alarm at the threat of Fascism and the prospect of war and indignation at the Government's treatment of the victims of poverty and unemployment stimulated a host of new intellectual and artistic movements. In May 1936 Victor Gollancz launched the Left Book Club, the membership of which reached 40,000 within nine months. On the committee which made the monthly selection, Gollancz and H.J. Laski were Labour Party members and only John Strachey was a Marxist, but its avowed policy was to build a British Popular Front; about a third of the books chosen were by Communists, and Communists played an active part in forming the Club's local groups. In the spring of 1936, the Bodley Head published the first volume of *New Writing* as an anthology of anti-Fascist work. Most of the British writers represented in it were drawn from the same categories as those who appeared in *Left Review* – members of the Auden group such as John Lehmann (the editor), Spender, Isherwood and Upward; Communists such as Fox, Wintringham and Alec Brown; and proletarian writers such as Ralph Bates and Gore Graham.

Similar movements were stirring in the theatre. The Group Theatre produced Auden and Isherwood's *The Dog Beneath the Skin* in January 1936, and the more openly Left Theatre put on Montagu Slater's *Easter 1916* in December 1935 and his *Stay Down Miner* five months later. More proletarian was the amateur Unity Theatre, which began its activities in February 1936. Surrealism made its belated appearance in Britain, with an exhibition of Surrealist art in London in June and the publication of the magazine *Contemporary Poetry and Prose*. Although British Marxists were sceptical of Surrealism, its leading literary advocates – Herbert Read, Hugh Sykes Davies, David Gascoyne and Roger Roughton – regarded themselves as revolutionists, politically as well as artistically. In other fields, both the Artists' International Association and the Workers' Musical Association were in effect Popular Front organizations. Of these publications, movements and organizations only *Left Review* and Unity Theatre were clearly under Communist control, but Communists and fellow-travellers were prominent in all of them. By 1936, in fact, the Communist Party, rather to its own surprise, found itself at the centre of something like an artistic Renaissance; *Left Review* chronicled it: it was largely conducted by the magazine's regular contributors.

The party strengthened control over the literary side of the movement by amalgamating Wishart & Co. with its own publishing business, Martin Lawrence.* Wishart & Co. had begun as a literary publishing house, but as Rickword, Garman and Wishart himself moved to the left their choice of books became increasingly political. Their list of publications for 1935 included, among others, the proletarian novel *Last Cage Down*, by the Communist miner Harold Heslop; political novels such as Montagu Slater's *Haunting Europe*, Walter Schoenstedt's *Shot Whilst Escaping* and Ramón Sender's *Earmarked for Hell*; Soviet books – Karl Radek's *Portraits and Pamphlets* and an anthology of Soviet literature; and directly political books, Wintringham's *The Coming World War* and Subhas Chandra Bose's *The Indian Struggle* among them. From King Street's point of view this was gratifying but also disturbing. Although Rickword had already joined the party and Garman and Wishart followed his example, probably in 1936, all three were still naïve politically; when they published books by Radek, Bose and the black revolutionary George Padmore they failed to appreciate that none of them was then in favour with the Kremlin. King Street's duty was clear; the Conditions of Adherence to the Communist International laid down that "all party publishing houses must be completely subordinated to the party Presidium", and that they "must not be allowed to abuse their independence and pursue a policy which is not wholly in accordance with the policy of the party".[17] By whatever means it was brought about, Wishart & Co. and Martin Lawrence were amalgamated on 27 February 1936 as Lawrence & Wishart, which became the party's official publishing house.

The board of directors consisted of Wishart, Rickword, Garman and

---

* "Martin Lawrence" was a code name; the initials ML stood for "Marx and Lenin".

three representatives of what had been Martin Lawrence, and at their first meeting on 4 March Wishart was elected chairman. Whereas Martin Lawrence had been almost exclusively a political publisher, the new firm at first continued Wishart's policy of combining political books with creative writing and literary criticism, and in 1936-37 published novels by John Sommerfield, Mulk Raj Anand, Paul Nizan and the Welsh miner Lewis Jones, plays by Slater and Gorky, and critical works by Fox, Alick West and T.A. Jackson. In the spring of 1937 it took over the publication of *New Writing* from the Bodley Head and reissued the first volume in a cheap edition. The outlook seemed fair for a publishing house which would promote progressive politics and avant-garde literature.

As editor of *Left Review* Rickword was as concerned with maintaining literary quality as he had been when editing the *Calendar*. After he took control it rapidly assumed a far more professional appearance, both in the writing and in the production. The issue for January 1936 introduced photographic illustrations for the first time, making possible the publication of serious art criticism. From the April issue onwards the layout was improved, and regular articles on the theatre and the cinema appeared; the size of each issue was increased from 48 to 64 pages. However welcome these changes might be, what really mattered to the editor was the quality of the writing.

Here the magazine's policy of devoting considerable space to proletarian literature presented a problem. Rickword believed in "this creative upsurge, this rapidly growing desire for, and power of, expression by the workers", and affirmed his commitment to it in an editorial.[18] He was largely responsible for the policy of publishing proletarian novels pursued by Wishart & Co, and continued by Lawrence & Wishart. Several notable working-class writers were published in *Left Review* for the first time while it was under his editorship, including Willy Goldman, Leslie Halward, Fred Urquhart, Lewis Jones, John Sommerfield and the dockyard apprentice Gordon Jeffrey. It was not enough for writing to be proletarian, however; Rickword insisted that contributions from working-class writers must come up to the same literary standards that he demanded from professional writers. In consequence, the amount of space devoted to proletarian writing fell from eleven pages out of 48 under his predecessors to seven and a half out of 64. There was a similar reduction in the amount of space devoted to competitions, no doubt because he was prepared to print only the best of the entries. In the first fifteen issues announcements and results of five competitions had occupied 53 pages; in the eighteen which he edited four competitions occupied 22. James Hanley, who judged a competition for stories about schooldays, spoke for the editor as well as himself when he wrote: "I judged these manuscripts by Miltonic canons, so to speak; that is, I was influenced by three things: clarity, simplicity, and sensuousness – or, in other words, feeling...I ruled out definitely propagandist matter."[19] He also ruled out class bias in favour of proletarian competitors, for one of the prize-winning stories depicted life in a middle-class girls' boarding school. This again was consistent with Rickword's policy of publishing stories by middle-class left-wing writers such as Storm Jameson and Pamela Hansford Johnson.

The poetry he published had less of the revolutionary rhetoric which had so often passed for poetry under his predecessors, and new names appeared among the contributors – H.B. Mallalieu, Herbert Read, William Soutar, John Cornford, Naomi Mitchison, Maurice Carpenter, John Pudney. Another poet whose work began to appear in *Left Review* was Jack Lindsay, a convert to Marxism in January 1936, who had re-established contact with Rickword. Shortly afterwards, infuriated by a statement in *The Times Literary Supplement* that a Marxist writer "does not understand the nature of the English people", he wrote a long poem on the English people's revolutionary traditions, "Not English?", which was published in the May issue of *Left Review*. Greeted with acclaim, it was reprinted as a penny pamphlet under the new title "Who are the English?". In January 1937 Unity Theatre put it on the stage as a group recitation divided between single voices and a chorus – an early example of mass declamation, an artistic form which had already been developed in Germany and the United States, and with which Unity Theatre had been experimenting.

With Rickword as editor, *Left Review* retained its vigorous radicalism. He affirmed his political creed in an editorial:

> There has taken place a process of growth giving rise in turn to the Liberal, the Labour, and the Communist Parties. In that growth all the friction between elder and younger, between sedate and fractious, between richer and poorer, is a part of history. But what is also a part of history is a core of liberal and democratic idealism which has been militant against reaction, at home and abroad, for well over a hundred years. It is this which may escape the memory of leaders eager to preserve the structure of party machinery and of party programmes, but it must not be allowed to escape the instinct of the British people...The People's Front is not a mere "manoeuvre" by Liberals or Communists, nor must it be rejected in the interests of a "pure" Labour Party or a "pure" Socialism. If it is developed with a nation-wide enthusiasm, it will affect not merely governmental policy, but our whole culture – just as a hundred years ago the continuous struggle to achieve democratic rights was reflected and encouraged by vigorous movements in religion, literature, and science.

Although editorials were written by a committee, the political idealism of this passage, the respect for national tradition and the conviction that culture and politics are inseparable are as typical of Rickword as is the ribald mockery of Mosley with which the editorial ends:

> Poor Blackshirts, poor "Tom" Mosley, poor Tom-a-Bedlam. "Poor Tom who hath had three suits to his back, six shirts to his body, horse to ride and weapon to wear," and now "in the fury of his heart, when the foul fiend rages, eats cowdung for sallets, swallows the old rat and the ditch-dog, drinks the green water of the standing pool, is whipped from tithing to tithing!"[20]

Under his editorship *Left Review* retained its cheerful irreverence towards the monarchy. On Edward VIII's abdication an editorial commented: "In spite of Tory attempts to show that the Throne has emerged with renewed authority from the royal crisis, we are not sorry to think that its prestige has been severely hit. Much false glamour and delusive fiction has been disposed of, and the exact nature of the loyalty and enthusiasm for monarchy of the upper classes has been made plain."[21] A later editorial described George VI's coronation procession as "a great show of all the forces of destruction which predatory Imperialism has at its command", and commented:

> Not the development of human culture, but its repression was the message which the most highly-developed capitalism in the world, endeavouring to disguise itself in the tawdry trappings of feudalism, conveyed to the impressionable minds of the tens of thousands of children lining the route. And in this they were nobly assisted by a servile press, from the *Times* to the *Daily Herald*. Only the *Daily Worker* brought the fresh air of common sense into the garish atmosphere.

The *Daily Worker* had celebrated the coronation by publishing comments from Bernard Shaw, who suggested that it might more appropriately have been held at Stonehenge, and Day Lewis (not yet Poet Laureate), who compared it to "the frantic window-dressing of a shop on the verge of bankruptcy".[22]

Rickword advocated the rights of nations to self-government and the development of their national cultures. The issue for April 1936 commemorated the twentieth anniversary of the Easter Rising with three articles on Irish questions, and India received even more attention. The September issue, after an editorial emphasizing that "the sincerity of our protests at fascist brutalities can only be measured by the strength of our efforts to secure the right of the colonial peoples to govern themselves",[23] contained an essay by Mulk Raj Anand on Indian literature, another on the struggle for civil liberties in India, two Indian short stories and a translation of an Indian poem. Over half the November issue was devoted to Scotland, with essays on the national question by Neil Gunn and James Barke, another on Burns by Edwin Muir, a poem by William Soutar and a story by Edward Scouller. It may seem ironic that Rickword's contribution to this issue was an essay entitled "Stalin on the National Question", but in 1936 the annexation of the Baltic republics, the wartime deportation of national minorities such as the Crimean Tartars, and the imposition of Soviet domination upon Eastern Europe still lay in the future. Stalin's theoretical statements on the subject, like those of many Western statesmen, were far more liberal than his practice.

Left Review under his editorship was more international in outlook than before. The first fifteen issues, apart from a report on the Paris Congress of Writers, contained only half a dozen items on the arts outside Britain and the Soviet Union; Rickword published extracts from novels by Ignazio Silone and an anonymous German writing in a concentration camp, short stories from South Africa and Australia, poems by Federico García Lorca and Pablo Neruda, essays by Romain Rolland on Beethoven and by Bertolt Brecht on German drama, an interview with Aragon, a report on a conference of the International Association of Writers for the Defence of Culture, with the full text of Malraux's speech, and essays on Erasmus, Heine, Ibsen, Lorca and Jules Romains. The first editors had devoted more space to the Soviet Union than to the rest of the outside world put together; Rickword published less Soviet material and far more from other countries, in an attempt to keep a sense of proportion.

Whether he succeeded is another question. His review of a book on the Soviet Union is lyrical in its enthusiasm:

> It is a book which should inspire poems, for it glows itself with imaginative fervour. It materializes a real body for that spirit which was vocal for a brief moment in English poetry at the end of the sixteenth century, when the discovery of new lands where life was more luxuriant than under our pale sun fired the minds of poets. But where then the new wealth was acquired by bloodshed and the extermination of cultures, here the sandy desert and the frozen wastes are brought to life, cities built on barren mountain sides and peoples given back their languages and their crafts.

Rickword is not alone in using this rhapsodic tone; if anything, it is exceeded by the enthusiasm with which Lehmann, writing from Tiflis, described the political freedom enjoyed by the Georgians, their growing prosperity, "the happiness and optimism anyone who has eyes and ears in his head will notice at once in Tiflis to-day". Nor was admiration for Soviet society in 1936-37 confined to Communists like Rickword, fellow-travellers like Lehmann or even Fabians like Sidney and Beatrice Webb, who in their *Soviet Communism*, according to *Left Review*, reached the conclusions "that Soviet democracy is true democracy, that Soviet progress is of a kind that the world has never witnessed before".

On the page before Rickword's review Hamilton Fyfe summarized the
view of Stalin expressed in *Inside Europe* by John Gunther, an American
and a non-Socialist: "Nor has he the hard insensitive ruthlessness which
Slavs so often display. He has stood forward as 'defender of the people's
rights, the champion of men as men'."[24]

The tone can be understood only if we bear in mind the date of
composition. The authors had witnessed the suffering inflicted on millions
of people by the Depression, the moral degradation of the Britain of
Baldwin, MacDonald and Chamberlain, the Fascist menace to civilized
values. They needed to believe that a society free from these evils was
possible; and they found it in the Soviet Union. Others found assurance
elsewhere: Blunden's description of Nazi Germany bears an ironic
resemblance to Rickword's and Lehmann's descriptions of the Soviet
Union. To many Communists the Soviet Union was what, in Marx's
phrase, religion is to a believer, "the kindliness of a heartless world".
The emotional basis of their attitude is apparent in a poem by Day
Lewis:

> U.S.S.R! The workers of every land
> And all who believe man's virtue inexhaustible
> Greet you to-day: you are their health, their home,
> The vision's proof, the lifting of despair.

Many of those who wrote admiringly of Soviet achievements had previously been harsh critics of Communism – Rickword himself, the
Webbs and Sir Bernard Pares, director of the London School of Slavonic
Studies. *Left Review* said of *Moscow Admits a Critic*: "Sir Bernard is
impressed by the general well-being, by the enthusiasm and seriousness
of Soviet youth who have such glorious chances of interesting careers,
by the amazing public services, the enormous support given by the
regime to science and learning".[25] These former critics contrasted the
chaos which followed the civil war and the Bolshevik regime's ruthless
suppression of opposition on the one hand, and the economic collapse
of the capitalist world and the destruction of liberty in the Fascist
countries on the other, with the Soviet Union's economic achievements
and the promise of freedom embodied in the 1936 constitution, with
its eloquent guarantees of human rights.

Those guarantees proved as illusory as Stalin's liberal sentiments on
the national question. In August 1936 Zinoviev, Kamenev and fourteen
other veteran Bolsheviks, in January 1937 Radek and sixteen others
and in March 1938 Bukharin, Rykov and nineteen others confessed at
public trials to charges of treason, terrorism, sabotage and spying. All
were found guilty, despite the absence of supporting evidence, and
almost all of them were shot. Only two explanations of these events
were possible: either men whose whole lives had been dedicated to the

Communist cause, many of whom had been among Lenin's closest
collaborators, had conspired with the enemies of Communism to
destroy their life's work, or Stalin was engaged in a monstrous plot to
wipe out the old Bolsheviks, many of whom had been induced to confess
to crimes of which they were not guilty. The vast majority of the world's
Communists accepted the first explanation; so did the American ambas-
sador to Moscow, *The Times* and the majority of foreign journalists
and lawyers who attended the trials. In the issue of *Left Review* for
March 1937, replying to the doubts expressed by Spender in his *Forward from Liberalism* about the first trial, Swingler declared:

> Spender will not admit the facts about the trial of Zinoviev, Kamenev,
> and others, not because they can be shown to be untrue. They are irrefut-
> able. Nor because he has studied them at all. They had not been published
> when he wrote that paragraph. But because his intelligence tells him
> that it has been insulted. Those who make this blind faith in their own
> intelligence the paramount criterion, and call that "disinterestedness"
> and "objectivity", have not progressed far from Liberal solipsism.

In fact, before this review appeared Spender had already announced in
the *Daily Worker* that, after studying the evidence at the trial, he had
become convinced "that there undoubtedly had been a gigantic plot
against the Soviet Government and that the evidence was true". In the
same issue of *Left Review* the veteran Communist T.A. Jackson, reviewing the verbatim report of the second trial, referred to its "scrupulous
fairness" and "the unquestionable and entire guiltiness of the accused".[26]

As editor Rickword must accept responsibility for the publication of
these reviews, but they did not necessarily express his own opinion on
the trials. The editorials in *Left Review* in 1936-37 regularly referred
to developments in the international struggle against Fascism, but none
of them mentioned the trials, although they were presented by Moscow
as frustrating a Fascist plot. In the draft of a letter written not earlier
than 1956, which has survived among his papers, he wrote: "We knew
that many of those close to the leadership were being executed, and
read avidly the official explanations which were wrapped in voluminous
minutiae". His only published reference to the trials suggests that by
1938 he had accepted them as genuine. "Contact such as Malraux had
established with the people's movement brings the whole of the world
situation into focus," he wrote in that year. "For the first time in history
we possess the whole sphere of human activity under our eyes. A crowd
fired on in India, a leader of the unemployed arrested in England, the
fall in the franc and the outcry about the Moscow trials, all this makes
sense and is not just a chaotic jumble of brutality and idealism." Here,
it will be noticed it is not the trials which need to be explained but the
"outcry" about them. Yet it is doubtful whether he was entirely convinced.

As he told Jack Beeching in the 1950s, for years he had recurrent night-mares of being on trial on political charges, similar to those from which Wordsworth suffered during and long after the Reign of Terror:

> the unbroken dream entangled me
> In long orations, which I strove to plead
> Before unjust tribunals.[27]

Rickword's nightmares, like Wordsworth's, may have arisen from a conflict between loyalty to a cause and horror at the crimes which he suspected were being committed in its name.

One new feature of *Left Review* during his period as editor was the publication of long critical studies of poets and novelists, written from a Marxist perspective. They included essays by Derek Kahn on Yeats, Garman on Tennyson, Spender on Joyce, West on Shakespeare and Spenser, Swingler on Blake, Jackson on Dickens, Day Lewis on Hopkins and Rex Warner on Swift. The best of these bear comparison with the criticism published in the *Calendar*. Two notable essays on art history also appeared during this period, a study of the crucifix as a symbol of medieval class struggle by F.D. Klingender and an essay on the sculptor Jules Dalou by the young Anthony Blunt.

Rickword devoted considerable space to Surrealism, a movement with which British Marxists generally had little sympathy. A review of Gascoyne's *Short Survey of Surrealism* by Viscount Hastings (Marxism had friends in high places in the 1930s) in the issue of January 1936 examined the Surrealists' programmes sympathetically, but decided that whilst the movement was "of revolutionary value", in that it attempted to destroy "the false standards and complete decay in bourgeois art", it remained "the complete expression of bourgeois decadence" – a classic example of how to have one's cake and eat it. The July issue contained an eight-page supplement on Surrealism, in which Read claimed that it was "the only true application of the principles of dialectical materialism"[28] and Blunt and West rejected his claim, reproductions of two Surrealist paintings and a very amusing drawing by James Boswell of visitors to the Surrealist exhibition.* An unsympathetic review of Read's *Surrealism* by A.L. Lloyd in the January 1937 issue was answered by Read and Sykes Davies a month later. Rickword considered the movement important enough to allow it to speak for itself, and to subject it to reasoned criticism.

His writing during this period was not confined to *Left Review*, for in June 1936 he expended his powers on *War and Culture: The Decline*

* No discussion of *Left Review* would be complete without a tribute to "the three Jameses" – James Boswell, James Fitton and James Holland – who presented the unacceptable faces of capitalism (they would have denied that there were any acceptable ones) with a satirical force that recalls now Daumier, now Hogarth.

of Culture Under Capitalism, published by the Communist Party as No. 6 in a series of penny pamphlets called the Peace Library. Hastily written (it quoted the *Sunday Times* of 21 June and was reviewed by the *Daily Worker* on 8 July), it began with a brief analysis of the place of culture under capitalism, when the mass of the people had become "consumers of culture, instead of partners in its production" and creative work had become more and more unreal, the Surrealists being adduced as an example. It then turned rather abruptly to the effect on culture of preparations for war – the perversion of science to produce weapons, restriction of intellectual freedom, glorification of war, rejection of humanitarianism, whether Christian or secular – and cited Nazi Germany as an example of the logical outcome of this process. After condemning the destruction of the national cultures of India and Africa by imperialism, it concluded with an appeal for the unity of workers and intellectuals in the struggle against war.[29] From May 1936 onwards he also wrote occasional articles and reviews for the *Daily Worker* which sometimes throw light on his character. He condemns the pleasure in killing animals expressed in Hemingway's *Green Hills of Africa*. His aesthetic criteria emerge in his comment on Philip Henderson's *The Novel Today*: "He understands that the novel must have social content (he has no use for the art for art's sake theory), but he does not see that it is not a matter of the novel having the content we want it to have that makes it a good novel; neither is its subject matter directly related to its value".[30] To make that point in a Communist paper required courage.

His most important contribution to the *Daily Worker* is the long obituary he wrote on Sir James Barrie. After writing his "scrutiny" for the *Calendar* he had had an unfortunate encounter with Barrie on a mild but windy day when he was walking along a narrow pavement, wearing a heavy overcoat which Nancy Cunard had given him as a present. He had flung it open, and the wind filled it out so that each side protruded about two feet. He hardly noticed a diminutive old gentleman approaching, until the wind blew the right side of the coat against him with such force that he staggered, but when the old gentleman looked up at him with a malevolent glare he was horrified to realize that he had unintentionally assaulted the creator of Peter Pan. His obituary on Barrie is as unsparing as his earlier essay, but there is in it a note of sadness. "It is not the journalism, as such, that is to blame for Barrie's frustrated genius," he wrote,

> but the intensive self-exploitation demanded of any periodical writer with the ambition to get on – and Barrie exploited his own most intimate feelings with the ruthlessness of a colliery-owner who has struck a rich but fiery seam. Barrie, the self-exploiter, got the stuff on the market, but Barrie, the writer, was destroyed in the process...As a writer Barrie

created nothing for which we can regret that he will write no more. In Barrie the man we deplore one more victim, though crowned with material success, of a system which perverts and distorts to its ignoble ends every natural gift of man.[31]

The first half of 1936 was probably among the happiest periods of Rickword's life. The political situation seemed to be improving; in June he could write optimistically that "in France and Spain, the strength of the People's Front, initiated by the Communist Parties, has definitely turned the scale".[32] His job with Lawrence & Wishart and his editorship of *Left Review* guaranteed him a regular income for work which he enjoyed and in which he believed. He had a satisfying private life with Jonny, with whom he shared a room on the top floor of a rambling old house near St Giles' Circus, and he had many friends. His friendship with Garman, who made some valuable contributions to *Left Review*, was particularly close at this time. Since John Holms's death in 1934 Garman had been living with Peggy Guggenheim, and their friendship was all the closer because Peggy and Jonny had got to know each other several years before, possibly in Paris. Peggy remembered Rickword in later years as "painfully introverted and very shy unless he was drunk", and Jonny as "a good-natured, lively girl who helped make Rickword more comfortable in the world by being natural, if not hearty". Having herself resisted all Garman's attempts to convert her to Communism, she was convinced that Jonny, "being the ideal wife, swallowed Communism whole to ensure having a peaceful life".[33] The four had a boating holiday together on the Norfolk Broads in the summer of 1936, and before Garman and Peggy separated in the following summer Rickword and Jonny stayed with them several times at their cottage near the border of Sussex and Hampshire.

XI. Spain

THE deepening anxiety with which Rickword followed the course of the Spanish Civil War from July 1936 onwards can be traced in his editorials in *Left Review*. At first, when throughout half of Spain the conspiracy of 18 July had been frustrated by a mass uprising of the common people, the situation did not seem too serious, and the August and September editorials refer to the war as merely one factor in a grave international situation. It was worrying enough, however, for most of the British residents to accept evacuation by the Royal Navy, among them two of Rickword's former friends. Robert Graves, having witnessed the beginning of the Fascist reign of terror in Majorca, arrived in England a Republican sympathizer, and attempted to open Winston Churchill's eyes to the threat to Britain presented by German and Italian aid to the rebels. Roy Campbell, who had witnessed the anti-clerical terror in Toledo, understandably supported Franco. He and his family were offered a temporary home in Sussex by Wishart, Mrs Campbell's brother-in-law, and there engaged in furious arguments with Wishart and Garman over politics in general and the Spanish war in particular. They later settled in Portugal, and Campbell spent a few weeks as a war correspondent in Spain, where his contact with the fighting was limited to a one-day visit to the front.

In the first week of September Rickword visited Brussels as a delegate to the International Peace Congress, which brought together over 4,000 delegates from 32 countries, including 750 from Britain. Conservative, Liberal, Radical, Socialist and Communist parties, Churches, trade unions and a host of other bodies were represented, although Europe's Fascist parties had refused to attend. For four days, beginning on 3 September, thirteen special commissions representing different occupations and professions discussed means of attaining the four aims of the congress: recognition of the sanctity of treaty obligations; the reduction and limitation of armaments by international agreement and suppression of the manufacture of and trade in arms; strengthening of the League of Nations for the prevention and stopping of war by the organization of collective security; and the establishment within the framework of the League of effective machinery for remedying international situations which might lead to war. Rickword presumably attended the commission on literature and the press, which proposed such forms of action as the exposure of newspapers which served or were subsidized by war interests, the conduct of propaganda for peace in the local and national press, and the formation of committees of eminent writers and journalists who would promote criticism of anti-peace propaganda. It was all very high-minded, and it accomplished nothing.

The congress had one fatal flaw: politics were banned. Although Fascism was a major threat to world peace, the word might not be mentioned; an American organization which described itself as "against War and Fascism" was not allowed to use its title. There was no doubt that the great majority of the delegates supported the Spanish Republic against Franco. Rickword was standing on the rear platform of a tram when someone shouted "San Sebastián has been taken"; most of the delegates among the passengers looked glum, and someone muttered "It will be a long job". On the first night of the congress, when a Spanish delegate mounted the platform shouts went up of *"Les avions pour l'Espagne!"* and clenched fists were raised in the Popular Front salute, whereupon the chairman reminded the demonstrators that the congress was entirely non-political. Hence the farcical situation arose that a congress supposedly discussing means of preserving world peace did not discuss the war which was then raging in Spain and threatened the peace of Europe.

Rickword realized the futility of the business. In his October editorial, after describing the congress in the opening sentence as "a sorely needed step forward in the consolidation of the work for peace", he immediately passed on to consider the European situation, and emphasized that "the Spanish Government's shortage of munitions renders a protracted civil war almost inevitable".[1] The same issue contained a report from Spain by Ralph Bates attempting to explain why the Catholic Church was so hated by so many Spaniards, a short story about the war and a tribute to Felicia Browne, a British artist who had joined the militia in Barcelona and had been killed in action – the first of a series of obituaries on victims of the war published in *Left Review*.

In the November issue the outstanding item on a Spanish theme was John Cornford's poem "Letter from Aragon". In normal times Cornford would have seemed destined to enjoy a successful career as a writer or historian amid idyllic surroundings. His father was Professor of Ancient Philosophy at Cambridge, his mother Frances a grand-daughter of Charles Darwin and a poet of the Georgian school. They named their eldest son Rupert John after their friend Rupert Brooke, but the "Rupert" was soon dropped. He proved academically brilliant, winning an open scholarship at sixteen to Trinity College, Cambridge, and receiving a starred first in the history tripos, for which he was awarded a research scholarship. But the times were not normal. At sixteen, while still at his public school, he was already a convinced Marxist, well-read in the Marxist classics, and at Cambridge he contributed more than any other man to the establishment of a strong Socialist movement in the universities. In August 1936 he joined a militia column in Aragon, with which he served for a month before being taken ill. He had written verse sporadically since he was fourteen, and while in Spain he wrote his last three poems. On returning to England he sent one of them to *Left Review*.

Other British volunteers besides Cornford and Felicia Browne had fought in Spain in the first weeks of the war. Tom Wintringham, then *Daily Worker* correspondent in Barcelona, emphasized the value of their contribution in a letter to Harry Pollitt, general secretary of the Communist Party, suggesting that more should be sent, and Cornford had returned with the intention of recruiting volunteers who would stiffen the ranks of the undisciplined militia. Shortly afterwards the formation of an International Brigade became the official policy of the Comintern, and recruiting for a British Battalion began in October. At first military experience was held to be essential, and ex-officers, particularly those with a knowledge of languages, were greatly in demand. Ex-officers, however, were very few indeed in the British Communist Party, and if Rickword had not lost an eye he would almost certainly have been given a command in the Brigade. Instead, he remained behind while Wintringham commanded the British Battalion in action, Fox served as a political commissar and inexperienced young volunteers were rushed into battle after a minimum of training. A sense of guilt and frustration at his inability to put his military experience to use contributed to the bitterness with which he wrote of the Spanish war.

In November Franco launched his offensive against Madrid. The Government fled to Valencia on 6 November, and the city was generally expected to fall. Two days later, however, the first units of the International Brigade marched along the Gran Vía – mostly Germans, Frenchmen, Belgians and Poles, but also including a few Britons, among them Cornford and the novelist John Sommerfield. Their arrival put new heart into the defenders, and after a fortnight of bloody hand-to-hand fighting Madrid did not fall. Rickword hailed the event in his December editorial as the turn of the tide, and declared that "by our mobilisation of public opinion against the National Government we can bring the Spanish Civil War to a swift, victorious conclusion".[2] In the issue for January 1937 he paid tribute to Fox and Wintringham, "both of whom are serving with the Brigade".[3]

In fact, when this issue appeared Fox was already dead. On Christmas Eve the newly-formed No. 1 Company of British volunteers, 145 strong, was ordered south to take part in an offensive on the Córdoba front. The offensive was badly bungled by the French officer commanding the battalion, and only 67 members of No. 1 Company survived, Fox and Cornford being among those killed. Fox's death came as a blow to Rickword, who had worked closely with him in the past three years. He wrote in the *Daily Worker*: "His wide knowledge and mental energy, combined with a quiet but penetrating wit, made him a most stimulating colleague", and in the editorial of the February *Left Review*: "His broad humanism and common sense were a valuable corrective against ultra-Left enthusiasm".[4] That he should have singled out these qualities for praise tells us a good deal about his own values. The news of Cornford's death, on his twenty-first birthday or the following day, did not reach England till a month later. A two-page tribute appeared in the March *Left Review*, together with another of the poems which he had written in Spain, "Full Moon at Tierz". Rickword greatly admired these poems, of which he later said: "the first poems written out of an understanding of Marxism, they are dialectically conceived, not abstract-revolutionary like those of his older contemporaries".[5] Is there a note of regret in this sentence, that so young a poet should have been able to write the kind of poetry which he would have liked to write himself?

The March issue, more than any other, was devoted to the Spanish struggle, from the sketch of a militiaman on the front cover to the appeal at the back for a fund set up in memory of Cornford. His poem was followed by a tribute to Federico García Lorca, one of Spain's greatest modern poets, murdered the previous August, and a translation of one of his poems. Rickword's editorial drew the moral from their deaths: "These men have re-established with their blood that unity between the creators of beauty and the masses of the people, for lack of which culture had become a petty play-word in the mouths of an isolated sect. By facing the enemy where he is strongest and most terrible, they have shown us, who have perhaps ignored earlier warnings, who and what he is."[6] The Spanish material was supplemented with an account by Sommerfield of his arrival with the first section of the International Brigade, and a long poem by Jack Lindsay, "On Guard for Spain", written at Rickword's suggestion. Like "Who Are the English?", this poem was used as a mass declamation; unlike its predecessor, it was written with this end in mind. The mass declamation, which Rickword saw as "a totally new break-through...a thing that could have come off only in a time of exceptional emotional intensity",[7] was a form which Lindsay took very seriously. In a later issue of *Left Review* he contended that "poetry has always found its vitalisation in a socially valuable relation to the speaking voice", citing the Homeric epic, Greek and Elizabethan drama, and Greek, medieval and Elizabethan lyrics in support of his argument: "only when capitalism started coming into its own was there driven a wedge between poetry and the speaking voice". With the emergence of a revolutionary proletariat it was possible again to identify a homogeneous audience for poetry, and mass declamation provided the direct contact with that audience from which new developments could stem; it was "the Thespis' cart, the miracle-play platform in the market-place, which is the prerequisite of a new depth of drama".[8] "On Guard for Spain" certainly found its audience; it was performed at Trafalgar Square and May Day demonstrations, political and trade union meetings, in theatres and public halls, from the tops of lorries and in the streets, sometimes before audiences numbered in their thousands. It is a cultural tragedy that the artistic energies of the Popular Front period never came to full fruition.

On 8 February Málaga was captured by Italian troops, and thousands of executions followed – four thousand in the first week, according to one account. About a hundred thousand men, women and children fled along the coast road to Almería, starving and exhausted, pursued by tanks, strafed and bombed by aircraft. A moving first-hand account by T.C. Worsley appeared in the April *Left Review*, together with Rex Warner's fiercely indignant poem "Arms in Spain" and a translation by Nancy Cunard of Pablo Neruda's "To the Mothers of the Dead Militia". Meanwhile Franco launched a second offensive south of Madrid, in an attempt to isolate the capital by cutting the road to Valencia. On 11 February his Moorish mercenaries and German gunners crossed the River Jarama, and the 600 men of the British Battalion were hurried to the front. For three days they held the line against superior odds, under Wintringham's command, until he was wounded at the end of the second day. Only 225 men survived the first day, but the line remained unbroken, the Valencia road open.

Among those killed was Christopher St John Sprigg, whose death was reported in the May *Left Review*. Born in 1907, the son and grandson of newspaper editors, he entered the family profession at fifteen, and between 1931 and 1937 published five books on aviation and seven detective stories under his own name and a serious novel, *This My Hand*, under the pen-name by which he is remembered, Christopher Caudwell. In 1934 he plunged into the study of Marxism and a year later joined the Communist Party. He enlisted in the International Brigade in December 1936, and was killed on his first day in action while covering with his machine-gun his comrades' withdrawal from a ridge aptly nicknamed "Suicide Hill". Sharing Jack Lindsay's ambition to reinterpret all branches of knowledge in Marxist terms, he had written in the last two years of his life the works which were published posthumously as *Illusion and Reality: A Study of the Sources of Poetry, Studies in a Dying Culture* and *The Crisis in Physics*. Although these books, which were hailed with enthusiasm on their first appearance, overshadowed the selection from his poems published in 1939, it is as a poet rather than as a critic or philosopher that he is remembered.

Rickword shared the general view of the relative merits of Caudwell's poetry and his theoretical writings. "It is hard to be critical of a poet who was killed fighting with the International Brigade," he wrote, "but

in one reader's opinion this volume of poems is not of the same order
of achievement as Christopher Caudwell's brilliant applications of
Marxism in the cultural and scientific fields". This judgment is surprising, for Caudwell's poems, in their tough-minded anti-Romanticism,
show a closer resemblance to Rickword's than those of any other poet
of the thirties. This may be due in part to affinities of temperament, in
part to a common debt to Donne and the Metaphysicals, but it is
difficult to believe that so omnivorous a reader and so dedicated a
Marxist as Caudwell was not familiar with the writings of the most
distinguished poet whom the Communist Party could boast. The affinity
between them is apparent in the continuation of Rickword's review,
much of which could be applied to his own poems:

> Caudwell's poems chiefly reflect the disillusionment and perplexity of
> the post-war generation, a state of mind which in other ways he has
> sweated out of himself by his many practical activities. At its most
> characteristic his verse is vigorous, even violent, and he faces his own
> psychological dilemmas with a saving sense of humour. He was not
> content to visualise himself as a moulting eagle in an age of decadence,
> and even in his obsession with the problem of death there is a healthy
> assertiveness, a confidence in the value of living as such, out of which
> might well have developed a materialist poetry.[9]

It is difficult to avoid the suspicion that Rickword's dissatisfaction is
not so much with Caudwell as with his own younger self, whom the
Caudwell revealed in the poems so closely resembled, and with his own
failure to advance beyond the poetry of disillusionment and perplexity
to "materialist poetry" similar to that written by Cornford.

The fighting along the Jarama continued throughout February; all
the Fascists' attempts to break through were repulsed. In the second
half of the month the American Lincoln Battalion of the International
Brigade came into action for the first time, fighting with conspicuous
gallantry. Among those killed in their ranks was Charles Donnelly, a
22-year-old Irish poet who had been an early contributor to *Left
Review*. A notice of his death appeared in the June issue, the fifth writer
dead in Spain to be commemorated in five months.

After Franco's attempt to encircle Madrid from the west had been
defeated on the Jarama, and an attempt by his Italian allies to encircle
it from the north had been averted at the battle of Guadalajara, he
turned his attention to the autonomous Basque Republic. The campaign
opened on 31 March with the bombing and machine-gunning of the
undefended country town of Durango. In order to starve the Basques
into surrender, the rebels threatened to prevent food supplies from
entering Bilbao, and the British Government co-operated by warning
British ships that if they tried to enter Bilbao the Royal Navy would

not protect them. Franco's bluff was finally called when four British ships sailed into Bilbao unharmed, and he reverted to the tactic of terror bombing. On 26 April the little town of Guernica, the historic home of Basque liberties, which was crowded with refugees and had no air defences, was bombed for three hours by German aircraft which left it a smouldering ruin, while German fighters, flying low, machine-gunned the population.

Rickword's rage at these events is clear in his June editorial, the last he was to write. After quoting a message expressing his horror at the destruction of Guernica, which he had sent to the President of the Basque Republic, he declared:

> There is no shadow of doubt that the cynical frightfulness of the German and Italian air forces which (as there is no longer any attempt to deny even in the reactionary press) are carrying out this mass slaughter, is encouraged by the benevolent attitude of the British National Government. This innocent blood is on our hands, we cannot escape responsibility.[10]

It was in this mood of anger and shame at the depths of degradation to which his country had been reduced by the Government's policy of appeasement that his poem "To the Wife of any Non-Intervention Statesman" was conceived.

Five days after the destruction of Guernica he marched in London's May Day demonstration – the largest since the General Strike. In January the Communist Party, the Independent Labour Party and the Socialist League, led by Sir Stafford Cripps, representing the left wing of the Labour Party, had reached agreement on a common programme, and although the Labour Party, which was to hold its own demonstration on the following day, officially took no part, the many thousands who marched displayed the strength of this embryonic Popular Front. Several factors combined to bring them on to the streets: a warm Saturday, a strike of London busmen who turned out in force, and above all anger at the crimes of Fascism in Spain and the British Government's collusion. Contingents from all over London, including a particularly large one from the East End, still celebrating its victory over Mosley the previous October, converged on the Embankment, where the procession assembled. One section consisted of printers, journalists, left-wing bookshops, the Left Book Club and Socialist periodicals. It included editorial staff, contributors and readers of *Left Review*, who marched behind their own banner and tableau. As they passed through the West End streets, already decorated in readiness for the coming coronation, on their way to Hyde Park, Sylvia Townsend Warner remarked to Julius Lipton, Jewish garment worker and poet, that "here for the first time writers and readers were combining, and what was

more, had found a unity of expression".[11] The objective Rickword had
pursued since the days of the *Calendar* seemed to have been achieved,
yet it is doubtful whether, even on what was apparently a day of
triumph, he was entirely happy.

His frame of mind in the spring of 1937 was very different from a
year before. Then the political situation seemed promising, and Lawrence & Wishart, of which he was both a director and a full-time
employee, was publishing fiction, poetry and criticism along with political books and Marxist classics. *New Writing*, which was anti-Fascist
in tone but did not demand party orthodoxy from its contributors, was
an especially hopeful sign. Encouraged by this, John Lehmann put forward a plan for a "New Writing Library" of novels, poetry and autobiographies by contributors to *New Writing*, among them Edward
Upward, Christopher Isherwood, James Stern, Willy Goldman, John
Sommerfield, B.L. Coombes, André Chamson, Jean Giono and Jean
Paul Sartre. Lawrence & Wishart appeared so interested in the idea
that early in 1937 Lehmann wrote to several of the authors assuring
them that the series would go ahead. Then came a sudden change; the
firm lost interest, not only in the "New Writing Library", but even in
renewing the contract to publish *New Writing*. This *volte-face* was part
of a wider change of policy. In 1937-38 political works almost completely ousted books of a more literary character. In the spring and
early summer the full-page advertisements for its books which regularly
appeared in *Left Review* announced the publication of novels by Mulk
Raj Anand, Paul Nizan and Lewis Jones and books on Dickens and
Diderot, as well as *New Writing* III, but from September onwards they
concentrated on the selected works of Lenin, *New Fashions in Wage
Theory* and *A History of the Civil War in the U.S.S.R.* Martin Lawrence
had routed Wishart & Co.

The explanation of this change can be found in the Moscow trials.
In accordance with the Popular Front policy, Communists had co-
operated in 1935-36 with anti-Fascists of all shades, Socialist, Anarchist,
Radical, Liberal and even Conservative, in an unprecedented atmosphere of tolerance. Wintringham translated a poem by Pedro Garfias
in which a Spanish Communist, addressing an Anarchist as "brother",
declares their past disputes to have been a crime and imagines Marx
and Bakunin embracing each other.[12] Unfortunately, this mood did not
last. After the Moscow trials of August 1936 and January 1937 a rigid
orthodoxy was once again imposed upon the international Communist
movement, and "Trotskyists" were hunted down with paranoid
ruthlessness. Typical of the mood of the time was the expulsion of
Wintringham from the Communist Party in July 1938 because he
refused to break with his American mistress, who was suspected
(wrongly, as it happened) of Trotskyism. Lawrence & Wishart dutifully

played its part by publishing in 1938 *Trotskyism in the Service of Franco* and *Traitors on Trial*, a verbatim report of the trial of the "bloc of rights and Trotskyists". In these circumstances it was unthinkable that it should publish books by Lehmann's contributors to *New Writing*, the majority of whom, anti-Fascist though they might be, were far from being orthodox Communists.

This was not a change with which Rickword could feel at ease. When Lehmann visited the firm's offices he always found him "sunk in profound and almost wordless gloom", and in May 1937 he gave up his post, while retaining his unpaid directorship. Whether he resigned or was dismissed is uncertain, and his comment in an interview with *Poetry Nation* does not make the point clear: "We started off our first year with a good list of general literature as well as political literature. That went phut; we hadn't got proper sales representation, and the Party side of it wasn't keen on having general books in. So it got dropped. After *Left Review* I sort of faded out; they hadn't got any work for me, really."[13] He clearly disagreed with the new policy, and probably resigned after the decision was taken, regarding himself as unfitted to carry it out. Without the regular income which his job had provided he knew that he would have to support himself by freelancing and might have to move to the country again. He gave up the editorship of *Left Review*. Political as well as economic factors may have helped bring about his resignation. Although during his editorship, as he later said, "there weren't any great pressures from the party to make us toe a conforming line",[14] under his successor the Communist Party increasingly assumed control of the journal's policy. It is possible that after his experience at Lawrence & Wishart he sensed that the party's policy of imposing strict ideological orthodoxy on all its publications would be extended to *Left Review*, and preferred to get out rather than compromise his independence.

Randall Swingler, who at his suggestion succeeded him as editor from June onwards, was eleven years his junior. The son of a rural dean and godson of an Archbishop of Canterbury, he was educated at Winchester, where he became head of his house, and New College, Oxford, where he obtained his blue as a runner. While earning his living as a teacher he wrote with furious energy, and by 1937 had published three collections of poems and a novel. A lover of music, he played the flute with the London Symphony Orchestra, married a concert pianist and wrote lyrics which were set to music by Benjamin Britten, Alan Bush and other composers. The turning-point in what had been a conventional enough career came when in 1934 he joined the Communist Party. After moving to London two years later he threw himself into a host of activities – writing, journalism, editing, public speaking, the Workers' Musical Association, Unity Theatre, the Left

Book Club. Gregarious, humorous, deeply sensitive yet free from sentimentality, he was sufficiently like and sufficiently unlike Rickword to form a close friendship with him, which lasted until his death thirty years later.

The sinister influence of the Moscow trials upon Communist thinking was sometimes apparent in *Left Review* during the period of his editorship, in a review describing the accused as "criminal puppets of the Fascists" and a cartoon depicting Trotsky as a snake. Particularly depressing was an article on Soviet poetry which asserted:

> It is significant to note that Bukharin, at the Conference of Writers, implied that the future development of Soviet poetry would be along the line of Pasternak, rather than Mayakovsky, and only after the recent Trials was it made clear that even on the front of culture was there a conscious attempt to stifle the genuine line of Soviet poetry – that is the line of Mayakovsky.[15]

In general, however, Swingler's policy as editor followed closely the lines laid down by Rickword. To celebrate the twentieth anniversary of the Bolshevik Revolution, the November 1937 issue was largely devoted to the arts in the Soviet Union, but the other ten issues which he edited contained only twenty-seven pages dealing with the subject. The review's international emphasis was strengthened; special issues were devoted to Spain and China, and material from or about Ireland, France, Germany, Austria, Italy, the Balkans, Palestine, India, Japan, South Africa, the United States, Canada, Australia, Jewish culture and Negro poets was published. The coverage of the arts was widened; more space was given to the cinema, architecture and especially music, which had been somewhat neglected in the past. Although stories and reviews by working-class writers continued to appear, the average amount of space per issue given to proletarian literature fell further, from seven and a half pages to five. This decline seems to have been caused, partly by Swingler's abandonment of the practice of holding competitions, partly by his insistence on high standards of writing. In an editorial he complained, like Wintringham before him, that although many stories by worker-writers were received, which were often excellently written, "in nearly every case the effect is uniformly depressing".[16]

Soon after giving up the editorship of *Left Review* Rickword paid a visit to Spain at short notice. At the Paris congress in June 1935 the Spanish delegation had invited the International Association of Writers for the Defence of Culture to meet in Madrid in two years' time, and when the association's executive committee met in London in June 1936 the invitation was repeated and officially accepted. A month later Spain was at war, but the Spanish writers insisted that the congress should proceed as planned. After an impressive delegation of British writers, including Auden, Lascelles Abercrombie, Slater, Lehmann and Strachey, had been assembled the Foreign Office intervened. Permits to enter Spain, an official announced at the last minute, would be granted only to accredited journalists, to businessmen and to those engaged on humanitarian work, and writers wishing to take part in a cultural congress did not fall into any of these categories. The distinguished writers who had been selected backed down, and it seemed that Britain would not be represented at the congress. Then an assurance was received from the French section of the association that the difficulty about passports could be overcome. A new delegation, consisting of Sylvia Townsend Warner, Valentine Ackland, Stephen Spender and Rickword, who took Jonny with him, was hastily assembled and gathered in Paris on 3 July.

Tensions soon developed inside the delegation. Rickword and the two women were Communist Party members, but no one seemed quite sure whether Spender was or not. According to his own account, after the publication in January of his *Forward from Liberalism* Harry Pollitt had personally invited him to join the party, despite his disagreement with it on certain points, and to write an article for the *Daily Worker* explaining his position. Spender accepted the offer, whereupon Pollitt issued him a membership card.* His article, which appeared on 19 February, in fact revealed no serious disagreement between him and the party; in particular, he withdrew the criticisms of the Zinoviev-Kamenev trial which had appeared in his book. Neither he nor his party branch made any attempt to contact each other, however, and as he paid no dues, apart from the original subscription which he paid to Pollitt, his membership presumably lapsed. After a visit to Spain he wrote an article for the *New Statesman*, "Heroes in Spain", in which he affirmed his full support for the social revolution in progress there, but caused some offence by deploring the heroic tone of left-wing propaganda about the war.† In his conversations with the other members of the delegation he worried a great deal about a friend who had been arrested after deserting from the International Brigade, and who he

* The story that Pollitt said at this meeting, "Go to Spain and get yourself killed, comrade, we need a Byron in the movement", is certainly untrue. It is not mentioned in either of Spender's two accounts of the interview in *The God that Failed* and *World Within World*, and he denied it in an interview with Hugh D. Ford (*A Poet's War*, 1965, p.289). It probably originated either as a piece of Cold War propaganda or as a joke at Spender's expense.

† *New Statesman*, No. 323 (1 May, 1937), p.714; reprinted in Valentine Cunningham, *The Penguin Book of Spanish Civil War Verse*, p.334. In *The God that Failed* (1950, p.249) and *World Within World* (1977 reprint, p.244) Spender claimed to have published an article in the *New Statesman* protesting against propaganda which attracted young men into the International Brigade without making clear that it was Communist-controlled. In fact this article, the only one which he contributed to the *New Statesman* in 1937, says nothing of the kind.

feared might be shot. Before they returned to England they learned that the young man had been repatriated at the request of Pollitt, to whom Spender had appealed on his friend's behalf.

Throughout the visit Spender maintained reasonably friendly relations with Rickword, with whom it was not easy to quarrel and whom he respected for his poetry, but he took an intense dislike to Sylvia Townsend Warner. Why this should have been is difficult to say. Her letters suggest that she found him trying (in one she described him as "an irritating idealist, always hatching a wounded feeling") but took an interest in his writing, as when she suggested in an unpublished letter to Rickword that his poetry had deteriorated because the party had given him too much journalistic work. Their incompatible temperaments are amusingly suggested by the impression which they made at the Congress on the American writer Malcolm Cowley, he "tall, slim, with wavy hair, a shirt open at the neck and a general look of being Shelley astray in the twentieth century", she "looking like a very pleasantly daft English spinster (say her own Lolly Willowes)".[17]

In Paris the English delegates were met at the Gare St Lazare by André Malraux, who had first organized the supply of aircraft to the Spanish Government and then formed and commanded in action an air squadron flown by foreign volunteers, and whom Rickword admired intensely both as a novelist and as a man of action. He conducted the party to their reserved carriage, where the French delegation, which also included Julien Benda and André Chamson, and the Latin American delegates were awaiting them. A passport control at Perpignan caused no difficulties, as Malraux had provided the English party with forged passports; Spender's described him as a Spanish citizen called Ramos Ramos, and the others were no doubt given equally improbable identities. In the early morning of 4 July they arrived at the Spanish town of Port Bou, which bore the scars of several bombing raids, and after the prolonged delays normal in Spain they were served with a meal which proved to have been worth waiting for. After being split up into fours and fives the delegates set out in the afternoon in a fleet of cars along the mountainous coastal road to Barcelona. The English delegation enjoyed a terrifying journey: the driver of the Rolls Royce in which they travelled was an enthusiast for speed, and it seemed that at any moment their car would join the wrecks which strewed the roadside. They reached Barcelona in the evening unharmed and were welcomed by the Catalan Minister of Propaganda, who asked whether they wished to stay the night or to continue their journey to Valencia. Sylvia Townsend Warner, who was exhausted, replied: "Of course we are quite willing to go on, but I think that out of consideration for this Mexican comrade, who has been travelling for ten days, we ought perhaps to stay the night". They were therefore accommodated at the best hotel in Barcelona as guests of the Catalan Government.

Although the delegates rose early next morning in the hope of reaching Valencia in time for the opening of the Congress, they had reckoned without the Spanish capacity for delay, and when they finally arrived the Congress had begun. The English party was met by Ralph Bates, now a political commissar with the International Brigade, and elected him leader of the delegation. Valencia, they found, had suffered from enemy bombing; at dawn that morning several rebel planes had flown low over the town and dropped some bombs, but had been driven away by anti-aircraft fire. The town hall, where the Congress met, was in ruins except for one wing; they climbed to the council chamber up a marble staircase which had been patched with concrete, and a bomb through the roof of the hall had narrowly missed two magnificent cut-glass chandeliers. On the wall were written in letters of gold the names of writers killed in the struggle, among them Lorca and Fox. The midsummer Spanish heat inside the hall was made even more unbearable by the blaze of lights for the cine camera.

No one seemed to know how many delegates were there (75? 80?) or how many countries were represented (26? 27? 28?). The uncertainty may have arisen from the fact that several, including Bates, the German Ludwig Renn and the Dutchman Jef Last, were on leave from the front and were unable to attend all the sessions. Some of the day's speeches lingered in Rickword's memory. The Catholic writer José Bergamín saw in the struggle the potentiality of "a complete intellectual and imaginative re-creation of Spain", and this theme was taken up by Bates, who hailed the end of "the legend of invertebrate Spain". Benda rejected the view that a writer should hold aloof from politics as a distortion of the theme of his book La trahison des clercs. "There is here a gross and more or less deliberate equivocation," he declared, "which is to confuse politics, defined in my book as submission to the basest individual interests, with morals, that is, with the defence of the highest moral values, principally those of justice and the rights of man, which include the rights of all nations to a free existence."[18]

Outside the Congress Rickword met Wintringham, still looking unwell after the wound he had received at Jarama and an attack of typhoid which had accompanied it. He had recently taken command of an officers' training school at Albacete, at which most of his students were Americans, and had been given short leave to attend the first session of the Congress. In a letter to Garman Rickword reported that Wintringham had said:

> articles like that of Spender's in the New Statesman did a lot of harm, as it is by no means simple keeping up morale in a struggle like the present one, especially as the comrades are necessarily out of touch with

home for stretches at a time. They haven't the sense of the whole community being behind them that the troops had in the 1914 war. Of course, they have something incredibly better, but it's more intellectual at present, a matter of will and understanding, and so needing external support as the grim business wears on. That's a realistic view, I think, and shouldn't be lost sight of.

The tired delegates got to bed late, and were awakened at 4 a.m. on 6 July by an air raid. Six hours later the motorcade left for Madrid. They stopped for lunch at a village called Minganilla, where after the usual wait they were served with a rural meal of omelettes, ham, cheese, garlic and white bread, delicious to taste but hard as a rock, washed down with excellent wine. While they were eating they heard the village children singing outside, first the *Internationale*, then the national anthem, "Riego's Hymn", and other Republican songs, and went to the window to applaud them. After the meal they came down into the square and watched the children dancing, while their mothers, many of them refugees from Madrid or Badajoz, the scene of one of the bloodiest massacres of the war, stood by in tears. There were no men – they were all at the front or working in the fields. After they left the village the road, which during the earlier part of the journey had run between orange groves and olive trees, suddenly descended steeply into the gorge of the Rio Gabriel, then rose again equally steeply. For many miles they circled the rim of an immense bowl of red earth from which the sun sent back its heat in great waves, painful to the eyes as they watched the movement of the almost treeless landscape. This was wheat-growing country, and for the first time the peasants, among whom the land had been divided when the land-owners fled, were reaping the harvest for themselves. Rickword watched fascinated as they reaped the corn with sickles and threshed it as it had been threshed in classical times, beating the grain out of the ears and then flinging it into the air so that the husks were blown away.

When they finally reached Madrid the cars turned into a park where three mounted sentries conducted them to a banquet. A secretary presented the apologies of General José Miaja Menant, the defender of Madrid, explaining that he was prevented from welcoming them personally by pressing business elsewhere. The general was indeed fully occupied, for at dawn that morning an offensive had been launched against the village of Brunete, with the aim of cutting off the besieging forces from the west, and within a few hours the Republicans had advanced nearly ten miles. The battle, fought in scorching heat under a pitiless sun, with both sides suffering agonies of thirst, continued for nearly three weeks, until most of the territory gained had been lost again. The rebels owed their success to their German and Italian bombers and fighters, which bombed and strafed everything that moved. Among

their victims was another English poet, Julian Bell, son of Clive and
Vanessa Bell and nephew of Virginia Woolf, who had given up an
academic post in China with the intention of joining the International
Brigade, but as a concession to his parents' pacifism had joined the
Spanish Medical Aid instead. He was mortally wounded on 18 July,
when a bomb hit the ambulance he was driving.

The delegates met in the University City, the scene of fierce fighting
the previous November. Part of it was still held by the enemy. Soldiers
stood guard on either side of the platform, and one session was interrupted when a party of soldiers rushed on to the platform waving two
enemy flags which they had captured. Speeches were often drowned
by the sound of gunfire. On one occasion the delegates and the citizens
of Madrid watched Republican fighters scatter a formation of Italian
bombers in a battle above the city. After dinner one evening, when the
Spanish delegates were singing Flamenco songs and clapping their
hands in time, the poet Rafael Alberti jumped on to a chair and shouted
that Madrid was being shelled. Rickword, Spender, Claud Cockburn,
the *Daily Worker* correspondent, and the French Communist writer
René Blech walked to the Puerta del Sol and watched the upper storeys
of the Ministry of the Interior, struck by an incendiary shell, burning.
Shrugging his shoulders, Blech turned away with the word "*Ignoble*".

War raged inside the Congress as well. The Soviet delegates besides
repeatedly denouncing Trotsky in their speeches, were anxious to force
through a resolution condemning André Gide's recently published
Retour de l'U.R.S.S. What strikes the reader today is not Gide's criticisms of aspects of Stalin's Russia – the gross inequalities of income,
the emergence of a new privileged class, the persecution of homosexuals,
the sycophantic cult of Stalin, the universal conformism, the absence
of any critical spirit and the complete suppression of all freedom of
thought – but the way in which he leans over backward to say everything
possible in favour of the regime, as if reluctant to part with his illusions.
This was not how the Russians and the more biddable foreign Communists saw it, and they intrigued behind the scenes to secure its condemnation, without success. Among those whom they approached was
Jef Last, who had accompanied Gide on his visit to the Soviet Union,
and considered his book morally courageous but inopportune in its
timing. He replied in his speech to the Congress, in a passage which
made no reference to Gide but of which the significance was unmistak-
able:

It sometimes happens that a doctor is the first to be infected with the
disease he is fighting against. Beware of infection. Let us have no more
betrayals of intellectuals, no more mechanical reactions and over-
simplified labels. Our job can never be merely to follow in the wake of
the journalists and orators. We have our own clearly defined task, which

is to extend and deepen the significance of the Homeric struggle in which we have the honour and the happiness to be taking part. Let it not be said of us that moral courage is a more difficult thing to exercise than the physical courage of the soldiers in the trenches.[19]

It is inconceivable that Rickword, with his interest in French literature and in the Soviet Union, had not read Gide's book. In the May issue of *Left Review* Pat Sloan, a professional apologist for the Soviet Union, had denounced it as "nonsense" and "utter confusion", and had justified Soviet conformism by the argument that "in such a society there is no longer reason for opposition and non-conformity".[20] The choice of reviewer was not necessarily Rickword's; in view of the nature of the book Sloan, who had just published a book called *Soviet Democracy*, may have been suggested by King Street as the obvious person to deal with it. It is significant that, in the article on the Congress which Rickword wrote for *Left Review*, he quoted more fully from Last's speech than from any other, including the passage cited above. In his quiet way, he took his stand on the side of Gide, Last and honesty.

After three nights in Madrid, in each of which their sleep was broken by the sound of shelling, the delegates returned to Valencia where, though there was an air raid alarm on their second evening, at least there was no bombardment. The most memorable event was a meeting on 10 July at which the Socialist professor and statesman Fernando de los Rios paid a tribute to his friend Lorca. Before they left Valencia the delegates were loaded with gifts of books published since the war began, among them a collection of some three hundred ballads of the war. On the road to Barcelona a tyre of the English delegation's car burst, and the spare tyre was found to be in no better condition; to pass the time while they awaited a replacement the driver gathered a large handful of walnuts and fed his passengers as they sat by the roadside.

In Barcelona, their last stopping-place in Spain, they were lodged in the same hotel as before, and Rickword and Jonny were able to enoy a little leisure together, sitting outside a café in the main avenue, the Rambla, or looking at the fishermen's boats in the harbour. An elegant young man who conducted them round an exhibition of war paintings remarked, pointing to one heroic canvas, "Our people never take cover, it's cowardly," to which Rickword replied, with an old soldier's realism, "People are more valuable alive than dead". There were more formal occasions – a concert conducted by Pablo Casals in the delegates' honour, a meeting in Barcelona's largest theatre, at which a representative of each delegation made a short speech. Before each speech the national anthem of the delegate's country was played, so that before Spender spoke on behalf of the English delegation the orchestra played "God Save the King" while the audience stood at attention giving the clenched fist salute. On leaving Barcelona the delegates received more gifts of books, in Catalan this time.

On 13 July they were driven to Port Bou, where they had to wait till evening for the Paris train. To pass the time Spender went into the sea for a swim, followed by Rickword. As he swam towards Spender he saw that he had clambered on to a rock, and heard him calling, "Oh, Edgell, do get out, there's a whole lot of nasty things coming towards you". Rickword then realized that the town sewer had been opened, and after a desperate struggle reached the shore a few seconds before its contents overtook him.

The delegates travelled to Paris in a special train consisting entirely of sleeping cars and arrived in time for the 14 July celebrations. Most of them were integrated into the main procession which marched, twenty abreast, to the Place de la Bastille. Rickword was deeply impressed by the gravity of the crowds, who marched in complete order without a policeman in sight and listened intently to the long and fiery speeches. Next day the Congress resumed its discussions, but although Auden and the other English writers who had been refused visas for Spain could easily have attended the closing sessions none of them took the trouble. As Spender bitterly commented,

> the English branch of the Writers' International can have no reason to feel complacent, or indeed anything but ashamed of its contribution to the Congress...The well-known English writers might at least have atoned for their absence in Spain by attending the last part of the Congress at Paris: they did not do so. The great democratic English writers have let go by unheeded a courageous demonstration of unity with the Spanish Republic by the writers of twenty-seven nations.[21]

At least one English writer was present in addition to the four delegates, however – Nancy Cunard, who was living in France, and had given to the Spanish Republican cause the same untiring devotion with which she had championed Negro rights. She showed her support for both causes by attending the Congress in company with three black poets, the American Langston Hughes, the Cuban Nicolás Guillén and the Haitian Jacques Roumain, all of whom had had poems in Negro. The final session met in the evening of 16 July at the Théâtre de la Porte St Martin under the auspices of the French Government, amid a great show of martial splendour, and on the following day the Congress issued a manifesto appealing to the writers of the world to take their stand in the struggle against Fascism and in defence of the Spanish Republic.

Shortly before the Congress Nancy Cunard had attempted to rally support for the Republic by sending out a questionnaire to British and Irish writers asking which side in the war they supported. The replies

pamphlet-poem antagonism, i.e. social struggle *versus* inner struggle, is a reflection of the poet's continuing isolation, falsifying the perspective of social development and delaying the re-integration of the poet into the body of society.[1]

Despite this criticism, Rickword greatly admired "Spain", and in later life spoke with contempt of the moral waywardness which led Auden first to mutilate and then to suppress it. Rickword saw this as a concession to conservative American opinion.

When writing this passage Rickword must have appreciated its relevance to his own position. He had thrown himself into the social struggle, he had written a pamphlet and political articles, he had attended countless meetings; but what had happened to his poetry? In the early months of 1938 it seemed for a moment that he had escaped his isolation and re-joined society not merely as a political being but as a poet. Despite his intense shyness he appeared as a public speaker; he spoke for literature at a meeting of the Arts Peace Campaign on 6 January, together with representatives of the other arts including Eric Gill and Anthony Asquith, and he addressed meetings of the Left Book Club Writers' and Readers' Group, which had recently been founded with the aim of bringing readers and writers into closer contact. He also published his first new poem for nearly seven years. It was his first purely political poem, "To the Wife of Any Non-Intervention Statesman". His *Left Review* editorials are evidence of the emotional impact which the Spanish war had upon him, and this was intensified by his visits to Valencia and Madrid, when for the first time since 1918 he found himself within sound of gunfire. The emotions aroused by the war provided the impulse for his return to poetry, and his memories of 1917-18 determined the form which his poem would take.

Although Britain was not directly involved in the war and only a little over two thousand Britons took part in it, it inspired a considerable number of poems, a surprisingly high proportion of which can still be read. Many of them were the work of men who served in the International Brigade or the British Medical Units: Cornford, Wintringham, Clive Branson, Miles Tomalin, John Lepper, T.A.R. Hyndman, Ewart Milne.* These men wrote poems remarkably free from heroics. As an old soldier Rickword had contempt for exhortations to courage and sacrifice written by people safely behind the line. He could not produce such verse himself. He preferred to fight his battle against the enemy at home, the men who were betraying both Spain and Britain, and that meant satire – satire in the manner of Swift ("a master for every revolutionary writer"), but also satire owing something to his old master Sassoon, who had first taught him how to write poetry about

* Charles Donnelly's poems all seem to have been written before he went to Spain.

war. In making, as he hoped, a new beginning as a poet he had returned to his original starting-point.

The butt of his satire was the cynical farce of "non-intervention", whereby Germany and Italy supplied troops, aircraft, tanks, artillery and other equipment to the rebels while the legal Spanish Government was denied its right under international law to purchase arms for its own defence against foreign invaders. It is possible that the writing of "To the Wife of Any Non-Intervention Statesman"* was spread over some months. It sometimes echoes the thought and even elements of the phrasing of *Left Review* editorials published in the spring of 1937, as when

> So time reveals the true intent
> Behind the Gentlemen's Agreement

is anticipated by "time will reveal to the full the responsibility of the National Government for the aggression of Japanese, German and Italian imperialism". The references in the earlier part of the poem are to events of the spring and summer – the blockade of Bilbao, the exploits of the blockade-runner "Potato Jones" and the destruction of Guernica in April, the attempted flight of the population of Santander before the advancing rebels in August. When Rickword wrote

> Euzkadi's mines supply the ore
> To feed the Nazi dogs of war

it is difficult to believe that he had not in mind, consciously or unconsciously, two sentences in Swingler's editorial in the July *Left Review*:

> It is evidence of capitalism's obliteration of the imagination that at the very thought of the agony inflicted upon the civilised Basque people, the general public in every European country do not rise up as one man in a fine indignation determined once and for all to kennel those two mad dogs of war...To-day the Basques are being wiped out because they stand between Krupps and Thyssen and the iron-ore of the Bilbao mines.[2]

The first 62 lines of the poem may have been written in the late summer, when Rickword's anger at the slaughter of the Basques had been followed by the inspiration of his visit to Madrid.

The poem was completed late in January 1938 or early in February. It refers to the capture of Teruel by the Republicans on 8 January and to the subsequent bombing of Barcelona by Italian aircraft, and the final impetus for its completion seems to have been provided by a raid on 19 January and two more on 30 January – the same raids which inspired George Barker's moving "Elegy on Spain". The lines

---

* Renamed "To the Wife of a Non-Intervenionist Statesman" in the 1947 *Collected Poems*.

On Barcelona slums he rains
German bombs from Fiat planes.
Five hundred dead in ninety seconds
Is the world record so far reckoned;
A hundred children in one street,
Their little hands and guts and feet,
Like offal round a butcher's stall,
Scattered where they'd been playing ball

appear to echo press reports: "Six large and fast Savoias (so they have been described) circled over the city and within ninety seconds had killed some three hundred civilians. Children were struck down in their playgrounds." "Scores of bodies, including many children, were pieced together in the mortuaries. Sometimes scraps of clothing were the only means of identification." These reports refer to the raid on 19 January. On those of 30 January the *Manchester Guardian* wrote of "the ruin and death which came to Barcelona in ninety seconds", and the *News Chronicle* reported:

> It was, in fact, the old town of Barcelona – the slums with their narrow streets and overcrowded dwelling-houses – that was singled out for the attack…One bomb crashed through a crèche, where working mothers had left their children for the day. When I passed the spot ten minutes later the street was littered with human fragments – the remains of more than seventy little ones.

Details of both raids – the bombed slums, hundreds dead within ninety seconds, children killed while at play, fragments of their mangled bodies littering the street – evidently came together in Rickword's mind, whilst the figure "five hundred" may have been suggested by a press report, afterwards denied, that 500 children had been killed in a raid on Valencia on 19 January.[3]

When he was satisfied with his poem he lost no time in getting it into print. He sent it to *Left Review* early in February. Swingler asked "Gabriel" (James Friell), the *Daily Worker* cartoonist, to supply illustrations, quoted it prominently on the front cover of the March issue and printed it inside immediately after the editorial. The suggestion on the back cover that *Left Review* readers should "win over non-intervention statesmen through their wives" by making dates with them was a joke decidedly out of place in such a grim context.

As the poem's original title made clear, it was not directed against any single individual but against a group. Anthony Eden as Foreign Secretary was the politician most closely associated with the non-intervention policy in the public mind, rather unfairly, as he sympathized with the Republicans and had proposed that the Navy should be used to prevent German and Italian intervention. Far more involved were

Sir Samuel Hoare, First Lord of the Admiralty, and Admiral Sir Ernle
Chatfield, the First Sea Lord, both of whom supported Franco and
succeeded in defeating Eden's plan. Neville Chamberlain, Prime Minister since May 1937, was the chief culprit, who in pursuit of his policy
of appeasement of Germany and Italy forced Eden to resign on 20
February 1938, just after Rickword completed his poem. His target
was far wider than the British Government, however, or even their
supporters in Parliament. If the poem returns to his starting-point as a
follower of Sassoon it also takes up again from where he left off writing
verse in 1931, and can be regarded as an extension into the political
field of the anti-bourgeois satire, "Hints for Making a Gentleman".
The comparatively light-hearted satire on the gentlemen produced by
the public school system, who know "to whom they can be safely rude",
is developed into a grim indictment of the "Gentlemen's Agreement"
with Mussolini of January 1937 and the political consequences of their
social attitudes:

> From small beginnings mighty ends,
> From calling rebel generals friends,
> From being taught at public schools
> To think the common people fools,
> Spain bleeds, and England wildly gambles
> To bribe the butcher in the shambles.

Such lines confirm that this is a profoundly patriotic poem, both in the
modern sense of the word and in the eighteenth-century sense: it is a
poem which speaks for the English people against their rulers. In kind
it recalls such poems as Marvell's "Last Instructions to a Painter",
which is patriotic in its protest against Charles II's misrule at home
and his appeasement of Louis XIV abroad.

"To the Wife of Any Non-Intervention Statesman" has a further
literary source. Its basic idea, that a wife should force her husband to
change his policy by means of a sex-strike, derives from the *Lysistrata*
of Aristophanes, to whose splendid sanity Rickword had paid tribute
in his foreword to *Women in Parliament*. The poem begins with suave
irony as the speaker imagines himself entering the lady's boudoir, and
its play on the words "volunteered" and "intervene" and the use of
colloquialisms such as "ballyhoo" and "yarns" give the impression
that this light tone will be maintained throughout, so that the sudden
outburst of anger at the betrayal of the Basques comes with the force
of an explosion. To the excuse that non-intervention has preserved the
peace of Europe he replies in lines that within three years were to prove
tragically prophetic:*

---

* The reference to Hull may have been suggested by a report in the *Daily Worker* on 5 January
1938, that there was widespread alarm in Hull at the lack of effective air-raid precautions.

> Euzkadi's mines supply the ore
> To feed the Nazi dogs of war:
> Guernika's thermite rain transpires
> In doom on Oxford's dreaming spires:
> In Hitler's frantic mental haze
> Already Hull and Cardiff blaze,
> And Paul's grey dome rocks to the blast
> Of air-torpedoes screaming past.

He then returns to the Lysistrata theme:

> Traitor and fool's a combination
> To lower wifely estimation,
> Although there's not an Act in force
> Making it grounds for a divorce:
> But canon law forbids at least
> Co-habitation with a beast.

Rickword's use of the word "beast" seems to have shocked the American critic Hugh D. Ford, who accuses him of having fabricated "a revolting monster". For him, the poem fails because "the statesman is false, an obvious 'hate symbol'". Ford does not understand the sort of animal intended. Perhaps he had not seen Gabriel's illustrations, the first of which shows the lady in bed with a rat, the usual symbol of treachery. The rat reappears in the other two, gnawing the hand of a corpse and licking a dead child's blood in bombed Barcelona. Ford's statement that "the only vivid impression is the author's own fury",[4] which implies that Rickword is making a fuss about nothing very much, is not supported by writers such as Hugh Thomas, author of a standard history of the war, who refers to the "justified bitterness" of his satire, and Valentine Cunningham, who finds it "terrifyingly harsh". Spender rightly emphasizes that the poem is a moral statement, in which the fundamental ideas prostituted by politicians, such as liberty and justice, "are turned against the politicians, in order to expose an imposture and a sham". Ford's distaste for the poem is an example of that prejudice, "based on a temporary social queasiness", against the expression of negative emotions in poetry to which Rickword had referred in his famous essay.[5]

If the poem was written in two stages, it may originally have ended with the word "beast" − a Swiftian climax, similar to the conclusion of "Hints for Making a Gentleman" with the equally Swiftian rhyming word "stinks". Not feeling entirely satisfied with it, he perhaps put it aside until the raids on Barcelona brought his anger to white heat and drove him to complete it. After his outburst of fury over the bombing, he again addresses the wife with an anger which is now firmly under control:

> Would not a thinking wife contemn
> The sneaking hand that held the pen
> And with a flourish signed the deed
> Whence all these hearts and bodies bleed?

The association of signing a document with death suggests that when writing these lines he may have had in mind Dylan Thomas's poem "The hand that signed the paper felled a city", published four years earlier. After this final condemnation, the poem returns to the note on which it opens, in "Thanks, my hat". For the first time Rickword had found a theme to command his satirical talents and produced one of the few great political satires in the language.

Another critic who failed to appreciate the poem was Potocki. His admiration of Rickword's poetry had survived their fundamental differences on politics; in earlier numbers of his *Right Review* he had referred to him as "the greatest of living English poets" and "the sole ornament" of *Left Review*. In his issue of July 1938, however, he wrote:

> In one of the last numbers of the *Left Review* appeared Edgell Rickword's first poem since "Twittingpan" (1931), date of his perversion to bolshevism. It is a longish attack on Franco, however one stupid attack more or less doesn't matter. What matters is this brilliant feat of bolshevic Kulcher in England. They have reduced our best poet to writing such drivelling doggerel that we took it for a piece of trotskyist sabotage. It looks more as if it had been written by Garman, or Wishart or the officeboy, than by Edgell.[6]

As the poem contains only two passing references to Franco in 94 lines, Potocki's description of it as "a longish attack on Franco" suggests that political bias drove him to condemn it without reading it.

His next attack on Rickword's verse was better justified. Whether his success with "To the Wife of Any Non-Intervention Statesman" encouraged Rickword to try his hand at a political poem of a more positive type or gave an editor the idea of commissioning one from him, a poem of his called "The National Question in the U.S.S.R." appeared in the June issue of *Soviet Life and Work*, the organ of the Society for Cultural Relations between the Peoples of the British Commonwealth and the U.S.S.R. The poem is uninspired, abounding in clichés such as "earth flowers beneath their eager hands" and "robber empires ruled by hate", and is largely a rehash of his review of N. Mikhaylov's *Soviet Geography* in the March 1936 *Left Review* and his article "Stalin on the National Question" in the November 1936 issue. The phrases "the sandy desert and the frozen wastes" and "peoples given back their languages and their crafts" in the former reappear in the poem as "from arctic ice to sun-burnt sands" and "old crafts and re-born cultures thrive", whilst the quotation from Stalin forming the epigraph to the poem had already appeared in the latter. Potocki quoted the poem in full in the October issue of *Right Review* in an article headed "Invocation to an Apostate Angel", and after describing it as "Edgell's Salvation Army hymn" commented: "It seems inconceivable that such a Poet as Edgell once was, could write this boring guff. Many of the lowest sort of hymns have more 'guts' and more beauty. Apollo deserts those who join in the communist conspiracy against the human race." Rickword seems to have come round to Potocki's view of his poem; not only did he not reprint it, but it is his only published poem which he never mentioned to Alan Young, who compiled a bibliography of his writings.

Potocki's attack on his poem was justifiable, but the libellous attack on Rickword which accompanied it was not. His article continued:

> And stay — what gullible goyish reader of the late left review would ever have dreamt that Edgell served the British Empire in the volunteer force known to the Irish as the *Black-and-Tans*, which the Editor of the *Right Review*, though an imperialist and a scion of a long line of warriors, would hardly like to have done. You would do better by your own soul, Edgell, former friend, if you were to leave the Gentiles to govern their own world, which their forefathers with such genius and such tribulation created on the soil of Europe. Those who obstruct the renewal of that work, deserve what they will get.[7]

As an intimation that his admiration for Rickword was at an end, the June 1939 issue of *Right Review* referred to Roy Campbell, who had published a volume of poems glorifying Franco, as "her (i.e. England's) greatest poet". In his high opinion of Campbell's rhetoric, as in his low opinion of "To the Wife of Any Non-Intervention Statesman", he was almost unique.

The story that Rickword had been a member of the Black and Tans (the force of British ex-servicemen employed on police duties in Ireland during the War of Independence in 1920-21, who became notorious for atrocities against the civilian population) seems to have circulated quite widely in the literary world at this time, although it was as baseless as Potocki's other allegation that he was a Jew. His sympathies with Irish republicanism, developed as early as 1916, would have made him the last man to volunteer for the Black and Tans; even if he had, a one-eyed man invalided out of the Army would not have been accepted; and in 1920-21 he was fully occupied, first in keeping his terms at Oxford, then in supporting his family by contributing to the *Daily Herald* and the *New Statesman*. The only foundation for the story seems to have been the fact that he had been stationed in Dublin with his regiment for two short periods in 1917-18.

In October he published his third political poem of the year, "The

Two Worlds", later renamed "Incompatible Worlds". An address to his master Swift, who

> preferred the tone satiric,
> Used but rarely panegyric,

it is in effect a synthesis of his two previous poems, combining the satire of "To the Wife of Any Non-Intervention Statesman" with the panegyric of "The National Question in the U.S.S.R." The use of themes from Swift to satirize Fascism may have been suggested to him by a letter published shortly before in the *Spectator*, which began: "The report of the physical fitness tests to which officials of the Fascist Party are now subjected, and which include jumping over upright rows of bayonets and diving through burning hoops, recalls a passage from *Gulliver's Travels*. At the court of Lilliput, officers and 'candidates for great employments' were obliged to demonstrate their physical dexterity by dancing on a rope..." He had already used *Gulliver* as a model for a satire on contemporary society in the Yahoo papers in the *Calendar*. The poem rests on the assumption that Swift's attacks on tyranny, injustice and war imply his belief in the possibility of a free, just and peaceful society, but the identity of the two worlds which represent the two sides of this antithesis is left vague. One world is clearly that of Fascism, where

> Laputan justice rules,
> Bombing fractious slums and schools –

in Barcelona, for example. It is not difficult to recognize Nazi Germany in the lines

> For the foulest pigmy crew
> Pullulates the half-world through,
> Crushing under bully heels
> All that finely grows or feels,
> And would dowse the spirit's lamp
> In a concentration camp.

More debatable is the identity of the second world, where

> the justice you invoke
> Men are building stroke by stroke,
> Where people are accounted wealth
> And liberty society's health.

Do these lines refer to the Western democracies, the Soviet Union or both? Were the builders of justice the Soviet people, who in the slogan of the day were "building Socialism" under Stalin's leadership, or those in every country who strove to build a more just society? Or were the two worlds the capitalist countries, whether Fascist or democratic, on the one hand, the Soviet Union on the other? Probably a comedy of errors occurred; Rickword intended his second world to represent both the Soviet Union and the democracies, which he hoped would form an alliance against Fascism, but a Conservative editor accepted the poem under the impression that it contrasted democracy with dictatorship, whether Fascist or Communist.[8]*

"The Two Worlds" appeared in the *Spectator*, not in *Left Review*, which had ceased publication in the previous May, though not, as Potocki suggested, because it had "found itself unable to sustain comparison with the Right Review".[9] Swingler's final editorial was optimistic in tone. The review was closing, he claimed, "not because it has proved a failure, or because its first success is declining. Precisely for the opposite reason. Paradoxically it comes to an end at the height of its success, and because of that success. Its history has been a gradually mounting graph of influence and position. Now it is felt by the Editorial Board that the present basis of editorial work, production and distribution, is too narrow to cope adequately with the job and the opportunities that press so urgently upon us." After summarizing its history at length, he concluded: "LEFT REVIEW as you have known it, and as it has established itself in the cultural world, will close, so that we may give all our energy in support of a wider project, which can reach a vastly greater mass of the people." On a later spread a full-page announcement appeared that a new pocket-sized and fully illustrated monthly review dealing comprehensively with the arts and sciences would commence publication in the following September.[10] In fact, no such magazine appeared, and the group of Marxist writers which included Rickword and Swingler had to wait until the publication of *Our Time* in 1941 before they again controlled a journal dealing comprehensively with literature and the other arts.

What had happened? The answer may be found in the last issue of *Left Review*, which contained articles by Allen Lane of Penguin Books and Donald Kitchin on the revolution in publishing which Penguins had already achieved. Lane was eager to include cultural journals, scientific as well as literary, in the Penguin list, and was later to publish *Penguin New Writing* and other periodicals. It would therefore appear that by May 1938 a *Penguin Left Review* had been planned, and that for reasons unknown the project fell through. According to Hugh D. Ford, who drew his information from Swingler, Victor Gollancz declined an invitation to take the journal over,[11] presumably after Lane had dropped the original plan.

Rickword's reviews for *Life and Letters To-day*, which probably formed his main source of income during 1938, all dealt with books on

* In a letter to David Holbrook written in 1962 Rickword says of this poem: "I fortunately struck out the stanza identifying the USSR of Stalin's day with the Ideal."

historical or political themes, and though they display his firm grasp
of realities are of little interest. His only contribution to the *Daily
Worker* in the course of the year was a review of Louis MacNeice's
The Earth Compels, to which he gave lukewarm praise: "Mr MacNeice
has the courage of his lack of convictions…He is at his best when he
can throw off his intellectual preoccupations and write straight out of
some sensuous experience; but what Mr MacNeice's poetry needs is
more mental energy." He seems to have revised his opinion of Mac-
Neice's verse by 1964, when he described much of it as "truly delight-
ful".[12]

The only important prose work which he published in 1938 – indeed,
his most important piece of critical writing of the 1930s – was an essay
on Malraux. This appeared in *New Writing*, which Lehmann had transferred to the Hogarth Press after his contract with Lawrence & Wishart
expired. "André Malraux: Action and Humanism" is at once Rickword's last study of a French writer (with the exception of a brief note
on Rimbaud published in 1948) and his first extended critical study
written from a Marxist viewpoint. The first three pages of this essay
abound in ideas each capable of being developed at length, as he traces
the development of the French tradition of humanism derived from the
writers of the Renaissance and the Enlightenment through the nineteenth and early twentieth centuries. The writers who were heirs of
that tradition, he suggests, reacted to the defeats which it suffered in
1830, 1848 and 1871, the Great War and the vindictive peace which
followed by retreat into an intenser subjectivism and the refinement of
technique, evolving Parnassianism, Symbolism, Naturalism, Dadaism
or Surrealism. Malraux is portrayed growing up in this mental climate
and escaping from it first through contact with the popular movements
in Indo-China and China, then through active participation in the struggle in Spain. This simple summary may suggest a mechanical attempt
to conform to a Marxist formula, but both the general argument and
the detailed analysis of the novels are developed with such subtlety that
one wishes Rickword had applied his Marxist critical technique to
other novelists, English as well as French. A particular combination of
circumstances evoked this brilliant essay: personal contact with Malraux in London in 1936 and in Spain in 1937; his visit to Spain, which
deepened his appreciation both of the significance of the war and of
Malraux's treatment of it in *L'Espoir*; and perhaps admiration of Malraux for having combined the roles of creative artist and man of action
as he would have liked to do, had he not been prevented by physical
disabilities and psychological inhibitions.

His income from occasional writings was not sufficient to cover the
cost of life in London, even when supplemented by his disability pension of £3 10s a week and Jonny's earnings. Another retreat to the

provinces became necessary, the first for over five years. In the spring of 1938 he and Jonny gave up their lodgings in Hampstead and moved in with her parents in the village of Hookpit, near Winchester. When Frederic Quilter died of a longstanding complaint in the Summer they accepted an invitation from the Irish novelist Jim Phelan, who had been a contributor to *Left Review*, to stay with him and his wife in a small village near Marseille, and took Mrs Quilter with them. On the way they spent a day or two in Paris, where she delighted in the French cuisine, which brought back memories of the early days of her marriage; in particular, she praised the quenelles in one restaurant as almost as exquisite as those which she had eaten on her honeymoon. All three enjoyed their stay in Provence; there was dancing in the village on Sundays, and Jonny's mother, who developed a taste for the wine of the region, passed much of her time in a blissful haze. After a while, however, they found money running short and the winds losing their warmth; reluctantly they returned to England, Mrs Quilter to Hookpit, Rickword and Jonny to rooms in Winchester. It was a beautiful town, rich in architecture and in memories, the resting-place of Izaak Walton and Jane Austen, with libraries where Rickword could carry on research, but not a very lively centre of Communist activities, though he did conduct political education classes for students at Southampton University.

At the end of 1938 he lost his mother. Despite the differences in their political and religious views, he had remained on good terms with his parents and seldom failed to return to Colchester for Christmas. This annual family reunion was all the more important to him as it gave him one of his rare opportunities to meet both his daughters. His Christmas presents to them often took the form of books, some of which his younger daughter still possesses, among them *Alice in Wonderland*, *The Arabian Nights* and a set of translations of Russian booklets for children on scientific topics. The first break in the Rickword family circle had occurred four years before, when George Rickword died on 23 November 1934, three days after his 78th birthday. He had remained a respected figure in Colchester, especially in its literary circles, until his death; only a month earlier he and Gerald had been among the Mayor's guests at the town's annual oyster feast. The mourners at his funeral service, in addition to his sons and daughters, included the Mayor of Colchester, the borough librarian and representatives of the Essex Archaeological Society, the Colchester Arts Club, the Colchester and Essex Museum, the Colchester branch of the National Association of Local Government Officers and the staff of the public library, which had largely been his creation.

During the four years that she survived her husband, the Christmas reunion became very important to Mabel Rickword and her family.

To her, as her son recalled in his memoirs, Christmas was a time when "the warmth of her nature had an opportunity to express itself", and as an Anglo-Catholic she must have appreciated what her son had written about Donne: "To deny the pleasures of the body would have been to him as great a blasphemy as to abuse them. The birthday of Christ is a day of rejoicing, not of mortification; and the celebration of Christmas as a feast is symbolic of the eternal joy to which humanity is admitted through the Incarnation."[13] On 27 December 1938, just before lunch, as she bent down to take a bottle of sherry from the sideboard cupboard, she gave a faint scream and collapsed on the floor. That same evening she died without pain, surrounded by her sons and daughters.

An interesting assessment of Rickword's verse had appeared earlier in the year in Herbert Palmer's *Post-Victorian Poetry*. Both as poet and critic Palmer was a traditionalist, but one of a highly individual type; violently hostile to all forms of Modernism, and especially to Eliot and Edith Sitwell, he was almost equally scathing about the Neo-Georgians of the Squirearchy. He was obviously intrigued by Rickword, without being quite sure whether he approved of him or not. After classifying him among "older poets standing outside the Georgian encampment... who have little or no affinity with the extreme modernists", he decided that "he is quite clearly not a satisfactory traditionalist, though tradition triumphs in his form", and finally summed him up as follows:

> An even more depressing pessimist than Thomas Hardy (but with whom, of course, he has little in common), he contemplates with both disapproval and cynical resignation many of the shattered values of this post-War age...But he can sometimes be a poet of pure beauty...He is, I am inclined to think, the only complete and satisfactory English Symbolist.[14]

XIII. The English Tradition

THE international Communist movement, which originated as a moral protest against the slaughter of the First World War, in its early days repudiated nationalism and even patriotism, except when they took the form of a revolt against colonialism, as sentiments liable to be exploited by imperialists in preparing new wars. By the 1930s, however, it had become obvious that by underestimating the strength of national feeling among the working class, rural workers and the petit bourgeoisie Communists had facilitated the propaganda of the Fascist parties. Georgi Dimitrov dealt with this problem in 1935 in his report to the Seventh World Congress of the Comintern, in which he laid down the strategy of the Popular Front. "The fascists are rummaging through the entire history of every nation," he pointed out

> so as to be able to pose as the heirs and continuators of all that was exalted and heroic in its past...Communists who suppose that all this has nothing to do with the cause of the working class, who do nothing to enlighten the masses on the past of their people, in a genuinely Marxist, a Leninist-Marxist, a Leninist-Stalinist spirit, who do nothing to *link up the present struggle with the people's revolutionary traditions and past* – voluntarily hand over to the fascist falsifiers all that is valuable in the historical past of the nation, that the fascists may dupe the masses.[1]

The Western Communist parties took his advice. The French Communists claimed to be the heirs, not only of the Communards, the Jacobins and the *philosophes*, but even of St Joan, the peasant girl who, as they delighted in recalling, after saving her country was deserted by the King and burned by the Church. They sang the *Marseillaise* (hitherto scorned as the song of French militarism and imperialism) as fervently as the *Internationale*, and flew the tricolour, like the *Marseillaise* a survival from the great Revolution, side by side with the red flag. The American Communists quoted Jefferson and Lincoln, and adopted the slogan "Communism is twentieth-century Americanism". The British party organized a March of English History on 20 September 1936, in which banners depicting scenes from the English people's struggle for freedom were carried through London. Over the next three years similar demonstrations took place in provincial cities and towns, scenes from local history depicted on the banners. In a march in Manchester, the Peterloo massacre figured. In 1937 an exhibition of Radical and Socialist history from John Wilkes to the General Strike, organized by G.D.H. Cole, was held in London; although Cole was a Labour Party member he supported the Popular Front, and Collet's bookshop, which assisted in the preparation of the exhibition, was Communist-controlled. Great emphasis was laid on the centenary of the Chartist movement in 1939; the London party staged a Pageant of Chartism at the Empress Hall, and pageants were held in South Wales to commemorate the centenary of the Newport rising. This glorification of the democratic and labour movements of the past was accompanied by a revival of interest in the radical tradition in English literature, and in 1936 the *Daily Worker* published a series of articles on radical writers, "The Past is Ours", in which among others Ralph Fox wrote on Fielding and Alick West on Shelley and Wordsworth.

The writers in the party enthusiastically supported this new development in its propaganda. Even before Dimitrov made his speech *Left Review* had published articles by Montagu Slater on the Leveller Richard Overton, by Allen Hutt on British Socialists of the early nineteenth century and by Rickword on Swift. Three writers in particular devoted themselves to the study of the English radical tradition in politics and literature: A.L. Morton, Jack Lindsay and Rickword. Morton published in 1938 *A People's History of England*, a pioneering attempt to reinterpret English history in Marxist terms, and this was followed over the next forty years by a number of valuable critical and historical studies. Lindsay, who had shown his interest in the radical tradition in "Who Are the English?", wrote a life of Bunyan and a trilogy of novels on English radical movements: *1649* (1938) on the Levellers, *Lost Birthright* (1940) on the Wilkesites and *Men of Forty-Eight* (written in 1939 but not published until 1948) on the Chartists. When Swingler, who had started a small publishing business called Fore Publications, asked him to develop the argument of "Who Are the English?" into a pamphlet, he produced a long essay on English revolutionary movements called *England my England*, which demonstrated that, in its closing words, "Communism is English". Published in 1939 as the first of a series of twopenny pamphlets, it sold 80,000 copies.

Apart from his essay on Swift, Rickword's first study of a radical writer was an article on Milton, which he contributed to the *Daily Worker*'s "The Past is Ours" series in December 1936. As in his review of Tillyard's book, it was Milton's continued relevance which he stressed. In the essay, which is headed "Milton Posed Problems That Still Remain", he wrote:

> Neither Milton's vision of truth and justice, nor the Levellers' attempt at economic equality on an agrarian basis, could be satisfied in a class society. But such ideas have never died; they have come to the surface at every time of stress, and have been voiced in some form or other by every considerable poet since...*Paradise Lost, Paradise Regained* and

Samson Agonistes (a dramatic poem) are the highest achievements of poetic genius in England outside the work of Shakespeare. There is no space to analyse them here, but let no one think that their Biblical mythology robs them of intellectual interest today. They pose problems of free-will and destiny that are still ours; and Milton was a strong and original thinker who was always breaking through the metaphysical habits of thought towards the dialectic that solves these problems.[2]

Milton and his times are the subject of two reviews published in the spring of 1938. When discussing David Daiches's *Literature and Society*, an attempt at a Marxist history of English literature, it is the inadequate treatment of Milton which Rickword criticizes most firmly, and both here and in a review of E. Wingfield-Stratford's *King Charles and the Conspirators* he hits out at the sentimental Tory-Anglican interpretations of history which had been dear to George Rickword.[3]

His first essay of any length on the radical tradition was "Culture, Progress, and English Tradition", written for *The Mind in Chains*, a symposium edited by Day Lewis and published in June 1937. Twelve left-wing writers discussed aspects of culture in their relationship to society from a Socialist, usually a Marxist, viewpoint, with Rickword's contribution as the conclusion and summing-up. After emphasizing that all culture is based on labour and quoting Langland's *Piers Plowman* as "a great poem in praise of social labour", he discusses the agrarian communism of John Ball, Sir Thomas More and the Diggers. The Levellers, Milton, Swift, Wilkes, Junius, Shelley, Byron, Cobbett and the Chartists are cited as spokesmen for "the ideals, so simple, so human, which are the core of the English, as of every popular tradition", and which can be realized only "if the productive forces of the country are in the hands of the producers themselves". Returning to his starting-point, that labour is the basis of culture, he suggests that many of the artist's problems arise from the divisions within society created by an increasing specialization and subdivision of labour, for which, he maintains, Socialism provides the solution. He stresses that a Socialist culture cannot repudiate the past, and rejects attempts "to erect a proletarian culture from 'first principles'". "In England to-day," he concludes,

> the preservation of culture in this Marxist sense is the responsibility of the adherents of the working class and democratic parties. As capitalism becomes more and more reactionary, the struggle to maintain the freedom of thought, the liberty of the subject, the toleration of opinion, which our ancestors won so hardly and which we thought we could enjoy without an effort, takes on again a revolutionary significance... The conditions of to-day, no less than the period of the building of socialism, require the assimilation and transformation of the past.[4]

It is an eloquent statement of his credo, marred only by a too trusting reference to the democracy promised by the new Soviet constitution, and a fitting prologue to the series of studies of English radicals which he was to write over the next forty years.

Late in 1938 or early in 1939 he reviewed two anthologies of historical documents for *Life and Letters To-day*: *Puritanism and Liberty*, a collection of Leveller documents edited by A.S.P. Woodhouse, including the Putney debates of 1647, which he had quoted in "Culture, Progress, and English Tradition", and *Writing and Action*, an anthology of prose passages on the development of political and intellectual freedom edited by Mary Palmer, which he described as "a book which one could recommend to a cabinet minister or some visitor from a totalitarian state who wanted to know what that freedom is that the English prize so highly".[5] Either of these books or Jack Lindsay's *England my England* may have suggested to him the idea of a comprehensive anthology of both prose and verse illustrating the struggle for freedom throughout English history. He secured the co-operation of Lindsay, who placed at his disposal the archive which he had collected while working on his pamphlet and his trilogy of novels; he then sifted through it, made some omissions and some additions and wrote an introduction "On English Freedom". In this form it was published by Lawrence & Wishart in May, with the title *A Handbook of Freedom*.

It is impossible to say which of the editors was responsible for the inclusion of most of the items; Rickword probably selected the extracts from Swift's poems, and Lindsay the poems by his Cumbrian poacher friends the Denwood family; but as they shared common interests and a common outlook the point is not important. Their picture of the growth of English freedom is very different from the Whig-Liberal version. In the first chapter a page is devoted to Magna Carta (which, Rickword points out, "confirmed its privileges only to the *free men* of England, who even at that late date were a bare quarter of the population") and half a page to Simon de Montfort, whereas the popular movement in London in 1196 led by William FitzOsbert receives nearly five pages and the Peasants' Revolt over eighteen. On the Revolution of 1688, which is represented only by the seven bishops' protest against the Declaration of Indulgence and Locke's justification of popular resistance, Rickword expresses a view very different from Macaulay's: "The 'glorious Revolution' of 1688 secured the new men of property, and the great landlords who had sloughed off their feudal rents in the form of an excise on the working-people's beer, against any threat to their wealth from the Crown. A wonderful age of plunder began." The only comment in the book on the 1832 Reform Bill is supplied by two extracts from *The Poor Man's Guardian*, pointing out that it would benefit the manufacturers but not the working class.

A consistent political philosophy runs through the book.

The plain necessity of having to work and fight through long centuries
for every advantage has fixed the strain, and has ingrained that deep
suspicion of the bosses which Froissart noted as making us a nation
very awkward to rule. Experience, too, bitter experience, has weaned
us from over-much enthusiasm for freedom in the abstract, for the freedom which is the climax of the politician's oratory. We have always
been concerned with freedom in some specific form, of association, of
expression or from arbitrary imprisonment, and such rights have proved
essential tactical positions when it comes to defending or extending the
material conditions which really measure the degree to which a society
is effectively democratic. Though we certainly haven't been indifferent
to the constitutional forms under which we have had to live, the profoun-
dest changes have had the bread and butter question at the root of them.
To be free and hungry is no doubt better than to be enslaved and hungry,
but we have always refused to believe that freedom and hunger can
subsist together... It was the most ethereal of our poets who expressed
this common-sense view of the matter, for that is how Shelley answered
the question, What is freedom? –

> For the labourer it is bread,
> And a comely table spread –

the necessities of life, and the amenities which are no less necessary to
human self-respect.

Rickword does not allow his insistence on the economic basis of freedom to lead him into the ultra-leftist position of despising constitutional
forms and democratic rights, however: "Democracy ensures us the
right to promote change, and those who sneer at its evident limitations
as we have it to-day, are repudiating the wisdom gathered from the
harsh but inspiring experience of twelve centuries".[6]

This explains the choice of the material included. Emphasis is placed
on the great national and regional movements of revolt: the Peasants'
Revolt, the Lollards, Cade's Rebellion, Kett's Rebellion, the Midlands
Rising of 1607, the Levellers, the Wilkesites, the naval mutinies of
1797, the Luddites, the Labourers' Revolt of 1831, the Chartists, the
New Unionism. Along with these we are shown the important local
and sectional struggles – primitive forms of trade unionism, from
medieval journeyman's guilds to Tolpuddle, resistance to enclosures
and impressment, food riots, the Dissenters' and freethinkers' struggle
for freedom of conscience, juries' defiance of bullying judges, the battle
for freedom of the press. The book does not deal only with popular
movements, however; the contribution of the poets, philosophers and
scientists is fully recognized. Extracts from *Piers Plowman* precede the
chroniclers' accounts of the Peasants' Revolt, speeches from *Timon* and
Coriolanus follow and implicitly comment on the report of the 1607
rising. Milton appears with Lilburne and Winstanley as a spokesman

for the Left in the English Revolution. Bunyan's narrative of the trial of
Faithful accompanies contemporary reports of the persecution of Quakers,
Samuel Bamford's eyewitness account of Peterloo is followed by passages
from Shelley's *Mask of Anarchy* and Keats's letters. The poems included
in themselves form a remarkable anthology, in which passages from major
poets are eloquently juxtaposed with anonymous ballads and the work
of little-known poets expressing, rudely but often forcefully, popular protest or popular aspirations.

The book had a favourable reception. J.B. Priestley described it as
"something really worth doing" and Philip Henderson as "an admirable
achievement". *The Times Literary Supplement* said: "the result of the
collaborators' wide and painstaking research is fascinating, and should
appeal not only to the progressive but also to the historian".[7] The historian
E.P. Thompson carried it with him throughout the war, and it contributed
to the researches which produced his classic *The Making of the English
Working Class*.[8] Yet the book seems to have aroused suspicions among
the Communist Party bureaucracy. The title was suspected of containing
a snide reference to Emile Burns's *A Handbook of Marxism* (a compilation
of extracts from the works of Marx, Engels, Lenin and Stalin), with the
implication that an English tradition of libertarian Communism existed
as an alternative to the authoritarian Communism of "the Four Great
Teachers", and a cheap edition published in 1941 was renamed *Spokesmen for Liberty*. When in the 1950s Rickword's friend Jack Beeching,
then a director of Lawrence & Wishart, suggested that it should be
reprinted the proposal was rejected. King Street's suspicions were probably
justified; in a letter to David Holbrook Rickword said in 1964 that the
book, "I suppose expresses my political position as well as it will ever
be", and significantly added: "Fortunately I did not hitch my ideals to
Stalin's Russia".

One offshoot of the book was Rickword's contribution to a series of
articles in the *Daily Worker* on "Books I would read again". He chose
as his subject Langland's *Piers Plowman*, which he had quoted in "Culture,
Progress, and English Tradition", and from which he had included five
pages of extracts in the *Handbook*.

> In his visionary way he saw that the bond of fellowship must supersede
> the sword of justice as the power holding society together, not only because
> that sword is liable to corruption, but because its existence is the sign that
> men are divided among themselves, that it is, as we should say, the instru-
> ment of an exploiting class...Piers Plowman is the spirit of comradeship
> permeating all the thoughts and actions of men in labour for the common
> good, all sects and pettiness laid aside.[9]

This may be nearer to Morris's philosophy than to Langland's; in its
rejection of sectarian intolerance and its recognition of the tendency

of state power to corrupt, it is certainly nearer to Morris's than to Stalin's.

Apart from this article and his review of Caudwell's poems, his only contribution to the *Daily Worker* in 1939 was a review of Eliot's *The Family Reunion*. He had praised Eliot's work ever since he reviewed *The Sacred Wood* in 1920, but his admiration had remained on this side of idolatry. After the review in the *Calendar* of *Poems, 1909-1929* his attitude had become increasingly unenthusiastic. He found the mood of "The Hollow Men" uncomfortably close to the "inclination towards nihilism" from which he had suffered in the later 1920s; he now found equally distasteful the religion in which Eliot had taken refuge from despair. In 1929 he wrote: "Some years ago it seemed that 'The Waste Land' might dominate the sensibility of a half-generation or so. But there was a definite weakening of influence when Mr Eliot expressed his vision of the way the world ends – 'not with a bang but a whimper', and since then the search has gone on for a more virile gesture." Reviewing *Selected Essays* in *Scrutiny*, he suggested that the literary sensibility of the earlier essays was not matched in the later ones.[10] Of *The Family Reunion* he wrote: "It is not surprising that Mr Eliot's poetic ability has wilted in this atmosphere of country-house vapidity. He knows that these people are parched at the root, but rather than face the fact, and its consequent action, he tries to inject them with a fabulous semi-Freudian, semi-religious significance."[11] The review – his last word on Eliot – is unsympathetic, yet one senses in it a note of regret for a lost leader.

His essay on Langland, with its appeal for human brotherhood, appeared six weeks before the outbreak of war. From the Anglo-French betrayal of Czechoslovakia at Munich and the British Government's rejection of plans for an Anglo-Soviet alliance Stalin concluded that the Western democracies were encouraging Hitler to expand to the East rather than to the West, and on 23 August concluded a non-aggression pact with Germany. Although this development shocked all sections of British opinion ("all the isms are now wasms", a humorist remarked), nowhere was the sense of shock greater than in the Communist Party. Party spokesmen produced ingenious explanations (that by dividing Germany from Italy the pact had "smashed the Axis") and declared an Anglo-Soviet alliance to be more urgently needed than ever, but few were convinced. On 2 September, the day after Germany invaded Poland, the Party issued a manifesto pledging its support for "all necessary measures to secure the victory of democracy over Fascism" and calling for "a struggle on two fronts, first to secure the military victory over Fascism, and second in order to achieve this, the political victory over Chamberlain and the enemies of democracy in this country". On 24 September, however, the British representative at the

Communist International, D.F. Springhall, arrived from Moscow with the news that the Comintern's official line was that the war was an imperialist war. After heated debates the Central Committee accepted the new policy, with only Harry Pollitt and J.R. Campbell dissenting, and a new manifesto issued on 7 October declared that the war was "not a war for democracy against Fascism" but "a fight between imperialist powers over profits, colonies and world domination".[12]

To regard this rapid change of policy merely as the supreme example of the party's subservience to Moscow, though understandable, would not be entirely just. Since 1800 the British Left has repeatedly found itself pulled in opposite directions by two of its strongest passions, hatred of tyranny and militarism on the one hand, hatred of war on the other. During the Napoleonic War, the Crimean War, the Balkan crisis of 1876-78, the two World Wars, the Korean War and the Falklands War Jacobins, Chartists, Radicals and Socialists successively were divided between those who saw the conflict as one against an aggressive tyranny and those who saw it as a sordid struggle for power and territory. Of the three major British Socialist parties in 1939, the Labour Party supported the war as just and necessary, the Independent Labour Party (as well as tiny sects like the Socialist Party of Great Britain) opposed it as an imperialist war, and the Communist Party first supported it and then opposed it. The opponents of the war had a case. Chamberlain, the man of appeasement, non-intervention and Munich, was not a convincing leader for an anti-Fascist crusade. He had admitted some opponents of appeasement, such as Churchill, to his Cabinet, but Churchill, the architect of British intervention in Russia and the leading opponent of self-government for India, was no hero to the Left. The British and French Governments seemed to regard Communism rather than Fascism as the enemy. While military action against Germany was virtually confined to the dropping of leaflets, the French Government devoted most of its energies to the persecution of Communists, and both Britain and France planned to assist Finland in its war against the Soviet Union – a piece of folly which, fortunately for Britain, was frustrated by the unexpectedly rapid Soviet victory.

Anti-war feeling was strengthened by the memory of the First World War. In 1914 volunteers were lured into the Army by assurances that this was a war to end war and to make the world safe for democracy and promises of an England fit for heroes to live in. Those who returned from the trenches found that the hard-faced men had done well out of the war, while the heroes rotted on the dole. Such memories led Rickword to accept the Communist Party's policy on the war. "I should say that the most important thing was to get peace, not to fight to a finish which will involve the deaths of millions," he wrote to his daughter Jane in June 1940.

And the first thing to do is to recognise our equal responsibility for the war – our holding on to "our" imperial possessions is just as wicked as Germany wanting to take them away, which is what the war is about and not about democracy and civilisation. I am inoculated against that form of propaganda by my experience of the last war for democracy.

He put his feelings about the war into a poem which appeared in *Poetry and the People*. This little magazine originated in 1938 as the organ of the Poetry Groups of the Left Book Club and appeared in mimeographed form until the autumn of 1939, when it doubled its price to sixpence and switched to print. Its contributors included Swingler, Lindsay, Morton, Idris Davies and Maurice Carpenter, who had published some poems in *Left Review*; Clive Branson and Ewart Milne, who had served in Spain; the Canadian Paul Potts, who could regularly be seen hawking his poems at political demonstrations; Roger Woddis, master of satirical light verse; the Apocalyptic Nicholas Moore and a number of young poets – the Australian John Manifold, Hubert Nicholson and Jack Beeching – who were to become Rickword's colleagues on *Our Time*. Some well-known names appeared in an appeal for financial support published in the issue for February 1940 – not only Communists such as Sommerfield, Swingler, Sylvia Townsend Warner and Alick West, but also Moore, William Soutar and Spender. Even after the Communist Party's change of policy and the Finnish War had bitterly divided the Left, co-operation between Communists and non-Communists was still possible in the literary world.

The issue for May 1940 contained Rickword's first poem for nearly two years: "Then and Now (Remembering school-friends killed in the 1914-18 war)". It was inspired by strong feelings as he recalled the useless sacrifice of Eric Brand and his other friends who had died, but feelings alone do not make a poem cohere. In attempting to address the widest possible audience he lapsed into rhetorical clichés ("lost generation", "storm-tossed", "prating slanders", etc.) and a jogtrot metre. Although moving, the poem is unsophisticated and even amateurish; his failure all the more glaring in contrast with Swingler's biting anti-war satire "Sixty Cubic Feet", printed in the same issue. Conscious that he had failed, he made no further serious attempt to write verse for fourteen years.

Three important essays appeared under the common title "War and Poetry: 1914-18" in the June, July and August numbers of *Life and Letters To-day*. Although they too were inspired by the outbreak of war, which recalled the earlier war, he does not attempt to draw a political moral. Instead he traces the development of the poetry of the war from the crude propaganda and muddled idealism of 1914 to the protests of Sassoon and Owen and leaves it to the reader to draw what inferences he will. He takes it for granted that the war was a product

218 The English Tradition

of the economic rivalries of the great powers and that they shared the
responsibility for it. Few people were likely to be shocked by such a
view in 1940. Far from being propaganda, these essays are among the
most subtle and sensitive of his critical studies. After quoting examples
of the rhetoric occasioned by the outbreak of war from William Watson,
Eden Philpotts, Herold Begbie and Alfred Noyes, he considers the "conspicuously undefined idealism" expressed in the early war poems of
Masefield and Brooke. He does not attempt to sneer; it was, in Masefield's phrase,

> some idea but dimly understood
> Of an English city never built by hands

which had sent sixteen-year-old Jack Rickword to try to enlist. Brooke's
1914 sonnets, which in the 1930s had been a joke among intellectuals
on the Left, are subjected to patient, not hostile analysis which illumi-
nates the mental conflicts underlying their apparent certainties. When,
for example, he points out that in the first sonnet "hardly a line follows
grammatically from the preceding one" the reader rereads the poem
with fresh eyes.[13]

The essays recognize that style and content are inseparable, and that
"terminology was an important factor in the creation of a genuine
war-poetry". The second essay traces how the trench poets, by trial
and error, finally evolved a style adequate to tell the truth about the
war as they saw it. The transition from rhetoric to realism is illustrated
by skilful quotations from the heroics of Julian Grenfell's "Into Battle";
W.N. Hodgson's "Back to Rest", conventional in style but realistic in
content; C.H. Sorley's "When you see millions of the mouthless dead",
with its unflinching contemplation of death; the imagist free verse of
Robert Nichols's "The Assault"; Edward Thomas's "Lights Out", in
which "the war theme is subtly suggested in the purely subjective reference"; the satirical free verse of Osbert Sitwell; and the realism of
Sassoon's "Suicide in Trenches", in which "the poetic diction has been
burnt out of the poet's consciousness by the permeation of war's reality". Although it was from Sassoon that Rickword had learned to write
war poetry, he does not hold him up as a single model; he recognizes
the "new experience...piercing the obvious rhetoric" in Hodgson's
poem, and the failure of Nichols's experiment does not prevent him
from declaring him "a real poet". (Nichols repaid the compliment three
years later, when he included "Winter Warfare" and "The Soldier
Addresses His Body" in his *Anthology of War Poetry, 1914-1918*.)
"Innovation there certainly was," he concludes, "but it was in the
variety of personal idiosyncrasy and not a new principle. The changes
in verse were like the changes in all organic things, which are at once
the same and different. No simple formula will cover all the modes of

expression that the new energy driving into English verse discovered. Realism is one way of wringing Rhetoric's neck, but it is not the only one." So in the final essay he passes on to pay his tribute to Sassoon and Owen, who in different ways gave voice to pity and anger against the carnage, and condemns the failure of the Labour leadership to develop the poets' protests "as part of the wider revolt against the primary cause of the evil which they challenged".[14]

While these essays were appearing, Rickword published another important critical study. In November 1939 he had received a letter from the young Oxford historian Christopher Hill, informing him that Lawrence & Wishart were planning "a series of symposia of articles on important subjects, beginning with one on the 17th century English revolution. We thought perhaps of one longish general political-economic background," the letter continued, "followed by say three articles of 5000 words (or two longer ones) on related subjects. How would you feel about doing something on Marvell or Milton? Or on what?" Hill, it will be noticed, thought first of Marvell rather than Milton as a possible subject for Rickword, perhaps because Garman, who suggested that he should be approached, had mentioned his interest in the Metaphysicals. On Marvell, however, he had already written: "There is not much to be said about Andrew Marvell. He was such a consummate poet that the content of his poems is all transmuted into poetry, and about that, of course, there really is nothing to be said, except to point to it with such expressions as shall best excite to admiration."[15] He therefore chose Milton for his subject, leaving it to Hill to produce the classical Marxist study of Marvell's poetry in his "Society and Andrew Marvell".

Rickword was drawn to Milton because he was a great poet; but his English poems are hardly mentioned in the essay "Milton: The Revolutionary Intellectual". The early poems are referred to in two passages, one of them a footnote; two of the sonnets are quoted and five others mentioned; and a subordinate clause in a sentence about Marvell speaks of "the epics in which his pent-up energies found expression". That is all. This silence is all the more astonishing because for years past Milton's poetry had been under attack from Eliot and Leavis, and by 1936 Leavis was able to proclaim triumphantly that "Milton's dislodgement, in the past decade, after two centuries of predominance, was effected with remarkably little fuss".[16] Rickword never accepted that Milton had been dislodged. He would have agreed with Edwin Muir's remark, in a review in the *Calendar* of Eliot's *Homage to John Dryden*, that "after one has encountered in all of the three essays in this volume an exasperated sentence on Milton, one begins to wonder if Mr Eliot is in reality capable of appreciating the greatness of Milton's poetry".[17] Shortly after Leavis announced Milton's dislodgement, Rickword defiantly proclaimed his epics and *Samson* "the highest achievements of poetic genius in England outside the work of Shakespeare". Whereas Eliot and Leavis depreciated Milton in order to glorify Donne and the Metaphysicals, Rickword, who yielded to no man in his admiration of the Metaphysicals, placed Milton's poetry on an altogether higher level than theirs.

In his essay, as in his contributions to the *Sunday Referee* and the *Daily Worker*, he emphasizes that Milton's ideas are still relevant.

> The continued vitality of Milton's work shows that the issues with which he was concerned have not even yet been decided. Though the terms of the controversies in which he engaged are rather remote from us, the principles he evolved demand a re-ordering of society for their realisation. That is why his fame is still the battle-ground of conflicting interests, and each successive book about him tends to turn into a polemic with its predecessors. The fog of mediaevalism which he swept aside is not unfamiliar to us to-day, in the form of a lack of confidence in human ability to expunge the evils of society.[18]

It was not so much Milton the poet on whom Eliot, the Anglo-Catholic and Royalist, and Leavis, who had long since abandoned his flirtation with Marxism, were waging war, he suggested, but Milton the revolutionist.

There are several reasons why he chose to write about the revolutionary intellectual rather than the poet. The book in which his essay appeared was intended to commemorate the tercentenary of the English Revolution of 1640, and it seemed appropriate that he should deal with Milton's contribution to the revolution rather than with his poems, most of which were written either before 1640 or after the Restoration. Over half the essay deals with the period of his life during which he had virtually abandoned poetry in order to devote himself to revolutionary propaganda (as Rickword himself had done). The essay, in fact, like his life of Rimbaud, contains an element of autobiography. When he wrote "We shall not understand Milton unless we remember that he thought of himself as no mere versifier, but as a conscious participant in this vital process", he may have had himself in mind as well as Milton.

> If ever a poet might have claimed to be excused from sharing in the political turmoil in order to devote himself to his art, that poet was Milton...Yet for nearly twenty years, from his thirty-third to his fiftieth year, Milton voluntarily devoted himself to quite different tasks...It was whilst the issue thus hung in the balance that Milton took the moral decision which had such far-reaching effects throughout his life... Milton accepted the obligation of actively participating in the social conflict.[19]

While in his thirties Rickword, as he saw it, had accepted the same obligation. As Milton had sacrificed his eyesight, "overplied in Liberty's defence, my noble task", so Rickword must have known that he was endangering the sight of his remaining eye by his literary work. In the end Milton's "pent-up energies" had found expression in his epics. Rickword perhaps cherished a hope that one day he too might return to poetry, his experience enriched, like Milton's, by his part in the political struggle.

His essay was published in June 1940 in *The English Revolution 1640*, together with a long essay by Hill from which the book took its title and a shorter essay by Margaret James on "Contemporary Materialist Interpretations of Society in the English Revolution". The book has had a curious history. Most of the reviews were unsympathetic. *The Times Literary Supplement*, which adopted a patronizing attitude towards all three contributions, said that "Mr Rickword, dutifully trying to exhibit Milton as a class warrior, soon finds himself carried away by the eloquence of a mind too aspiring for consistent materialism".[20] George Orwell, who reviewed the book in the *New Statesman*, used it as a pretext for firing a few shots in his private war against the Communist Party. *Labour Monthly*, while praising Rickword's essay, devoted practically all its review to questioning Hill's interpretation of the English Revolution, and thus set off a controversy which rumbled on in the Marxist press until well into the 1950s. After being twice reprinted, the book appeared in a revised edition in 1949 with a new preface by Hill. Thereafter, Lawrence & Wishart continued to reprint Hill's essay (which became the canonical Marxist version of the Revolution at just about the time that Hill was abandoning the theories contained in it, at least in the form in which they appeared there), but without Rickword's and Margaret James's contributions. It was Hill who paid the most generous tribute to "Milton: The Revolutionary Intellectual", nearly forty years after its publication:

> I did not appreciate quite how superlative it was until I came to write a book of my own on *Milton and the English Revolution*, published in 1977. Edgell Rickword's essay of 1940 must have sunk deep into my consciousness, but I did not re-read it until I had finished the first draft of my book. I then realized that though I had expanded some factual points, and had dealt more fully with Milton's last great poems than Edgell Rickword did, in all essentials I had merely elaborated arguments which he had stated with beautiful brevity and clarity in 1940...Rickword's thirty pages of 1940 contain more sense and insight than most of the many books that have been written about Milton.[21]

When *The English Revolution* appeared the two productive Winchester years, in which Rickword had written the essays on Malraux, Milton and the war poets and edited *A Handbook of Freedom*, were coming to an end. Mrs Quilter died on 19 April, and Jonny decided to devote what money she had left and the proceeds of selling the cottage at Hookpit to running a café. She found one at Marlow, Buckinghamshire, a former farmhouse with a garden and outhouses, which stood opposite the local cinema and was already a going concern. She and Rickword took over the business in the late summer, and on 26 September he wrote to Jane: "I am helping to run a restaurant here, quite a change for me, chef, waiter and gardener all in one". He was in fact an excellent cook, especially skilful in preparing fish dishes. To augment their food supplies they kept rabbits and chickens in one of the outhouses, which involved additional work. He wrote to Jane in February 1941: "This café is now a flourishing business but it involves 12 or 14 hours a day and does not leave much time for contemplation. Which is rather a blessing just now."

Air raids on London began soon after they moved to Marlow, and one evening the town suddenly filled with refugees, most of them from the East End. As the café buildings included a large spare room they were able to shelter a fair number of them, making them more welcome than some of the inhabitants of Marlow, who resented their intrusion. Rickword made his contribution to the war effort by joining the fire service, which involved turning out for training on Sunday mornings in full uniform, complete with fire axe, and sleeping at the fire station on alert every few weeks. The Marlow firemen were required now and then to man the fire boat which was responsible for their section of the Thames, and one Sunday they took part in an exercise involving Clive-den House, then notorious among left-wingers as the headquarters of the allegedly pro-Nazi "Cliveden Set".

The work of running a café, the bombing and the war situation made this a depressing period, but he found some relief in corresponding with his daughters. To Jane, who had decided to join the Society of Friends, he wrote in September 1940:

> I was very pleased to get such a long and interesting letter from you last month. It somewhat reminded me of the beginning of the memoirs of an earlier Friend, Thomas Ellwood, which I have just been reading, and his peregrinations from one Meeting to another. You at least have escaped one of his ordeals, which was to be continually beaten by his father for wearing his hat in his presence. I have also been reading George Fox's Journals with great admiration. It is as pioneers in the struggle for social justice that the non-conforming elements of the time attract me, and of these the Friends are certainly the purest, though extraordinary fortitude and courage seems to have been widespread among the sects. But I suppose I should have been a Fifth Monarchy man in those days.

This letter, with its sympathetic approach to religious convictions which he did not himself share, suggests that his work on *A Handbook of Freedom* and his Milton essay had broadened his knowledge of the seventeenth-century sectaries, one of the main sources of the English radical tradition.

Early in 1941 Jane wrote to tell him that she had decided to study medicine, a decision which he welcomed. "I was very glad to hear that you have found your vocation," he wrote to her in February.

It is refreshing to find the spirit of constructive effort expressing itself in spite of the present concentration on murderous activities. I trust you will grow up to exercise your knowledge in a society which has eradicated the root causes of these inter-imperialist conflicts. I think you are wise to look towards the public health services, there is a measure of mumbo-jumbo in private practice which you would find repugnant but which is hardly separable from the business of making the individual's investment of capital show a profitable return. And there is every possibility in the increase of the communal principle in medical treatment, so that the number of openings for a qualified woman should be greater in five or six years' time. So if you can face up to the hard graft the training demands there is every chance of your finding a useful and inspiring field to apply your skill. I am sure you have thought it all out very fully and I have every confidence that you have the capacity to carry through on your ambitious course.

His confidence in her proved fully justified.

About the beginning of 1941 he received a letter from Swingler, who had never given up the idea of founding the Marxist journal of the arts which had been promised in the last number of *Left Review*. Under wartime regulations paper supplies were rationed and starting a new magazine was illegal, but it was possible to take over an existing magazine, thereby acquiring its paper ration. In accordance with this process Fore Publications had taken over *Poetry and the People*, the last issue of which had appeared in September 1940, but which was shortly to reappear under the new title *Our Time*. Outlining his plans, Swingler wrote:

This paper will cover architecture, medicine, education, art, literature, etc., and the general plan is to devote the space to four or five quite substantial pieces per month rather than attempt by scraps and bits to cover the whole ground every time. One should, for instance, include a central article every month up to about 6,000 words, with critical and constructive work really thoroughly done...The difficulty has been to find people with both the time and the ability to work on it in an editorial capacity. Some of my efforts have been rather disappointing: Montagu is always helpful but without startling initiative, and the student movement does not seem to have developed the younger people who ought now to be coming forward to take our place with new ideas. The great thing is that the field is now ours undisputed. Poor doddering old *Horizon* gives out a plaintive moan this month about nobody really liking them and if somebody doesn't buy a copy soon they will have to shut down! We can make a go of this paper in spite of the fact that our resources are now so scattered.

The first number of *Our Time*, which appeared in February, was an unexciting pocket-sized magazine which fell short of Swingler's objectives. After producing seven issues he was called up, and over the next year his wife Geraldine and the actress Beatrix Lehmann took charge. Rickword's only contribution during this period, an essay called "Poetry and Two Wars" which was published in the April issue, was provoked by two articles in *The Times Literary Supplement*, one by Lord David Cecil entitled "The Author in a Suffering World", the other a leader entitled "Authors and the War". Lord David complained that writers seemed "equally incapable of Brooke's passionate fighting spirit or Owen's passionate pacifism", and reached the startling conclusion that "the numbness of spirit which hampers so many writers to-day is due in part to the fact that, bred as they are in the tradition of the prosperous and progressive nineteenth century, they look on suffering as an unmixed evil". This doctrine of salvation through masochism did not please the leader-writer, who declared: "never more than now was there a nobler opportunity for poets and novelists to show writing at its full stature... The war may mean a renaissance of English literature, which for years has threatened to pass away in fatuous experiments."[22] In his essay Rickword rejected both views. "War," he maintained, "is the result of the same human will that condemns the people to a low and precarious standard of life whether engaged with an external foe or not... The true poets of this war... see the war not as a temporary disease, but as the culminating criminality of a system."[23]

Within three months of the publication of this essay the political situation was transformed by the German invasion of the Soviet Union and Churchill's immediate promise of British support for the Soviet people. The Communist Party decided that the war was not an imperialist war but an anti-Fascist war after all, and issued a new manifesto calling for a "united national front".[24] Harry Pollitt, who had been dropped from the general secretaryship after the previous change of line, was reinstated, and almost overnight Communists became supporters of the war effort and advocates of national unity. Suggestions that the party should break the political truce by contesting by-elections in which the Government candidate was a Conservative were frowned on, and strikes were denounced as the work of Trotskyist saboteurs. Hardly less remarkable than the party's political somersault was the transformation of the popular view of the Soviet Union. When the Wehrmacht failed to go through the Red Army, in the phrase generally used, "like a knife through butter" popular enthusiasm for the Soviet Union broke all bounds, and Stalin became as great a hero to the man in the street as Churchill was to the Communist Party. Recruits flooded into the party, which by the end of 1942 had 56,000 members. The old-established members viewed the newcomers, whom they nick-named "Red Army sympathizers", with a reserve which was largely justified, for most of them were politically naïve and drifted out of the party almost as rapidly as they had drifted in.

Rickword's attitude to these developments is difficult to assess. Reactions among his former collaborators on *Left Review* varied widely. Wintringham throughout the war advocated the policy of a struggle on two fronts which the Communist Party had proposed in 1939 and then abandoned; he put his military experience at the service of the Home Guard, and in 1942 helped to found Common Wealth, a party which was both Socialist and patriotic. Ralph Bates had broken with the Communist Party over the Finnish War. After defending the Nazi-Soviet pact and supporting the party's attitude to the war, Strachey denounced its policy in April 1940 as defeatist. Lindsay, while accepting its anti-war policy, maintained even before June 1941 that the war was bound to develop an anti-Fascist character. Alick West, on the other hand, was deeply sceptical about the party's switch to a pro-war position. More than most Communists Rickword, with his memories of the Western Front, must have been torn between hatred of war and hatred of Fascism. When he wrote early in 1941 that "in the ruin of individual hopes it is difficult not to succumb to a sense of the malignancy of human life itself",[25] he was surely speaking of himself. The mood of deep depression suggested in his letter to Jane of February 1941, rather than the demands made by the café on his time and energies, was probably responsible for the fact that after the early weeks of 1941 he seems to have written nothing for some two and a half years. He resigned his directorship at Lawrence & Wishart in May 1942.

In time Jonny came to share his depression. The café was proving less profitable than they had hoped, and wartime Marlow was decidedly boring, although the boredom was sometimes relieved by visits from London friends. Nina Hamnett, who stayed with them in December 1942, found their home "most comfortable, with warm baths, lots of food and a session at the pub not long enough to get drunk".[26] Such visits became increasingly infrequent, however, as more and more of their friends were called up or drawn into war work. By the summer of 1943 Jonny felt that she could not face another winter at Marlow and formed the idea of opening a guest house in London. During a visit of exploration to Hampstead she found an empty house in Arkwright Road with three floors, a basement, a garage, a conservatory and a fair-sized garden which seemed suitable for the purpose, and almost at the same time they received a good offer for the café. They jumped at it, and in August returned to Hampstead.

Furnishing the house was no great problem; they brought some furniture from Marlow and some more from their previous Hampstead flat; the second-hand shops often had pieces rescued from bombed houses, and a careless removal van brought them a dresser which was not strictly theirs. When they opened their boarding house Rickword, as in Marlow, did some of the cooking, and in the evenings officiated at the tables with a serviette over his arm. Jack Lindsay, who lodged in the house for a time, has left an amusing picture of life there. "One evening in the kitchen something he said or did annoyed Jonny. He went on talking to me, and Jonny, infuriated, started throwing plates at him. He caught them one by one, put them down, and went on all the while unperturbed with the conversation. Somehow this anecdote seems to tell a lot about him."[27]

His assistance in running the guest house did not take up all his time, and because of the paper shortage there were fewer outlets for freelance writers. One day he met a journalist friend who was employed by the Soviet embassy, and at his suggestion he applied for and got a job which mainly consisted of checking translations sent from the Soviet Union. On one occasion he failed to notice a misprint in a list of battle honours, so that honours given to the 11th Regiment of Guards were mistakenly attributed to the 10th Regiment. He only discovered this when his boss rushed into the room waving the list in a shaking hand and shouted "Suppose Stalin sees this! Can he fail to do so?"

Despite the boring nature of this work, by the end of 1943 he had broken through the block which for over two years prevented him from writing. The turning of the tide after the victories of El Alamein and Stalingrad, the Allied advances on the Russian and Italian fronts and the fall of Mussolini, which brought new hope of the overthrow of Fascism and the return of peace, combined with the intellectual stimulus of London life and the renewal of literary friendships to dissipate the cloud of depression and revive his will to write. He returned to his old theme, the English radical tradition, but he now approached it from a new angle. Whereas in the past he had written studies of Milton and the First World War poets, as well as shorter pieces on Langland, Bunyan and Swift, almost all his writings on this subject after 1943 dealt with the writers and artists of the half-century between 1780 and 1830 which witnessed the Industrial Revolution, the French Revolution, the Romantic movement and the birth of the British democratic and Socialist movements. He was to write on Wordsworth and Thelwall, who opposed the war against revolutionary France but supported that against Napoleon, and Hazlitt, who, as Rickword put it, "opposed the renewal of the war with France after the Treaty of Amiens as being

in fact motivated by a desire to destroy the democratic gains of the
French Revolution and at the same time seize more colonial territory
for commercial exploitation". It had been possible for honest men (and
if Wordsworth abandoned his democratic beliefs neither Thelwall nor
Hazlitt did) to disagree on whether the Napoleonic War was a defensive
war against an aggressive dictator or an imperialist war, and whether
Napoleon was the continuator or the betrayer of the French Revolution.

His first essay on this period was "William Hazlitt – An English
Jacobin", which he contributed under the transparent pseudonym
"John Edgell" to the issue of *Our Time* for January 1944. *Our Time*,
to which Jack Lindsay and its assistant editor, Arnold Rattenbury,
persuaded him to become a contributor, was conscious of the radical
tradition and ran a regular feature called "Heritage", consisting of
snippets mostly taken from *A Handbook of Freedom*. What attracted
Rickword to Hazlitt was his integrity, the sturdy independence which
enabled him to remain faithful to his Radical principles even when they
exposed him to persecution and slander. Some sentences in Rickword's
characterization throw light on his own political attitudes: "Hazlitt
was that kind of a Jacobin in whom the principle (always with him the
fruit of incessant intellectual labour, for he was no lazy doctrinaire)
was converted into a passion...But he understood the mixed nature of
men as they actually are, and did not believe that the alteration of
political institutions would automatically usher in the Millennium." In
the first sentence was he rebuking those lazy doctrinaires who always
swallowed the party line whole, without considering whether it corresponded to the facts? Was the second aimed at those who criticized the
Soviet Union for not having established Utopia in 26 years, or at those
party members who believed that it already had? Whatever the answer,
there is no doubt that he had some contemporaries in mind when he
quoted Hazlitt on the Lake Poets:

> All the authority that they have as poets and men of genius must be
> thrown into the scale of Revolution and Reform, their Jacobin principles,
> indeed, gave rise to their Jacobin poetry. Since they gave up the first,
> their poetical powers have flagged and been comparatively or wholly
> "in a state of suspended animation"...Poet-Laureates are courtiers by
> profession, but we say that poets are naturally Jacobins. The poets...
> are with us while they are worth keeping.

Rickword's comment is pointed: " 'It is worth attending to', this collapse of the poetic power when it is 'at variance with the spirit of the
age'. We might, making allowances for the time-lag in mental processes,
for the hangover of old enthusiasms, see the making of a general law
of it."[28] He was probably thinking of the degeneration of Roy Campbell
from the author of "The Zulu Girl" to the man who wrote in praise

of Franco, and perhaps also of some members of the Auden generation.

A study by "John Edgell" of a less famous Regency Radical, William Hone, appeared in *Our Time* in September. Although he was to deal more fully with Hone in *Radical Squibs and Loyal Ripostes*, the earlier essay, written with spirit and humour, is an admirable introduction. He was thoroughly in sympathy with Hone's personality, courageous, humorous, irreverent, the dedicated enemy of all cruelty and injustice. Both were thorough bookmen; Hone recalled that even as a boy "I was in the habit of making my own every bit of printed and written paper, whether from cheesemonger's or other shops", just as Rickword, according to Rattenbury, "could never see a book in his vicinity without handling it". In *Our Time* he concentrated on the story of Hone's three trials for blasphemy and his acquittal, giving little more than a mention to the satires which he later published in book form. The conclusion of the essay makes clear the significance which the radical tradition possessed for him. After quoting Hone's account of how moved he had been as a boy by reading John Lilburne's trial, he continues: "The memory of this reading may well have fortified him when, ill and unaided, he struggled for three days against the Government's law-officers and the toughest judge that could be put on the Bench. The judge it was that died. Such is the reality of Heritage."[29]

An even more striking declaration of his libertarian principles was his essay "An Important Jubilee", published in December in a Russian translation. One outcome of the Anglo-Soviet alliance was the publication in Moscow of *British Ally*, a periodical dealing with the British war effort and British life and culture, to which he contributed this article and another on English translations of Gorky. He took as his theme the tercentenary of the publication of Milton's *Areopagitica*, which he set in the context of the struggle for freedom of the press from the Reformation down to the nineteenth-century Radicals and Chartists. Milton's belief that the people would be able to judge rightly if the facts were placed before them, he emphasized, was one of the bases of democracy, and even in the war against Hitler, when the British people had to give up many freedoms, freedom of the press had not been one of them. The most striking feature of this praise of "the liberty to know, to utter, and to argue freely according to conscience" is that it was addressed to a Russian audience. Unless Rickword was so naïve as to take seriously the guarantee of press freedom in the Soviet constitution of 1936, he must have realized that his argument was profoundly subversive by Stalinist standards, and that only exceptional wartime circumstances made it possible for them to be published in Moscow. In any event, he unfurled the banner of the English radical tradition in the capital of Stalinism.

The summer of 1944 marked a major turning-point in his private life, haunted for over twenty years by the pathetic figure of Peggy. His poems leave no doubt that he had loved her. At first he hoped that she might be cured, but with the passing years that hope had faded. A man who needed a woman's support, he found himself neither married nor a widower, and her living death denied him the solace of hope and the finality of physical death, which could be mourned and accepted. This blocking of the channels of grief contributed both to the difficulty he found in communicating with other people and to the withering of his poetic impulse. He loved Jonny deeply, he shared thirty years of his life with her (ten times as long as he spent with Peggy), yet he addressed no love poems to her. In 1940 Dr Back had applied for a divorce on the grounds of adultery, citing Rickword as co-respondent, and had been granted a decree nisi which was made absolute on 18 November. Although Rickword could then have obtained a divorce from Peggy on the ground of incurable insanity in order to marry Jonny, he seems to have made no attempt to do so. He and Jonny, whose life together had the qualities of a successful marriage, may have regarded a formalization as unnecessary, but in view of later developments this seems improbable. He attached great importance to loyalty, and it may have been a sense of loyalty to Peggy which prevented him from ending his marriage to her.

She died of tuberculosis at the age of 45 on 22 June 1944 – in Colchester, where she had been moved to a mental hospital. Just over a month later, on 24 July, Rickword married Jonny at Hampstead register office. She once told a friend that the only reason they decided to marry was that, while they were on holiday, their landlady refused to let them sleep together on discovering that there were different names on their ration books. But the fact that he married her so soon after Peggy's death suggests that he considered himself under a moral obligation to do so. On the marriage register he described himself as an author, although in the previous three years he had published only one essay; evidently he hoped to resume his literary career after this long interruption.

By leaving London before the war he and Jonny had escaped the bombing of 1940-41, but they returned in time for the flying bombs. The first to fall on Hampstead hit a hostel for Jewish refugees on 19 June 1944, and by the end of August seven more had fallen on the borough and twelve just outside its boundaries, killing 21 people, seriously injuring 80 and destroying 79 houses. When an evacuation scheme for children and their mothers was introduced, so many left that the local paper reported that "There's no more queuing in Hampstead since the flying bombs started".[30] Although the boarding house escaped serious damage a nearby bomb brought a piece of the ceiling down on the pillow where Jonny's head would have been. She was away at the time. The Rickwords' decision to get married was perhaps influenced by the imminent threat of death.

XIV. *Our Time*

THE history of *Our Time*, like that of *Left Review*, can be divided into three periods: early growing pains, Rickword's editorship, when it achieved its greatest distinction, and a final period. *Our Time* survived over twice as long as its predecessor, however, and its editorial history is far more complex. In the last number which appeared under their editorship Geraldine Swingler and Beatrix Lehmann defined its aims as follows:

> A positive contribution will be a stocktaking of the cultural activities taking place at the present time. Far more is happening in the country than many of us suspect, and unless we know what forces are to hand, we can neither assess their value nor make any attempt to develop them as a movement. And this will take us farther back. No new and vital culture can spring from its own roots; we must know as much as there is to know about the cultures of the past.[1]

"Far more is happening in the country than many of us suspect..." Cultural life, which the outbreak of war seemed to have brought to a standstill, not only survived, but by 1942 was flourishing. The Council for the Encouragement of Music and the Arts (CEMA) was founded in 1940 with a Government grant, despite the protests of the *Daily Express*, which declared: "The government gives £50,000 to help wartime culture. What madness is this? There is no such thing as culture in wartime."[2] It gradually extended its operations to sponsoring symphony orchestras, drama, opera and ballet companies, and art exhibitions, while the Entertainments National Service Association (ENSA) organized light entertainment for the troops as well as plays and symphony concerts in garrison theatres, hospitals and factories.

Because of paper rationing and the destruction of publishers' stocks in air raids, fewer books were available; but the black-out, long railway journeys and the absence of other forms of entertainment ensured that people read far more than in peacetime. There was a new demand for poetry; under the stress of war many people in and outside the forces who would never have done so in peacetime found emotional release in writing and reading verse. Publishers welcomed collections of poems because they consumed less paper than novels. Music, like poetry, met an emotional need, and concert-going became more popular than before. The London Philharmonic Orchestra, taken over by its players when it was threatened with disbanding, regularly visited over a hundred towns and played before more than a million people, not only in concert halls but in music-halls, cinemas and factory canteens. Important new works were composed and performed, among them Michael Tippett's oratorio *A Child of Our Time* and Benjamin Britten's opera *Peter Grimes*.

Painters were employed by the Ministry of Information to record all aspects of the war effort, and the results, from Henry Moore's sleepers in the Underground to Stanley Spencer's shipyard workers, were exhibited in the National Gallery. Other exhibitions, organized by the Artists' International Association (AIA), were held in factories, British restaurants and Underground stations. Theatre companies toured army camps, war workers' hostels and mining villages, and the Army Bureau of Current Affairs (ABCA) formed its own Theatre Group, which performed plays specially written by J.B. Priestley and "living newspapers" dramatizing topical political issues. It was accepted that cultural activities must be subsidized by state and local authorities, and drama, classical music and painting were reaching a larger public than they had ever done before.

These developments were welcomed and chronicled by *Our Time*, both in articles and on the monthly "Notes and Comments" page. Jack Lindsay in later years recalled "the great cultural gains during the war, in so far as the idea of an anti-fascist war had gripped the people", and "the new possibilities of writing based upon what was active and concrete in this release of the human spirit, something that made the ideas of peace and brotherhood cease to be abstractions and become at long last the valid material of art". Rickword and the group gathered round *Our Time*, he pointed out, sought to make it "the mouthpiece of the new spirit – what we called, half in joke, half in delighted earnest, the Cultural Upsurge".[3] Among the aspects of the "Cultural Upsurge" which it reported or discussed during the last eighteen months of the war were the London Philharmonic Orchestra; the Nottingham Harmonic Society; the ABCA Theatre Group; the paintings of Leslie Hurry, L.S. Lowry and John Armstrong; the Edinburgh Film Guild; amateur drama at Toynbee Hall; exhibitions at the AIA's Charlotte Street centre; plays and concerts sponsored by ENSA; Alun Lewis's poetry; the war artists' exhibition at the National Gallery; John Gielgud's production of *Love for Love*; the documentary films of Humphrey Jennings; the formation of the National Book League; the National Building Record; children's theatres; local orchestras; the British Drama League; community centres; adult education at Morley College and the City Literary Institute; the Society for the Promotion of New Music; the Council for Industrial Design; a ballet festival at Salisbury; a film workers' conference; municipal concerts in Portsmouth; the Ballet Rambert and much more.

Communists and others on the left associated with *Our Time* made a considerable contribution to the "Cultural Upsurge", which in many aspects continued the anti-Fascist artistic movements of the Popular Front period. The AIA was founded in 1934 as an anti-Fascist organization, and the director of its Charlotte Street centre was F.D. Klingender, the magazine's art editor. When the Amalgamated Engineering Union celebrated its silver jubilee in 1945, he organized an exhibition, "The Engineer in British Life", which gave him the idea for his book *Art and the Industrial Revolution*. The same occasion was celebrated by a production of *Century for George*, a play by Montagu Slater, theatre editor of *Our Time*, who also wrote the libretto for *Peter Grimes*. The living newspaper form used by the ABCA Theatre Group, which originated in the United States, had been introduced to Britain before the war by Unity Theatre. Among the ABCA script-writers was Jack Lindsay, who as the only private working in the War Office was allocated a room to himself, as no officer could be expected to share one with him. When the London Philharmonic Orchestra was taken over by its members they elected as secretary a viola-player named Thomas Russell, who organized its tours and other activities, and who later became a member of the editorial committee of *Our Time*.

Support for activities which brought world culture to the widest possible British audience: all those associated with *Our Time* agreed on that objective, if on very little else. Alfred Sharp, who edited the issues from November 1942 to July 1943, was considered too "abstruse" and "theoretical", and a campaign to give the magazine more popular appeal was launched at Unity Theatre and in the Workers' Musical Association. As a result Peter Phillips and Honor Arundel became joint editors, and in August the magazine appeared in a new large format with a photograph, a list of contents and an editorial statement on the cover. After three issues they were succeeded by Vernon Beste as editor. A leading member of Unity Theatre, in order to legitimize what had been virtually a hijacking operation by Unity, he established close relations with Emile Burns, the Communist Party official mainly responsible for cultural matters. In its new format, designed to catch the eye on bookstalls, *Our Time* achieved popular success, but at a price. Arnold Rattenbury, a young Cambridge man invalided out of the Army, who joined the staff as assistant editor at the same time as Beste, summed up the policy at this time as "State it simply or working men and women won't understand",[4] and much of the material published, particularly the verse and short stories, was of poor quality. Pressure to conform to the required standard of simplicity was exercised through the correspondence column, much of which Beste was suspected, perhaps unjustly, of writing himself. Letters appeared complaining that "I cannot understand the poetry you publish... Write for the people... Can't you put some guts into your stuff?"[5] The May 1944 issue, which in

Beste's absence Rattenbury edited with Lindsay's assistance as an example of what they would like *Our Time* to be, included Dylan Thomas's "Ceremony after a Fire Raid" (which its author pressed upon Rattenbury because, he said, he wanted to advertise that he remained a Socialist), part of David Gascoyne's "Ecce Homo", and poems by Hugh MacDiarmid, Paul Potts, Geoffrey Matthews and Lindsay. Although none of these poems, with the possible exception of Thomas's, could be described as obscure, a letter in the next issue maintained that as the writer "could not make head or tail of them" they were "a waste of paper". This view was supported in another letter by Pat Sloan, who demanded that *Our Time* should "print nothing that would not be understood by the ordinary reader who picks up the magazine on W.H. Smith's bookstall".[6]

By March 1944 many of the writers associated with *Our Time*, including Lindsay, Slater and Rattenbury, were convinced that a new editor was urgently needed, and Rickword was the obvious man. He was reluctant to undertake it, partly because he felt himself ill-equipped to edit a journal aimed at a broader popular readership than the *Calendar* or even *Left Review*, partly because he planned to concentrate on research into the radical tradition in English literature. On 29 August, however, Lindsay wrote urging him to "come to the rescue", and a few days later he wrote on the envelope: "'I guess all authors must be half-witted.' Report P.G. Wodehouse. Daily Sketch 1.9.44" as a wry comment on his decision to accept. Events moved fast. Mrs Swingler appointed a new board of directors for Fore Publications, which formally removed Beste and appointed Rickword, who accepted on the understanding that his was purely a stopgap wartime appointment.

The effects of the change were immediately obvious. The fussy front cover design was replaced by a large photograph or drawing, with the titles of three of the major articles underneath. The cover picture of the November issue, the first which Rickword edited, showed Picasso conversing with French Communist leaders, making it clear that under its new editor *Our Time* was to be as international in outlook as *Left Review* had been. Although "Notes and Comments" on page 3 was normally the joint work of the editor and the associate editors, who contributed paragraphs on the particular aspects of culture for which they were responsible, the opening here, which echoes the argument of Rickword's essay on Malraux, is unmistakably his:

> The photograph on our cover vividly expresses the way in which liberated France re-assumes her essential place in European culture. In modern France the cleavage between the intellectuals and the community, result of the bloody repression of popular strivings throughout the past century, had been carried through with a ruthless logic which did not shrink from the extremes of imbecility (timidly copied by our contemporary

art-for-art's-sake, anarcho-pacifist escapists). Yet a great painter, Gus-
tave Courbet, was honoured by, and was honoured to work for, the
heroic short-lived Commune, and now French democracy honours and
is honoured by a greater painter than Courbet. The adherence of Pablo
Picasso to the French Communist Party is a tribute to the leadership of
that Party in the struggle for national freedom... The intellectuals have
found their way back to the people along a trail of blood and in the
common struggle each has learnt to know the other and to realise that
their interests are inseparable.[7]

This editorial was followed by Nancy Cunard's article on the role of
the intellectuals in the French resistance movement. After heroic efforts
on behalf of Spanish refugees in France she had sailed for Chile in 1940
as the guest of Pablo Neruda, but returned to England in the following
year and worked for the Free French radio. Although she settled in
France in 1945, she continued to contribute articles to *Our Time* on
aspects of French and Spanish culture.

In general the journal's policy remained as it had been under Rickword's predecessors. Many aspects of contemporary cultural life, in
the broadest sense, were considered not only in "Notes and Comments"
but in articles on such topics as pottery design, radio drama and town
planning. Most issues included a study of a writer of the past, among
them essays on Mrs Gaskell by Sylvia Townsend Warner, Trollope by
Julian Symons and Wordsworth by Roy Fuller. If there was greater
emphasis on European culture, this was in part the result of the liberation of occupied Europe and the return of peace. What Rickword
brought to *Our Time* was an insistence on quality. He was prepared
to publish poems and short stories only of the standard he demanded,
and if none good enough were submitted the issue appeared without
them. Beste had published at least one story and from two to six poems
in every issue; but of the 34 edited by Rickword, poems appeared in
twelve and short stories in only nine, unless one counts as stories a
number of narratives from liberated Europe which could better be
described as reportage. No more letters complaining about obscure
verse were received, or if they were they were not printed.

Rickword used his literary contacts to draw on a wide range of
contributors. There were several Marxist writers on whom he could
rely – Lindsay, Slater, Morton, Sylvia Townsend Warner, Mulk Raj
Anand, Alick West, Hugh Sykes Davies, and later Sommerfield and
Swingler – as well as a group of younger Marxists such as Rattenbury,
Jack Beeching, Edward Thompson, David Holbrook, John Manifold
and Maurice Carpenter. He also recruited writers who held left-wing
views but were not Marxists, including Julian Symons and Arthur Calder-
Marshall, who became frequent contributors, as well as a number of
well-known non-Communist writers whose work appeared once or

twice in *Our Time*, among them V.S. Pritchett, Rex Warner, Philip Henderson, William Empson, Edith Sitwell (who reviewed Dylan Thomas's *Deaths and Entrances*), J.B. Priestley, Storm Jameson, Pamela Hansford Johnson, Charles Madge and Douglas Goldring. The magazine maintained a high standard of art work, especially cover drawings supplied by Feliks Topolski, James Boswell, James Holland, James Fitton, Elizabeth Shaw and Ronald Searle, among others. The work of "the three Jameses", reflecting the short-lived euphoria that accompanied and succeeded military victory and the election of a Labour Government, had a cheerful good humour very different from their bitter drawings for *Left Review*.

In *Our Time* Rickword combined high standards with popular appeal. Circulation rose from about 3,000 in 1942 to 18,000 in 1945 – "a larger circulation", he could proudly boast, "than any Left-wing cultural magazine" in Britain had ever achieved.[8] The tribute to his success which gave him most pleasure was a letter from Corporal Randall Swingler, who wrote:

> *Our Time* is like a child grown up, to me. I mean it has really grown into an adult, authoritative, and I think most distinctive magazine. I was glad when I heard you'd come back to it. It has achieved what we never before really managed, the right balance between "news", information, and theory. It is really covering the field at last, and not just the little "left" corner. People out here find it interesting and new to them, but most important they find it "approachable", as easy to read and to look at as *Picture Post*. It's all right, it is "for us", not obviously just for the highbrows.

There was a genial atmosphere, despite Rickword's habitual silence, in the *Our Time* office in Southampton Street, just off Covent Garden. Rattenbury, who spent more time there with him than anyone else, recalls:

> He did a stupid question the same cautious honour as a wise one, looking all round its possible supplementaries before answering. This was for everyone, even for visitors a response to whom I had thought already agreed, to the point that I often left for the outer office in despair of any answer ever coming...Sometimes, certainly, silence alone was enough, as in that exceedingly rare case of a goading from communist headquarters in King Street; sometimes not, as when he wished an author to remove some entirely unsolicited bigotry from an article. But the answer always came in effect.

When after his lunch hour Rattenbury brought back a book he had picked up in Charing Cross Road – John Galt's novels, Marvell's poems, a novel by Gorky, Hone's *Trials* – Rickword would examine it with interest, and then talk about its author so that Rattenbury thought him encyclopaedic. Elizabeth Shaw remembers him as the most helpful and considerate editor for whom she ever worked. Contributors would drop in from time to time, bringing a friend who hoped to write for *Our Time*. Early in 1945 Symons introduced Roy Fuller, an old admirer of Rickword's poems, who was then working at the Admiralty, and Fuller contributed several articles and reviews over the next two years. He was struck by Rickword's "almost inaudible voice, an absence of small talk,...not precluding a sudden succinct and acute literary judgment". "The Southampton Street premises had no attractions of their own," he recalled nearly forty years later, "but their association in my memory with a general movement towards a pub would have arisen in any case from Edgell's own inclination. I never knew him the worse for drink, but the saloon bar was very much his habitat, perhaps stemming, like his earliest verse, from the pub poets of the Nineties." John Mortimer was introduced in the same way by James Holland, and for most of 1946 acted as one of the magazine's film critics. He has since claimed that he "didn't realize it was a Communist magazine".[9] As he was a friend of Swingler, who was not a man to conceal his opinions, this is surprising, but in view of Rickword's freedom from political bigotry and the high proportion of non-Communists among the contributors, it is not impossible.

In most of the articles in *Our Time* politics was a matter of approach and tone; direct political statement was usually confined to the opening paragraphs of "Notes and Comments", as a rule written by Rickword. His comments on the momentous events of 1945, in which he dealt with politics in terms of culture and culture in terms of politics, contain perhaps the fullest statement of his views on the social function of the arts, as a few extracts make clear:

> The twelve months of 1945 will hold more possibilities of good or evil for more generations to come than we dare attempt to reckon. All the power the arts have to tilt the balance towards good must be thrown into the scale. Through our feelings, the arts direct our energies towards creation, towards fuller living. They are the dissolvent of that inertia, expressed in the vulgarity and third-rateness of commercialised existence, which is the only basis on which the forces of destruction can rear their nightmare puppets...

> How many of those who, in these weeks of Allied triumphs, have been shaken by the visual proofs of the bestial nature of Fascism, remember the photographs of the Burning of the Books in Berlin? It was in 1933, the ceremonial inauguration of the Nazi reign of terror. It may have seemed then a mere theatrical stunt, yet it was the first symbolic step in a ruthless logic of human debasement. Before the German nation could be fitted for a vile destiny, the very memory of the finest achievements of the human reason and imagination had to be rooted out of their

consciousness, as their finest individuals had to be hunted out and destroyed. Such a terrible tribute to the formative virtues of culture in conditioning behaviour will not be wasted on a liberated world. It is through art that the anarchic impulses can be directed to creative ends and disparate individual appetites harmonised with the needs of a humane social order.[10]

Following the Labour victory in the general election, a Labour Government was formed on 26 July. Ten years of agitation and propaganda by Communists and their political allies through *Left Review*, the Left Book Club, Unity Theatre, the AIA, the Workers' Musical Association, Fore Publications and *Our Time* had certainly contributed to this event. Within a fortnight the first atomic bomb was dropped on Hiroshima on 6 August, and the second on Nagasaki three days later. At the time most people were too relieved at the surrender of Japan to grasp the implications; but one exception was Rickword, who for a week after hearing of the destruction of Hiroshima could not sleep for distress. About the middle of August he wrote an editorial for *Our Time* entitled "The Atom and the Arts", the opening and final paragraphs of which are worth quoting for their lucid expression of his humanist philosophy:

We have shown ourselves of late years to be an adaptable people; and in these recent weeks, too, we have certainly needed to be. The election of the Labour Government and the end of the last phase of the war burst like coloured rockets over a happy nation; but the atom bomb cast its immense shadow, and renewed expressions of antipathy from powerful interests to the new governments that have grown up out of the anti-fascist struggle also darkened a brilliant scene. What will be the pattern of our national life for the next decade? From day to day we adjust ourselves, as we must, to external change, but we also assimilate more slowly, by one means or another, the deeper significance of events and thus bend our energies to the task of mastering them for practical purposes...

It was in this sense because we had assimilated the war that we voted as we did: but how do we respond to the atom bomb? There is no need to succumb to the forebodings of speculative publicists, for what men have invented they can control: but it is easier to talk about a new era than to understand what it means to us. At this point we may as well remember that the arts are one of the greatest instruments of human adaptation: in the age of the Atom and of similar developments science will become more important than ever, but then art becomes more important also. Art can solve the new equations set to the feelings and the personality, can stimulate the love of life and the expansion of human values: it does this on the music hall stage as well as in the study; and we shall need artistic inventiveness and integrity no less than their scientific counterparts. During the immediate future, moreover, we have to discover increasingly the links between artist and scientist within the good society...

Here, then, lies part of the answer to the atom bomb. Scientific research we must have at all costs – but not at the cost of the arts, or it will be wasted. The human qualities that enable us to control it – energy, wisdom, courage, faith in human destiny – can be developed in all forms of collective effort, but not least in the writers' groups, Little Theatres, orchestras, evening classes, poetry circles and film societies that taken singly may seem small and ineffectual. And if, so far, these activities fall behind our scientific achievements, these coming years of peace are our opportunity to redress the balance. André Malraux, the great French writer and fighter, expressed for us years ago this belief that art is an act that takes possession of life, when he said that "All art is a means to gain a hold on destiny".[11]

Apart from these editorials, Rickword contributed at least five reviews to *Our Time*, all signed "John Edgell", while he was in charge. As he had first choice of which books he wished to review, his selection is interesting: Sean O'Casey's *Drums Under the Windows*; two autobiographical books, each dealing with a London childhood; two collections of Gorky's writings; a volume of Swingler's poems; and a life of Thomas Paine. O'Casey and Gorky were both favourites of his; in his review of O'Casey he speaks of their "spiritual kinship", their love of humanity, their determination to "show the grim truth of life", and their comic spirit which is "the necessary sanity-preserver".[12] His respect for the radical tradition, and especially for the English Jacobins, emerges in his choice of a life of Paine for review, in concluding his review of O'Casey with a quotation from Thomas Holcroft, and in his delight in a ballad on the punishment meted out to the notorious General Haynau by Barclay and Perkins' draymen. In addition to these, he probably wrote a review of Jack Lindsay's *British Achievement in Art and Music*, which is signed ".J.E." and closely resembles his editorials in style and thought: "Not that culture is the sugar-icing sweetening the bitterness of war. It is an integral part of the whole human relationship which made possible the victory of the United Nations."[13]

When Swingler returned to London after being demobilized, he was in no condition to resume the editorship of *Our Time*. He had served in Tunisia and throughout the Italian campaign, and several of his war poems are dated from the fronts where the fighting was most bitter: "Salerno Bay, September 1943"; "Monte Cassino, October 1943"; "River Garigliano, January 1944"; "Anzio, March 1944"; "the Gothic Line, September 1944"; "Faenza, Christmas 1944". He ended the war at Gradisca, near the Yugoslav border, and afterwards came into contact with Tito's partisans. His reactions to the war were complex. Regarding it as just and necessary, he yet found it abhorrent; twice

awarded the Military Medal for bravery, he repeatedly rejected suggestions from both the Army authorities and the Communist Party that
he should accept a commission. His horror was deepened by the nature
of the war in Italy, fought at times in conditions not unlike the trench
warfare of 1914-18. He emerged psychologically crippled. Out of the
conflict between his conviction that the war must be won and his instinc-
tive loathing of the means necessary for victory came some of the most
powerful poems of the war:

> No, it will never be worth it...
> Only this pride we have, both now and after,
> Because we have grasped the fate ourselves created,
> And to have been the centre of contradiction
> And not to have failed, and still to have found it hateful.[14]

War experiences created a bond between Swingler and Rickword, who
printed three of his war poems in *Our Time* and wrote in a review of
The Years of Anger, the collection in which they appeared: "For those
who have looked across the frontiers of non-existence where the troops
inhabit, they will speak much".[15] This bond remained strong when
Swingler finally returned to *Our Time* as joint editor in July 1946.
"Not the least of the many tensions at Southampton Street," Rattenbury
has recalled in a letter, "was that the pair of them kept disappearing
into secret huddles or mutual silences, and none of the rest of us could
get much sense out of them."

Other Communist writers, most of them of a younger generation
than Swingler, were released from the forces in the later months of
1945 or early in 1946. From the Army came John Manifold and Hamish
Henderson, some of whose best poems were inspired by the war,
Edward Thompson (son of the Edward Thompson whose book on the
Indian Mutiny had been praised in the *Calendar* and whose poems
Rickword had reviewed unenthusiastically in the *Sunday Referee*) and
David Holbrook. From the Navy came Jack Beeching, and from the
R.A.F. John Sommerfield, who had written some sharp stories of service
life in India and Burma. Most of them settled in London, temporarily
or permanently, and all became contributors to *Our Time*. Outside its
offices and the nearby pubs, they found a rendezvous at the Communist
Party Writers' Group, recently organized, together with similar groups
for historians and other intellectuals, with King Street's encouragement
(an ironic reversal of the policy advocated by Dutt in 1932). Monthly
meetings, usually held at the "Salisbury" in St Martin's Lane, were
informal, convivial and refreshingly free of dogmatism and sectarianism.
The most serious division was a controversy between the Neo-Romantics
led by Maurice Carpenter, whose poetic heroes were Dylan Thomas,
Edith Sitwell and George Barker, and the Neo-Classicals led by Manifold,

whose models were Pope, Byron and Australian bush ballads. Rickword took no part in their disputes, although his sympathies, unlike Lindsay's, were probably more with the Neo-Classicals. At the group's meetings he said little, except when he was appealed to for a judgment on a disputed point, and even then he would confine himself to few words. As the oldest and most distinguished member of the group he enjoyed respect, but it never occurred to him to expect it. When a brash young man declared that *Our Time* must avoid the left-sectarian errors of *Left Review* he gave his characteristic quiet chuckle; it was Swingler who roared with laughter and remarked that it was time the young were taught respect for their elders.

Swingler's return to *Our Time* enabled Rickword to give more attention to his own affairs. In the course of his researches into the radical tradition he had begun, while still living at Marlow, to take an interest in booksellers' catalogues, especially those which included books on political and sociological subjects, and he was increasingly attracted by the idea of opening a secondhand bookshop. He was encouraged by Jonny, who sensed that he was unhappy at *Our Time* and herself preferred living outside London. She began looking for a new home and suitable premises for a bookshop and found both at Deal, Kent — a fisherman's cottage and a corner shop in a passage leading to the sea. Having sold the guest house, in October 1946 they moved into the cottage and opened their shop, the Book Corner. For the next nine months he lived with the Swinglers in their flat in Islington during the week and joined Jonny at Deal for the weekends. He did not enjoy the arrangement. The cost of keeping two homes going on his scanty editorial salary was intolerable, and he was anxious to end it.

When Swingler returned from the Army, Fore Publications was flourishing. He had plans to expand its activities. *Our Time* was selling well, its financial position assisted by the eloquence of its sales representative who managed to give potential advertisers the impression of a circulation far larger than it really was. *Seven*, a more popular magazine which Fore Publications had taken over, sold even better and made a useful profit. The time had come to launch a project which had long been discussed, the publication of separate quarterlies devoted to each of the arts. The first of these, *Theatre Today*, began to appear in March 1946 under Slater's editorship; preliminary work began on *Film Today*, and two other magazines, *Music Today* and *Art Today*, were under consideration. By 1947, however, Fore Publications was in serious financial difficulties. The readership of *Our Time* had fallen away rapidly to only half of what it had been two years before. Sales and advertisements together were no long sufficient to cover its modest overheads and to enable the staff to be paid a living wage. In the spring *Theatre Today* and the rights to *Film Today* were sold to the Saturn

Press, and the proposed quarterlies on music and art never appeared. *Seven* had been sold to another publisher.

Although all cultural journals were suffering a falling circulation at this time, when the abnormal demand for reading matter created by the war no longer existed, *Our Time*'s difficulties were compounded by the deteriorating international situation. The Communist parties' contribution to the defeat of Fascism earned mass support, reflected in election results, and in 1944-45 they entered coalition Governments in many countries of Eastern and Western Europe. On the assumption that a similar situation would soon exist in the United Kingdom, the British party in March 1945 advocated the continuation of all-party government after the war, but its dreams of a solid block of Communist M.P.s and possible Communist representation in the Government were disappointed when it won only two seats in the July election. Putting the best face it could on the situation, it adopted an attitude of critical support for the Labour Government, campaigned for increased production in the factories and mines, and even supported the continuation of conscription in peacetime, contrary to the Labour movement's libertarian and pacifist traditions. By 1947, however, it was finding this position difficult to maintain. The United States and the Soviet Union were entering the period of Cold War, and the Labour Government consistently followed Washington on foreign policy issues. Between March and May the Communist ministers were dropped from the Governments of Belgium, Luxembourg, France and Italy, while in Eastern Europe it was becoming obvious that "people's democracy" was merely a euphemism for Stalinist dictatorship. After the formation of the Cominform in September the British party virtually abandoned its policy of support for the Government and demanded "a complete reversal of the Government's policy and new men in the leading Government positions".[16] This political polarization adversely affected both the party's membership, which had fallen from 56,000 in 1942 to 43,000, and the sales of pro-Communist periodicals such as *Our Time*.

By the early summer of 1947 two views existed on how it should increase its circulation. Rickword believed that it should extend its appeal by drawing more widely than before upon all shades of progressive opinion. On the other hand, Rattenbury and his ex-army friends Thompson and Holbrook, then completing courses at Cambridge after demobilization, maintained that such an in-gathering of progressive opinion would only follow upon a more aggressive and polemical editorial policy, and that to ensure that this policy was vigorously put into effect the younger generation (themselves) should be represented on the editorial board. Slater and Sommerfield supported this view, and Swingler and Lindsay were not unsympathetic. The differences were in danger of becoming acrimonious and Rickword was anxious to leave. Swingler, as proprietor of *Our Time*, called in the party to arbitrate.

The meeting took place at King Street, in late June or early July, with Emile Burns presiding. He was a man with a grievance. Although the Comintern had been put out of its misery four years earlier, in his view the principle which it had laid down, that "all party publishing houses must be completely subordinated to the party Presidium", still held good. As he saw it, Beste, who had followed his advice, had been removed by a conspiracy among the intellectuals and replaced by Rickword, who had consistently ignored it, which he resented. Beside him, facing the meeting, sat Garman, who, his *Calendar* days far behind him, was now a fulltime party official responsible for political education. Rickword and Swingler sat to one side, looking, Thompson thought, like the accused in the dock, the rest of those present, among them Lindsay, Rattenbury, Holbrook and Thompson, faced Burns like schoolboys before their master. After Rickword and Swingler had been grilled on the journal's falling circulation figures and desperate financial position, and the younger men had voiced their criticisms of Rickword's policy in strong terms (which they afterwards regretted), Burns delivered his verdict, finding Rickword and Swingler guilty of every sin in the Stalinist calendar. Neither made any reply to this tirade, which Rickword accepted as an excuse for resignation, while the others present listened in stunned silence. Garman also remained silent, but probably through his influence Burns was subsequently relieved by the party of his responsibility for cultural matters.

Next day Lindsay wrote to Rickword deploring "the pretty dreadful display all round" and dissociating himself from "the wretchedly discourteous (to use too mild a word) behaviour of the rebels and the rest". "I think the attitude to you who built the paper up into a national paper with general respect from all sides was absolutely disgraceful," he continued. "I admit that initially I wanted to see the young chaps given a chance to take over and see what they could do – even if it was only to learn a lesson. But the result of yesterday has been to wither away any desires on my part to help them." It is characteristic of Rickword that he did not bear any grudge against Rattenbury, Holbrook and Thompson, the first two of whom remained lifelong friends. As for his other critics, he wrote in 1969 in a letter to Holbrook: "That milieu offers rich opportunities for the exercise of Gogolesque fantasy, I mean the King St bureaucracy and Emile and all that".

He prepared the August issue of *Our Time* with Holbrook's assistance, and then left for Deal. The paper's later history can be briefly summarized. The next issue, which did not appear until October, bore the names of an editorial commission in which Slater, Sommerfield and George Marrin represented the older men and Rattenbury, Beeching and I the younger generation, with Holbrook, nominally "assistant editor", discharging the day-to-day functions of editorship. The paper's size was increased from 20 pages to 28, and its price from sixpence to a shilling. In tone it became more polemical, devoting much space to denunciation of the anti-Communist witch-hunt in the United States. Its attitude towards Zhdanov's campaign in the Soviet Union against "decadent bourgeois literature" was an equivocal one; it did not defend it, as King Street would have wished, but printed letters from Soviet writers which did, as well as a lengthy exposition of the biological theories of the charlatan T.D. Lysenko. Satire figured prominently in its pages, outstanding examples being the short stories of Sylvia Townsend Warner and the poems of the young American Tom McGrath. The continued influence of Rickword, who contributed a number of reviews, was clear in the spring of 1948, when the party was celebrating the centenary of *The Communist Manifesto*: the editorial commission (at my suggestion) chose rather to devote the April issue to a celebration of the centenary of the Chartist campaign of 1848, greatly to King Street's annoyance. From this issue onwards Holbrook was replaced as editor by Frank Jellinek, a journalist who had written a valuable history of the Paris Commune, although Holbrook remained a member of the editorial commission. In the autumn, when Jellinek took a job abroad and Rattenbury temporarily acted as editor, Swingler wrote to Rickword: "*Our Time*...ironically enough, seems to be reverting on to my hands. Frank has commuted (I think that's the word) to Switzerland, leaving everything to Arnold who is going to live in Bristol next week. As Edward Thompson is now settled in Middlesbrough, that also answers the question about the new life, fresh talent, younger generation, and what not." A single issue appeared for November and December, in which no editor's name was given, and from January 1949 Swingler resumed the editorship. The magazine regained much of the good-humoured tone and literary standard which had characterized Rickword's day; although it remained political, there was none of the bad temper which marred the 1948 issues. By then, however, the decline in circulation, to which both the polemical tone and the increased price had contributed, had gone too far, and although the price was reduced to sixpence in June in a desperate bid to arrest it, the next issue was the last.

When he gave up the editorship Rickword's mind was occupied with his new life as a bookseller and with the forthcoming appearance of his collected poems. His three previous collections, the latest of which had appeared sixteen years earlier, had been out of print for many years, and were unknown to the great majority of the poetry-reading public. An article on "Poetry Between the Wars" published in *The Times Literary Supplement*, which suggested that his poems should be reprinted, made clear the obscurity into which they had fallen. "Future selectors will find the period not least worth study in the neglected writers – and there are always many who in the fullness of time are recalled," it remarked, adding as examples of such neglected writers: "When shall we ourselves have leisure to recollect such voices as Alan Porter, Edgell Rickword, or Frank Prewett?"[17] To suggest that he fell into the same category as Porter and Prewett emphasized how much his work was underestimated.

When Lindsay, whose books were then being published by the Bodley Head, persuaded the firm to issue a collected edition of Rickword's poems, he jumped at the chance to re-establish his poetic presence. He went through his earlier work with extreme care, excluding everything which failed to satisfy him. Of the 36 poems in *Behind the Eyes* he suppressed 26, including the two poems dedicated to Peggy, "The Gift" and "Grave Joys", perhaps because of their painful associations, such Romantic poems as "Reverie", "Blindness", "Desire", "Dead of Night", "Winter Prophecies" and "Keepsake", and even the more mature "Complaint of a Tadpole", "Outline of History" and "Meditation on Beds". The only survivors of this drastic purge were the four war poems, the two "Regrets", "Intimacy", "Passion" (renamed "Obsession"), "Cosmogony" and "Complaint after Psycho-analysis". Of the poems in *Invocations to Angels* he rejected, more surprisingly, "Earth and Age", "Race Day", "Necropolis", "Regrets for Certain Blind Alleys" and the exquisite "Beyond Good and Evil", yet he included "Memory", which was dropped from his two subsequent collections. He omitted "The Contemporary Muse", "Answer to an Invitation to Love" and "Advice to a Girl from the War and Afterwards" from *Twittingpan*, and added "To the Wife of a Non-Interventionist Statesman". The 49 poems which survived this sifting process were stated on the jacket to be all those that the author wished to republish. They were at first printed in the order in which they had appeared in the original editions, with "To the Wife..." at the end, but Rickword later rearranged them so that the book began with the war poems and ended with "The Happy New Year".

When *Collected Poems* appeared in November, with a dedication to Jack Lindsay and his wife Ann, it had a mixed reception. The anonymous reviewer in *The Times Literary Supplement* commented that Rickword had always been out of tune with poetic fashion, a poet of the town in the days of the bucolic Georgians, "a poet of the world of bohemian individualism" in the political 1930s, and continued:

> Mr Rickword, in fact, had an eye for what is shabby and hopeless, and at the same time for what is original and eccentric, in the moral atmosphere of Soho; he was a poet of the bad nerves of London...His poems convey the atmosphere of a special society, at once down-to-earth and passionately and ornately literary, at once consciously disreputable and

jauntily stylish... Yet, bitterly aware as he is of the vices and follies of the London literary man, Mr Rickword also exemplifies his virtues. In his satirical pieces he attacks shams and cruelties, not on any low plane of personal interest, not from any sudden surge of warm emotion, but from the high and rigid standpoint of truth and justice.

A patronizing review in *The Listener* treated the book as a quaint period piece, describing it as "an interesting document of the period" which displayed "the rusted edge of pre-war acuity", and neither *The Times Literary Supplement* review nor Roy Fuller's in *Tribune* resisted the temptation to assume that because most of the poems were over twenty years old they were primarily of historical interest. Fuller chided Rickword and his generation for their "irritatingly and weakly pre-Marxian" failure to appreciate the social origins of their malaise, but praised his poems for possessing "qualities which are badly needed now – intellect, form, bitterness".

Lindsay also reviewed the poems from a historical standpoint, but assessed their value more generously. In *Adam* he hailed Rickword as "the most important poet of the 'twenties who came forward to work in the space cleared by the Sitwells and T.S. Eliot", and suggested that if he had continued to write poetry in the 1930s the socially-oriented verse of the Auden school and the neo-Romantic verse of Edith Sitwell and Dylan Thomas might have been integrated into a single movement, to the advantage of both. In the *Daily Worker*, as might be expected, he related the poems to the political rather than the poetic developments of the inter-war years. "They reveal a man," he wrote, "who by the whole necessity of his poetry finds himself a Communist; he finds that his poems and the revolutionary movement are going in the same direction, the vindication of human freedom in all its fullness...By their subtle creative tenacity, their faith in life, the poems break through 'to all men's Harvest-Home'." Beeching's review in *Our Time* analysed the poems in similar terms as a record of the poet's progress from the trenches to Communism.[18]

"You know what I think of your poems," Swingler wrote to Rickword, "so I won't say more now than that their technical richness is a perpetual exhilaration, and couldn't be more salutary to the state of literature at the moment. I hope people wake up to the importance of their appearance as they should." This hope was unfulfilled, for the book was largely ignored; the *Sunday Times*, the *Observer*, the *New Statesman* and the *Spectator* did not review it. Its failure was so complete that Rickword bought up the unsold copies himself, planning to reissue it at a more propitious time. There are several reasons for its poor sales. The appearance of the book was uninviting; the coarse greyish paper may have been the best that could be obtained in those days of austerity, but the black binding and drab olive-green jacket did not help. More serious was the silence of the quality Sunday papers and the weeklies, which could make or break a book, and here political prejudice played a part; at a time when Britain was entering the Cold War editors were reluctant to publicize the writings of a known Communist. In choosing to publish his poems in 1947 Rickword displayed that tendency to be out of tune with the times on which *The Times Literary Supplement* remarked. He was not only a Communist when Communism was no longer fashionable or tolerated; he was a poet of intelligence and a meticulous craftsman when much of the poetry in demand was characterized by a formless emotionalism. The qualities of his verse, as both Fuller and Swingler recognized, were precisely those which the poetry of the day needed, but they were not calculated to win recognition. His selection according to his own standards may also have contributed to its failure; by omitting many of his warmer and more colourful early poems, while retaining those written in the nihilistic mood of the later 1920s and the acid epigrams from *Twitting-pan*, he gave the impression that he was a coldly cerebral and forbidding poet with a negative outlook on life. He seems to have recognized this mistake himself, for he readmitted fifteen of the excluded poems to the selection published in 1970 and nine more to the collected edition of 1976. This lay in the future, however; for the time being, an apparent failure both as an editor and as a poet, he resolved to concentrate on bookselling.

XV. Bookselling

BY the end of July 1947 Rickword was settled with Jonny in their cottage at Deal, planning to make a success of the Book Corner, where in addition to new and second-hand books they sold music, prints and curios. It was a good time to enter the book trade. After the interruption to sales caused by the war, more books were coming on to the market; the larger booksellers could not afford to buy the range of rarities which turned up, and small dealers could pick up eighteenth and even seventeenth century books at a reasonable price. Selling proved a slower process, and to extend his clientèle he began issuing catalogues twice a year.

Deal was only a few miles from Dover and Folkestone, and friends going to or returning from the Continent sometimes broke their journey to visit the Rickwords. David Holbrook and his wife Margot looked in when returning from their honeymoon and, as Holbrook afterwards remembers, were treated by Jonny with "kindness alternating between fierceness and gentleness". Nancy Cunard paid a visit, and spent most of the night typing letters by candle-light, squatting on the floor as the spare bedroom was too small to leave room for a table. Rickword found congenial company in Deal, notably the writer Douglas Goldring, whom he persuaded to review for *Our Time*. Goldring had long admired his verse and in his book *The Nineteen Twenties* included Rickword among neglected poets of the period who "still await their almost inevitable re-discovery".[1] Not all his friends were literary. Deal was on the edge of the Kentish coalfield: some of the fishermen's cottages had been taken over by miners, and Rickword formed a close friendship with a trade union activist who had educated himself with the help of the Everyman series and the extensive library of the South Wales area of the National Union of Mineworkers.

He had settled in Deal with the intention of combining bookselling with writing and research, and some of his work was published in 1948, although the only book with his name on the title-page contained none of his writing. He was a member of the committee of the Writers' Group of the Society for Cultural Relations with the U.S.S.R. It is symptomatic of the friendly attitude of most British people towards the Soviet Union in the brief interval between the end of the war and the onset of the Cold War that his fellow-members included Richard Church, Ifor Evans, Compton Mackenzie, V.S. Pritchett and Stephen Spender, who were not Communist sympathizers. Members of the Group had sent questions on subjects of interest to writers to the Literary

Section of VOKS, the Soviet organization for cultural relations with foreign countries, and the Russians' replies were published in a booklet called *Soviet Writers Reply to English Writers' Questions* which Rickword edited.

To commemorate the centenary of the revolutions of 1848 Fore Publications planned to issue a series of booklets under the title "The Birth of Socialism". *The German Revolution of 1848* by Roy Pascal appeared in July 1948, and *The French Revolution of 1848* by the French historian Albert Soboul followed shortly after. Rickword translated this while living with the Swinglers, and undertook to write the third of the series, *The Struggle for Democracy in Britain, 1848*. His surviving notes, which include extracts from R.G. Gammage's *History of the Chartist Movement*, the Chartist newspaper *The Northern Star, The Times, The Quarterly Review* and the letters of Queen Victoria, Prince Albert, Lord John Russell, Lord Palmerston and Matthew Arnold, show that he planned to emphasize the Socialist elements in Chartism (he took copies of several long articles in *The Northern Star* by or about Robert Owen and his followers) and its connection with European revolutionary movements, and especially with the French Socialists. Although the pamphlet was apparently completed, or almost so, by July, when an advertisement in *Our Time* announced that it would be "ready shortly", it was never published, presumably because the sales of the first two booklets proved disappointing, and the manuscript has disappeared.

Rickword's reviews in *Life and Letters To-day* and *Our Time* in 1948 were of less interest than one published in *Tribune*, in which he dealt with the poems of Robert Bloomfield and Matthew Arnold and books by Jane Austen, Charlotte Brontë, Anthony Trollope, George Gissing and Richard Jefferies. He wove his comments on these very different writers, who between them span the nineteenth century, into a unity by relating them to the transformation of English society brought about by the Industrial Revolution. How successfully he combined the Marxist sociological approach to literature with the aesthetic criticism which reacts to a writer's use of words is apparent in his comment on *Emma*:

> It is very rarely that Jane Austen's characters express themselves passionately, however deeply they may feel; it would offend against decorum. There is an outburst in *Emma*, though, when Jane Fairfax refers to the profession of governess, for which she seems destined, as a trade in flesh, and compares it unfavourably with the African slave trade. It is very unusual for Jane Austen to refer to flesh. She must have intended to bring the protest home to the most obtuse.[2]

The only work which Rickword published in 1949 was a preface to a new collection of essays by Christopher Caudwell, *Further Studies in a Dying Culture.* It states his Marxist beliefs, casting light on his own intellectual development and on Caudwell's:

> The garish boom of the late 20's suddenly collapsed into slump…Hungry men and empty factories existed alongside men whose unsatisfied elemental needs those factories and workless men could have supplied… Whatever one studied in those days, the course of events always dragged back the attention to the realism of economics, the material reproduction of our means of existence, as the basis of social organisation…Marxism was a light that radiated hope through the gloom of Britain's depressed areas…Having the clue, he set out to explore with its aid deeply into contemporary reality…And it was clear to him that he could not do this as the contemplative philosopher, in a secluded study. He became a member of the Communist party…The dozen years that have passed have immensely emphasised the world-pattern which he discerned.[3]

Whatever grievances Rickword might have against individual Communists, his attachment to his principles remained unshaken.

In November 1949 the Rickwords moved south along the Kentish coast to Sandgate, virtually a suburb of Folkestone. Life went on there all the year round, whereas Deal seemed to fall asleep in winter, and the new shop was ideally situated on the coast road from Folkestone to Rye and Hastings, facing the best hotel. Business was so brisk that Rickword could afford to engage an assistant, a young man with some experience of the book trade, and as he owned a car he was able to attend sales more easily than Rickword had been able to do. In July 1951 he reported in a letter to his daughter Jane that he had leased a second shop along the coast at Hythe, and although the narrow one-way street in which it stood was very noisy "we hope to hold enough visitors to ransom to compensate us for the discomfort". As business expanded, in 1951 he began issuing catalogues three times a year instead of twice.

Between 1949 and 1953 he published only one piece of writing, but it was a notable one. After the war the Army Bureau of Current Affairs had been converted into a civilian organization, the Bureau of Current Affairs, which issued pamphlets on political and social questions for use in adult education classes, as well as occasional pamphlets on literary themes. Holbrook had joined the Bureau after leaving *Our Time*, and at his suggestion Boris Ford, the editor of its pamphlets, commissioned one from Rickword to mark the centenary of Wordsworth's death. The resulting essay, published in April 1950 and intended for readers with little knowledge of the poet's work, forms as good an introduction as any in the language, but it is much more than a piece of popularization. The first section in particular abounds in critical insights which enable us to read Wordsworth with a deeper understanding and appreciation.

There is in ["Hart-Leap Well"] the Wordsworthian power of throwing
over natural objects a sense of organic being. This plastic or informing
power is quite different from the purely descriptive or pictorial faculty,
such as Spenser had in such a high degree, and Tennyson afterwards.
One of Wordsworth's favourite painters was Rembrandt, who has the
not dissimilar faculty of transforming common objects by the contrast
of light and shade, because of the intensity with which they are felt. It
may be noted how very rarely he uses a colour adjective; there is much
more of movement in his verse, of clouds, winds, waterfalls, and rivers...
"I have at all times," he justly claimed, "endeavoured to look steadily
at my subject." And as that subject is generally psychological rather
than material ("the feelings arising from the situation and action"), so
the language is verbal, following the movements of the mind, rather
than adjectival, for the adjective is necessarily static... As he is so sparing
of colour, when he does put in a splash it has tremendous effect.

Rickword goes on to trace Wordsworth's intellectual development up
to 1800, dismissing the last fifty years of his life in a paragraph.
Although he deals at some length with the impact of the French Revolution on Wordsworth, he does not over-emphasize his early Jacobinism,
as if anxious to disprove the allegation that Marxist critics are primarily
concerned with a writer's politics. The final section contains an
enlightening analysis of Wordsworth's literary theories and a balanced
discussion of his claim to be a philosophic poet. Rickword's conclusion
– "he remains the most modern of our poets"[4] – comes as something
of a shock, for Wordsworth's poetry would seem to have little in common with that of the Modernists of the 1920s or with Rickword's own,
yet it emerges logically from the argument of the essay.

   In the early months of 1950 Rickword passed through a period of
indecision over his future as a writer. On 8 March he wrote to the
Society of Authors, of which he had been a member since 1939, "I am
not now engaged in authorship and feel that I must give up my membership of the Society".[5] Yet on 21 April he announced in a letter to Jane
that "I hope to start in on a long book soon, a sort of historico-literary
study of some of the more obscure figures of the early Wordsworth
period". What had happened, apart from the publication of his essay
on Wordsworth, to make him decide, only six weeks after giving notice
of his abandonment of authorship, to undertake his first full-length
prose work since *Rimbaud*?

   The explanation may lie in his discovery of John Thelwall, the minor
poet and friend of Coleridge and Wordsworth whom Edward Thompson
has described as the most important political theorist among the English
Jacobins.[6] At some time in 1950 he bought for two or three pounds
eight letters from Thelwall to Thomas Hardy, secretary of the London
Corresponding Society, which he had seen advertised in a bookseller's

catalogue, and also bought for 1s. 6d. a volume of Thelwall's verse. These purchases suggested to him the idea of a book of essays on radical poets of the late eighteenth and early nineteenth centuries, some indications of the scope of which are given by notes among his papers written on index cards. One card, obviously referring to Thelwall, has: "Evidence from Letters. To Coleridge on the Sonnet to Priestley. Priestley's reputation – Riots in Birmingham, Part 2, Appendix. Gillray's cartoon The Fourteenth of July. His friendships – he mixed consistently with democrats – though without breaking with Wordsworth and Southey." Another, which has merely "Robert Merry, a Butterfly on the Wheel", suggests that he considered devoting a chapter to the Della Cruscans. A third, written not earlier than 1957, reads: "Coleridge and Gogol. Compare their attitude to Landowners. Lay Sermon, Select Letters. cf. Magarschak, Gogol." For the time being, however, the only outcome of the plan was an article on Thelwall's letters published in *The Times Literary Supplement* in June 1953.

At an uncertain date he modified his plan, and drew up proposals for a book provisionally entitled *Five Prison Poets. Essays in Practical Democracy, with Selections of Poems*. This was to include biographical essays on Thelwall, the Lancashire Radical Samuel Bamford and the Chartists Robert Peddie, Thomas Cooper and Ernest Jones, all of whom published collections of poems written while they were in prison for advocating extension of the franchise. "These five men," Rickword wrote,

> represent different phases of the democratic movement from its first considerable upsurge in the early 1790s, through the tumultuous, post-war, anti-Castlereagh years, to the birth, climax and decline of Chartism, which ends a historical cycle. The men are all extremely interesting, even if their poems are not intrinsically of great value. But they are scattered in editions that are hard to come by (except for Cooper) and such a book would have a certain value as a work of reference.

At the bottom of the typed page he added in ink: "Say an average of 24 pp for poems & 35,000 prose = 272 pp." There is no indication among his correspondence that he ever submitted his plan to a publisher, however, and nothing came of it.

Meanwhile his hopes of establishing a flourishing business in Sandgate were frustrated by lack of capital and his inability to establish his claim to the tenancy of his premises. His belief that they were on a ten-year lease proved to be unfounded, and in 1953 it became necessary to move again. At this point Jonny had an idea so outrageous, in conventional eyes, that it could only have originated with her. Dr Back, her former husband, had a two-storey flat near Swiss Cottage, large enough to provide living space for all three of them and ample premises for a bookselling business as well: why not move in with him? He was approached and proved amenable. Rickword found himself selling books ("business by post or appointment only") from Dr Back's house in Buckland Crescent. This *ménage à trois* raised some eyebrows, even in literary Hampstead, but it was generally accepted that such unconventional behaviour was what could be expected from three survivors from the bohemian 1920s. Although on the surface Rickword and Dr Back accepted the situation philosophically, and occasionally Jonny was escorted to their local pub by both her husbands, there is evidence that Rickword suffered at times from an agonizing jealousy. Among his manuscripts in the British Library is a sheet of paper on which he has written drafts of two poems, the first of which reads:

> When I have used you
> As my lusts wish
> Till the skin lies loose
> On your tired flesh
>
> You little old woman
> With sunken eyes
> Loving the bed
> Where your girlhood lies
>
> Shall be to me
> As the sooty ember
> One kicks to flame
> In a grey November.
>
> The sparks that fly
> Shall be stars that burned
> In the blue of your hair...

The mood of the second, which begins with the words "You pulled your skirt up", is less ambiguous. Throughout the first eleven lines Rickword tortures himself by imagining in detail how in the past Jonny had allowed other men to make love to her, then his agitation subsides into a deep unhappiness:

> Though you have given me an autumn love,
> A gentle life and clear companionship,
> These will not let me rest, these memories
> Of your strong girlish lust by men appeased
> Before my time. And though you turn to mine
> All you remember that was given you,
> Though he who took your maidenhead had not
> That whole of you that rests with me each night,
> Fantasy cannot ease me, we grow old
> And I with half my youth wrenched from me seek

Still Lethe that my senses may be dimmed
And I in the green world out of the sunlight
Find love in gloomy pools where no sound comes.[7]

The references to age in this poem suggest that Rickword can hardly
have written it before his middle fifties, and the situation in Buckland
Crescent would seem to provide the occasion for it. If this is so, these
drafts were the first poems he had written since 1940, and the first
which he had ever addressed to Jonny. It is significant of the depth of
his feeling for her that when jealousy at last forced him to break his
silence he automatically returned to the imagery of woodland pools
through which he had expressed his love for Peggy over thirty years
before.

Rickword and Jonny had no difficulty in forming a social circle in
their new surroundings, which were not far from their old home in
Arkwright Road. They spent most of their evenings at the Adelaide
(now demolished) in Chalk Farm, where they would meet his old friend
Hayter Preston, then editing a glossy three-shilling monthly called
Courier. Rickword and Preston spent hours happily discussing their
favourite authors, for example George Gissing, for whom lives spent
in New Grub Street had given them a special sympathy, or James Joyce.
At times the Rickwords would accompany Preston and his wife Vera
to his club, the Renaissance in South Kensington, for the pleasure of
hearing him recite Yeats in his cups. Among other men of literary tastes
who often joined them at the Adelaide were Henry Savage, an aged
poet who had been the friend and biographer of the unfortunate poet
Richard Middleton; Paul Allen, Preston's young assistant at *Courier*,
and his friend Igor Chroustchoff, a Ukrainian by descent with a gift
for discovering rare books. Sharing Rickword's love of Russian literature, admiring his poems and hating his Communism, he would often
drop in with another early Soviet author for his collection. When he
nicknamed Rickword "the quilted man", declaring that he had put
himself to bed for many years like Goncharov's Oblomov, Rickword
merely chuckled.

After some months in London he was forced in the spring of 1954
to admit that he had not enough capital to make a success of his bookselling business. The stock was sold off, what little money was left went
to Jonny's account, and he began a depressing journey round the
second-hand bookshops of Central London in search of work, beginning at Foyle's. After a pleasant chat about his experiences Miss Chris-
tina Foyle told him that the firm was not prepared to pay him the £10
a week which he asked, and other shops were even less encouraging,
offering him £6 less insurance. It was probably at this time that he had
to sell his Thelwall letters. One day, finding himself literally penniless,

he was obliged to pawn for £4 a gold ring which his grandmother had given him on his twenty-first birthday; when he went to redeem it he was asked £6, and decided that he could do without it. Fortunately there were other ways of raising money. Jonny returned to her old craft of dressmaking, though her exotic creations were not to everyone's taste. "He's a poet, you see," she would explain, adding: "My other husbands were much better off." In fact, Dr Back was the only other husband she had had, but she had certainly lived with other men before settling down with Rickword. He himself wrote two essays which Preston published in *Courier*, and for each of which he received £10. One was on the bibliography of cricket; he took little interest in the game, but his catalogues show that many books on sport had passed through his hands in his bookselling days. The other, "Grub Street Epicures", gave a lively picture of the bohemian eating-houses of London in the 1920s, and he thought highly enough of it to quote liberally from it in his memoirs.*

At this point he was fortunate enough to meet an old acquaintance, then manager of Collet's bookshop in Charing Cross Road, who told him that the firm was looking for a manager for its Hampstead branch. He applied for the job, was accepted, and found himself in charge of a double-fronted shop on Haverstock Hill at a salary of £9 a week, with the promise of an annual rise of £1 if he gave satisfaction. Although not princely, this at least guaranteed him a certain security, especially when Jonny's earnings were added, and the shop had the additional advantage of being within walking distance of Buckland Crescent.

His assistant was Peter Chalk, a lively young man of working-class origin with a love of books. Something like a father-son relationship developed between them. They would spend an evening at the pub now and then with William Empson, who lived in the neighbourhood, but as he was almost as taciturn as Rickword, Chalk's hopes of hearing some literary discussion were usually disappointed. Half an hour would sometimes pass without a word being spoken, then one of them would remark, "Not a bad pint this". The other would agree, and after another long silence add, "But I've drunk better". Rickword nevertheless made a remark on occasion which lingered in Chalk's memory. As a birthday present Chalk gave him a first edition of Swinburne which had been marked down from 10s. to 2s. 6d., and mischievously commented "You see what happens to classics, they get marked down". "Yes," Rickword agreed, "but he still remains a classic." His birthday present to Chalk was a copy of Cobbett's autobiography, in the front of which he had written: "There were giants on the earth in those days". Another assistant, a young woman, was so impressed with him that she called her

* An extract is included in Chapter VI above.

eldest son Edgell, an unusual name which the boy found rather embarrassing when he was old enough to go to school.

During the years between Rickword's departure from *Our Time* and his taking over the Hampstead shop the Cold War was at its height. Yugoslavia's expulsion from the Cominform was followed by a series of show trials of "Titoists", complete with detailed confessions by the accused to incredible crimes – the Rajk trial in Hungary, the Kostov trial in Bulgaria, the Slansky trial in Czechoslovakia. The outlook in the Western world was hardly more encouraging. The United States had its own show trials, at which batches of Communists were imprisoned on dubious evidence. The division of Europe assumed institutional form in 1949 with the partition of Germany and the establishment of NATO, and when a rearmed Western Germany entered NATO in 1955 the Soviet Union retaliated with the formation of the Warsaw Pact alliance. A third World War seemed only a matter of time.

If the pressures on Communist intellectuals in Britain during this period were mild compared with those to which American intellectuals were subjected (to say nothing of Eastern Europeans), they were no less real. A Marxist academic, Eric Hobsbawm, has said: "The test was when you got in. If you made it before the Berlin Crisis of May 1948, well, you didn't get promotion for ten years, but nobody threw you out."[8] For some this was not enough. A review in *The Times Literary Supplement* of Jack Lindsay's *Byzantium into Europe* demanded that Communists should be banned from teaching history, and this call for a purge of the universities was supported by an editorial denouncing the "confused liberalism" of those who opposed it.[9] The demand that distinguished historians such as Christopher Hill, Rodney Hilton, Eric Hobsbawm, Edward Thompson, John Saville, Victor Kiernan and George Rudé be banned illustrates how British McCarthyism threatened academic standards as well as intellectual freedom. Against Communist intellectuals any slander was legitimate. A book published as late as 1959 asserted that Rickword believed that "certainty no longer existed, except the certainty that one line of behaviour was no better than another". In fact in the passage referred to Rickword had said that Joyce, Eliot, Huxley or Virginia Woolf left the reader, "if with any certainty, then the certainty that no line of behaviour is better than any other".[10] His statement had been distorted to suggest that Communists denied moral values.

Some intellectuals left the Communist Party during this period. Claud Cockburn went, concluding that the 1945 election results had shown that it was no longer politically relevant. Holbrook resigned soon after leaving *Our Time*. Edward Upward departed in 1948, believing that the party's support for the Labour Government proved that it was no longer a Leninist party. J.B.S. Haldane was forced out by King Street's insistence that he should defend Lysenko's biological theories. But the majority of the intellectuals in the party remained. If the Soviet bloc under Stalin presented an unacceptable face, what could be said of the Western bloc, waging its colonial wars in Indonesia, Vietnam, Morocco, Tunisia, Algeria, Malaya, Kenya and Cyprus, and destroying democracy in British Guiana and Guatemala? Many Communists would have taken Sartre's view, who denounced Soviet labour camps and the Rajk and Kostov trials, but supported the Communist Party after 1952 because he believed that the main threat to peace came not from the Soviet Union but from the Atlantic Alliance.

Another thing helped to keep Communist intellectuals inside the party: the emergence of professional ex-Communists. In the McCarthyite atmosphere persons who had been or claimed to have been Communists made a living out of recantation, and those who claimed to have undergone a religious conversion did particularly well. A group of some eighty professional ex-Communists toured the United States, appearing as expert witnesses at show trials and indulging in perjuries which would have aroused the admiration of Titus Oates. Anything was better, many intellectuals felt, than to find themselves in such company, and those who like Haldane left the party out of honest conviction were careful to keep quiet about it.

Rickword's relations with the party leadership had been strained ever since the *Our Time* episode, and the political developments of the years that followed deepened his unease. To him as to many others the Rajk, Kostov and Slansky trials were particularly disturbing, reviving painful memories of the Soviet trials of 1936-38. Sensing the party's mood, the leadership called in James Klugmann, a King Street propagandist who had served with the British military mission to the Yugoslav partisans during the war and had since written copiously in praise of Tito in *Our Time* and elsewhere. This did not prevent him from publishing in 1951 *From Trotsky to Tito*, in which he accepted all the grotesque allegations made against the Yugoslav leaders at the trials as historical fact. Rickword bought a copy, but the presence among his books of *Revision of Marxism-Leninism on the Question of the Liberation War in Yugoslavia* by Colonel-General Kocha Popovich, the Yugoslav Chief of Staff, suggests that he was not prepared to swallow the party line without examining the evidence on both sides. His increasing doubts about Stalin may have stimulated his interest in Thelwall, whose letters record his gradual disillusionment with "the tyrant Buonaparte, who has destroyed, perhaps for ever, all my glorious speculations of the improvability of man, and blasted the best hopes of Europe".[11]

His doubts were more than confirmed when the full text of Khrushchev's report on Stalin's excesses was published in the *Observer* on

10 June 1956. Faced with a rising storm inside the party, the leadership set up a commission "to examine and report upon problems of inner-party democracy, including congress procedure", but as ten of the fifteen members were full-time party officials, including Burns and Klugmann, little could be hoped from it. In July Thompson and Saville began publishing *The Reasoner*, contributors to which included Doris Lessing, Professor Hyman Levy and Rodney Hilton. Ordered to cease publication of this embarrassingly independent journal, the editors defiantly issued a second number. In October came a new shock, with the popular uprising in Hungary, followed in November by its brutal suppression by the Soviet Army. The British party leadership reacted as might have been expected; the *Daily Worker* suppressed the eyewitness reports of its Budapest correspondent, who was expelled from the party for publishing them in book form, and the executive adopted a resolution defending the Soviet intervention. When a third issue of *The Reasoner* called on the executive to repudiate the invasion, Thompson and Saville were suspended from membership, whereupon both resigned. Fifteen other intellectuals, including Lindsay, MacDiarmid, Doris Lessing, Levy, Hill, Hobsbawm, Hilton and Kiernan, signed a letter to the *Daily Worker* condemning the Soviet aggression, and when it was refused publication sent it to *Tribune* and the *New Statesman*. A special party congress in April 1957 approved the invasion, accepted the majority report on party democracy and rejected a minority report signed by Hill and two others, which called for greater freedom of discussion within the party and the right to dissent from official policy.

With this congress the crisis ended. Most of the dissidents who had not already resigned decided that there was no hope of reforming the party from within, and left it. Membership fell from over 33,000 at the beginning of 1956 to under 25,000 two years later. Among the intellectuals who resigned were Hill, Hilton, Levy, Doris Lessing, the composer Rutland Boughton and Rickword's friends Swingler and Beeching. Most of them left quietly, having no desire to issue noisy recriminations. Not all the dissidents resigned; Hobsbawm, Lindsay and MacDiarmid, among others, believing that the party's Marxist principles were more important than the shortcomings of its leaders, stayed on. In the past Communists who resigned or were expelled and those who remained had regarded each other with suspicion. But "the friendship and comradeship of the years before 1956", as Hobsbawm has put it, "survived the tensions and disputes of the time and the more permanent divergences of political allegiance".[12] Each side understood the other's motives.

Among those who left the party was Rickword. Taciturn as ever, he did so even more quietly than his friends. Beeching, with whom he was in frequent contact personally or by letter, continued to believe that he was still a member until 1978, when Rickword told him that he had made his decision after the invasion of Hungary. He remained on friendly terms with Lindsay, Morton, Alick West, Garman and others who had chosen to stay, and occasionally wrote for the party publications, the *Daily Worker*, its successor the *Morning Star* and *Labour Monthly*. He still called himself a Marxist, although he no longer accepted Moscow or King Street as sole interpreters of Marxism; it is significant that he bought a copy of the 1957 edition of Trotsky's *The Revolution Betrayed*. Many years later he wrote on an odd scrap of paper "When rulers who call themselves Marxists behave as brutally as capitalists it is time to think again". He had joined the party because he hated cruelty and injustice, he left it for the same reason.

In March 1957 he received a letter from Swingler. "Edward Thompson and John Saville are about to produce a quarterly review of 'Socialist Humanism' called The New Reasoner, and I am giving them a hand with it," he wrote.

> They intend to come out sometime in May and they are very anxious to include a piece about the origins of Left Review, as a sort of occasion to recall the kind of enthusiasm and exploration that was going on then, and to revive some of the best things that were involved in the 'Thirties business, before we all got hag-ridden with purges and pacts and so on. Would it be possible for you to do something on this? I think it would be worth saying now, and some of the early stuff in L.R. was vigorous and sane.

Through Rickword's reply one can discern his mental anguish:

> I have begun a letter to you four times to say that I wouldn't be able to write the article you wanted, so I have to ask your forbearance. It's a very complex matter – and the subject isn't one for me. I think it should be written from the outside – by someone who was aware of what was going on, but not involved in the activities to any responsible extent. There are so many revaluations to make and the whole situation is so fluid. Difficult but hopeful. I wish you would get in touch with me next time you are in London, there is so much to discuss which is better not written down. *Voici le temps des Assassins.*

Although he declined this invitation, he produced at about the same time his first important piece of writing since the Wordsworth essay. Among his regular customers at the bookshop was Boris Ford, who had commissioned that essay and was now seeking contributors for *The Pelican Guide to English Literature*. Hoping to enrol Rickword, he has written, "I raised the notion with him in a tentative way one day, when I was buying a book, and he gave me his familiar hesitating, ambiguous, smiling reply. Some time later he said he had been thinking about this idea and would like to 'have a shot' at something on the

Romantics, perhaps something on the background to the Romantics."[13]
The outcome was "The Social Setting, 1780-1830", which appeared
as the opening chapter of the volume *From Blake to Byron*. A model
of compression, it covers in some fifteen pages the momentous political,
economic and social developments of half a century and their impact
on the literary world. Readers, however familiar with the history and
literature of the period, came away with a deepened understanding; it
is to be lamented that his planned book on the radical writers of the
period was never completed.

In the summer of 1958 the Rickwords bought a cottage in the small
Essex town of Halstead for £800 and left Buckland Crescent. Jonny
moved in to the cottage, while Rickword took lodgings with Peter
Chalk and his young wife Irene, joining Jonny for the weekends. As
there seemed to be little demand for dressmakers at Halstead, she took
a job slaughtering chickens at a broiler house packing plant. One of
the attractions of Halstead was its nearness to several relations and
friends living in northern Essex or just over the Suffolk border: Gerald
Rickword at Colchester, Swingler at Pebmarsh, Lindsay at Castle
Hedingham and Morton at Clare, where he lived in a Norman chapel
converted into a house. Edmund Blunden settled in the same neighbourhood, at Long Melford, in 1964, and he and Rickword resumed their
former friendship, the political differences of the 1930s forgotten.

Rickword wrote to Jane in the summer of 1959: "We have had a
Hampstead Festival of the Arts and we did our window up specially
with paintings by local artists and books by others. We took second
prize. A certificate (and a bottle of sherry) of merit! quite like being at
school again." But it was becoming clear that the shop was not paying
its way, largely, he thought, because he tended to overstock with books.
Collet's sold the shop but had another opening for him. The basement
of the main branch in Charing Cross Road, which had been used as a
store for new books, was converted into an out-of-print and rare books
department, which opened in the autumn with Rickword as manager.
By October he was installed in what he called "my lair, den, earth,
burrow, warren or whatever", drawing up an annotated catalogue of
the more interesting items. He had many visitors in his cellar, among
them Paul Allen, who thought he looked "glad to be free from glossy
new covers and back in his element among the books of 30 years ago",[14]
and wrote a lively pen-portrait of him for the *Guardian*. John Betjeman
found him out when he called and left a note saying "I have long been
a fervent admirer of your poetry". Although Rickword had a certain
prejudice against him, when at last they met he was overwhelmed by
Betjeman's kindness. After standing him an excellent lunch, Betjeman
took him to a nearby antiquarian bookseller, and there insisted on
buying him a first edition of Isaac Rosenberg's poems, which he had

coveted but which was far beyond his pocket.

These visitors to his cellar suggested that his years of obscurity were coming to an end. He had never been entirely forgotten. *The Penguin Book of Comic and Curious Verse* (1952) reprinted "The Encounter", "Martyrs: Modern Style" and "A Glimpse of the Great Beyond", rather to his annoyance, for as he told Peter Chalk he considered them "not representative of my verse". He was better pleased to be represented in *The Faber Book of Twentieth Century Verse* (1953) by "Cosmogony" and "The Cascade", and in *The Chatto Book of Modern Poetry* (1956) by "The Cascade" and "Rimbaud in Africa". In 1954 the Institute of Contemporary Arts paid him the compliment of inviting him to chair a meeting to commemorate the centenary of the birth of Rimbaud, at which his translation of "Le Bateau Ivre" was read. The rediscovery of his poetry, however, may be said to have begun with a 25-minute broadcast on 23 July 1960, for which Roy Fuller was responsible. In a note on the programme the *Radio Times* found it necessary to explain that Rickword was "a poet, still living, but now almost totally neglected" who had "written virtually no poetry since 1931".[15] The reading evidently made some impact, for in a letter of thanks to Fuller he said that he had "heard nothing but appreciation of it".

It may have been the consciousness that his poetry was beginning to reach an audience that moved him about this time to make some attempts at verse. In his 1961 diary he wrote on 8 January:

> Hazlitt, Marvell, Stendhal, Donne
> Blest the bed I laid upon.

During the course of the month he jotted down two more lines – "The green slats sheltering nests of lust" and "I can no longer in your languor rocked" – but did not succeed in developing them into a poem. Then, after an interval of nearly two years, he wrote in December 1962 a poem which he originally called "On the difficulty of finding a Christmas card for my beloved Jonny", and after her death renamed first "On choosing a Christmas card for a close friend" and then "Instead of a Christmas Card". In this, the only published poem addressed to Jonny, he envisages her as a huntress of the woods, or at the very least a witch's familiar, an embodiment of energy, in contrast to himself, the sleepy bear.

At this time he was under pressure from Holbrook to publish a collection of his critical writings. The smallness of his output, caused partly by the diffidence which made him so taciturn in conversation, partly by a streak of indolence in his disposition, irritated the energetic and self-confident Holbrook, 25 years his junior, whose production of verse, novels, criticism and educational works almost rivalled Lindsay's. He nicknamed Rickword "Lazy Old Bugger" (usually abbreviated to

LOB) which he applied to him in their correspondence, and Rickword took in good part. In 1960 he wrote:

> You are a Lazy Old Bugger not to have done a book of critical essays. What about it? Towards standards is o.p. So are Scrutinies. But there's some marvellous stuff buried in those. Include possibly some of your cousin's C.H. Rickword's pieces? And your preface to that book on Verlaine, something from your book on Rimbaud. Search through Left Review and Our Time for things which caught the old authority.

The pressure for republication of his critical writings was strengthened by a study of *The Calendar of Modern Letters* by Malcolm Bradbury in *The London Magazine* of October 1961, the opening shot in the campaign for recognition. Although his critical essays were not republished until 1974, he was spurred on to revise *Rimbaud: The Boy and the Poet* for a reprint published by Jack Lindsay in September 1963.

Holbrook meanwhile turned his attention to publicizing his poetry. He busied himself with selling copies of the 1947 *Collected Poems* in academic and literary circles, and reported to Rickword in 1961 that his customers included the poets A. Alvarez and Anthony Thwaite. His most valuable contribution, however, was "The Poetic Mind of Edgell Rickword", published in *Essays in Criticism* in July 1962. In this study he demonstrated the distinctive qualities of his verse – "a profound tragic sense...an awareness such as Donne's of man's predicament... authority, poise, a flavour of wisdom...a Horatian fullness of eroticism, acceptance and knowledge of sexual reality, which yet never loses its tenderness, nor its profound respect for the mysteries of love...deep urbane civilised feeling...great variety in texture and rhythm...acute wit...tough metaphorical, metaphysical combination of thought and feeling and tone, without hysteria, but nonetheless angry and penetrating ...a convincing compassionate sincerity" – through a detailed analysis of "To the Sun and Another Dancer", "The Soldier Addresses his Body", "Birthday Ruminations", "Assuagement", "Ode to a Train-de-Luxe", "The Encounter" and "To the Wife of a Non-Interventionist Statesman". The essay concluded with an affirmation of Rickword's continued relevance:

> If there is any literary life left in us, any possibility for a vital effective English language culture, then the work of this urbane civilised minor poet of our time must be dragged from its shadows, for our own benefit ...For our creative needs now he demonstrates acute metaphorical responsibility wedded to deep feeling and a profound metaphysical preoccupation – neglected by a world which needs these perhaps more than anything else.[16]

The letter in which Rickword thanked Holbrook for his "very subtle and perceptive exegesis" reveals the man, in its combination of modesty and poetic dedication, perhaps as fully as anything which he ever wrote:

> You have done LOB proud! I'm warmly moved by your understanding, and thankful for your sensitiveness to the poetic virtue in the words. I know they have, those you quoted, poetic virtue. I'm not vain about it, though I'm pleased to have been the medium through which it was done. If they haven't that, they are dust and ashes, and the writing about them is dustier dust and ashen ashes. In fact, it becomes "literature"...I stopped writing poetry because the words wouldn't come (or the emotions that would have caused the words to come) as what I would accept as poetic. The later work in couplets is much lower on the poetical level. So I stopped. If I can start again I shall. But "success" would have ruined me. That has never been more the case than now, when the microphones gape and all that. Dylan would have been better off as Clare was...I've been thoroughly egotistical, but what can you expect if you will give me such a shot in the arm? I'll write more soberly soon.

In response to a note at the end of Holbrook's essay, that copies of *Collected Poems* could be obtained from the author, Rickword received several orders, including one from Charles Tomlinson, who asked if he could have a signed copy, as he greatly admired his poetry and criticism, and another from his Oxford friend Vivian de Sola Pinto. Acknowledging the inscribed copy which Rickword sent him, Pinto wrote:

> I'm glad to renew my acquaintance with some of my old favourites like the splendid "Intimacy" and "Winter Warfare" and to discover such delights as "The Encounter" (which I think the Earl of Rochester would have enjoyed) and the magnificent address "To the Wife of a Non-Interventionist Statesman", the lovely "Cascade" and others. I am astonished at the way in which the critics seem to have ignored the book and I sincerely hope that Holbrook's article will do something towards remedying the neglect of some of the best verse of our time.

Soon after his essay was published, Holbrook was invited to submit a selection of his verse for inclusion in a series called Penguin Modern Poets, each volume of which contained poems by three living writers. He strongly recommended that Rickword should be included in the same volume, but his suggestion was rejected by the publishers. Rickword wrote: "I'm grateful for your attempt to get me in the Penguin Anthols. I don't want to start on about publishers, as I shall get worked up and it is a blissful sort of Indian Summer morning. Of course, they have to think about sales, but I think a judicious selection of my pieces has every chance of becoming 'popular'."

His pleasure in the growing appreciation of his work was overshadowed by his anxiety about Jonny, whose health deteriorated seriously from 1960 onwards. Long afflicted with asthma, to which her heavy smoking contributed, she underwent two major operations, and in 1963 broke her leg. Early in the new year she suffered a brain haemorrhage and was admitted to Black Notley Hospital, Braintree. On 6 February, as he sat by her bedside, she opened her eyes, looked at him, gave a sigh and died. She was 64.

Her death was not unexpected, but he was heartbroken. When he spoke of her to Jack Beeching in Charing Cross Road he wept openly. In a letter to David and Margot Holbrook thanking them for their message of sympathy he wrote:

For her sake I could not have wished the unequal struggle to be prolonged, and it is only in the minds of the few friends aware of her rare individuality that some measure of consolation can be found. The gods paid her out in triple measure for her intransigence – only Pan she revered, of whom she had a very old bronze mask to which she would sometimes pour libations of (Algerian) burgundy. But she seemed to have lost touch with him, latterly…I knew that she would not have wanted any dog-collars at the cremation, so asked Randall to read some pieces (which he did most sensitively)…The local took up a collection in her memory and instead of flowers sent it to the Blind Institution in which she was interested. But there we are, she would have been pleased with that, but cannot know it. We do not, fortunately, have to believe that *Les morts, les pauvres morts, ont de grandes douleurs*, though the yearning for survival will never be absolutely eradicated…

XVI. Recognition

RICKWORD tried to fill the gap Jonny left by work, and by seeking female companionship. He had picked up a report of an eighteenth-century trial which had dramatic possibilities and suggested to Swingler that they should together turn it into a radio play. The story is conveniently summarized on the title-page of the pamphlet:

> The Tryals of Haagen Swendsen, Sarah Baynton, John Hartwell and John Spurr. For Feloniously Stealing Mrs Pleasant Rawlins, A Virgin and Heiress of a Considerable Fortune: With An Intent to Cause and Procure the said *Pleasant Rawlins* against her Will, to Marry the said *Haagen Swendsen*. At the *Queens Bench Bar* at *Westminster*, Nov. 25. 1702. Before The Right Honourable the Lord Chief Justice *Holt*, and the rest of the Judges of the said Court, of which Fact the said *Haagen Swendsen* and *Sarah Baynton* were found Guilty, and the said *Swendsen* was executed for the same, Decemb. 9th following. The said *Baynton* being with Child was Reprieved after Sentence.

Rickword drew up a synopsis of his play, which he provisionally entitled *The Abused Heiress*, in April 1964 and worked on it with Swingler. By July they were in contact with a B.B.C. producer, but there is no evidence that the play was ever broadcast or even completed.

Rickword was still discussing with Holbrook the possibility of a collection of his critical essays. He wrote in June: "I would rather come out with a book of literary-political or politico-literary essays, rather than lit.-crit.", and suggested as possible items revised versions of his essays on Milton and First World War poetry, together with new ones on Auguste Barbier, Ebenezer Elliott and possibly Ernest Jones and John Clare. In notes for his essay on Barbier he remarked that he had taken no interest in him, even after acquiring a copy of his poems, until he discovered by chance that Baudelaire had described him as "grand poète". There was another reason for his interest in Barbier; the poems in his *Lazare* (1837), written after a visit to England, present a vivid and terrifying picture of the society produced by the Industrial Revolution from which Chartism emerged. "His verse is shrill with horror," Rickword had written in an essay on the Victorian novelists in 1962, "as he describes the unending vistas of petty dwellings and low workshops belching smoke, lit only by the glare of furnace flames. The Thames winds its oily sluggish way like some river in the Inferno."[1] Unfortunately his essay on Barbier remained unwritten, like those on Elliott, Jones and Clare.

There are indications that he was drinking more heavily than usual at this time. In a letter to Swingler he wrote in July: "Re Jordan, T. (deceased) 'Tis certain post mortem / Nulla voluptas.' Refute this, if possible, in the same number of words. Edgell (Blind drunk again). I was so tight I came back to Halstead just to prove to Peter I was not tight." That five months after Jonny's death his thoughts should turn to Thomas Jordan's great drinking song, with its warning that the most beautiful woman "will be damnable mouldy a hundred years hence", is not surprising in the author of "A Dead Mistress" and "Grave Joys". The obsession with death and corruption which haunted him ever since the trenches was still powerful.

He found some respite from that obsession in his relationship with Peter and Irene Chalk. Having lived with them for six years, he had become an integral part of the family, and when tensions developed between them his gentle tact smoothed over their differences. He regularly took their small son to school and allowed himself to be diverted into the sweet shop on the way. During the months after Jonny's death his affection for Irene Chalk became more intense. The daughter of an East End docker, she had won scholarships first to grammar school and then to Camberwell College of Art and was hoping to get a job as an art teacher. For this attractive and gifted woman, nearly forty years younger than himself, he cherished a feeling that was partly paternal, partly sexual and, as he knew, completely hopeless. He gave her a copy of Jean Cocteau's book on the making of the film *La belle et la bête*; he saw himself in the role of the beast in their relationship. She and her husband were aware of his feelings for her, but never referred to them. In conversation, she compared his passion to that of the troubadours for the mistresses whom they worshipped from afar, more appropriately than she realized, for in his letters to Swingler and Holbrook he always referred to her as "Laura", after Petrarch's idealized lady. Conscious of the dangers of his infatuation, he remarked in a letter to Holbrook that he kept in mind the "dreadful example" of Hazlitt's obsession with a woman much younger than himself, as chronicled in *Liber Amoris*.

From the emotional turmoil caused by his grief for Jonny and his passion for "Laura" emerged "The Age Gap", the first poem which he had written for over a year:

> What can her kindness and my love ever breed?
> Not monsters, maybe, but Petrarchan whimsies
> (Handling reactor-rods by remote control,
> that elseways sear the flesh and drive to frenzy).
>
> Dream-shackled addict, how could I breathe without
> the mescalin of her bright morning laugh,
> her lithe, brave battling with the household chores!
> Child of the bomb-raked street, blinded lamp-posts.

> Sit in the sun, old man, and mumble prayers
> (soon you will slobber and much worse besides);
> best sink into some Northampton of the mind
> and roam with Clare his sweetheart-haunted lanes.
> So you would spare her friendship's last ordeal,
> having no choice but pity or disgust.

He wrote the first two drafts of this poem at 6.30 and 7.30 on the morning of 23 April, and sent them to Holbrook on the same day, with a letter (dated "Bard's Day") in which he said: "Had a brief encounter with the Muse this morning. Inconclusive. We were both rather embarrassed after such a long absence... Not the Rickword timbre yet. Too much raw emotion in it. Must keep slogging." Holbrook replied enthusiastically: "Many thanks for your poignant poem – full of surprising *Invocations* strengths. You must suffer at 6.30 a.m. more frequently. Say no more – but if you write all your strict maps of inward agonies down there'll be a booklet in a couple of years. How marvellous that would be!" On 8 May Rickword wrote: "I haven't waked up early to attract the Muse. Capricious bitch. But Laura is being sweet and kind, so maybe she's jealous. N.B. I don't mean 'kind' in the technical amatory sense." Meanwhile he continued to work on "The Age Gap". In reply to some criticisms by Holbrook he wrote on 27 May: "I agree with most of your judgments on the latest draft of *Age-Gap*, but still not satisfied with much of it. Trouble is I have been writing from too high a level of consciousness, not tapping the archetypal images. I have in mind an essay on idealistic poetry called 'Petrarch didn't have to live in the Castle'." *

Into a quatrain which he wrote on 1 June he poured his feelings about his old love for Jonny and his new love for "Laura":

> In flighty youth we thought love no great matter,
> girls were as flowers to pluck, leaving no sting.
> No one believed love could be long, or bitter,
> an all-consuming, ineradicable thing.

On the following day, while returning to London from a weekend at Halstead, he wrote to Holbrook: "Did you know that Hobbes wrote a love poem at 95? It is better than my *Age Gap*, more mature. But then he had 30 years advantage of me. I've still time to catch up. It is printed by Aubrey in his *Brief Lives*. I've not seen it anywhere else. I am writing this in the train over a can of beer. Haven't seen Laura for 3 days. Purgatory." Another brief meditation on the nature of love, which he called "Presumption", was written on 7 June:

* The text of "The Age Gap" printed above is dated 24 May, and probably represents Rickword's final version.

Incalculable, ungovernable!
No man may rest at ease with love.
He thinks: "She is mine. Rich harvest our year's yield."
Before the thought's finished she is gone;
the green ears mashed to puddle. No harvest home!

He was again separated from "Laura" in August, when she took her
little boy to Jersey for a holiday. After receiving a post card from her
he wrote a poem which he called first "Holiday Season" and then "Isles
of Illusion":

Beyond desert life's favoured me –
a postcard, in her girlish hand,
with sage-green bays and violet sea,
and, for her laughing feet, gold sand.

Such heavens in a drop of ink!
Paradise from a printer's ramp!
Our mimic world's all false, I think,
except the tongue that licked this stamp.

On the first draft of this poem he noted: "23/8/64. 7.30-8.25 a.m.
Post-card received 7 p.m. yesterday. Sub-conscious at work all night.
By Betjeman out of Coventry Patmore."

Meanwhile events were conspiring to bring this episode to an end.
Among the letters of sympathy he received after Jonny's death was one
from Douglas Garman, who expressed regret at "how far apart we have
grown" and invited him to stay at his cottage in Dorset. He had resigned
his Communist Party job on the advice of his doctor, who told him that
he should move out of London, and since 1950 he and his wife Paddy had
lived near Wareham, where after spells of farming and clerical work he
was supporting himself by translating books from the French. He repeated
his invitation in April, suggesting that Rickword should come for a long
weekend at Whitsun. "A friend of Paddy's, a woman, would like to come
then and would be driving down if she did," he added. "If you'd like to
come with her, it could easily be arranged." In fact the visit took place
before Whitsun, on 2 May, and Rickword travelled to Wareham by train.
He and Paddy's friend Beatrix found they enjoyed each other's company,
and at the end of their visit she drove him back to London. After their
return he wrote to her inviting her out to a film, a meal or both with
him; as he had addressed the letter wrongly their first evening together
was delayed for a week, but after that they began going often to a
theatre or cinema together. He reduced his drinking.

Beatrix, an attractive widow some years younger than he, with two
sons, was the youngest daughter of a divided family. Her father, the
son of a butcher, was a Socialist in politics and later became a Communist;
her mother was middle-class, Conservative, Anglo-Catholic, with a

sense of social superiority to her husband. Six of their eight children accepted their mother's social, political and religious outlook; only Beatrix and one of her brothers took their father's side. The political views she inherited from him were similar to Rickword's and helped to bring them together. A journalist by profession, she had worked for *Picture Post* among other papers, and shared his tastes and interests. If her knowledge of literature was less than his, she had a deeper know-ledge of music, which she had taught as a young woman. She was strikingly different from her predecessors in his affections, Jonny, Nancy Cunard and Betty May, all forceful personalities in violent revolt against society. She was no more prepared than they to be a slave to convention, but she conducted her private rebellion against her mother's values with a quiet gentleness that belied the strength of her will-power. Why was she attracted to him? "He was so gentle and considerate." This says as much about her as about him, for she possessed the qualities she valued in him. After the exhilarating but strenuous years with Jonny he must have found her company restful; it is difficult to imagine her throwing plates at him, whatever the provocation.

As the weeks passed they saw more and more of each other. His poor sight prevented him from ever learning to drive a car; but she was a good driver and enjoyed driving. When they spent a weekend with the Garmans it was natural that they should travel down together. It was also natural that she should invite him to her house in Islington, after warning him that he might find it full of teenagers. With a show of nervousness he replied, "They don't actually attack one, do they?" Her sons at the time were passing through an awkward phase; one had just failed his examinations, although he was later to have a distin-guished academic record, and the other had incurred the attention of the police by his activities as a member of the Gnomes' Liberation Front, which specialized in releasing (or, as the police put it, stealing) gnomes from front gardens. Remembering his own exploits with Town and Brand, Rickword was prepared to take an indulgent view of such peccadillos and established excellent relations with both of them.

Then Beatrix spent a night or a weekend at Halstead. The first time this happened he came downstairs wearing a green silk dressing gown, a present from Jonny, and said apologetically "I feel like Noel Coward". One weekend in March 1965 they arrived to find the cottage full of butterflies, an incident which inspired the lovely poem, addressed to Beatrix, "Rhapsody on Red Admirals":

> Let your tawny images float in her deep eyes
> till we've forgotten autumnal storms must rage.
> Only each busy heart, tapping the breast,
> links us with time and travail, seasons, grief –
> when your shrivelled husks shall litter dusty sills.

That spring was the most poetically productive period for many years. In April he wrote "The Washerwoman of Eight Ash Green", his only poem mentioning Colchester, inspired by a visit there or by talking to Beatrix about his childhood. Two fragments date from this period, the exultant cry

> I have slept in all the beds in all the world
> And seen dawn from the beggar's gutter,

and the pensive

> Dearest, we cannot but bring our ghosts
> along with us, should we mix it.
> Not you, nor I, would have it otherwise;
> the present does not blaspheme the past,
> nor late joys invalidate the earlier.
> Could we but all foregather, at the end,
> in that Garden men thought of, and called Eden!

Here he is clearly seeking to reconcile their love with his continued fidelity to Jonny's memory, and hers to her husband's.*

Love and reviving poetic powers: a third cause for happiness was new proofs of public recognition. Thirteen years of Conservative rule had recently ended, and there was a new radicalism in the air. Many people looked back with a new interest to the 1930s, which by comparison with the affluent 1950s looked like a heroic age. *The Review* had devoted its July 1964 issue to the 1930s and published an interview with Rickword as a signficant figure of the decade – the first of several which were to appear in various journals. *Up the Line to Death: The War Poets 1914-1918*, an anthology published in the same month, reprinted "Winter Warfare" and contained a foreword by Blunden in which he spoke warmly of his old friend. Now, in the spring of 1965, the Arts Council was acquiring contemporary writers' manuscripts for national libraries, and at Holbrook's suggestion its assistant secretary, Eric Walter White, approached Rickword, who showed him a batch of manuscripts. Asked to name a price for them, he suggested £150. White felt this figure to be too modest, and he raised his price to £200. When White showed the manuscripts to the Arts Council's Poetry Committee they felt even this price to be too low, and offered Rickword £250. For this sum the British Library acquired manuscript or typed drafts of the poems included in *Invocations to Angels*; the printer's copy

---

* A manuscript of "Rhapsody for Red Admirals" has a note reading "2nd draft 06.30-05.88 31.3.65." The other poems can be dated by his habit of drafting poems on the back of envelopes. A draft of "The Washerwoman" is on an envelope postmarked 23 April 1965, and "I have slept…" on one postmarked 6 May 1965. "Dearest, we cannot…" is written on an envelope postmarked 1965; the rest of the date is illegible, but it is addressed to Collet's, where he ceased to work in May.

for *Twittingpan* and *Collected Poems*; drafts of many unpublished poems and fragments; a list of poems for a projected collection, probably drawn up in 1924; and the exercise book containing notes for *Rimbaud*, on the unused or half-used pages of which he had drafted the Faustus play.

He received White's letter informing him of the Arts Council's offer at the end of April or the beginning of May. That same weekend, a year after they had met, Beatrix agreed to live with him. On 3 May he wrote to Holbrook, whom he and Beatrix had visited a few weeks earlier:

> You will not be altogether surprised to hear that Beatrix and I have teamed up. It was on the brink when we came to see you. Petrarchan whimsies sunk without trace. She is really a most marvellous gift to the L.O.B. Why me? What have the gods got piling up? Won't they want to cut me down to size? You must compose a *Carmen nuptiale*...Last week I heard from Eric White that the Poetry Committee of the Arts Council had recommended that the B.L. buy my manuscripts for £250. Will it really happen, do you think? At any other time, this would have seemed tremendous, but after my first piece of news it sinks into relative insignificance. Life before literature!

That May was a time of upheaval for Rickword. He left Collet's, which had decided to close down its rare books department, with a small pension, and took a job for four days a week with a West End bookseller, as he explained to Holbrook, "to keep body and soul in liqueur – spiritual wine and juice of the grape". Shortly afterwards he moved out of the Chalks' flat and into Beatrix's house, which was to be his main home for the rest of his life, although every Friday, which Beatrix regarded as "the nicest day of the week", they drove down to Halstead for the weekend. In this atmosphere of domesticity he temporarily relaxed; he seems to have written nothing in the second half of 1965 except four lines which he jotted down on the back of an envelope postmarked 24 November:

> "I cannot come to terms with death," she said.
> "Nor I," I said. "Why raise the question now?
> It's been unanswered a long time," I said.
> "If it much worries us, we're better dead."

A few weeks before White had asked him to write one of his poems in a book which he kept for contributions by the poets among his friends, and in which Day Lewis, Spender, Lehmann, Roy Fuller, Plomer, Eliot, Auden, Robert Lowell and R.S. Thomas had already written. Rickword chose "Invocation to Angels". The next contributor was Blunden, who wrote a poem beginning:

How unangelic must a verse of mine
Follow the voice of Edgell my old friend.

Was Rickword's mind turned to verse again by chagrin at his failure
to provide a new poem for White's book?

In June 1966 the publishing house of Frank Cass & Co. brought out
a reprint of *The Calendar of Modern Letters*, with Malcolm Bradbury's
essay as a preface. The standard of its contents seems to have come as
something of a shock to the reviewers, who compared it favourably
with more recent literary journals. *The Times Literary Supplement*
decided that it had had "precisely the general qualities that one looks
for, unsuccessfully, in current publications"; Donald Davie observed
in the *Guardian* that "if Edgell Rickword in the 'Calendar' was indeed
a pioneer of our literary criticism, he was so by virtue of marking and
avoiding some pitfalls which his successors have fallen into"; and Frank
Kermode in the *New Statesman* came to the conclusion that *The Calendar*
had died because it was "rather too good for any possible audience".[2]

Another recognition came in November when the Literature Panel
of the Arts Council decided to award four prizes of £1,000 to a novelist,
a short story writer, a historian and a poet. The prize for the novel
went to Rayner Heppenstall, for the short story to James Stern, for
history to John Bowle and the prize for poetry, on the recommendation
of Cecil Day Lewis, chairman of the Literature Panel, to Rickword.
The awards were presented on 4 December by Jennie Lee, Minister for
the Arts, who emphasized in her speech that there had been no political
direction of any kind or any consideration of the recipients' circumstances, but that the prizes were intended as honours. In the same month
Rickword's poem to Jonny appeared under the title "On choosing a
Christmas card for a close friend" in *The Christmas Poetry Supplement
of the Poetry Book Society*, edited by Eric White. He repaid the compliment by sending White, his neighbour in Islington, a poem as a
Christmas card. Unfortunately this seems to have survived only in rough
draft, with many alterations and alternative readings:

> "An Islington" in Cowley's ode*
> stood for a rustic solitude
> with fruits and syllabubs for food.
>
> Somewhere round here a battered plaque
> on Lamb's old dwelling sets its mark
> whose Wednesdays were quite a lark.
>
> We rehabilitate our squares
> and wits and eggheads cram the stairs
> but something's missing that was theirs

* Refers to the phrase "a village less than Islington" in the poem at the end of Abraham
Cowley's essay "Of Solitude".

> when sloppy hooves on cobbles rung
> a friendly tune and whiffs of dung
> from heaps of rubbish pell-mell flung...
>
> A park, a pub, a dancing floor,
> a prison with an open door
> and euthanasia for the poor.
>
> These rhymes came just a shade too late
> to fit the Christmas schedule date
> so please accept, though incomplete.

For the greater part of the year he had been working, in collaboration with Swingler, on a play about the Irish patriot Theobald Wolfe Tone, a theme uniting his longstanding interest in Irish republicanism and the British Jacobins. In his notes for the play, provisionally called *How they brought the Good News*, he wrote: "The development will be musical, not epical. There will be three movements, two themes. Spiral not linear. Two themes (1) Tone and his comrades. (2) British repression." He found Tone's personality and politics attractive; he emphasized that Tone's aim was an independent Ireland with "no king, no aristocracy, no established religion", and summed up his character: "A man of the Enlightenment. Attitude to aristocracy, religion. Romantic but sophisticated. Humour. Wide reading. Exuberant." Against Tone and the United Irishmen, who represented the positive values of the Enlightenment, he set the barbarities of British repression in Ireland, the floggings, pitch-cappings and hangings. This antithesis corresponded to something fundamental in his political outlook. Before the Great War, when he was just beginning to regard himself as a Socialist, the Irish question was at the heart of British politics. His first political poem had protested against the shooting of the Easter Week martyrs. Ireland was associated in his mind with his love for Peggy and Jonny, the atrocities of the Black and Tans and Swift's championing of Irish liberties. His feelings were deepened by his research for the play, which uncovered the tortures inflicted on the Irish in 1798 that afterwards gave him recurrent nightmares. Long after he put his play aside Ireland remained a symbol for the oppressed everywhere; in 1972 he cut out and kept press reports of the shooting of thirteen people by the British Army in Derry on Bloody Sunday.

His earliest surviving reference to the play is in a letter to Holbrook of March 1966 in which he mentioned that he was giving up his job at the bookseller's and added: "Time is getting short. I want to do a play about the '98 in Ireland." Swingler was later drawn into the project, but Rickword made himself responsible for the preliminary work; with his pensions to live on he could afford the time for research, while Swingler was dependent on lecturing and reviewing for his livelihood.

He read everything he could find on the events of 1798, and in his search for materials corresponded with Irish booksellers about early literature on the subject. In the summer he toured Ireland with Beatrix, in order to study the sites associated with Tone and the United Irishmen; after a short stay in Dublin they drove up the west coast from Galway to Donegal, and made a special visit to Killala Bay, where General Humbert's troops had landed. By the following summer he had completed his research and drafted a synopsis of the play. The first "movement" or act, set mainly in France, was to deal with Tone's interviews with Hoche and Carnot and his embarkation with the French expedition to Ireland, and to conclude ominously with a "march past of a British column with portable gallows and pitch caps". The second act portrayed the landing of the French, their early successes and the proclamation of a Provisional Government, and ended with patriotic songs. In the third act the French were routed, and Tone, captured and condemned to death, committed suicide in his cell, defiant to the last. The final scene was to show a dinner party of the Anglo-Irish establishment under a portrait of George III, at which "the guests act and sit like dummies".

On 19 June 1967, when everything was ready for the actual writing of the play, Swingler dropped dead in the street. His death was a blow to Rickword. They had been close friends ever since *Left Review* days; their war experiences, their collaboration on *Our Time*, their common disillusionment with the Communist Party and their continued adherence to libertarian Marxist principles had drawn them even closer together. For a few weeks Rickword attempted to continue work on *How they brought the Good News* (Garman wrote on 1 August: "It's good to hear the Irish play is proceeding"), but in the end he confessed to Beatrix: "I can't write dialogue without Randall". Another item joined the growing pile of abandoned projects.

Swingler's death reminded him of his advancing age. Of his other colleagues on *Left Review*, Tom Wintringham had died in 1949, Montagu Slater in 1956. On the other side of the political fence, his former friends Roy Campbell and Wyndham Lewis had both been dead since 1957. Apart from Swingler's, the death that moved him most deeply was Nancy Cunard's in a Paris hospital on 16 March 1965, working, she told the nurses on her deathbed, on a long poem against all wars. Nearly ten years later, in 1974, he wrote in a volume of her poems which he gave to Holbrook as a Christmas present:

"In Memoriam N.C.

A fiery Soule, that working out its Waye,
Fretted the Pigmie Bodie to Decaye.

Christmas. Human Rights Year."

In August 1967 he and Beatrix visited East Germany at the invitation of one of her friends living near Berlin with her Austrian husband. The long letter to Jane in which he described his first visit to a Communist country is detached in tone, noting the positive features of life there but displaying no great enthusiasm.

> Everything for ordinary living is readily obtainable, and necessities are cheaper than with us, but of course choice is rather limited at present. Priorities are on housing and necessities, cars ranking as luxuries so far. Berlin is still war-stricken and a lot of the new building is rather garish, and amenities like cafés and cinemas are scarce. Unfortunately the theatres were closed as usual in August, as that is one of their best achievements. The original university quarter, XVIIIth century, has been well restored and is spacious and elegant, and the rebuilt R.C. Cathedral is very striking and yet restrained. Some awful imperial-baroque monstrosities are being pulled down, and these are pointed out to bus loads of western visitors as instances of religious persecution. We came back by a more southerly route which passed through some delightful country (our in-route was rather flat and monotonous). We looked round Leipzig, on which they are concentrating a lot of their efforts as it is a city where international exhibitions are held. The new opera is a fine building and fits in with the 18th cent. university buildings near it. J.S. Bach's church is in unspoilt condition and v. austere. We had a rush round Weimar, which is still quite redolent of Goethe's time, and we would have liked to stay there, but had to move on...

Although the plan for a play had failed, in 1967 Rickword's poems found a wider audience. Early in the year he got to know the booksellers Eric and Joan Stevens, who agreed to reissue his *Collected Poems* at 18s., and fifty signed copies with the author's manuscript revisions at 63s. Always a perfectionist, he had been revising the text of his poems for years. In 1966, for example, he had asked Holbrook to substitute "a huckster by his empty cart" for "a kike conversing with a tart" in the last stanza of "Race Day", one of the poems excluded from *Collected Poems*. "This gets rid of the anti-semitic suggestion (which some maniacs might even read into the title)," he explained, "and integrates with the ambient atmosphere of debasement, i.e. he has sold all his trashy stuff, choc-bars and kitty kats and kupies, and the wrappings have been flung down among the rest of the litter."

The book received an enthusiastic review from *The Times Literary Supplement*, which recalled its history and added:

> Who knows, if the public do not respond this time, the poems may go into hiding again. This sibylline state of affairs should not be allowed to continue: Mr Rickword should be read. Now... The volume deploys an urgent and humane wit of which literary histories are already bemoaning the absence in the period (1918 to 1930) in which all but one

of these poems were written. Mr Rickword shares some of the erotic, ornate and rhetorical delicacy of the 1920s; there are even suggestions of undigested "Prufrock" or Sitwellian Queen Anne: but this goes for nothing. Mr Rickword is superbly intelligent and musical, and echoes bow before him, not accuse. His masters are the Jacobeans, his subject modern life and love. The poised beauty of his lines gives great sadness to the wryness which organizes his arguments. Anyone trying to think of the best English poet between Eliot and Empson need look no farther.[3]

Three weeks after the publication of this review the Stevens were able to report to Rickword's daughter Jane that "sales are going extremely well".

1967 was also the year in which the anthologists discovered Rickword. *Poetry of the 1920s*, edited by Sydney Bolt, represented him by three poems from *Behind the Eyes* (the two "Regrets" and "Complaint after Psychoanalysis"), four from *Invocations to Angels* ("Terminology", "Annihilation", "Farewell to Fancy" and "Assuagement") and four from *Twittingpan* ("The Encounter", "Hints for Making a Gentleman", "A Glimpse into the Great Beyond" and "Provincial Nightpiece"), a representative selection. *Poetry of the First World War*, edited by Maurice Hussey and published in the same year, included "The Soldier Addresses his Body", "Trench Poets", "War and Peace" and "Winter Warfare" – four of Rickword's six war poems. From this time on his poems appeared more frequently in anthologies, but editors rarely showed originality in their selections. No anthology of World War I poetry was complete without "Winter Warfare", for which he developed a strong dislike. Anthologists also proved fond of the later satirical poems, while ignoring his best work, the lyrics in *Invocations to Angels*.

He rebelled in 1971 when Philip Larkin proposed to represent him in *The Oxford Book of Twentieth Century Verse* by "Winter Warfare" and "The Encounter". "Your selection of 'Twittingpan, or The Encounter'," he wrote,

> is only balanced, or rather is not balanced, by the juvenile trifle "Winter Warfare", and so gives a misleading impression of my social attitude and of my verse generally. Had it been any other anthology I would probably have made no objection, indeed it has appeared in one or two with my consent, but the *Oxford Books of...* have a special authority and will be read by countless people who will perhaps be ignorant of everything else the poet has written. In these circumstances, a little harmless fun at the expense of a type of intellectual poseur will no doubt be learnedly annotated as an expression of anti-homosexual prejudice in Georgian English circles.

In his reply Larkin explained that if "The Encounter" was omitted it would not be possible to replace it by another poem of Rickword's, and continued:

> If I may soften this somewhat bleak presentation of alternatives, how-
> ever, I do welcome an opportunity to say how much I like both the
> poems by you which I have chosen, and have indeed liked them since
> my schooldays (I remember reading "Twittingpan" in that delightful
> anthology *Whips and Scorpions*). If "Winter Warfare" is a trifle, then
> your trifles are more substantial than many people's epics; and I must
> say I hadn't really thought of "Twittingpan" simply as a satire on
> homosexuality – I see it as much as a piece of literary history, and very
> evocative of the period of which it treats.

Rickword allowed the two poems to be printed, but he later confided
his private opinion of the anthology to a piece of paper on which he
wrote: "Larkin's *Oxford Book* shows that Eliot's influence has hardly
scratched the surface".

One anthology caused him some amusement. This was *Moderni
Anglicka Poezie*, a collection of Polish translations of twentieth-century
English poems, including "To the Wife of a Non-Interventionist Statesman", published in 1964. The names of women poets were given a
Polish feminine form (e.g. Edith Sitwellova, Elizabeth Jenningsova),
and Rickword's name appeared as "Edgell Rickwordova", possibly
because the translator or editor had confused the names Edgell and
Ethel. Rickword signed his copy, which he gave to Holbrook, "David
from Edgellova", and wrote underneath: "What fantastic exercise of
unreason led them to feminise my name?"

Early in 1968 Cass & Co. followed up the reprint of the *Calendar*
by republishing *Left Review* in eight handsome volumes. The revival
of the fiery poems, stories and essays of thirty years earlier must have
been embarrassing for some of the contributors, especially Cecil Day
Lewis, who had just been appointed Poet Laureate. "The wildest rebel
of the thirties has allowed himself to be lassoed with a cord that may
be silken, but which I really wouldn't have thought was all that strong,"
Garman commented in a letter to Rickword. *Left Review* reappeared
at an opportune time, for 1968 was a year of revolt – the year of the
"Prague Spring", the French general strike, student demonstrations
from Poland to California, black riots in the United States, worldwide
demonstrations against the American actions in Vietnam, the Civil
Rights Movement in Northern Ireland, the Pakistani revolt against
military dictatorship. Even the British Communist Party, taking an
increasingly independent attitude, protested when the Soviet Army
invaded Czechoslovakia. In another letter Garman remarked in September on the new situation which made *Left Review* relevant again:

> There is, I think a good deal of hopeful significance in the changed
> assessment of the 'thirties that is taking place – such a relief from the

mixture of knowing despondency and brittle condescension of the
affluent society generation. It ties up with the very impressive and
courageous, resurgence among the students and youth in general, which
seems to me the most hopeful and encouraging phenomenon in a general
situation that provides all too many grounds for disillusionment and
withdrawal.

The most perceptive tribute to *Left Review*'s achievement came from
Raymond Williams. "It began in 1934," he wrote,

> with the formation in Britain of a section of the Writers' International
> to oppose fascism, imperialism and war. For nearly four years, through
> an intensifying crisis, it worked with extraordinary energy to make lit-
> erature effective in that kind of struggle; to publish new Socialist and
> popular writing from many countries; to define, in a Marxist tradition,
> humane and literary values; to build, by discussion and organisation, a
> democratic culture...It is a necessary landmark of a brave, urgent, and
> humane struggle...and at the same time of a substantial confusion and
> failure...In the retrospective complacency of the late forties and fifties
> the struggle itself was made to seem absurd or malign. In the sixties,
> faced by a comparable crisis, that safe, self-regarding dismissal is not
> seriously available. To fail to respond, with that urgency, seems now
> the absurd and malign act.[4]

In March 1968 a short article by Rickword, "Public Poetry and Social
Advance", appeared in *Labour Monthly*, which for nearly fifty years
had been under R. Palme Dutt's editorship, the jealous guardian of
Marxist orthodoxy. It was appropriate that it appeared when it did,
for it took up themes with which *Left Review* often dealt: the importance of spoken verse and the public role of the poet as a spokesman
for his fellows. Rickword contrasted the poor performance of the British
and American poets at the International Poetry Festival held in London
in the previous summer with that of "those poets whose cultures had
roots in civilisations on the shores of the Mediterranean", Pablo Neruda
for example, who had "the confident stance and delivery of men accus-
tomed to exhort and argue face to face with their fellow-citizens, in
sun-drenched public places". "To Neruda," he continued, "as to all
contemporary poets of his stature, I would say, there can be no intelligent differentiation between political themes and others. All experience
is political and all reflection involves a philosophy of history. It is the
treatment that differs, where the emphasis falls."[5] And he went on to
illustrate his point from the work of poets from three continents –
Nazim Hikmet the Turk, Menelaos Londemis the Greek and Amado
Hernandez the Filipino.

The trouble Rickword took with this essay, dealing as it did with themes
dear to him, is clear from the notes among his papers, which include three
draft openings quite different from the final printed version. One begins:

In periods of crisis poetry comes into its own. The trivialities of television and the press become unbearable. It is discovered to be a necessity. And since the social condition is the focus of awareness, themes of public concern are looked to. For many of my generation, this was brought home to us in the violent years leading to the Second World War, but in this country the tradition of spoken verse had slipped so far as to be virtually irrecoverable. It was not so in pre-industrial communities, as there was a tremendous production of topical poems brought forth by the War of Intervention; nor in Turkey, though we did not know it then, nor in Martinique, where Aimé Césaire was composing his volcanic (a blank in the manuscript) of the pain and re-birth of the Negro consciousness. And in Greece without any pause – But invidious to particularise. Oppression does not naturally, automatically, stimulate the lyric impulse. Grunts and groans and belches may be extorted by unbearable pressures, and final imbecility. Only the intelligence bred in struggle can give form to the emotion. Of all public themes resistance and commemoration have the widest resonance; the latter requires a mood or breathing space of tranquillity. In our community to be serious or dignified was to invite contempt. So Edward Thomas, transcribing one of his poems in a letter to a friend, felt compelled to disguise the fact that he was writing verse by running on the lines like prose. The music-hall song, the half-mocking ballad, a satirical marching song, were all that could be tolerated by stomachs debauched by cheap print. To face up to the crisis, we require an emotional organiser, something richer, that touches the exhortations of statesmen.

These disjointed jottings are clearly the product of a mind so overflowing with ideas on the subject that Rickword found it necessary to write them down immediately.

When he wrote this essay he was no less an internationalist than when he edited *Left Review*. The reference to Césaire and the "re-birth of the Negro consciousness" is particularly significant. Ever since he worked on *Negro* he had been interested in black writing in the British and French colonies in Africa, the West Indies and the United States, although it was not until the 1960s that the subject became of major importance to him. In 1967 he remarked in a letter that David Jones's poems "and the Africans are the extent of my reading now". For years he worked on an essay variously entitled "Black Breakthrough. A New Dimension in World Literature" and "The Black Breakthrough in Creative Writing", until the failure of his eyesight finally compelled him to abandon the idea.

Just before Christmas he received a letter from Norman Hidden, chairman of the Poetry Society, who had been asked to submit the names of poets who might be considered for the award of a Civil List pension, asking whether he wished his name to be put forward. After some hesitation he filled in the questionnaire on the last day of 1968, giving details of his income and state of health ("Not robust – rheumatic heart, arthritis. Bad sight of remaining eye makes getting about alone difficult, especially at night"), and naming Holbrook, Fuller and Rattenbury as referees. In a letter to Holbrook he was apologetic about his application. "The attempt to extort charity from the Civil List was not on my own initiative," he explained. "I had never conceived any success possible in such an enterprise. But although I have about three times as much as a normal O.A.P., thinking of possible dilapidations and becoming a burden all round, a few extra pounds might do something to alleviate the indignities consequent, so I consented to Norman Hidden's suggestion." In March 1969 he learned that the application had been successful and he was granted a small pension. The subsequent arrival of a monthly letter from Downing Street impressed the postman.

In 1967 he took up Holbrook's idea of collecting his critical writings for publication, and began searching through the files of *The Times Literary Supplement* and *New Statesman* for reviews and articles. "If you thought it a publishing proposition to select enough for a 30/- volume," he wrote to Holbrook, "nothing would give me greater pleasure than for the selection to be yours. But not if it would hold up any creative work of yours and only on condition that we would *halve* the receipts, jointly making the agreement." Holbrook welcomed the idea, and repeated his earlier suggestion that some of Cecil Rickword's critical writings should be included, but was later forced to withdraw from the project by the pressure of his other activities. Meanwhile Rickword and Rattenbury, who had lost touch for some years, resumed friendly relations. Rattenbury was hoping to publish a collection of his poems, and after he had shown them to Rickword, who was enthusiastic, turned to Roy Fuller for a second opinion. As he explained, "Edgell is probably just too damn nice to be nasty. (He calls me Dear Boy. He calls you Young Fuller, come to that.)" Fuller's opinion, though more critical, was also favourable, and in 1968 the poems were accepted by Chatto and Windus. In his letter of congratulation Rickword mentioned that "I've begun to dig out some of my old literary articles which carefully pruned might make a volume", and over the months following Rattenbury and Fuller were drawn into the project. Chatto and Windus were approached without success. The project hung fire for a year or so.

While collecting his critical writings and studying black literature, Rickword found time for work on the radical tradition. In March 1968 he mentioned in a letter to Holbrook that he had persuaded Cass & Co. to reprint Cobbett's *Twopenny Trash* ("magnificent stuff"), with a preface by himself. Unfortunately the publishers later reversed their decision, and his preface was not printed until 1978. A letter from Garman to Rickword, also written in March 1968, shows that he was trying to find a publisher for a reprint of Hone's satirical pamphlets, with Cruikshank's illustrations, in which he had been interested since his essay on Hone appeared in *Our Time* in 1944. In April 1969 he reported to Holbrook that a friend, Tony Adams, had agreed to publish the pamphlets, and described the editorial work involved as "a not too intellectually strenuous assignment and great fun". The book, with a long biographical essay on Hone, was published in 1971 under the title *Radical Squibs and Loyal Ripostes: Satirical Pamphlets of the Regency Period, 1819-1821.* Although *The Times Literary Supplement* praised it as "valuable" and commended the "useful and enthusiastic" introduction,[6] it did not sell well, and was later remaindered.

1969 was for Rickword a year of endings and beginnings. In January he sat beside the bed where his brother Gerald lay dying, holding his hand. Gerald had retained his active interest in local history to the last; his particular enthusiasm had been military history, but his unpublished biography of another Essex man, Dick Turpin, probably appealed more to Rickword, who presented it to the County Record Office. In June he had a holiday in Italy with Beatrix, staying at Torbole, on Lake Garda. A poet's first visit to Italy is normally a major event, but the only evidence that this was so in his case is a sentence in a letter to Rattenbury: "I was ravished by Italy". In December came the news of the death of Douglas Garman, his friend for 48 years, collaborator on the *Calendar* and *Left Review*, and companion on the road to Communism. If they had drifted apart, Garman's responsibility for his introduction to Beatrix had forged a new bond between them, and for the past five years they had remained in close contact, personally or by letter. Not long afterwards he had news of his other collaborator on the *Calendar*, Bertram Higgins, whom Holbrook met on a visit to Australia, and who expressed the hope in a letter to Holbrook that Rickword's Indian summer would be "devoted to a reflorescence of poems rather than a thesis-like book".

Joan Stevens, who with her husband had reissued the *Collected Poems*, pressed Rickword in the early months of 1969 to publish a selection from his poems in a limited edition. After some hesitation he agreed. The poems, which they picked in consultation with Fuller and Holbrook, make a curious list. To the ten poems from *Behind the Eyes* which had already appeared in *Collected Poems* were added "The Tired Lover", "Blindness", "Complaint of a Tadpole", "Winter Prophecies" and "Meditation on Beds". Rickword was doubtful about a number of other poems; he included "Dead of Night" on Holbrook's recommendation and "Lovers" despite his objections, but dropped "A Child" after Fuller had queried it. The poems from *Invocations to Angels* were less generously represented than in the previous selection; "Dream and Poetry", "Sir Oran Haut-ton at Vespers", "Absences", "Memory", "Circus", "The Deluge", "Theme for *The Pseudo-Faustus*" and "The

Happy New Year" were all dropped, although "Earth and Age", "Race Day", "Necropolis", "Beyond Good and Evil" and "Regrets for Certain Blind Alleys" were reinstated. The only major disagreement over the selection arose when Holbrook wished to include "The Encounter", "The Handmaid of Religion" and "Hints for Making a Gentleman", to which Rickword objected "because we may not have many pages, and they have circulated quite widely – in Penguin's *Comic and Curious Verse* and the recent *Satirical Verse* etc.* And truly I'm a bit bored with them. But a couple, perhaps." "Hints for Making a Gentleman" was accordingly omitted and the other two included. Of the other *Twittingpan* poems, "Martyrs: Modern Style", "A Glimpse into the Great Beyond", "An Old Rhyme Re-rhymed", "Provincial Night-piece", "Strange Party" and "The Lousy Astrologer" went out, and "The Contemporary Muse", "Answer to an Invitation to Love" and "Advice to a Girl from the War and Later", omitted in 1947, came back. "To the Wife of a Non-Intervention Statesman" was left out, but "Incompatible Worlds" (much revised) and "Instead of a Christmas Card" appeared in book form for the first time.

Rickword considered putting in his 1940 poem "Then and Now"; in reply to Holbrook's objections he wrote: "Remembering the occasion I think it had a point and I have improved a couple of lines – but it doesn't have to go in". He does not seem to have considered including the "Laura" poems, "Rhapsody on Red Admirals", "The Washerwoman of Eight Ash Green" or his Christmas poem for Eric White. Although he may have omitted "The Age Gap" and "Isles of Illusion" as too personal, there was no objection to the others, and it is possible that, encouraged by having written seven poems in 1964-66, he hoped that they would form the nucleus of a new collection. If so, he was disappointed. Two lines –

> Whose high romance and tragic woes
> Haunt a suburban universe –

written on the back of a letter dated 13 May 1969, seem to be the only scrap of verse among his papers which can certainly be attributed to the late 1960s.

Fifty Poems was published by the Enitharmon Press in September 1970, in a signed edition of 362 copies, at what was then the high price of three guineas. It was a handsome volume, in striking contrast to *Collected Poems*, beautifully printed on good paper, with a pencil portrait by Nina Hamnett as its frontispiece. Roy Fuller contributed the introduction: he described Rickword's poetic career as "Rimbaudian" and compared it with Hart Crane's. In some jottings on an envelope

---

* Rickword was in fact represented in *The Penguin Book of Satirical Verse* (1967) by "To the Wife of a Non-Interventionist Statesman".

Rickword commented: "I think the epithet Rimbaudian not quite plausible, and besides too exalted. The parallelism with Hart Crane is much
more fitting, though in me the self-destructive instinct could be curbed
– by timidity perhaps". He sent a copy of the book to Blunden, who
was recovering from a serious illness. In a letter of thanks Blunden's
wife, Claire, wrote: "Ever since I first knew him he has spoken with
special regard of your work, and this volume has been one of the few
things to reach through to him for a long time". Another copy he sent
to Betjeman, who called the poems "rich and varied beyond words".*

The book provoked little comment, with the exception of an enthusiastic review in *Adam* by Hugo Manning, who suggested that "it is time
for some justice to be done, not necessarily for Rickword's sake alone
but mainly to ensure that people who would find him more worthwhile
than some over-estimated contemporary poets are not deprived of an
acquaintance with his work because of the barrier of neglect".[7] That
barrier was not easy to break down. *The New Cambridge Bibliography
of English Literature, 1900-1950,* published in 1972, contained no
entry for Rickword, presumably because the editor considered him a
less important poet than Harold Acton, Frank Kendon, E.V. Knox,
Margot Ruddock or Sheila Claude Wingfield, each of whom was given
a full bibliography. He received more generous treatment from the
reference book *Contemporary Poets of the English Language,* first published in 1970, which contained a discerning appreciation of his work
by Bernard Bergonzi. In his reply to the questionnaire sent to him by
the publishers, with his usual taciturn modesty, he answered "No" to
the two questions "Do you consider yourself primarily a poet?" and
"Do you recognize yourself as belonging to a particular 'school' of
poetry?", and when asked to give a critical analysis of his verse summed
it up in the two words "traditional idiosyncratic".

The first important critical account of his verse after Holbrook's
essay appeared in 1971, in C.H. Sisson's *English Poetry 1900-1950,* a
contribution to literary history as eccentric as Herbert Palmer's. Sisson
considered only 35 poets, and not all commanded his approval; Dylan
Thomas got in because of his bad influence on the poetry of the 1940s.
Famous names – most of the Georgians, the Sitwells, Edwin Muir,
MacNeice – were ignored. Rickword was allotted four whole pages,
emphasizing the anti-humanist element in his writing of the 1920s –
the influence of Wyndham Lewis and de Sade, the contempt for "the
loutish mass" – which he later repudiated. But Holbrook's and Sisson's
were the only critical studies of his poetry that he thought worth mentioning in his entry in later editions of *Contemporary Poets*: he

* The Enitharmon Press published in 1974 Rickword's translations of two prose poems
by Ronald Firbank, *La Princesse aux Soleils* and *Harmonie,* in a limited edition of two
hundred copies.

appreciated the validity of Sisson's comments.

Just before *Fifty Poems* was published he received an offer from Michael Katanka, a bookseller who wished to develop a publishing side to his business, to bring out a book of his literary essays, which, he thought, "would go well in these days of neo-Rickwordian revival". Rickword still harboured doubts about the wisdom of publishing his "bits and pieces" and suggested in a letter to Roy Fuller that "their reception would be greatly facilitated if a preliminary essay were to put them in perspective, in the transition from the aftermath of Victorianism to the birth of the nuclear epoch". He therefore proposed to Fuller's son John, himself a poet and critic, that he should contribute an introduction to the collection. In a courteous reply John Fuller said:

> I had doubts: mainly of my ability to write such an introduction, and secondly (not insignificantly) of the propriety of Fuller *fils* joining Fuller *père* as a parasite upon the works of Rickword – it might look like a family business, or, from your point of view, a rather limited range of critical commendation. However, the chief objection seemed to me that you need no such introduction, that your position is well known.

The project made no further progress at this time.

In the summer of 1971 Rickword and Rattenbury planned a new bi-monthly literary journal for which Rattenbury drew up several sets of detailed proposals. It was to hark back "beyond the popularizations of *Our Time* to the rather tougher intellectual standards of Edgell's *Calendar of Modern Letters* in the twenties", and to "provide a tough, serious, progressive but not over-solemn journal, attached to no clique, dealing with contemporary and historical literature in the broadest sense, under the direction of a small Board of eminent but not stuffy academics and literary persons working through an editor". Each issue was to contain seven or eight articles of two to six thousand words, plus two or three major reviews, and there might be "some deliberate revaluations of fake literary reputations" similar to the "Scrutinies" in the *Calendar*. The journal was not to be political "except in the sense that its critical values, as happened with the original *Calendar*, begin to project their own politics", or, as Rickword put it in a letter to Tom McGrath, "not politically political in the parliamentary sense, but certainly involved in the contemporary struggle". His own list of principles for the conduct of the journal was short and pithy: "No jargon. Keep it short. Hate hate." Roy Fuller and William Empson agreed to serve on the editorial board, and lists of possible contributors were drawn up, including both Marxists and sometime-Marxists (Edward Thompson, Christopher Hill, Sylvia Townsend Warner, Geoffrey Matthews, Mulk Raj Anand, Hugh Sykes Davies and Paul Foot), and others thought likely to be sympathetic (John Arden, Edward Bond, Geoffrey

Grigson, John Lucas, David Caute, John Prebble, John Fuller, Seamus
Heaney, John Berger and Julian Symons). The name of the journal was
much debated, but after Rickword had suggested *Doxy* ("my orthodoxy is your heterodoxy"), *Axis* or *Motives* and Rattenbury *Magazine,
Compass, Wheels, Parameters* or *Touchpapers*, it was finally agreed
that it should be *The New Calendar*.

Originally the launch was planned for spring 1972, but progress was
delayed by failure to find a financial backer. In the summer came the
news that the Arts Council was planning to subsidize a new monthly
literary journal for three years. The plan was discussed at a dinner
party given by Eric White, to which he invited Rickword, Frank Kermode, the former editor of *Encounter*, Ian Hamilton, editor of *The
Review*, and a young man named Michael Schmidt who was starting
his own literary magazine. Empson and Fuller favoured co-operating
with the new journal, on the ground that two magazines of similar
character might damage each other; Rickword was inclined to agree
with them, but Rattenbury strongly advocated going ahead with *The
New Calendar*. There were long delays before the Arts Council finally
decided to subsidize Hamilton's *New Review*, and meanwhile the fate
of *The New Calendar* hung in the balance. As late as February 1974
Rickword optimistically suggested to Rattenbury that it might be possible to launch it in a year or two, but the inflation of the 1970s at last
killed the idea.

Rickword's only important piece of writing while this project was
under discussion was an essay on George Cruikshank, published in July
1973 in the same volume as an essay on James Gillray by Katanka as one
of a series of popular illustrated biographies. This was his only study
of an artist, though he had a lifelong interest in art. He had visited a
Turner exhibition with Rattenbury, inspiring a poem,[8] and at a Van Gogh
exhibition he told Holbrook he found "great joy in many of the pieces
wrung out of his torment. Not even the most often reproduced seemed
hackneyed." The English caricaturists and engravers of the eighteenth
and early nineteenth centuries gave him particular pleasure; he refers
to Bewick's "exquisitely truthful wood-engravings", "the lyrical grace
which refines Rowlandson's robust humour" and "the care-free insolence
of Gillray's immense grotesqueness" as aspects of Romanticism, and
compares Rowlandson and Gillray to Cobbett. He had been familiar
with Cruikshank's work since childhood, when he pored over the illustrations to Grimm's fairy tales or his father's copy of *Oliver Twist*, and
his interest was rekindled by the reprint of Hone's pamphlets. Cruikshank's right to appear in his gallery of radicals is debatable. As a young
man he drew political cartoons for whoever paid him, Radical or Tory;
his illustrations to W.H. Maxwell's *History of the Irish Rebellion of
1798* depict the Irish as subhuman savages; and his last etching was

an attack on the Paris Commune. None of these facts, of which Rickword was aware, detract from his achievement as a scourge of social evils and a chronicler of London life who "stayed always, like Steinlen and Phil May, with the multitude".[9] Rickword clearly had a fellow-feeling for Cruikshank (who went through a period of neglect and straitened circumstances, and was given a Civil List pension when over seventy) which made him ready to forgive much.

We catch a glimpse of how Rickword struck a contemporary at this time in an article which appeared in the local Halstead paper. In it he appears as "this genial gentleman enjoying a quiet drink with his wife, Beatrix…in the Napier Arms in Halstead. Or the Cock at Maplestead. Or the Three Pigeons at Mount Hill, Halstead…Quiet. Unassuming. Fitting into the Colne Valley like the river itself."[10] Sending a copy of the article to Jane, he remarked: "As you can see, our pub movements are well observed!"

XVII. The Last Years

IN an April 1973 letter to Jack Beeching Rickword wrote: "I have been corresponding with a man called Michael Schmidt who is behind a new firm called The Carcanet Press, and is planning a journal called *Poetry Nation*. I don't like the name." When Rickword and Schmidt met at Eric White's neither had made much impression on the other; Schmidt had had "only the vaguest notion who this quiet and humorous man was",[1] and Rickword had not mentioned him when writing to Beeching about the dinner party. Among Schmidt's friends in Manchester, where he was a special lecturer at the university, however, was Alan Young, head of the English faculty at the Didsbury College of Further Education, who in the course of research into the literary journals of the inter-war years had come across poems, stories and critical essays signed Edgell Rickword which had impressed him. While discussing the contents of the first issue of *Poetry Nation* he suggested that it should include an interview with Rickword, and Schmidt, who by this time had read *Fifty Poems*, agreed.

One snowy day in the early summer of 1973 Schmidt and Young drove from Manchester to Rickword's home in Islington, where Beatrix welcomed them. The interview covered a wide range of subjects, including his war poems and other early verse; his reading of English and French poetry; his reactions to the other war poets, the Georgians ("I very soon lost interest in them"), the Imagists ("they didn't really amount to much"); post-war Oxford; his youthful political opinions; the Oxford bus strike; the *Calendar*; Eliot's *Criterion* ("a bit of a rag-bag"); the élitism of Eliot and Wyndham Lewis ("believing themselves cut off from common humanity"); "negative emotions" in poetry; "Scrutinies"; Barrie ("People actually wept. Ghastly!"); de Sade ("He was really very dreadful"); political verse ("you can't really write with conviction unless you believe that it will have some effect"); Auden's statement that his poems had not saved a single Jew from the gas-chambers ("how can he tell, anyway?"); his abandonment of poetry ("It was dissatisfaction, I imagine, at myself"); the possibility of a genuinely popular literature; the relevance of the literature of the past ("If you don't enjoy reading the past, the past is dead")... "The interview was all we could have wished," Young remembered. "His quiet voice was sometimes inaudible on our portable tape-recorder, and his gentle diffidence made him think long and hard before answering some of our questions and points. But the mind was wonderfully alert and balanced." The interview as printed in *Poetry Nation* I, which covered

seventeen pages, was considerably cut; only two sentences refer to African literature, for example, although Young recalled that he "showed
great interest in the concept of 'negritude' and obviously had read all
the recent literature on the subject".[2] One discovery which the inter-
viewers made was that a large body of critical essays and reviews by
Rickword existed which had never been reprinted, and on their return
to Manchester Schmidt agreed to Young's suggestion that Carcanet
should publish a volume of his criticism, as well as a new collected
edition of the poems.

That summer Rickword and Beatrix took a holiday in the Lake District, making Keswick their base. "We paid homage to Wordsworth in
Grasmere churchyard (Grasmere was like a Bank Holiday) and on the
outside of Dove Cottage," he wrote to Jane. "I was disappointed not
to be able to get into the Museum, but there had been a power-failure,
and the elaborate security precautions around the exhibits were not
working. No one has yet thought of having loud-speakers in the trees
to relay the poems. In fact, there was nowhere any visible indication
that he had written poetry." Another literary shrine which they visited
was Beatrix Potter's house ("charming, but a bit over-devout"), where
the lady custodian was almost overcome at hearing that Beatrix was
Beatrix Potter's god-daughter. They broke their return journey in Manchester, where they visited Schmidt ("he has promised to bring out
some criticism of mine next year") and spent the night at Young's house.

They were to see a great deal more of Young during the coming
months, as he and Rickword got down to collecting the critical essays.
"We had a hilarious time at the Colindale Newspaper Library," Young
has written, "largely because Edgell kept finding a superb review by,
say, Richard Aldington, or I would come across an early reference to
Surrealism, and we forgot completely that Michael Schmidt was biting
his nails in his Manchester office."[3] Although Rickword's contributions
to the *Calendar* were easily accessible since its republication, and he
had collected most of his reviews from *The Times Literary Supplement*
and the *New Statesman* several years before at Holbrook's insistence,
there was still material to be hunted down, such as his reviews for the
Sunday Referee. Understandably, he found it impossible to remember
everything which he had written half a century earlier; he remembered
his contributions to the *Daily Herald* only after the book had reached
the page-proof stage, and as the best of them were too good to be
omitted a small selection had to be added as an appendix. His contributions to the *Spectator* seem to have slipped his memory entirely. Always
a perfectionist, he insisted on making minor stylistic improvements to
the essays as originally published and correcting errors of fact. While
they were engaged on this work, the friendship between Rickword and
Young developed rapidly. They shared common interests in art and

especially music as well as literature, and they visited exhibitions, attended concerts and listened to records together. Young spent several weekends at Halstead, and on these occasions Beatrix would bring a carrier-bag of records from Islington and take back others from the Halstead collection when they returned to London.

Rickword, who had at first been slightly suspicious of the group around the Carcanet Press, became increasingly fond of them as he got to know them. After years of disappointment and neglect, it was gratifying to meet people who not only admired his work but were eager to publish it; moreover, the orientation of *Poetry Nation* at that time was, in Schmidt's words, "Marxising if not Marxist". Of Schmidt himself Rickword wrote to Holbrook: "He is both intelligent and humorous, an ideal combination, and works like a nuclear reaction". His letters to Beeching were equally enthusiastic. "Carcanet are or is a very nice crowd...These boys really care about poetry." "They are good lads, but only mildly pro-Marxist at present...But they will develop well, there is reason to hope, when they have shaken themselves clear of the academics who were useful as preliminary supporters." "I think Carcanet must be supported. It would be fine to have a cultural revival based on Manchester instead of Oxbridge. But, my god, the city is a ghastly dump."

Essays and Opinions, a selection of the criticism which Rickword had published between 1920, when he began writing for the *Daily Herald*, and 1931, when he edited *Scrutinies II*, including substantial extracts from *Rimbaud*, appeared in November 1974. In it he discharged two debts of gratitude; he included Cecil Rickword's "A Note on Fiction", which had appeared in the *Calendar* nearly fifty years earlier, and he dedicated the book "To David Holbrook, Friend of Many Seasons", who had first pressed him to publish his criticism. The reviewers' first reaction to the book was surprise – the first word of Gabriel Pearson's review in the *Guardian* was "astonishingly". Rickword, he pointed out, "displays the methods and attitudes of what we now think of as modern criticism, already formulated, grasped and consistently and flexibly applied". Clive James in the *New Statesman* admitted that "there are issues Rickword raised fifty years ago that we have not yet dealt with". Bernard Bergonzi in the *Observer* praised his "keen, iconoclastic intelligence and independence of judgment", and compared his achievement with Edmund Wilson's. In the *Listener* Elaine Feinstein wrote: "Edgell Rickword's great strength was to assist that fruitful fertilisation from other cultures – Russian and American as well as French – from which English culture has always gained... He always wrote as if he cared, passionately, that what he said should be true." It was unfortunate, however, that the book stopped at 1931 without making clear that a second volume was in preparation, for it gave critics an opportunity to sneer at Rickword's later Marxism. "His kind of secular integrity, inquisitive, principled and omnivorous, seems to have been a casualty of the crisis politics of the thirties." "The terminal date of 1931 might seem arbitrary. The odds are that just as Rickword more or less stopped writing poetry at about that time, he ceased to be an interesting critic then too." "It has long been known that Edgell Rickword's conversion to Marxism in the Thirties was a form of intellectual suicide. *Essays and Opinions*...intensifies one's regret by making apparent the height from which he jumped."[4]

Three months before the book was published Rickword and Beatrix had toured the Soviet Union as the guests of the Novosti news agency, for which Beatrix had worked, visiting Moscow, Leningrad and Yalta. His reactions were very different from what they would have been thirty or forty years earlier. In his letters to Holbrook and Beeching he said very little about the politics and economics, apart from a comment on Leningrad: "Fascinating to walk among the crowds down the Nevsky Prospekt thinking of *The Overcoat* and *The Nose*. Nothing there has really changed very much, only Gogol would have had to be published underground." On the other hand, he praised the generous hospitality which they had received and the "very lovable" people whom they had met, especially the "marvellous" girls – "my poor old heart was wrenched this way and that". The men by comparison had seemed "a bit cloddish", although the husband of their "lovely and lively" guide from the Novosti staff had been an exception. When he summed up the holiday as "a very worth-while experience" he was thinking of individuals, not of a political system which he no longer supported.

A typed fragment among his papers, which may date from this period, tells us something of his attitude towards the Soviet Union:

> Karl and Rosa
>   dans le noir canal
>   and sealed Lenin's fate
>   whether or not he finally succumbed to
> one of Joe's peppery prescriptions.

The murder of Karl Liebknecht and Rosa Luxemburg and the defeat of the German Spartacists, he suggests, doomed the Russian revolution to failure. His respect for Stalin belonged to the distant past; the last two lines accept as a possibility that he poisoned Lenin, and in a letter of March 1974 to Beeching he accepted that he was responsible for the assassination of Kirov, which provided the pretext for the purges.

His relations with the British Communist Party were not unfriendly, especially after it condemned the imprisonment of dissident Soviet writers and the Soviet invasion of Czechoslovakia. In 1978 he sent £10 to the *Morning Star*'s fighting fund. His occasional contributions to the party press were mostly popular essays on aspects of literary history, similar to those which he had written for the *Daily Worker* in the 1930s, or reviews of books by his friends; he reviewed Alick West's *The Mountain in the Sunlight* for the *Daily Worker* in 1958, *One Man in his Time* for *Labour Monthly* in 1971, and A.L. Morton's *Collected Poems* for *Red Letters* in 1977. For the French Communist Party, which was less independent than the British, he had little respect. "The spectacle of the E.C. of the French C.P. proclaiming themselves democrats makes me give a hollow laugh," he wrote to Beeching in 1972. In the absence of anything better to vote for he continued to vote Labour, as he had always done, but with little enthusiasm. "The prospect of a Labour Government headed by Wilson brings joy to none," he wrote in 1972. On the question of Britain's entry into the Common Market he remained sceptical. In reply to Beeching's arguments in favour of entry he commented: "I know that just coyly standing aside won't do any good, but with social-demo influence preponderant will it not be the same old story of essentially co-operation with big capital still?" He remained, after shedding his illusions about the Soviet Union, the libertarian Marxist he had been since the 1930s.

In the 1970s, especially after the publication of *Essays and Opinions*, Rickword found himself in demand as an authority on the literature of World War I, the 1920s and the 1930s. He was approached or interviewed by writers on all three subjects, and by biographers of his old friends and enemies – Nancy Cunard, Roy Campbell, Wyndham Lewis, Philip Heseltine and Hugh MacDiarmid. He took part in symposiums on the 1930s with William Empson, Stephen Spender and Cyril Connolly at the University of Sussex in 1972, and with Empson, Spender and David Gascoyne at Norwich University in 1976. When a radio programme on his verse, written and presented by Alan Young, was broadcast in 1977 the producer, Fraser Steel, was struck by his modesty, which he defined as "gentle scepticism towards any pretentious claims made on his behalf", and afterwards commented: "I suspect that the only talent in which (he) has been conspicuously surpassed by many of his contemporaries is the talent for advertisement".[5]

John Lucas, who interviewed him for *Renaissance and Modern Studies* in 1975, has given us a Rembrandtesque portrait of his later years.

> The walls of the downstairs room where we talked were lined with books, piles of books and records spilled across the floor, were heaped on chairs, on and under tables. A coal fire poured out heat, pushing back the cold of a December afternoon. Rickword's thick mass of grey-white hair is combed back from a high forehead, and he moves slowly, perhaps because of physical frailty – he is, after all, in his late seventies –

or more probably because he is very nearly blind. When he spoke his voice fluttered, died, sprang to sudden life, and it was some time before I could be sure I was understanding him aright. But of two things I was in no doubt. One, that for all the apparent guardedness of his speech he was full of mischievous wit. Two, the energy of his commitment to the cause of letters as well as the cause of Marxism in the thirties and beyond, and the fact that such commitment followed in a clear line from the days when he had edited the *Calendar of Modern Letters*.[6]

As soon as *Essays and Opinions* had gone to press, Schmidt turned his attention to the collected edition of Rickword's poems. In July 1974 Rickword wrote to Holbrook:

> My publisher is bubbling over with energy, is whipping me on to prepare a "complete" poems, is insisting on seeing every fragment, willing to argue, but not to accept my single judgment. On hearing that you had some unpublished ramblings he became frantically insistent that I should ask you to send them all to him. Like Donne exhorting his lady, he insists on utter nakedness, though I emphasise the sores and ulcers such frankness must disclose. So, if you can without a large waste of time, put your hands on the bits and pieces I sent you in the 60's please do so.

Holbrook complied with this request, and in August Rickword wrote to him: "Thanks so much for digging out those pieces. They need a lot of work on them."

Behind the Eyes: Selected Poems and Translations, as the collection was rather confusingly called,* was published in August 1976. It contained 78 poems, in addition to the translations from Rimbaud. 24 of the 36 poems in the 1921 *Behind the Eyes* were included – all the 17 reprinted in *Fifty Poems* except "Regret for the Depopulation of Rural Districts", plus "Reverie" (renamed "Sea Sash"), "Desire", "Keepsake", "Dalliance", "A Child", "Yegor", "Outline of History" and "Grave Joys", none of which had been reprinted since 1921. All the poems in *Invocations to Angels* except "Moonrise over Battlefield" and "Memory", and all the *Twittingpan* poems and three later poems ("To the Wife of a Non-Intervention Statesman", "Incompatible Worlds" and "Instead of a Christmas Card") were included, together with most of the translations from *Rimbaud*. Finally, six poems were published for the first time: "How Nikolai Gogol Failed to Save His Soul", "Human Rights Year 1974", "Ancestor Worship", "The Washerwoman of Eight Ash Green", "Memo to Lord Snow C.B.E." and "Rhapsody on Red Admirals". The book thus offered a much wider selection from Rickword's verse than either of the previous collections, but there were still regrettable omissions. "Moonrise over Battlefield" was left out by mistake, to Rickword's annoyance, but it is difficult to explain why "Regret for the Depopulation of Rural Districts", which

---

* The dust-jacket has "collected" for "selected".

had appeared in both the previous collections, was dropped. Although the inclusion of eight more poems from the 1921 volume was to be welcomed, they do not seem to have been selected on any particular principle; why, for example, were the comparatively feeble "A Child" and "Yegor" given preference over "The Gift"?

"Human Rights Year 1974", the most important of the previously unpublished poems, demonstrated that when he was in his mid-seventies his poetic powers, though less often exercised, were as vigorous as ever. His use of an alliterative metre, with which he had previously experimented in the second section of "Prelude, Dream and Divagation", was no doubt suggested by his conception of Langland as the poet of human fellowship, which he had expounded in his *Daily Worker* article on *Piers Plowman*. In this poem he appears for the last time in the triple role of libertarian, satirist and metrical technician. "Rhapsody on Red Admirals" and "The Washerwoman" we know to have been written in 1965, but the other three poems cannot be dated even approximately, apart from the fact that "Gogol" was written after the publication of David Magarshak's biography in 1957 and the trivial "Memo to Lord Snow", which was hardly worth printing, after the publication of Snow's *The Two Cultures* in 1959. "The Age Gap", a much better poem than either, was presumably omitted as too personal. The book contained a charming dedication, referring to "Rhapsody for Red Admirals": "The butterflies are for Beatrix".

The only verse of Rickword's which can certainly be dated between 1969 and 1974 is two lines written in the margin of a letter dated 30 October 1972:

> The douche-bag shadow bobbing through the glass
> And swish of water is the last of love,

but Schmidt's proposal to collect his poems seems to have stimulated his poetic plans. In his contribution to *World Authors 1950-1970* he said: "I still look forward to writing something more comprehensive than I've done so far, a philosophical jest-book or an heroic farce, perhaps. I cannot imagine there would be anything more to live for after completing a *Samson Agonistes* or *Rape of the Lock*."[7] It is a remarkable statement for a man of 75, and hard to reconcile with the theory that he wrote little verse after 1930 because "he knew when had nothing more to say in verse".[8] These two seemingly casual sentences suggest intriguing possibilities; when he speaks of "an heroic farce", for instance, he seems to be taking up an idea at which he had hinted fifty years earlier in his essay "The Returning Hero". None of these plans was achieved, though two entries in a notebook apparently dating from this period may be intended for a "philosophical jest-book" or *dictionnaire philosophique*:

Academe
A port-soaked don unutterably bored.

Armistice
A mounted policeman by the cenotaph.

Two more items seem to be meant for a verse self-portrait:

A clean old chap, polite to callers, even
Reasonably grateful for a pint of bitter.

But the rest, apart from the poems in the 1976 collection, is silence.

The reviews of *Behind the Eyes* were generally enthusiastic. Julian
Symons in the *Sunday Times* called it "a selection from one of the
wittiest, most stylish, and least-appreciated poets of the Twenties", and
Robert Nye in *The Times* found it "an impressive reminder of a neglected talent", praising alike the "war poems quite unlike anyone
else's", the "notable erotic lyrics" and "To the Wife of a Non-Interventionist Statesman" ("one of the very few good twentieth-century poems
to have been written out of a political passion"). Desmond Graham in
Stand saw in the poems "energy, wit, and sinewed intelligence...robust,
masculine sexuality, caustic disposal of cant, uncluttered compassion
and political commitment of great force". Holbrook, reviewing *Essays
and Opinions* and *Behind the Eyes* together in *New Universities Quarterly*, combined a sensitive appreciation of the poems with an attack
on Rickword's Marxism, and made the surprising assertion that "there
was no ambition in Rickword, as in Sartre, to humanize communism".
Eric Homberger, who also reviewed the two books together, gave a
more sympathetic survey of his whole career in *The Times Literary
Supplement*, stressing the continuity between the *Calendar* and his later
writings, which sprang from "his aspiration for a more completely
realized and fulfilled life".[9]

The best reply to those who sneered at his adherence to his principles
was provided by Alan Young's collection of his prose writings since
1932, *Literature in Society*, which appeared in November 1978. Three
items from the early 1930s – "Verlaine in England", the *Scrutiny* review
of Eliot's criticism and his contribution to *Negro* – were followed by
a selection from his writings in his early days in the Communist Party.
There were some omissions (understandably, "Stalin on the National
Question" was not reprinted), but no attempt to hush up his political
activities of this period as if he were ashamed of them. This section
ended with the essay on Malraux and the introduction to *A Handbook
of Freedom*. After the study of the poets of 1914-18, enlarged by the
insertion of a tribute to Isaac Rosenberg, came the essays on Milton,
Wordsworth, Hazlitt, Hone and Cruikshank, together with "The Social
Setting, 1780-1830". The preface to *Twopenny Trash* appeared here

for the first time, together with an essay on Thelwall enlarged from the article on his letters in *The Times Literary Supplement*. The book ended with a selection from Rickword's reviews for *Life and Letters To-day* and *Our Time*, and a review of a life of Keith Douglas which appeared in *Stand* in 1975. This sympathetic tribute from one soldier-poet to another, which commended his resolution to write "true things" rather than "musical or sonorous" verse, formed a fitting conclusion. In gratitude for the many services his editor had done him, Rickword dedicated the book to Alan Young and his wife Irene, "whose friendship opened new paths".

The book answered his critics. Eric Homberger described him in *The Times Literary Supplement* as "the most attractive and most intelligent Marxist critic of the interwar years", Robert Giddings in *Tribune* as "one of the few really outstanding critical intelligences of the far Left"; Arnold Kettle in *New Universities Quarterly* remarked "how little his judgments and procedures were adversely affected by the cruder kinds of dogmatism which, we are always being told, were the main characteristics of the Left of the period". The reviewers also paid tribute to his contribution to that rediscovery of the English radical tradition which, Homberger pointed out, "was a distinctive part of Popular Front culture in the late 1930s". Derek Mahon's review in the *New Statesman* was so patronizing as to provoke an angry protest from Schmidt, yet even he was forced to end with a high tribute: "He does not by any means reject the English literary and artistic traditions. Like Blake (and it would be interesting to read him on Blake) he seeks to modify and expand them in accordance with his vision of what England should be. This is in itself a long and honourable English tradition, and one to which Rickword's contribution may in time appear rather more considerable than it does at present."[10]

In his last years Rickword was not without honour in his own country. The conferment of an honorary doctorate on him by the University of Essex on 20 July 1978 gave him great pleasure. It was the only academic honour which he had ever received, and the other person honoured on this occasion was the journalist James Cameron, a libertarian radical of his own type and a former colleague of Beatrix on *Picture Post*. He was also pleased with Dr Simon Collier's oration when presenting him to the Chancellor of the University, Lord Butler. Recalling that he was born in Colchester, the seat of the university, Dr Collier commented: "In science, and in music, we can point to some very eminent Colcestrians in times gone by, but Edgell Rickword has no rivals among the town's gifts to English literature". He described his war poems as "poetry with a sharper cutting edge, a more savage bite, perhaps, than was common even among the poets of *that* terrible time", and after recalling *The Times Literary Supplement*'s suggestion that he was the most important English poet in the period between Eliot and Empson he continued: "That such a judgment can be proposed at all is an eloquent tribute to any man, and although *The Times Literary Supplement* is not quite infallible (except to those who write for it) there seems no good reason to take exception to this considered opinion. Edgell Rickword's finest poems... are very definitely part of the literary cargo we would like to send into the future from our century. And I feel certain that they will get there." For his achievement as a critic he claimed: "Without Edgell Rickword, without the *Calendar of Modern Letters*, there might well have been no *Scrutiny*, no significant and (one hopes) permanent elevation of critical awareness in this country. All modern critics, whether they know it or not, whether they like it or not, are in some measure indebted to Edgell Rickword...The hateful tides of fashion," the oration concluded, "often seem to condemn writers to strange, unpredictable cycles of esteem and relative neglect, but true value invariably reasserts itself...A younger generation of readers is discovering, once again, the sensitive (if sometimes barbed) poetry, the marvellous Rimbaud translations, the percipient essays and reviews – in short, the notable integrity of a very distinctive voice, a very English voice, which deserves to be heard not once but again and again."[11]

Some of his friends had reached the age at which a writer becomes a public institution. In 1979 he contributed his essay on Cobbett's *Twopenny Trash*, in a slightly revised version, to *Rebels and their Causes*, a collection of essays issued in honour of A.L. Morton's 75th birthday, to which Eric Hobsbawm, Christopher Hill, Margot Heinemann, John Saville, Victor Kiernan, Jack Lindsay and Arnold Kettle also contributed. In 1980 it was Lindsay's turn to receive homage on his eightieth birthday, in a booklet called *A Garland for Jack Lindsay*, which provided the occasion for a last parade of the Marxist old guard of the *Our Time* period – Rickword, represented by his last published work, a whimsical reminiscence of his early friendship with Lindsay, Holbrook, Rattenbury, McGrath, Beeching and Manifold. Among the other contributors were Doris Lessing, Naomi Mitchison, Alan Sillitoe and Roy Fuller.

Rickword himself had already had his *festschrift*, in the form of a supplement to the March 1979 issue of *PN Review* (the successor to *Poetry Nation*) edited by Alan Munton. This began with an abridged version of Dr Collier's oration, followed by a selection of Rickword's writings: eight of the poems ("Birthday Ruminations", "War and Peace", "Farewell to Fancy", "Absences", "Rimbaud in Africa", "Luxury", "Don Juan Queasy" and "Theme for *The Pseudo-Faustus*"), the short story "The Cow", the reviews of Hugh l'Anson Fausset's life of Donne and *The Waste Land*, and the essay "The Re-creation of Poetry". It was a reasonably representative selection, apart from the fact that nothing later than 1927 was included. Then came tributes by twenty friends, colleagues and acquaintances from most stages of his career – Lindsay, Morton and Empson from the 1920s, Hill from the 1930s, Julian Symons, Beeching, Rattenbury, Holbrook, Thompson and Fuller from the *Our Time* period, Boris Ford and Betjeman from the 1950s, Eric White from the 1960s, David Gascoyne, Alan Young and Michael Schmidt from the 1970s. Such a symposium enabled his achievement to be appreciated from different and sometimes opposing viewpoints; Symons's condescending suggestion, for example, that by joining the Communist Party Rickword

> born for the universe, narrowed his mind
> And to party gave up what was meant for mankind

was devastatingly answered in John Coombes's study of his criticism in *Left Review* and Thompson's tribute to him as one of the sources of the post-Stalinist regeneration of Marxism. There was some penetrating criticism, as in Empson's contribution and Gabriel Pearson's analysis of "The Happy New Year", and Hill and Thompson gave an unexpected view by emphasizing the value of his essay on Milton and *A Handbook of Freedom* to them as practising historians. Although some errors of fact had to be corrected before publication, such as Beeching's assumption that he was still a Communist Party member, and one or two of the contributions irritated him, as a whole the symposium gave him pleasure.

So did two other tributes which he received in 1979. To celebrate the publication of Jon Silkin's *Penguin Book of First World War Poetry*, in which "The Soldier Addresses his Body" and the inevitable "Winter Warfare" were included, a reading was held at the Poetry Society on 25 July at which, as the only person present who was represented in the anthology, he was the guest of honour. Among the other trench poets Robert Nichols had died in 1944, W.J. Turner in 1946, Richard Aldington in 1962, Siegfried Sassoon in 1967, Herbert Read in 1968, Osbert Sitwell in 1969, and Edmund Blunden and David Jones in 1974; the only survivors were Robert Graves, who was living in Majorca, and Rickword, the youngest of them. In September a student working for a degree in performing arts asked his permission to put on a private production of "The Happy New Year", using dancers and musicians. In his reply he said: "In the more than fifty years since it was printed I have had hardly any comments one way or the other on its appreciation or otherwise. I welcome this unexpected opportunity to procure a wider interest in it." The epigraph from Seneca, he added, "does indicate the main theme of the work, which is dominated by the parallel slaughter of the Western Front in which I participated to a small extent."

The years of neglect over, he was enjoying

> that which should accompany old age,
> As honour, love, obedience, troops of friends.

But old age as a rule is also accompanied by bodily infirmities. Ever since he lost one eye he had been haunted by that fear of blindness which finds expression in one of his earliest and most poignant poems. In later years he suffered from glaucoma, and although he was given drops with which to bathe his eye he did not remember to apply them as often as he should. In August 1975 he wrote to John Saville, who had invited him to contribute an essay on *Left Review* to a symposium: "The recent deterioration of my sight...makes reading and writing virtually impracticable for long spells. I'm hoping to get round this by dictation, but have so far not got on good terms with it."[12] By 1976 he was completely blind. As soon as he was formally registered as a blind person Islington's social services sprang into action; he was measured for his white stick, and a young woman came to the house to teach him touch-typing. He declined an offer to teach him braille, saying sadly, "I'm too old to learn a new language".

In 1979 he and Beatrix reluctantly decided to give up their house at Halstead. Before it was sold they had to sort out their furniture, books and other belongings for which there was no room in the Islington house. Among the books with which he parted were many of Hone's works, his edition of Southey's *Wat Tyler* with Hazlitt's preface, collections of poems by Ebenezer Elliott, Samuel Bamford, Thomas Cooper, Ernest Jones and Ebenezer Jones, and prose works by William Godwin, Mary Wollstonecraft, Thomas Holcroft, Jeremy Bentham, Hazlitt, Leigh Hunt, Richard Carlile and Jacob Holyoake. That he let them go was an admission that the book on the English Jacobins, Radicals and Chartists which he had had in mind for nearly thirty years would never be written. To show his gratitude to the University of Essex for the honour which it had conferred on him, he donated 34 books and 13 pamphlets, most of them by or relating to Hone, to its library.

Despite his blindness, he still hoped to continue writing. He worked on his essay on black writers, some drafts of which are touch-typed, but his only sustained literary effort was the writing of his memoirs. He had this idea in mind at least since 1973, when he asked Holbrook to look out some material for him; but it was not until 1979 that, encouraged by Schmidt's enthusiasm for the project, he seriously got down to work. His blindness made it impossible for him to consult written sources, however, even with Beatrix's help, and his memory proved fallible. His record of his service on the Western Front is particularly disappointing, for he set down incidents as he remembered them without attempting to relate them to the course of the war. The weeks of fighting after he returned to the front in September 1918 are dismissed in three short sentences, and the episode in which he won his M.C. is not even mentioned. His mastery of touch-typing was less complete than he imagined, and many passages were almost incomprehensible. As an alternative method of composition Beatrix bought him a tape-recorder which he used to dictate passages, but as he sometimes pressed the wrong knob some tapes which he believed to contain a record of his dictation were blank. Beatrix undertook the task of translating his touch-typing into English, transcribing his tape-recordings and fitting the fragments together into a continuous narrative. The resulting narrative, which covers his life up to his retirement from Collet's, contains vivid passages and flashes of wit and insight, and forms the essential foundation for any biography. But it is the work of an old man. When after his death Schmidt read it he had to admit that it was unpublishable.

Despite his blindness, his last years were not unhappy. In the words of *The Times*, "the devotion of his family and his many friends, and, not least, his own general tolerance and good humour, helped keep alive to the end his modest yet enquiring spirit".[13] He may have recalled the lines written in his blindness by his beloved Milton:

> What supports me, dost thou ask?
> The conscience, friend, to have lost them overplied
> In Liberty's defence, my noble task.

And he had other consolations. If he could not read, he had the radio and a large library of records. He maintained a lively interest in the literary and political worlds. Above all, he had Beatrix, always ready to read to him, to play records, to converse, and do what was possible to make his life enjoyable.

From 1980 his health declined rapidly. He was taken to the Whittington Hospital, Highgate, suffering from a heart complaint from which he nearly died, and was fitted with a pacemaker. Early in March 1982 he complained of internal pains. His doctor diagnosed cancer of the liver which, he said, was inoperable. He was taken back to the Whittington Hospital to die. Holbrook visited him there, and pressed his hand as a farewell gesture. "It was like Pip saying goodbye to Magwitch," he later wrote, "a gentle pressure on my hand the only indication that he understood what I was saying. It was like talking to someone at the bottom of a well, but Edgell Rickword surfaced enough, once or twice, to murmur a response to family news."[14] Rattenbury came to stay in the Islington house, keeping Beatrix company. On 15 March the telephone rang, and as she was upstairs at the time he answered it. When she came down he put his arms round her and said "He's gone".

At the funeral a week later Jane spoke of her memories of her father, and Holbrook read some of his poems: "Birthday Ruminations" and "In Sight of Chaos", meditations on the power of time and death, and "Rhapsody on Red Admirals", in which love triumphs over both. He also read the lines from Wordsworth which Rickword had printed at the beginning of *A Handbook of Freedom*:

> Not in Utopia, subterranean fields,
> Or in some secret island, Heaven knows where!
> But in the very world, which is the world
> Of all of us, the place where in the end
> We find our happiness or not at all!

There were some generous tributes in the press. *The Times* commented that under his editorship *Our Time* had "argued, by example, for a popular culture which insisted upon the highest standards of discrimination and intellectual honesty", and that he "represented a humane and intelligently progressive brand of Marxism, one which rejected formulae, dogmas and closed perspectives". Schmidt described him in the *Guardian* as "one of those unobtrusive men of letters who help set the tone of their age". Another friend, Laurence Coupe, writing in the *Morning Star*, saw him as "trying to move toward a new meaning, a new order, a new humanity", and declared: "We cannot fault him either for the strength of his imagination or the sincerity of his struggle for change". Holbrook in *The Cambridge Review* called his criticism "intransigent, independent, confident, heart-felt and witty", and praised above all his "essential honesty".[15] But perhaps the most satisfying account of his achievement had already been given in the *PN Review* Supplement by Arnold Rattenbury, his former assistant editor and friend for many years, who summarized what he had learned from him:

> For all there are no quick and easy answers to anything, society is constantly intolerable, revolt against it the only possible dignity, change essential. Communism cannot be bigotry except it dishonour itself. Forms in verse and prose are things that men and women have haggled, manhandled into being to express not actually dissimilar thoughts, and need the utmost respect therefore. Formlessness will always tend to thoughtlessness. Poetry is passionate intellectual communication, not emotional morass. Traditions matter. Every kind of information, however seemingly arcane, matters – for how else understand Tradition? Art is a sort of revolution conducted in the soul of whoever receives it. Neither can Art be bigotry. Society and poetry will change, doubtless by violence, doubtless by innovation, but only stepping from past to future, only knowing how they got where they are.
>
> I doubt if Edgell would recognize himself as the teacher of all this. But there it is in the poems, the journals, the *Essays and Opinions*, the

friendship, fitting snugly beside the elderly gentleman who sits and chuckles now at his growing recognition, or spits with practised venom at some atrocious news of inhumanity that comes his way, or some (and he finds it often) plain intellectual deceit...Such an account as this – indeed all accounts of himself – I see him regarding, hand round another pint I think, with another considerate, drift-laden silence alert for change.[16]

Sources and Bibliography

MY primary sources have been Edgell Rickword's unpublished memoirs and the collected editions of his writings: *Behind the Eyes: Selected Poems and Translations* (1976), *Essays and Opinions 1921-1931* (1974) and *Literature in Society. Essays and Opinions (II) 1931-1978* (1978), the last two of which were edited by Alan Young. The entry on Rickword in *World Authors 1950-1970*, edited by John Wakeman (New York 1975), which is largely in his own words, gives a useful summary of his career. Interviews with him containing much auto-biographical information were published in *The Review* 11-13 (July 1964), *Poetry Nation* I (1973), *Renaissance and Modern Studies* XX (1976) and *Artery* 18 (1980); of these the second and third are particularly valuable. A slightly revised text of the *Renaissance and Modern Studies* interview appears in *The 1930s: A Challenge to Orthodoxy*, edited by John Lucas (1978). A unique source of information on all stages of Rickword's career since the 1920s is "Edgell Rickword. A Celebration", edited by Alan Munton and published as a supplement to *PN Review* 6.1 (March 1979), which contains contributions by twenty-two of his friends and acquaintances. The bibliography of his writings in *Seven Writers of the English Left. A Bibliography of Literature and Politics, 1916-1980* (1981), compiled by Alan Munton and Alan Young has proved invaluable.

My information on the Rickword family is derived from George Rickword's unpublished *Annals of a Family of No Importance: Materials for a History of the Rickword Family and its Connections*. The description of Colchester is mainly derived from *The Victoria History of Essex*, Volume II (1907) and the files of the *Colchester Gazette*. For Rickword's education, in addition to his memoirs, I have used the files of *The Colcestrian*, the Colchester Royal Grammar School magazine. Letters from several of his boyhood friends are among his private papers.

Details of Rickword's military service have been supplied by the Army Records Centre. The War Diary of the 5th Battalion, Royal Berkshire Regiment, is in the Public Record Office at Kew (P.R.O. – W.O. 95 – 1850, 1856). Published sources include *The Regimental Roll of Honour and War Record of the Artists' Rifles* (1922); F. Loraine Petre, *The Royal Berkshire Regiment* (Reading 1925), in which Chapter XXXI deals withthe 5th Battalion; Major-General Sir Arthur B. Scott, *History of the 12th (Eastern) Division in the Great War, 1914-1918* (1923); *Official History of the Great War – Military Operations France and Belgium 1918*, Volumes IV and V; Barrie Pitt, *1918: The Last Act* (1984).

My account of university life in 1919-20 and the Oxford bus strike is derived mainly from the *Oxford Chronicle*. There are references to Rickword in the autobiographies of several of his contemporaries at Oxford, including Vera Brittain, *Testament of Youth* (1933), Roy Campbell, *Broken Record* (1934), A.E. Coppard, *It's Me, O Lord!* (1957) and Vivian de Sola Pinto, *The City that Shone* (1969). For Campbell see Peter Alexander, *Roy Campbell: A Critical Biography* (1982).

The Calendar of Modern Letters was reprinted in three volumes in 1966. There are entries on *The Calendar, Left Review* and *Our Time* in *British Literary Magazines: The Modern Age 1914-1984*, edited by Alan Sullivan (1986). For Wyndham Lewis see Jeffrey Meyers, *The Enemy: A Biography of Wyndham Lewis* (1980). Rickword's unsuccessful attempt to publish a passage from *Finnegans Wake* is described in Sylvia Beach, *Shakespeare and Company* (1960).

Jack Lindsay, *Fanfrolico and After* (1962) is an important source for Rickword's life during the years 1928-30. Betty May's (ghosted) autobiography *Tiger-Woman* (1929) breaks off before her meeting with Rickword. For his relations with Hart Crane see John Unterecker, *Voyager: A Life of Hart Crane* (1970) and *The Letters of Hart Crane 1916-1932*, edited by Brom Weber (University of California Press, 1965).

For the Potocki case see the *Daily Telegraph*, 9 February 1932; *The Right Review*, Nos. 2 and 3 (1937); Gilbert Armitage, *Banned in England. An Examination of the Law Relating to Obscene Publications* (1932); Count Potocki of Montalk, *Snobbery with Violence. A Poet in Gaol* (1932). There is a good biography of Nancy Cunard by Anne Chisholm (1979).

Left Review was republished in eight volumes in 1968. Noreen Branson, *History of the Communist Party of Great Britain, 1927-1941* (1981) is useful and reasonably objective. *Culture and Crisis in Britain in the Thirties*, edited by Jon Clark, Margot Heinemann, David Margolies and Carole Snee (1979), deals with several aspects of left-wing cultural activities. For Rickword's Communist friends see the entry on Tom Wintringham in the *Dictionary of Labour Biography*, Volume VII, edited by Joyce Bellamy and John Saville (1984); *Ralph Fox: A Writer in Arms*, edited by John Lehmann, T.A. Jackson and C. Day Lewis (1937); Wendy Mulford, *This Narrow Place. Sylvia Townsend Warner and Valentine Ackland: Life, Letters and Politics, 1930-1951* (1988); *Rebels and Their Causes: Essays in Honour of A.L. Morton* (1978), edited by Maurice Cornforth; and Alick West, *One Man in His Time: An Autobiography* (1969). Arnold Rattenbury, "Total

Attainder and the Helots" in *The 1930s: A Challenge to Orthodoxy* and the sections on Montagu Slater and Randall Swingler in the same volume, which are also by Rattenbury, are particularly valuable. Peggy Guggenheim, *Out of this Century* (1980) gives glimpses of Garman and Rickword. Neal Wood, *Communism and British Intellectuals* (1959) is Cold War propaganda. For Fascist sympathizers in the literary world see Richard Griffith, *Fellow Travellers of the Right* (1980).

On the Spanish war I have found the following useful: Hugh Thomas, *The Spanish Civil War* (1977); Jill Edwards, *The British Government and the Spanish Civil War, 1936-1939* (1979); Tom Wintringham, *English Captain* (1939); Hugh D. Ford, *A Poets' War: British Poets and the Spanish Civil War* (1965); Valentine Cunningham (editor), *The Penguin Book of Spanish Civil War Verse* (1980) and *Spanish Front* (1986). For Cornford, Bell and Caudwell see *John Cornford: A Memoir*, edited by Pat Sloan (1938); Peter Stansky and William Abrahams, *Journey to the Frontier* (1966); and Alan Young's introduction to Christopher Caudwell, *Collected Poems 1924-1936* (1986). Accounts of the 1937 writers' congress include Rickword's articles in *Left Review*, August and September 1937; Stephen Spender, "Spain Invites the World's Writers" (in *Spanish Front*) and "The International Writers' Congress" (*London Mercury*, August 1937); Sylvia Townsend Warner, "Harvest in 1937" (in *The Penguin Book of Spanish Civil War Verse*) and passages in her letters, edited by William Maxwell (1982); Valentine Ackland, "Writers in Madrid" (*Daily Worker*, 21 July 1937); Malcolm Cowley, "To Madrid" (*New Republic*, New York, 15 September 1937). Spender's later accounts in *The God that Failed* (1950) and *World Within World* (1951) are unreliable.

Robert Hewison, *Under Siege: Literary Life in London 1939-1945* (1977) is excellent. Noreen Branson's book deals with Communist attitudes to the war. There are glimpses of Rickword at *Our Time* in Roy Fuller, *Home and Dry* (1984) and John Mortimer, *Clinging to the Wreckage* (1982), but by far the best account is Arnold Rattenbury's in the Supplement to *PN Review* 6.1.

For Rickword in the 1950s see Paul Allen, "More Homage to Pasternak" (*Guardian*, 1 October 1959), "In the time of Hey Presto" (*London Magazine*, April/May 1988) and "All Praise for Magliabechi" (*London Magazine*, December 1988/January 1989). The impact of the events of 1956 on Communist intellectuals is dealt with in Eric Hobsbawm, "The Historians' Group of the Communist Party" in *Rebels and Their Causes*.

Rickword's memoirs end with his retirement from Collet's, and my main written sources for his later years have been his private papers, his correspondence with Douglas Garman, David Holbrook, Arnold

Rattenbury, Jack Beeching and other friends, and contributions to the Supplement to *PN Review* 6.1, notably those by Eric Walter White, Alan Young and Michael Schmidt.

References

I: Colchester

1 *Poetry Nation* I (1973), p.77.
2 John Wakeman (editor), *World Authors 1950-1970* (New York 1975), p.1212.
3 *Poetry Nation* I, p.74.
4 *World Authors*, p.1212.
5 *Literature in Society*, p.307.
6 Ibid., p.146.
7 *Poetry Nation* I, p.76.
8 *Literature in Society*, p.307.
9 *Colchester Gazette*, 17 May 1916.

II: War

1 Wilfred Owen, *Collected Letters*, edited by Harold Owen and John Bell (1967), p.347.
2 *Spectator*, 3 February 1923, p.189.
3 *Literature in Society*, p.64.
4 Owen, *Collected Letters*, pp.583, 585-6.
5 Dominic Hibberd and John Onions (editors), *Poetry of the Great War* (1986), pp.31, 36, 175.
6 *Literature in Society*, p.156.

III: Oxford and Marriage

1 *World Authors*, p.1212.
2 *Literature in Society*, p.14.
3 *Essays and Opinions*, p.85.
4 Edgell Rickword, *Love One Another* (1929), p.94.
5 Roy Campbell, *Broken Record* (1934), p.126.
6 Peter Alexander, *Roy Campbell: A Critical Biography* (1982), p.25.
7 *Broken Record*, pp.35-7, 41.
8 Ibid., p.40.
9 *Spectator* 18 August 1923, p.227.
10 *Broken Record*, p.37.
11 *Poetry Nation* I, p.75.
12 *Dictionary of National Biography, 1941-1950* (1959), p.67.
13 *Oxford Chronicle*, 19 November 1920.
14 Ibid., 21 May, 1920.
15 Ibid., 4 June, 1920.

IV: *Behind the Eyes*
1 *Daily Herald*, 20 October 1920, p.7.
2 *Essays and Opinions*, p.312.
3 Ibid., p.314.
4 Ibid., p.315.
5 *Daily Herald*, 19 January 1921, p.7.
6 Ibid., 28 July 1920, p.7.
7 Ibid., 12 August 1920, p.7.
8 Ibid., 13 October 1920, p.7.
9 Ibid., 11 January 1922, p.7.
10 *New Statesman*, 6 August 1921, p.500.
11 *Love One Another*, p.77.
12 *Poetry Nation* I, p.74.
13 Ibid.
14 *Broken Record*, pp.35-7.
15 *In Broken Images: Selected Letters of Robert Graves 1914-1946*, edited by Paul O'Prey (1982), p.135.
16 W.J. Turner, *Selected Poems 1916-1936* (1939), p.36.
17 *Daily Herald*, 7 June 1922, p.7.
18 *Essays and Opinions*, pp.316, 318.
19 *World Authors*, p.1213.

V: *Reviewing and Rimbaud*
1 *London Mercury* IX, 50, p.165.
2 *Poetry Nation* I, p.76.
3 *Spectator*, 2 December 1922, p.792.
4 Ibid., 15 July 1922, p.85.
5 Peter Alexander, *Roy Campbell*, p.34.
6 *Spectator*, 30 December 1922, p.1011.
7 Ibid., 6 January 1923, p.14.
8 Ibid., 3 June 1922, p.696.
9 *Rimbaud*, pp.43-44. Unless otherwise stated, all references are to the first edition of 1924.
10 *New Statesman*, 24 March 1923, p.723.
11 Michael Grant (editor), *T.S. Eliot: The Critical Heritage* (1982), Volume I, pp.194, 191-2.
12 Siegfried Sassoon, *Diaries 1923-1925* (1985), p.55.
13 Grant, op. cit., pp.198, 176, 178, 135, 143, 161.
14 *Essays and Opinions*, pp.42-43.
15 *Spectator*, 3 November 1923, p.660.
16 Ibid., 30 June 1923, p.1087.
17 Ibid., 10 February 1923, p.247.
18 Ibid., 5 May 1923, p.761.
19 Ibid., 3 November 1923, p.654.

20 Ibid., 19 January 1924, p.91.
21 *The Isis*, 1 February 1922, p.14.
22 *London Mercury* IX, 50, pp.166, 168, 169, 171.
23 *Rimbaud*, pp.5, 23, 30.
24 *Rimbaud* (1963), pp.175-6.
25 *Rimbaud* (1924), pp.112, 78.
26 *Sunday Times*, 6 July 1924, p.5.
27 *London Mercury* IX, 50, pp.168, 172.
28 *Rimbaud* (1963), p.177.
29 *Rimbaud* (1924), pp.134-5, 143, 118, 185.
30 Ibid., pp.94, 168, 171; (1963), pp.68, 127, 129.
31 TLS, 19 June 1924, p.385.
32 *Observer*, 15 June 1924, p.4.
33 *Spectator*, 30 August 1924, p.295.
34 *New Statesman*, 28 June 1924, p.352.
35 *Sunday Times*, 6 July 1924, p.6.
36 *Adam* Nos. 244-46 (1954), p.7.
37 Rimbaud, *Collected Poems*, edited by Oliver Bernard (1986), p.234.
38 Ibid., p.11.
39 *Rimbaud*, p.xii.
40 *Calendar* II, p.287.

VI: *The Calendar of Modern Letters*

1   *Poetry Nation* I, p.78.
2   Sylvia Beach, *Shakespeare and Company* (1960), p.173.
3   *T.P.'s and Cassell's Weekly*, 28 February 1925, p.699.
4   *Calendar* I, pp.70-71; reproduced in part in *Essays and Opinions*, pp.169-70.
5   *Calendar* I, p.80.
6   TLS, 5 March 1925, p.158.
7   *Poetry Nation* I, p.81.
8   Sassoon, *Diaries 1923-1925* (1985), p.220.
9   *Calendar* I, pp.156-9; II, pp.62, 364-6.
10 John Gross, *The Rise and Fall of the Man of Letters* (1969), p.255.
11 *Calendar* I, p.393; II, pp.288, 47, 49.
12 Ibid., III, pp.247-8.
13 Lewis, *The Art of Being Ruled* (1926), pp.369, 49, 69, 67-8.
14 *Calendar* II, p.418.
15 *The Enemy*, No. 2, pp.xxx, 102.
16 *Calendar* II, pp.427-30; *Essays and Opinions*, pp.219-22.
17 *Calendar* III, pp.150-51.
18 *Artery* 18, p.22.
19 *Calendar* III, p.72.

20 *PN Review* 6, 1, Supplement XIX.
21 *Calendar* IV, p.169.
22 Ibid., IV, pp.175-6.
23 John Lucas (editor), *The 1930s: A Challenge to Orthodoxy* (1978), p.144.
24 TLS, 27 May 1926, p.358.
25 *Calendar* I, p.336.
26 Ibid., I, p.392.
27 *Poetry Nation* I, p.78.
28 *Calendar* III, p.321; *Essays and Opinions*, p.177.
29 *PN Review* 6, 1, Supplement I.
30 *Calendar* I, p.236; *Essays and Opinions*, p.170.
31 *Poetry Nation* I, p.80.
32 *Calendar* II, p.210.
33 Ibid., II, p.71.
34 *Essays and Opinions*, p.3.
35 *Calendar* II, pp.278-81; *Essays and Opinions*, pp.180-84.
36 *Calendar* III, pp.76, 157; *Essays and Opinions*, pp.188, 190.
37 *Calendar* I, pp.165-6; II, pp.66-68; *Essays and Opinions*, pp.186-87.
38 *Calendar* I, p.391; IV, p.156.

VII: Scrutinies and Poetry

1 Jack Lindsay, *Fanfrolico and After* (1962), p.138.
2 *The Letters of Hart Crane 1916-1932* (University of California Press, 1965), p.283.
3 TLS, 16 August 1928, p.590.
4 *Scrutinies* I, pp.v-vii; *Essays and Opinions*, pp.275-6.
5 *Spectator*, 31 March 1928, p.502; TLS, 10 May 1928, p.362; *New Statesman*, 12 May 1928, pp.162, 164; *Observer*, 1 July 1928, p.7; *Calendar* III, p.81; *Essays and Opinions*, p.202.
6 *Scrutinies* I, pp.v, 11, 87, 27. Rickword deleted his remark on courage from the reprint of his essay on Barrie in *Essays and Opinions*.
7 *London Aphrodite* (1928-29), p.224.
8 Lindsay, op. cit., pp.279, 275; *A Garland for Jack Lindsay*, (1980), edited by James Corbett, p.13.
9 *The Mandrake Press* (catalogue of an exhibition held at the Cambridge University Library, 1985), p.1.
10 Lindsay, op. cit., p.137.
11 Ibid., p.138.
12 *Calendar* II, p.324.
13 *Poetry Book Society Bulletin* 88 (Spring 1976), p.3.

14 *London Aphrodite*, p.472; *New Statesman*, 2 March 1929, p.669; *Spectator*, 9 March 1929, p.377; TLS, 17 January 1929, p.40; *Calendar* III, p.159; *Essays and Opinions*, p.193; *Observer*, 27 January 1929, p.7; *Sunday Times*, 10 March 1929, p.10.
15 *PN Review* 6, 1, Supplement XVI.
16 Roy Fuller, *Home and Dry* (1984), p.143.
17 *Essays and Opinions*, pp.245, 248, 253, 255, 257, 262; *Sunday Referee*, 14 September 1930, p.6.
18 Ibid., 18 May 1930, p.6.
19 *Essays and Opinions*, pp.302-3, 308.
20 Lindsay, op. cit., p.154.
21 Ibid., p.140.
22 Ibid., p.155.
23 *Spectator*, 18 August 1923, p.226.
24 *Times*, 6 March 1929, p.11.
25 Ibid., 9 August 1929, p.9.
26 *Observer*, 8 December 1929, p.5.
27 Lewis, *The Apes of God* (Santa Barbara, 1981), pp.165-66.

VIII: Scrutinies and Satire

1   *Scrutinies* II, p.v; *Essays and Opinions*, p.287.
2   *Scrutinies* II, p.247.
3   *New Statesman*, 14 March 1931, p.118.
4   *Scrutinies* II, pp.vi, 142, 160, 161; *Essays and Opinions*, pp.287, 289, 299, 300.
5   TLS, 19 March 1931, p.226; *Spectator*, 14 March 1931, p.427; *New Statesman*, 14 March 1931, p.118.
6   *Towards Standards of Criticism*, edited by F.R. Leavis (1933), p.22.
7   *Rimbaud*, p.82n.
8   *Poetry Book Society Bulletin* 88, p.3.
9   *Scrutinies* II, pp.154, 149-50; *Essays and Opinions*, pp.296, 293-4.
10 *Poetry Nation* I, p.86.
11 Ibid., p.85.
12 TLS, 3 December 1931, p.986; *Sunday Times*, 1 December 1931, p.9.
13 *PN Review* 6, 1, Supplement XXII; *New Universities Quarterly*, Spring 1977, pp.248-9; *Stand* 22, 3, p.43; *Our Time* 7, 6 (March 1948), p.145.
14 *Poetry Nation* I, p.86.
15 Lucas, *The 1930s*, pp.9-10.
16 *The Living Poet – Edgell Rickword* (typescript of an interview broadcast on 23 February 1977), p.15.

17 *World Authors*, p.1213; *Poetry Nation* I, p.86.
18 Lindsay, op. cit., p.183.
19 *Front* 3 (April 1931), p.221.
20 *Literature in Society*, pp.1, 5.

IX: The Road to Communism

1   *The Right Review*, Nos. 2 (February 1937) and 3 (May 1937); *Daily Telegraph*, 9 February 1932, p.6.
2   Potocki, *Snobbery with Violence* (1932), pp.9, 51.
3   *Daily Herald*, 23 March 1921, p.7.
4   *Essays and Opinions*, p.39.
5   *New Statesman*, 28 January 1933, p.104.
6   *Scrutiny* (1963 reprint), Vol. XX, p.3.
7   *Scrutiny* I. i, p.2.
8   *Towards Standards*, p.1.
9   TLS, 15 June 1933, p.414; *Scrutiny* II. iii, p.305.
10 Ibid., I. i, pp.3, 6.
11 Ibid., I. iv, p.320.
12 *Towards Standards*, pp.11-14.
13 Anne Chisholm, *Nancy Cunard* (1979), pp.30, 60, 76, 202, 271, 287.
14 *Daily Worker*, 28 February 1934, p.4; *New Statesman*, 10 March 1934, p.352.
15 *Labour Monthly*, May 1971, pp.234-5.
16 *The Review* 11-12 (1964), p.18; *Poetry Nation* I, p.82.
17 TLS, 22 October 1976, p.1322.
18 See *Literature in Society*, p.78.
19 Lucas, *The 1930s*, p.11.

X: Left Review

1   Lucas, *The 1930s*, p.8; Peter Alexander, *Roy Campbell*, p.156.
2   *The Review* 11-12 (July 1964), pp.17-18.
3   Richard Griffiths, *Fellow Travellers of the Right* (1980), pp.24, 362; John Lucas, "An Interview with Edgell Rickword", in *Rennaissance and Modern Studies* XX (1976), p.10. This sentence is omitted from the interview as reprinted in *The 1930s*.
4   *Left Review* I. 1 (October 1934), p.38.
5   Noreen Branson, *History of the Communist Party of Great Britain, 1927-1941* (1985), p.207.
6   *Left Review* I. 11 (August 1935), p.479; *Literature in Society*, p.52.
7   Lucas, *The 1930s*, p.5.
8   *Left Review*, I. 9 (June 1935), p.366.
9   *The Review* 11-12, p.19.
10 *Left Review*, I. 1, p.37.

11 *Literature in Society*, p.86; *Left Review* I. 5 (February 1935), p.169; I. 8, p.291.

12 Ibid., I. 3 (December 1934), pp.75-7; I. 4, pp.125-7; I. 5, p.179; I. 6, p.223.

13 Ibid., I. 2 (November 1934), p.35; I. 3, p.69; I. 4, pp.101, 123; I. 7, p.255; I. 10, pp.396, 430; I. 12, p.505.

14 Ibid., I. 1 (October 1934), pp.19-25; *Literature in Society*, pp.39-45.

15 *Left Review* II. 3, (December 1935), p.118; *Literature in Society*, p.65.

16 *Left Review* I. 6 (March 1935), p.237; *Literature in Society*, p.50.

17 Charles Hobday (editor), *Communist and Marxist Parties of the World* (1986), pp.433-4.

18 *Left Review* II. 9 (June 1936), p.417.

19 Ibid., II. 7 (April 1936), p.305.

20 Ibid., II. 14 (November 1936), pp.730-31.

21 Ibid., II. 16 (January 1937), p.858.

22 Ibid., III. 5 (June 1937), p.258; *Daily Worker*, 12 May 1937, p.3.

23 *Left Review* II. 12 (September 1936), p.601.

24 Ibid., II. 6 (March 1936), pp.282-3; III. 1 (February 1937), p.10; II. 8, p.395.

25 C. Day Lewis, "On the Twentieth Anniversary of Soviet Power", in *In Letters of Red*, ed. E. Allen Osborne (1938), p.155; *Left Review*, II. 11 (August 1936), p.591.

26 Ibid., III. 2 (March 1937), pp.112, 116; *Spanish Front*, ed. Valentine Cunningham (1986), p.8.

27 *Literature in Society*, p.116; *The Prelude*, Book X, lines 410-12.

28 *Left Review* II. 4 (January 1936), pp.186-7; II. 10, p.ii.

29 *War and Culture* is reprinted in *Literature in Society*, p.80.

30 *Daily Worker*, 23 December 1936, p.7.

31 Ibid., 21 June 1937, p.5.

32 *Literature in Society*, p.91.

33 Peggy Guggenheim, *Out of this Century* (1980), pp.145, 153.

XI: Spain

1 *Left Review* II. 13 (October 1936), pp.665-6.

2 Ibid., II. 15 (December 1936), p.793.

3 Ibid., II. 16 (January 1937), p.857.

4 *Daily Worker*, 6 January 1937, p.4; *Left Review* III. 1 (February 1937), p.1.

5 *Life and Letters To-day*, Vol. 17, No. 10 (Winter 1937), p.163.

6 *Left Review* III. 2 (March 1937), p.65.

7 *The Review* 11-12 (1964), p.19.

8 *Left Review* III. 9 (October 1937), pp.511-17.

9   *Daily Worker*, 22 November 1939, p.3.
10 *Left Review* III. 5 (June 1937), p.257.
11 Ibid., III. 15 (April 1938), pp.937-8.
12 *Poems for Spain* (1939), edited by Stephen Spender and John Lehmann, pp.93-4; *The Penguin Book of Spanish Civil War Verse* (1980), edited by Valentine Cunningham, pp.280-81.
13 John Lehmann, *The Whispering Gallery* (1955), p.251; *Poetry Nation* I, p.82.
14 Lucas, *The 1930s*, p.12.
15 *Left Review* III. 10 (November 1937) p.600; III. 11 (December 1937), p.688; III. 13 (February 1938), p.767.
16 Ibid., III. 12 (January 1938), p.702.
17 S.T. Warner, *Letters*, edited by William Maxwell (1982), p.49; *New Republic*, Vol. LXXXXII, No. 1189 (15 September 1937), p.154.
18 *Left Review* III. 8 (September 1937), pp.447-9.
19 Ibid., III. 8, pp.450-51.
20 Ibid., III. 4 (May 1937), pp.242-4.
21 *London Mercury*, Vol. XXXVI, No. 214 (August 1937), p.573.
22 *Authors Take Sides on the Spanish War* (1937), p.23; Valentine Cunningham (editor), *Spanish Front* (1986), p.55.

XII: Poetry and Politics

1   *New Verse*, Nos. 26-27 (November 1937), pp.10, 21-2; *Literature in Society*, p.104.
2   *Left Review* III. 4 (May 1937), p.193; III. 6 (July 1937), pp.317-8.
3   *Manchester Guardian*, 22 January 1938, p.10; 31 January, p.8; 20 January, p.11; *News Chronicle*, 20 January 1938, pp.1-2; 31 January, pp.1-2.
4   *A Poets' War: British Poets and the Spanish Civil War* (1965), p.145.
5   Hugh Thomas, *The Spanish Civil War* (1977), p.796; Cunningham, *The Penguin Book of Spanish Civil War Verse*, p.71n; Spender and Lehmann, *Poems for Spain*, p.10; *Essays and Opinions*, p.171.
6   *The Right Review*, Nos. 1, 2, 4 and 6. This journal, which Potocki printed himself, is not paginated.
7   Ibid., No. 7.
8   *Spectator*, 8 July 1938, p.65; 7 October, p.557. "The Two Worlds" is quoted from the original text, not from Rickword's later revision.
9   *Right Review*, No. 6.
10 *Left Review* III. 16 (May 1938), pp.957, 960, 967.
11 Ford, op. cit., pp.81, 278.
12 *Daily Worker* 18 May 1938, p.7; *The Review* 11-12 (1964), p.18.

13 *Essays and Opinions*, p.30.
14 Palmer, *Post-Victorian Poetry* (1938), pp.256-8.

XIII: The English Tradition

1 Georgi Dimitrov, *Selected Articles and Speeches* (1951), pp.99-100.
2 *Daily Worker*, 2 December 1936, Christmas Book Supplement, p.iv.
3 *Left Review* III. 14 (March 1938), pp.888-9; *Life and Letters To-day*, Vol. 18, No. 11 (Spring 1938), pp.154-6; *Literature in Society*, pp.301-3.
4 *The Mind in Chains* (1937), pp.238, 245, 253, 255; *Literature in Society*, pp.93, 97, 103, 104.
5 *Life and Letters To-day*, Vol. 21, No. 19 (March 1939), p.106.
6 *A Handbook of Freedom* (1939), pp.vii, xvi, ix-x, xxi; *Literature in Society*, pp.123, 129, 124-5, 132.
7 *New Statesman* 27 May 1939, p.829; 19 August 1939, p.286; *Times Literary Supplement* 8 July 1939, p.410.
8 *PN Review*, Vol. 6, No. 1, Supplement XXVIII.
9 *Daily Worker*, 19 July 1939, p.7.
10 *Essays and Opinions*, p.249; *Literature in Society*, pp.16-17.
11 *Daily Worker*, 19 April 1939, p.7.
12 Ibid., 2 September 1939, p.3; 7 October 1939, p.2.
13 *Literature in Society*, pp.141, 143.
14 Ibid., pp.148-50, 155.
15 *Essays and Opinions*, pp.247-8.
16 Leavis, *Revaluation* (1967 edition), p.42.
17 *The Calendar*, Vol. I, p.243.
18 *The English Revolution* (1940), p.131; *Literature in Society*, p.182.
19 *The English Revolution*, pp.101-2, 115, 118-9; *Literature in Society*, pp.165, 173, 175.
20 *Times Literary Supplement*, 7 September 1940, p.436.
21 *PN Review*, Vol. 6, No. 1, Supplement XXII, XXIII.
22 *Times Literary Supplement*, 11 January 1941, pp.18, 19.
23 *Literature in Society*, pp.159, 161.
24 Noreen Branson, *History of the Communist Party of Great Britain, 1927-1941* (1985), p.333.
25 *Literature in Society*, p.159.
26 Nina Hamnett, *Is She a Lady? A Problem in Autobiography* (1955), p.142.
27 *Artery*, Vol. 6, No. 1, p.31.
28 *Literature in Society*, pp.246-8.
29 *Our Time*, Vol. 4, No. 2 (September 1944), p.9; *PN Review* Vol. 6, No. 1, Supplement XXIV.
30 *Hampstead and Highgate Express*, 21 July 1944, p.1.

XIV: *Our Time*

1 *Our Time* 2.6 (October 1942), p.2.
2 Quoted in Robert Hewison, *Under Siege: Literary Life in London 1939-1945* (1977), p.23. This paragraph is largely based on Mr Hewison's book.
3 Jack Lindsay, *Meetings with Poets* (1968), p.65.
4 *PN Review* Vol. 6, No. 1, Supplement XXIV.
5 *Our Time* 3.7 (February 1944), p.5.
6 Ibid., 3.11 (June 1944), p.8; 4.1 (August 1944), p.19.
7 Ibid., 4.4 (November 1944), p.3.
8 *The Review* 11-12 (1964), p.20.
9 *PN Review* 6.1, Supplement XXIV; Roy Fuller, *Home and Dry* (1984), p.144; John Mortimer, *Clinging to the Wreckage* (1982) p.88.
10 *Our Time* 4.6 (January 1945), p.3; 4.10 (May 1945), p.3.
11 Ibid., 5.2 (September 1945), p.23.
12 Ibid., 5.5 (December 1945), pp.97-98; *Literature in Society*, p.308.
13 *Our Time* 5.2 (September 1945), p.39.
14 Ibid., 5.7 (February 1946), p.143; Randall Swingler, *The Years of Anger* (1947), p.41.
15 *Our Time* 6.7 (February 1947), p.165; *Literature in Society*, p.313.
16 *Daily Worker*, 18 October 1947, p.1.
17 TLS, 16 March 1946, p.123.
18 Ibid., 7 February 1948, p.80; *Listener*, 12 February 1948, p.271; *Tribune*, 23 January 1948, p.17; *Adam*, No. 179 (February 1948), p.18; *Daily Worker*, 11 December 1947, p.4; *Our Time*, 7.6 (March 1948), p.144.

XV: *Bookselling*

1 Douglas Goldring, *The Nineteen Twenties* (1945), p.103.
2 *Tribune*, 28 May 1948, p.18.
3 Christopher Caudwell, *Further Studies in a Dying Culture* (1949), pp.7-10.
4 *Literature in Society*, pp.226, 245.
5 B.L. Add. Ms. 63321,
6 E.P. Thompson, *The Making of the English Working Class* (1965), p.157.
7 B.L. Add. Ms. 54200A, p.163.
8 *Guardian*, 26 February 1988, p.25.
9 TLS, 12 December 1952, p.816; 2 January 1953, p.9.
10 Neal Wood, *Communism and British Intellectuals* (1959), p.100; *The Mind in Chains*, p.250; *Literature in Society*, p.101.
11 *Literature in Society*, p.224.

12 Hobsbawm, "The Historians' Group of the Communist Party", in *Rebels and Their Causes* (1978), edited by Maurice Cornforth, p.42.
13 *PN Review* Vol. 6, No. 1, Supplement XX.
14 *Guardian*, 1 October 1959.
15 *Radio Times*, 15 July 1960, p.47.
16 *Essays in Criticism*, Vol. XII, No.3, pp.274, 275, 278, 282, 284, 285, 289, 291.

XVI: Recognition

1 From Rickword's rough draft of an essay published in the *Daily Worker*, 14 June 1962, p.2. The published text is shortened.
2 TLS, 21 July 1966, p.635; *Guardian*, 8 July 1966, p.11; *New Statesman*, 2 September 1966, p.320.
3 TLS, 9 November 1967, p.1059.
4 *Guardian*, 22 March 1968, p.9.
5 *Labour Monthly*, March 1968, p.123.
6 TLS, 23 April 1971, p.473.
7 *Adam*, Nos. 367-369 (1972), p.51.
8 Arnold Rattenbury, *Man Thinking* (Nottingham, 1972), p.37.
9 *Literature in Society*, pp.185, 201, 297.
10 *Halstead Advertiser*, 18 January 1973, p.6.

XVII: The Last Years

1 *PN Review* 6, 1, Supplement XXXII.
2 Ibid., XXX, XXXI; *Poetry Nation* I, pp.73, 77, 78, 79, 81, 85, 86, 89.
3 *PN Review* 6, 1, Supplement XXXI.
4 *Guardian*, 28 November 1974, p.16; *New Statesman*, 21 February, 1975, pp.243, 246; *Observer*, 12 January 1975; *Listener*, 1 May 1975, p.590.
5 *PN Review* 6, 1, Supplement XXX.
6 *Renaissance and Modern Studies* XX (1976), p.5; *John Lucas* (ed.), *The 1930s: A Challenge to Orthodoxy* (1978), p.3.
7 *World Authors 1950-1970*, John Wakeman (New York 1975), p.1213.
8 *PN Review* 6, 1, Supplement XXXII.
9 *Sunday Times*, 14 November 1976, p.41; *Times*, 10 February 1977, p.12; *Stand*, 18, No. 2, p.73; *New Universities Quarterly*, Spring 1977, pp.248-9; TLS, 22 October 1976, p.1322.
10 TLS, 18 January 1980, p.69; *Tribune*, 5 January 1979, p.6; *New Universities Quarterly*, Autumn 1979, p.502; *New Statesman*, 10 November 1978, p.630.

11 The oration, slightly abbreviated, is reprinted in *PN Review* 6, 1, Supplement I-II.
12 This letter and that mentioned in the previous paragraph are quoted from drafts among Rickword's papers.
13 *Times*, 16 March 1982, p.12.
14 *Cambridge Review*, 4 June 1982, p.252.
15 *Times*, 16 March 1982, p.12; *Guardian*, 16 March 1982, p.9; *Morning Star*, 17 March 1982, p.2; *Cambridge Review*, 4 June 1982, p.254.
16 *PN Review* 6, 1, Supplement XXIV.

Index

Index